PATIENCE IS A VIRTUE...

Ken-ichi Sakura

Lately I feel like I'm not getting enough thrills and excitement. If I don't get some soon, Takumi's going to leave me in the dust! Somebody come on an adventure with Saken!!

Ken-ichi Sakura's manga debut was *Fabre Tanteiki*, which was published in a special edition of *Monthly Shonen Jump* in 2000. Serialization of *Dragon Drive* began in the March 2001 issue of *Monthly Shonen Jump* and the hugely successful series has inspired video games and an animated TV show. Sakura's latest title, *Kotokuri*, began running in the March 2006 issue of *Monthly Shonen Jump*. *Dragon Drive* and *Kotokuri* have both become tremendously popular in Japan because of Sakura's unique sense of humor and dynamic portrayal of feisty teen characters.

DRAGON DRIVE

DRAGON DRIVE
VOLUME II

The SHONEN JUMP Manga Edition

STORY AND ART BY
KEN-ICHI SAKURA

Translation/Martin Hunt, HC Language Solutions, Inc.
English Adaptation/Ian Reid, HC Language Solutions, Inc.
Touch-up Art & Lettering/Jim Keefe
Cover Design/Mark Griffin
Interior Design/Frances O. Liddell
Editor/Shaenon K. Garrity

Editor in Chief, Books/Alvin Lu
Editor in Chief, Magazines/Marc Weidenbaum
VP of Publishing Licensing/Rika Inouye
VP of Sales/Gonzalo Ferreyra
Sr. VP of Marketing/Liza Coppola
Publisher/Hyoe Narita

Printed in the U.S.A.

Published by VIZ Media, LLC
P.O. Box 77010
San Francisco, CA 94107

SHONEN JUMP Manga Edition
10 9 8 7 6 5 4 3 2 1
First printing, December 2008

www.viz.com

THE WORLD'S
MOST POPULAR MANGA

www.shonenjump.com

DRAGON DRIVE

SHONEN JUMP MANGA EDITION

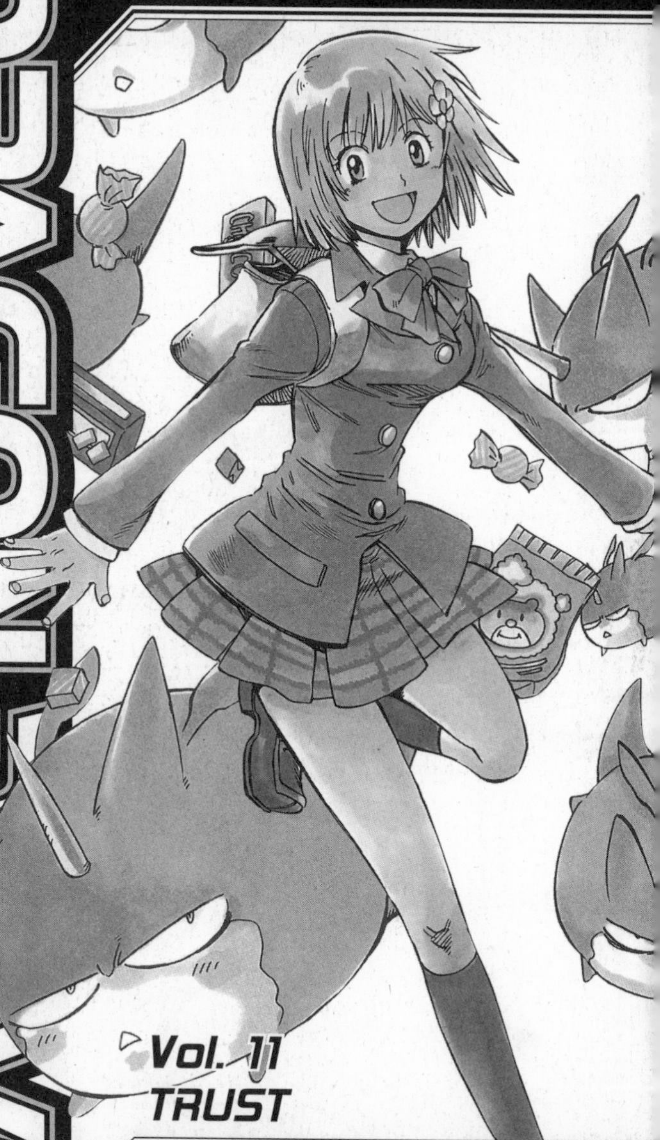

Vol. 11
TRUST

STORY & ART BY
KEN-ICHI SAKURA
IN COLLABORATION WITH BANDAI • CHAN'S • ORG

CHARACTERS

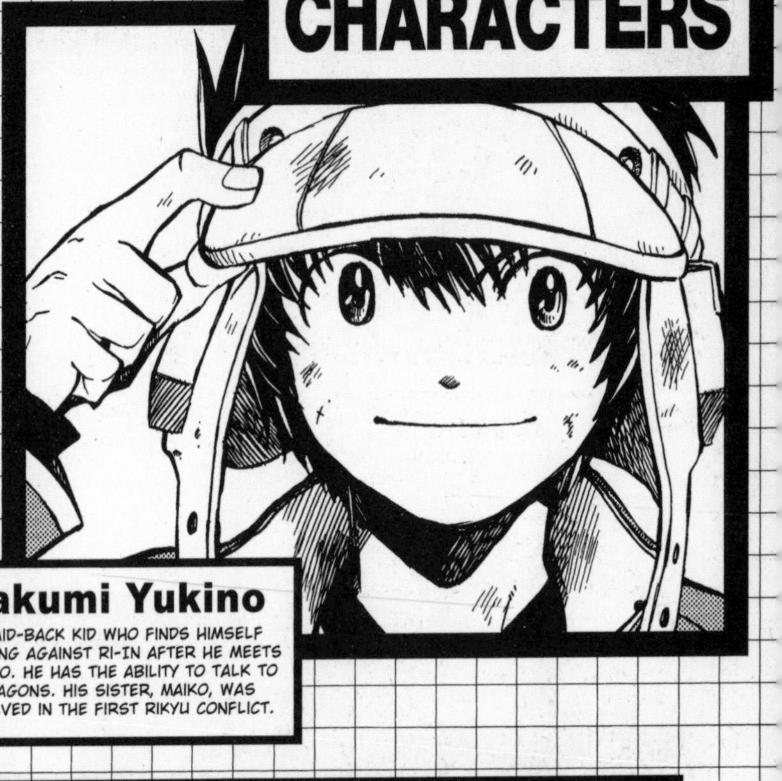

Takumi Yukino

A LAID-BACK KID WHO FINDS HIMSELF IGHTING AGAINST RI-IN AFTER HE MEETS RAIKOO. HE HAS THE ABILITY TO TALK TO DRAGONS. HIS SISTER, MAIKO, WAS INVOLVED IN THE FIRST RIKYU CONFLICT.

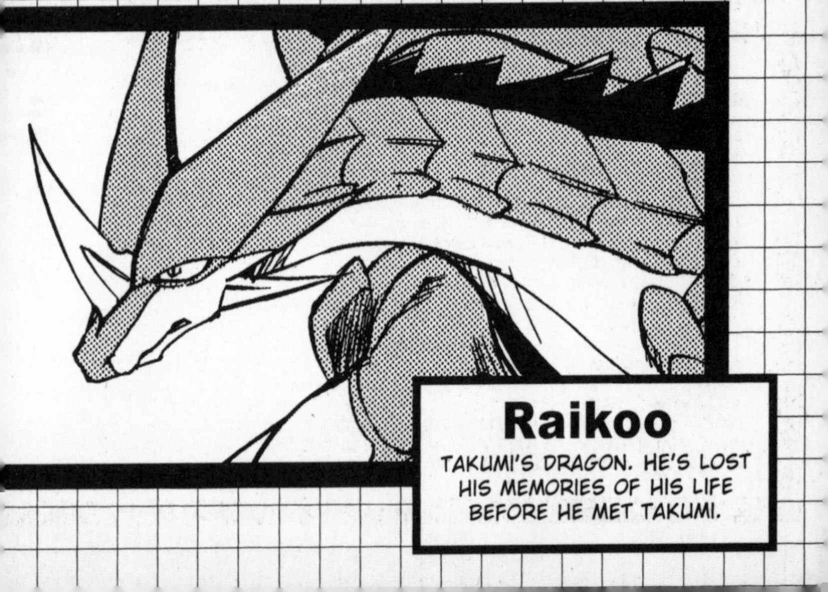

Raikoo

TAKUMI'S DRAGON. HE'S LOST HIS MEMORIES OF HIS LIFE BEFORE HE MET TAKUMI.

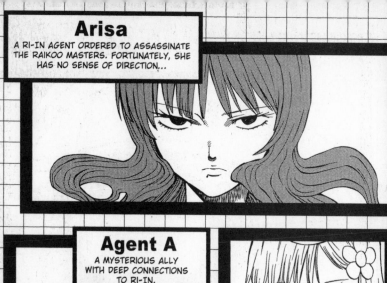

Arisa

A RI-IN AGENT ORDERED TO ASSASSINATE THE RAIKOO MASTERS. FORTUNATELY, SHE HAS NO SENSE OF DIRECTION...

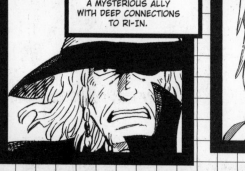

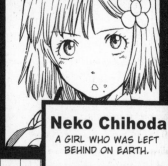

Neko Chihoda

A GIRL WHO WAS LEFT BEHIND ON EARTH.

Agent A

A MYSTERIOUS ALLY WITH DEEP CONNECTIONS TO RI-IN.

STORY

A GAME CALLED DRAGON DRIVE IS WILDLY POPULAR WITH KIDS ALL OVER THE WORLD. ONE DAY, TAKUMI YUKINO RECEIVES A DECK OF D.D. CARDS FROM AGENT A AND JOINS A TOURNAMENT. EVEN THOUGH HE'S NEVER PLAYED BEFORE, HE MANAGES TO MAKE IT TO THE NATIONAL FINALS WITH THE HELP OF HIS DRAGON, RAIKOO.

BEFORE THE FINALS, TAKUMI HAS A STRANGE DREAM. HE'S TOLD THAT TO AWAKEN THE TRUE RAIKOO FROM AMONG THE 99 RAIKOO CARDS, ALL THE RAIKOOS MUST FIGHT EACH OTHER. THE DREAM WORRIES TAKUMI, BUT HE HEADS FOR THE FINALS ANYWAY, HOPING TO RESTORE RAIKOO'S LOST MEMORIES. HOWEVER, AFTER REALIZING HOW MUCH HE STILL HAS TO LEARN, HE DROPS OUT OF THE TOURNAMENT TO CONCENTRATE ON HIS TRAINING.

A WEEK LATER, AN ORGANIZATION CALLED RI-IN HACKS INTO THE D.D. COMPUTER SYSTEM. THE D-ZONE DRAGONS TRADE PLACES WITH THE PEOPLE OF EARTH. ONLY THE PEOPLE WHO WERE INSIDE A D.D. CENTER AT THE TIME ARE LEFT BEHIND. WHILE FLEEING THE AGENTS OF RI-IN, TAKUMI AND HIS FRIENDS SEARCH FOR A WAY TO REVERSE THE DISASTER. TAKUMI GETS A PHONE CALL FROM HIS SISTER MAIKO, WHO TELLS HIM THAT HE HAS TO FIND THE OTHER RAIKOO MASTERS AND HELP THEM ESCAPE RI-IN...

Vol. 11 TRUST

CONTENTS

DRAGON DRIVE

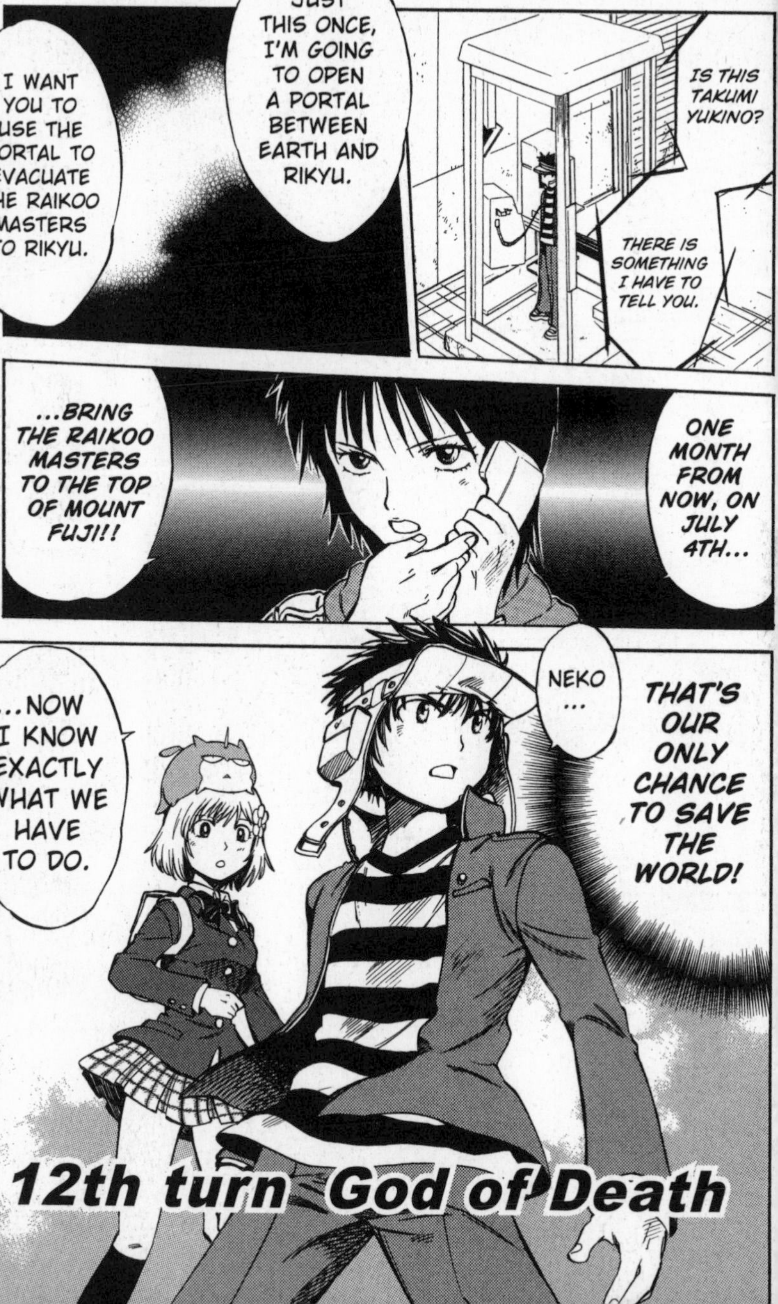
IS THIS TAKUMI YUKINO?
THERE IS SOMETHING I HAVE TO TELL YOU.
JUST THIS ONCE, I'M GOING TO OPEN A PORTAL BETWEEN EARTH AND RIKYU.
I WANT YOU TO USE THE PORTAL TO EVACUATE THE RAIKOO MASTERS TO RIKYU.
ONE MONTH FROM NOW, ON JULY 4TH...
...BRING THE RAIKOO MASTERS TO THE TOP OF MOUNT FUJI!!
THAT'S OUR ONLY CHANCE TO SAVE THE WORLD!
NEKO...
...NOW I KNOW EXACTLY WHAT WE HAVE TO DO.

12th turn God of Death

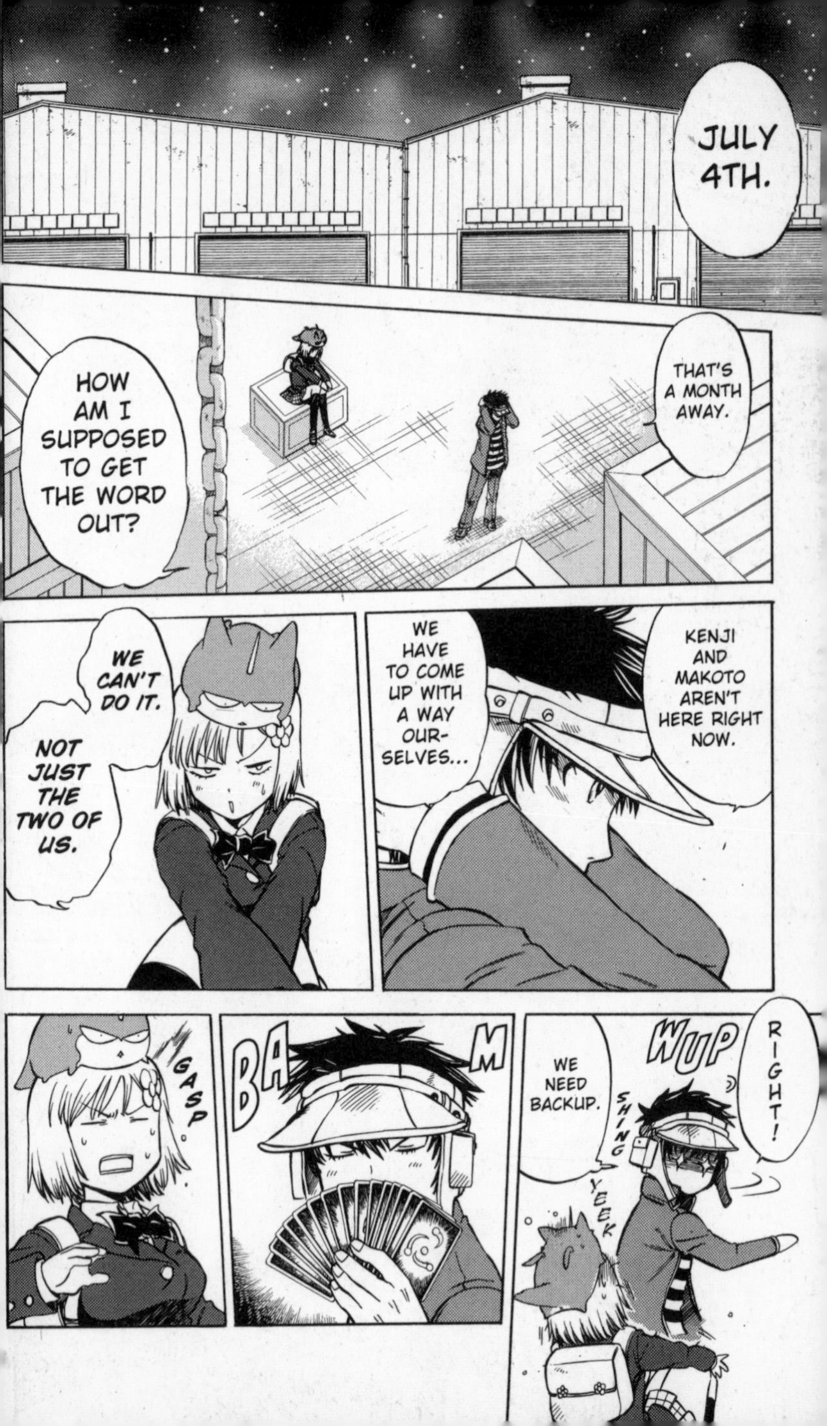
JULY 4TH.
THAT'S A MONTH AWAY.
HOW AM I SUPPOSED TO GET THE WORD OUT?
KENJI AND MAKOTO AREN'T HERE RIGHT NOW.
WE HAVE TO COME UP WITH A WAY OUR-SELVES...
WE CAN'T DO IT.
NOT JUST THE TWO OF US.
RIGHT!
WUP
WE NEED BACKUP.
SHING
YEEK
BAM
GASP

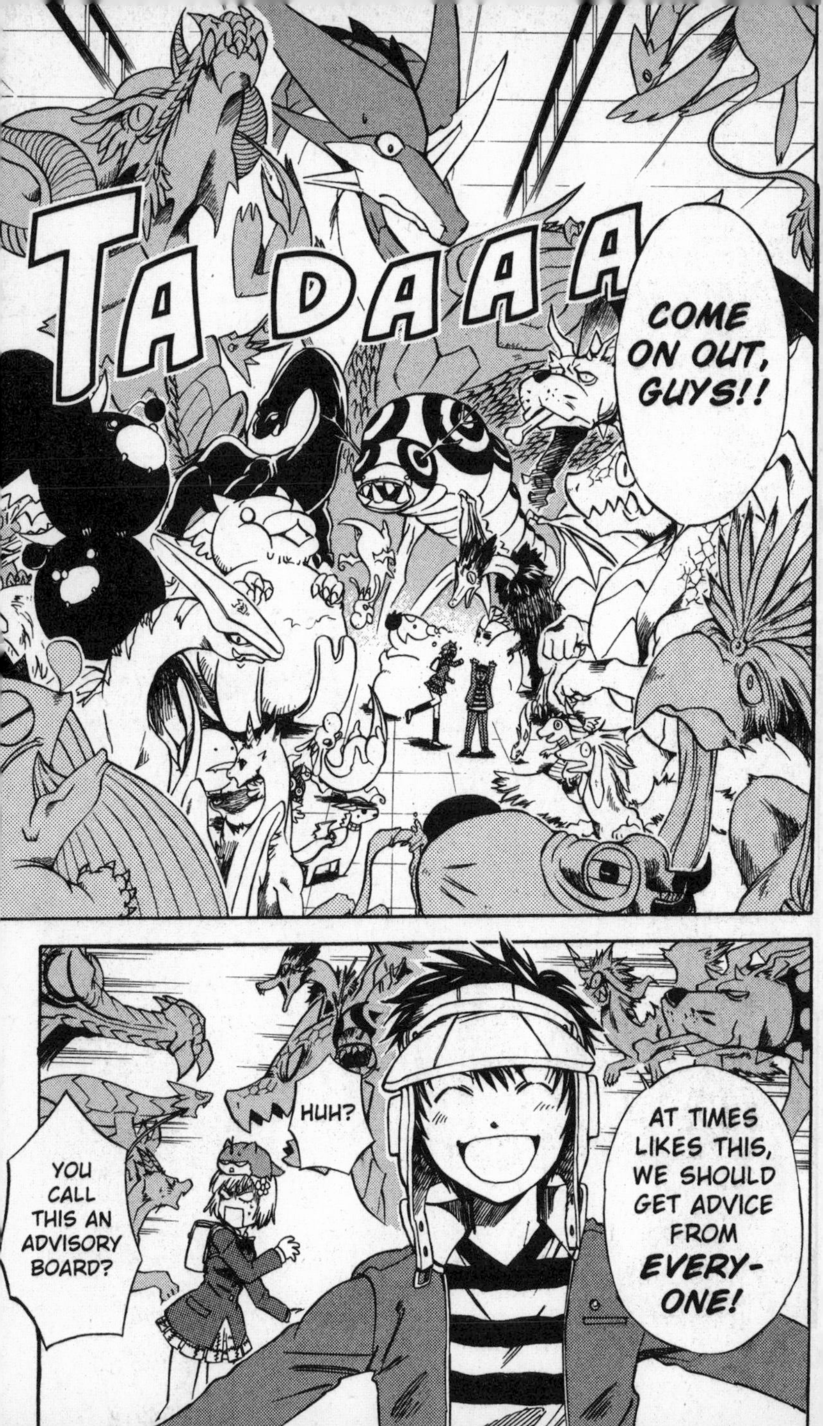
COME ON OUT, GUYS!!
TADAAA
AT TIMES LIKES THIS, WE SHOULD GET ADVICE FROM EVERY-ONE!
HUH?
YOU CALL THIS AN ADVISORY BOARD?

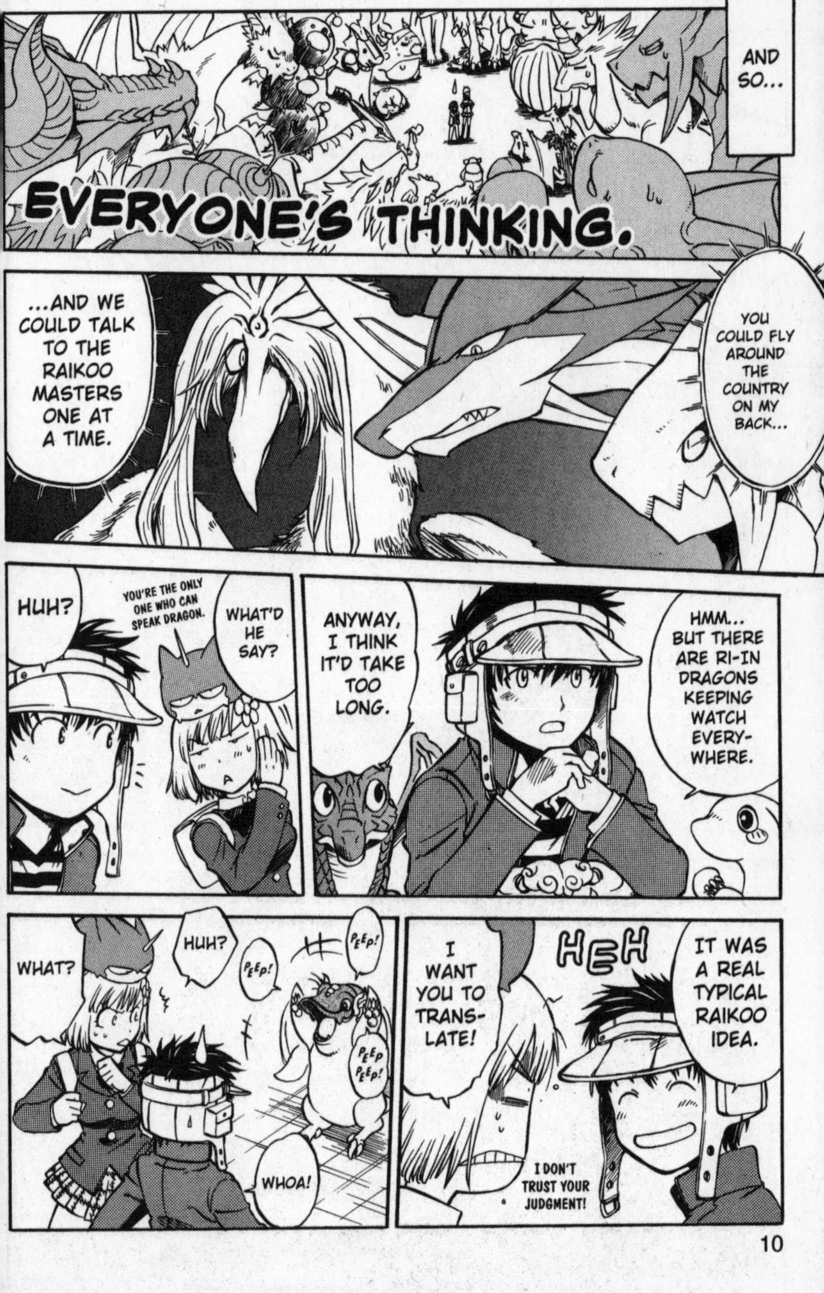
AND SO...
EVERYONE'S THINKING.
YOU COULD FLY AROUND THE COUNTRY ON MY BACK...
...AND WE COULD TALK TO THE RAIKOO MASTERS ONE AT A TIME.
HMM... BUT THERE ARE RI-IN DRAGONS KEEPING WATCH EVERY-WHERE.
ANYWAY, I THINK IT'D TAKE TOO LONG.
WHAT'D HE SAY?
YOU'RE THE ONLY ONE WHO CAN SPEAK DRAGON.
HUH?
IT WAS A REAL TYPICAL RAIKOO IDEA.
HEH
I WANT YOU TO TRANS-LATE!
I DON'T TRUST YOUR JUDGMENT!
PEEP!
PEEP PEEP!
PEEP!
HUH?
WHAT?
WHOA!

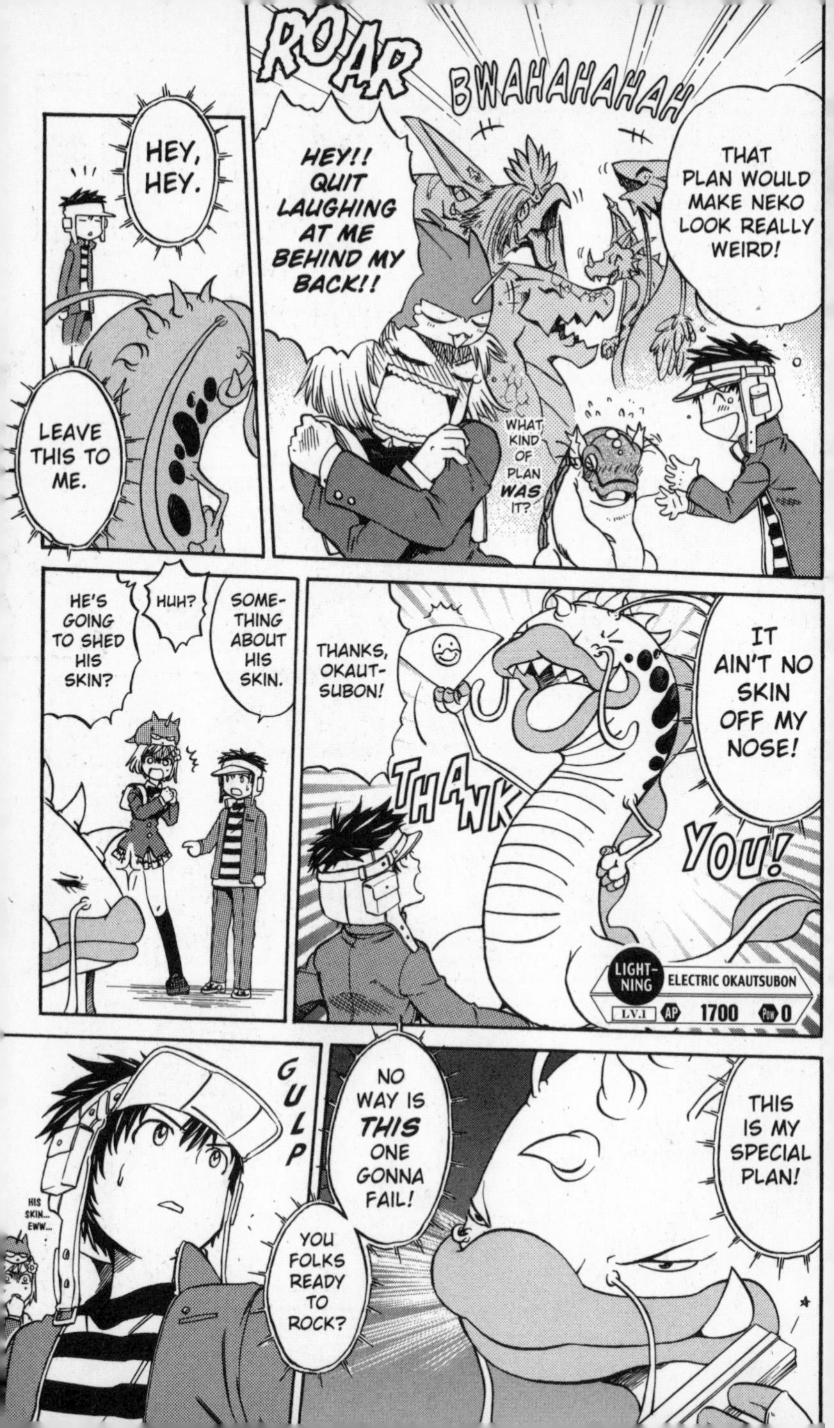
ROAR
BWAHAHAHAHAH
THAT PLAN WOULD MAKE NEKO LOOK REALLY WEIRD!
HEY!! QUIT LAUGHING AT ME BEHIND MY BACK!!
WHAT KIND OF PLAN WAS IT?
HEY, HEY.
LEAVE THIS TO ME.
IT AIN'T NO SKIN OFF MY NOSE!
THANKS, OKAUT-SUBON!
THANK
YOU!
LIGHT-NING
ELECTRIC OKAUTSUBON
LV.1
AP
1700
Pow
0
SOME-THING ABOUT HIS SKIN.
HUH?
HE'S GOING TO SHED HIS SKIN?
THIS IS MY SPECIAL PLAN!
NO WAY IS THIS ONE GONNA FAIL!
YOU FOLKS READY TO ROCK?
GULP
HIS SKIN... EWW...

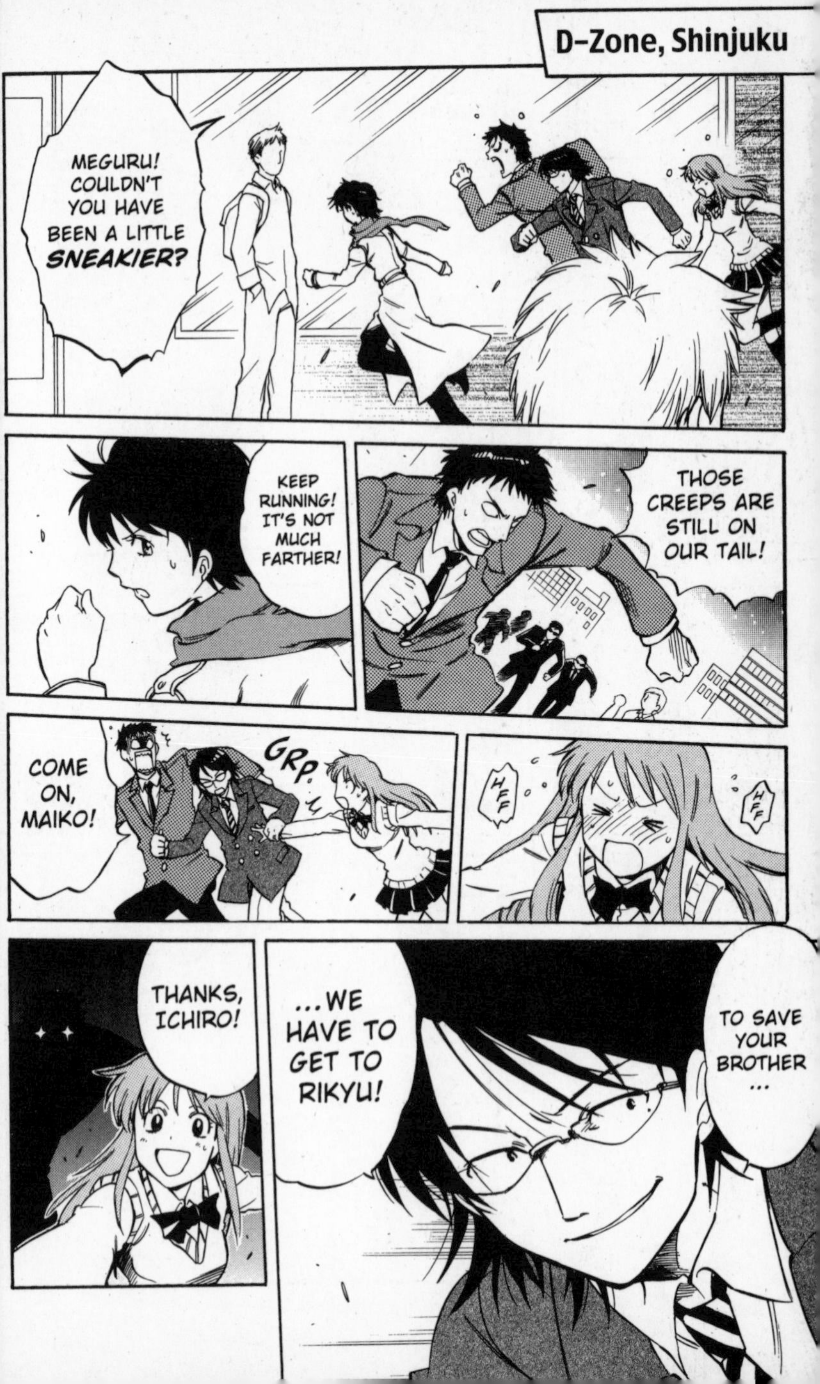
D-Zone, Shinjuku
MEGURU! COULDN'T YOU HAVE BEEN A LITTLE SNEAKIER?
THOSE CREEPS ARE STILL ON OUR TAIL!
KEEP RUNNING! IT'S NOT MUCH FARTHER!
HFF
HFF
GRP
COME ON, MAIKO!
TO SAVE YOUR BROTHER ...
...WE HAVE TO GET TO RIKYU!
THANKS, ICHIRO!

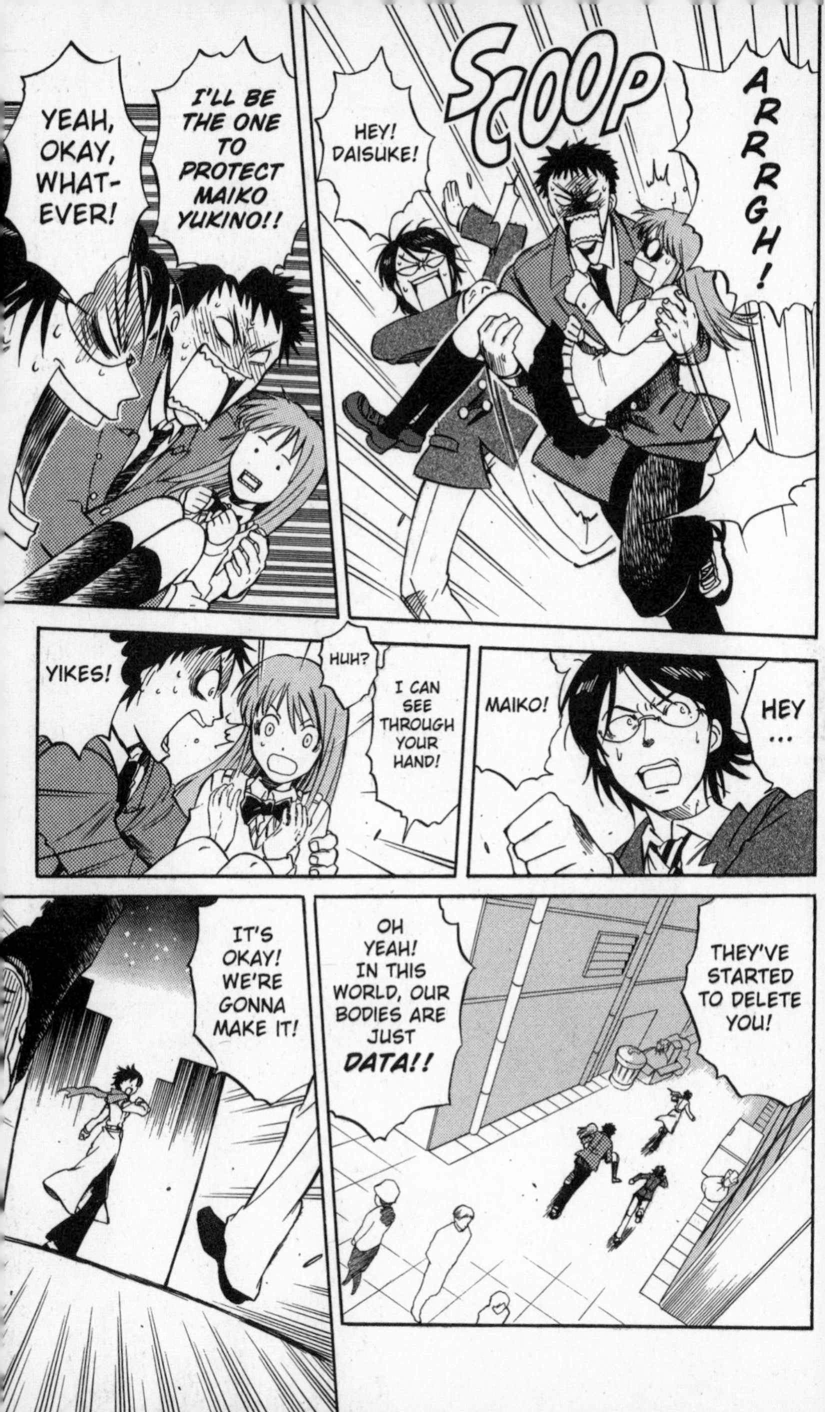
ARRRGH!
SCOOP
HEY! DAISUKE!
I'LL BE THE ONE TO PROTECT MAIKO YUKINO!!
YEAH, OKAY, WHAT-EVER!
HEY ...
MAIKO!
HUH?
I CAN SEE THROUGH YOUR HAND!
YIKES!
THEY'VE STARTED TO DELETE YOU!
OH YEAH! IN THIS WORLD, OUR BODIES ARE JUST DATA!!
IT'S OKAY! WE'RE GONNA MAKE IT!

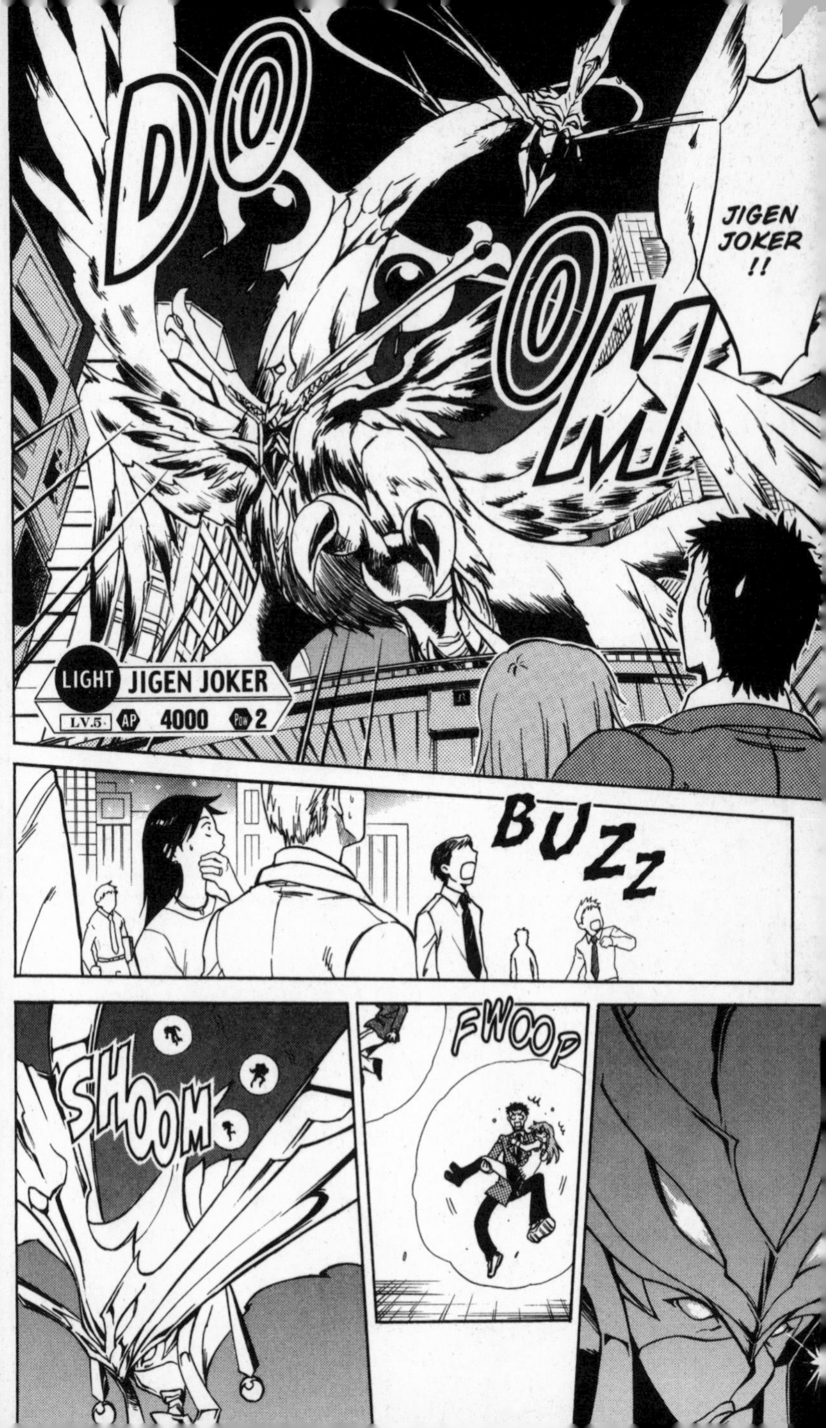
JIGEN JOKER !!
DOOOM
LIGHT JIGEN JOKER
LV.5 AP 4000 POW 2
BUZZ
FWOOP
SHOOM

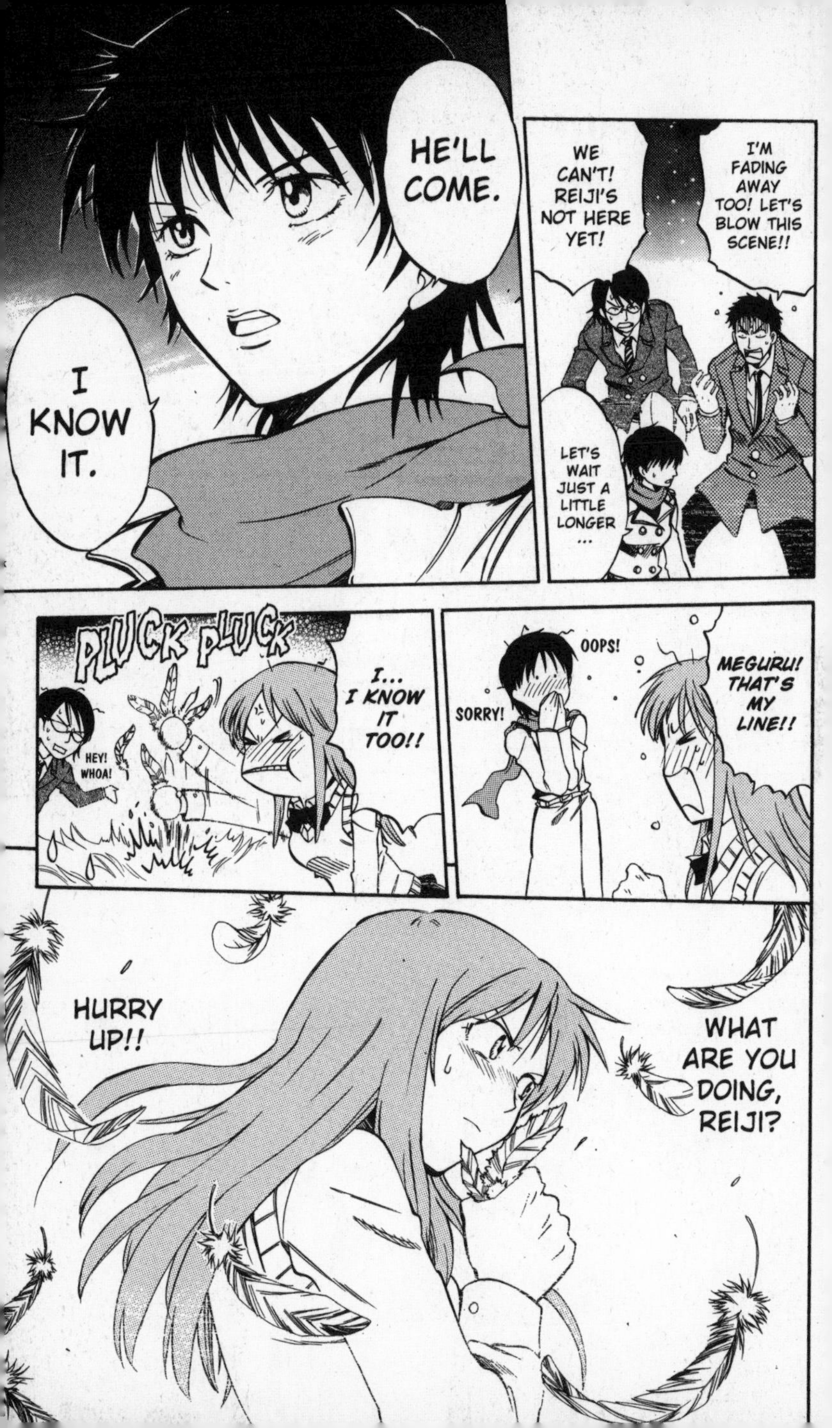
I'M FADING AWAY TOO! LET'S BLOW THIS SCENE!!
WE CAN'T! REIJI'S NOT HERE YET!
LET'S WAIT JUST A LITTLE LONGER ...
HE'LL COME.
I KNOW IT.
MEGURU! THAT'S MY LINE!!
OOPS!
SORRY!
I... I KNOW IT TOO!!
PLUCK PLUCK
HEY! WHOA!
WHAT ARE YOU DOING, REIJI?
HURRY UP!!

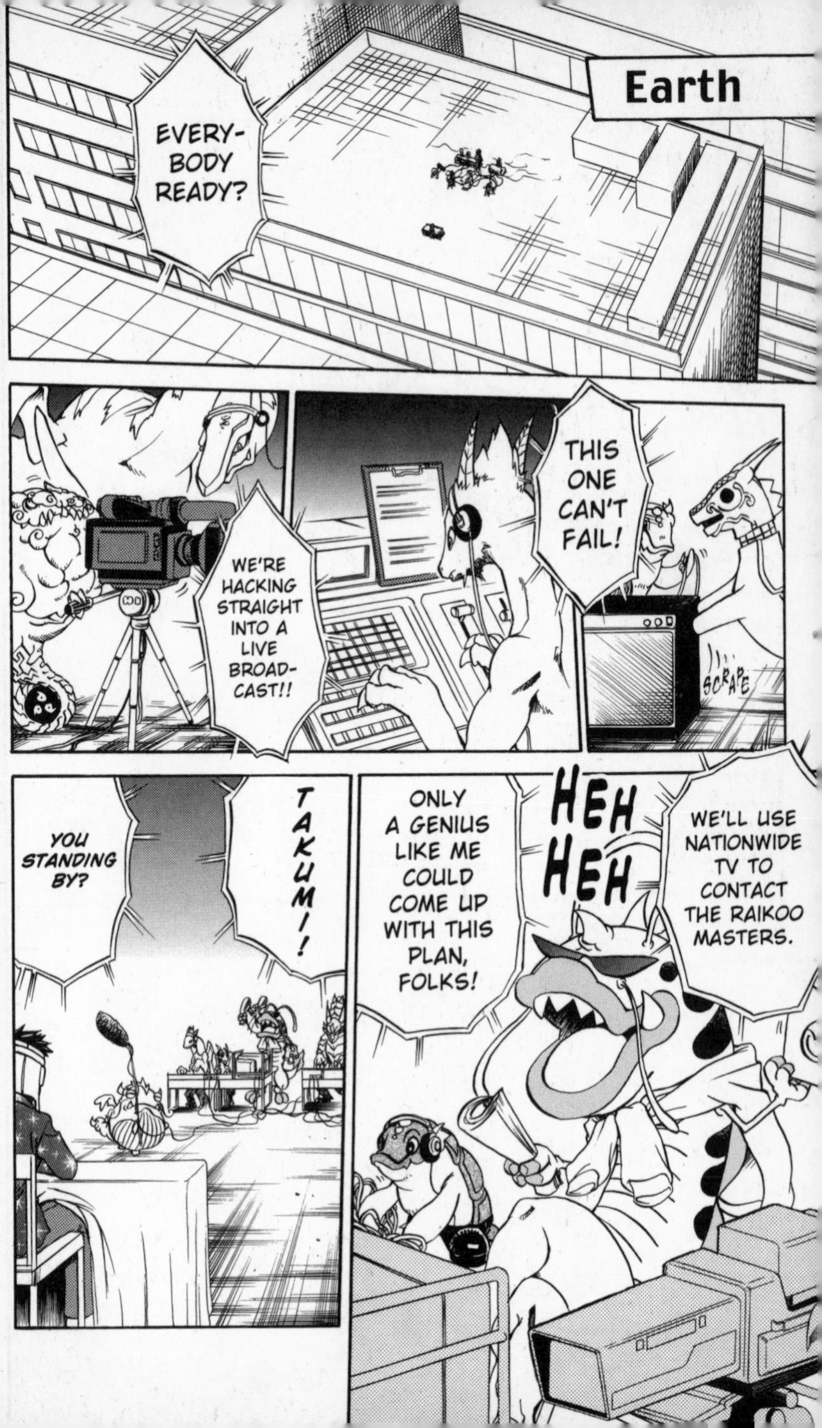

Earth
EVERY-BODY READY?
THIS ONE CAN'T FAIL!
SCRAPE
WE'RE HACKING STRAIGHT INTO A LIVE BROAD-CAST!!
WE'LL USE NATIONWIDE TV TO CONTACT THE RAIKOO MASTERS.
HEH HEH
ONLY A GENIUS LIKE ME COULD COME UP WITH THIS PLAN, FOLKS!
TAKUMI!
YOU STANDING BY?

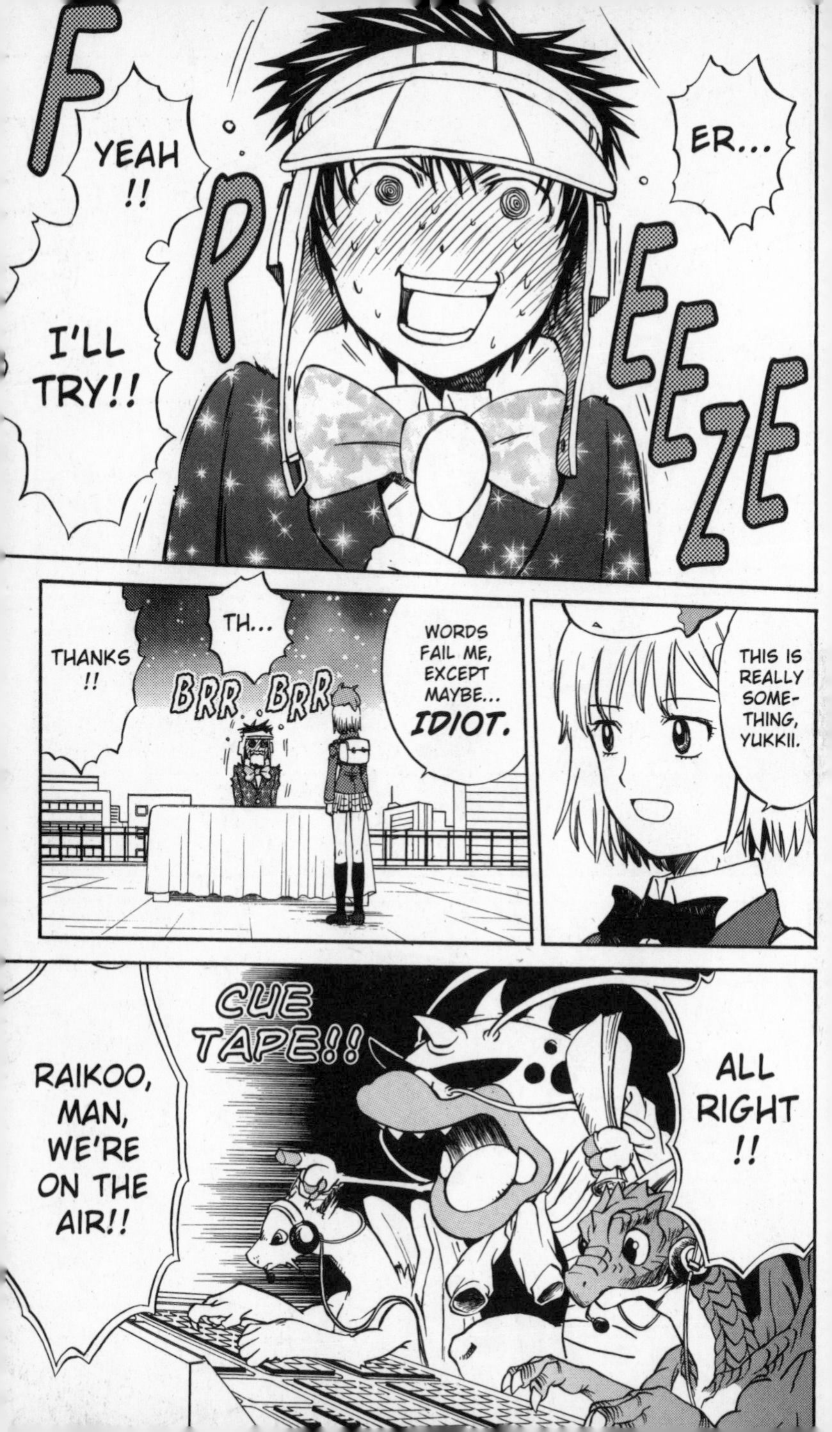
ER...
FREEZE
YEAH !!
I'LL TRY!!
THIS IS REALLY SOMETHING, YUKKII.
WORDS FAIL ME, EXCEPT MAYBE... IDIOT.
TH...
BRR BRR
THANKS !!
ALL RIGHT !!
CUE TAPE!!
RAIKOO, MAN, WE'RE ON THE AIR!!

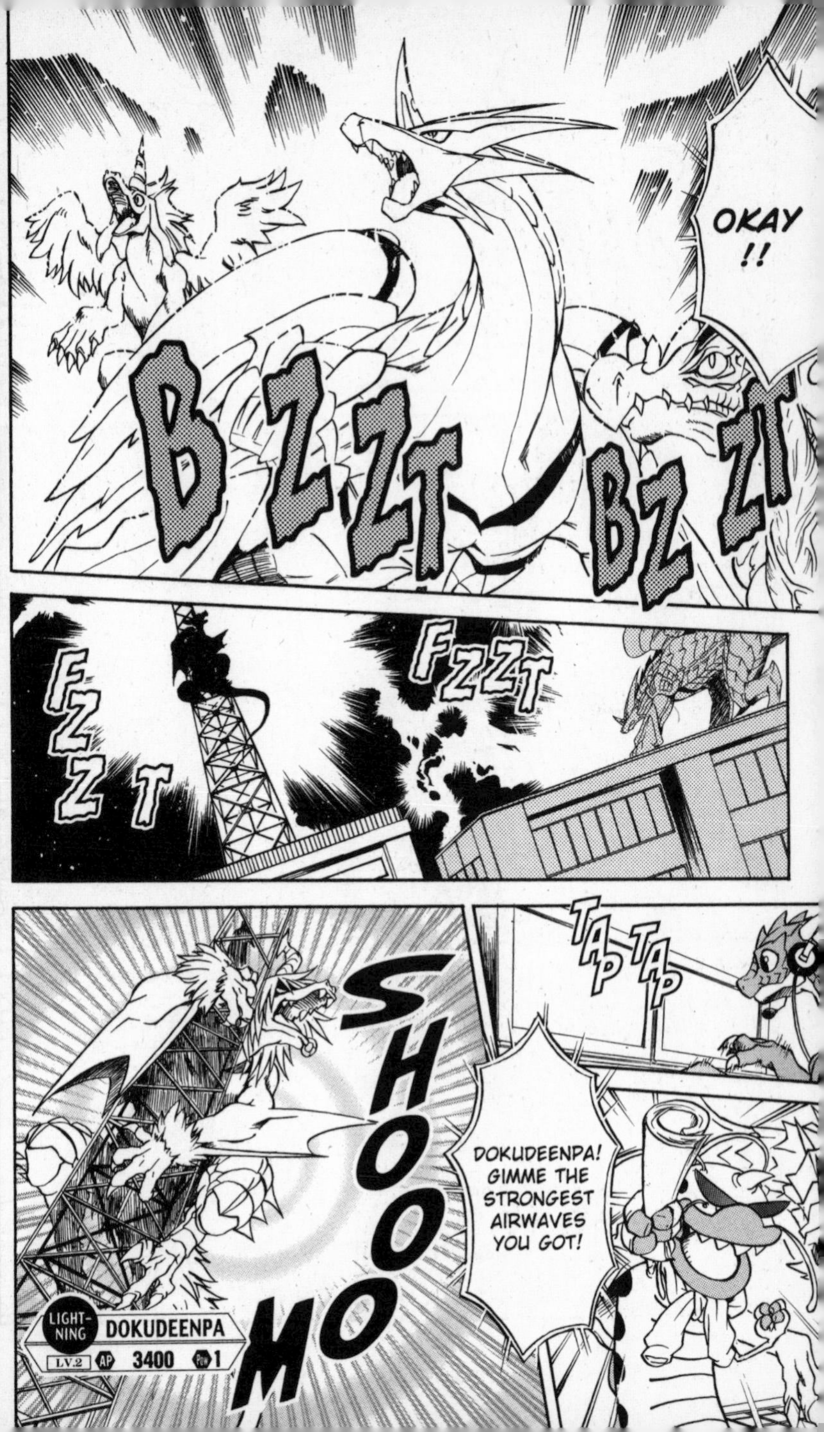
OKAY !!
BZZT BZZT
FZZZT
FZZT
TAP TAP
DOKUDEENPA! GIMME THE STRONGEST AIRWAVES YOU GOT!
SHOOOOM
LIGHT-NING DOKUDEENPA
LV.2 AP 3400 1

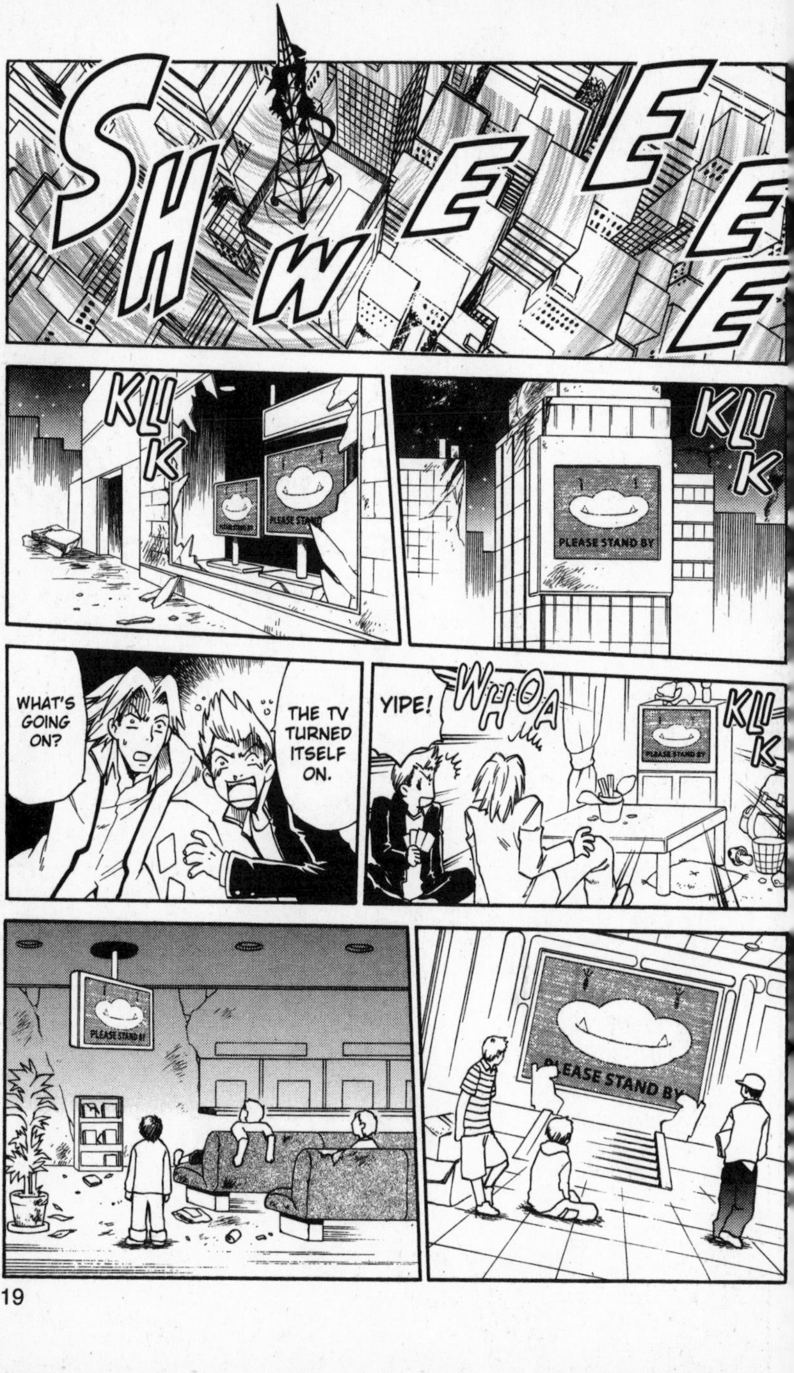

SHWEEEEE
KLIK
PLEASE STAND BY
KLIK
PLEASE STAND
KLIK
WHOA
YIPE!
THE TV TURNED ITSELF ON.
WHAT'S GOING ON?
PLEASE STAND BY
PLEASE STAND BY

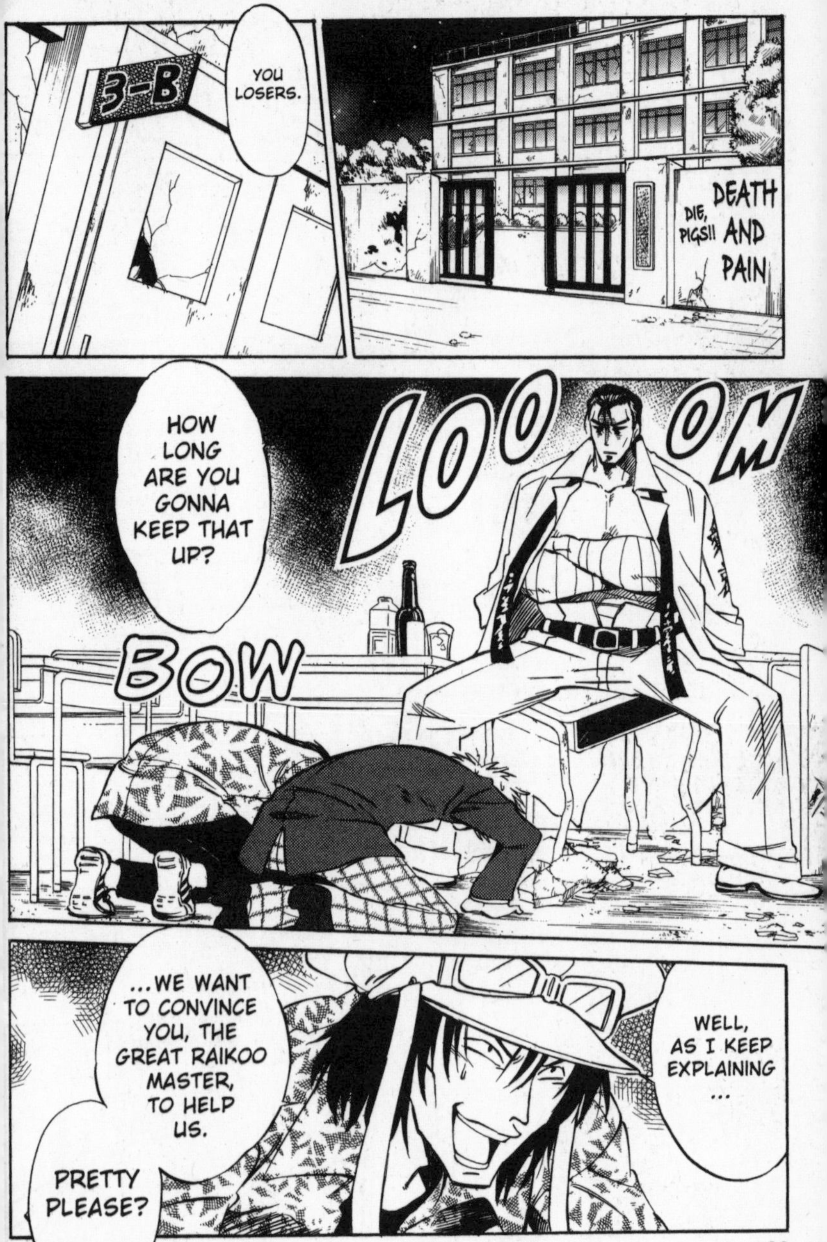
DEATH AND PAIN
DIE, PIGS!!
3-B
YOU LOSERS.
LOOOM
HOW LONG ARE YOU GONNA KEEP THAT UP?
BOW
WELL, AS I KEEP EXPLAINING...
...WE WANT TO CONVINCE YOU, THE GREAT RAIKOO MASTER, TO HELP US.
PRETTY PLEASE?

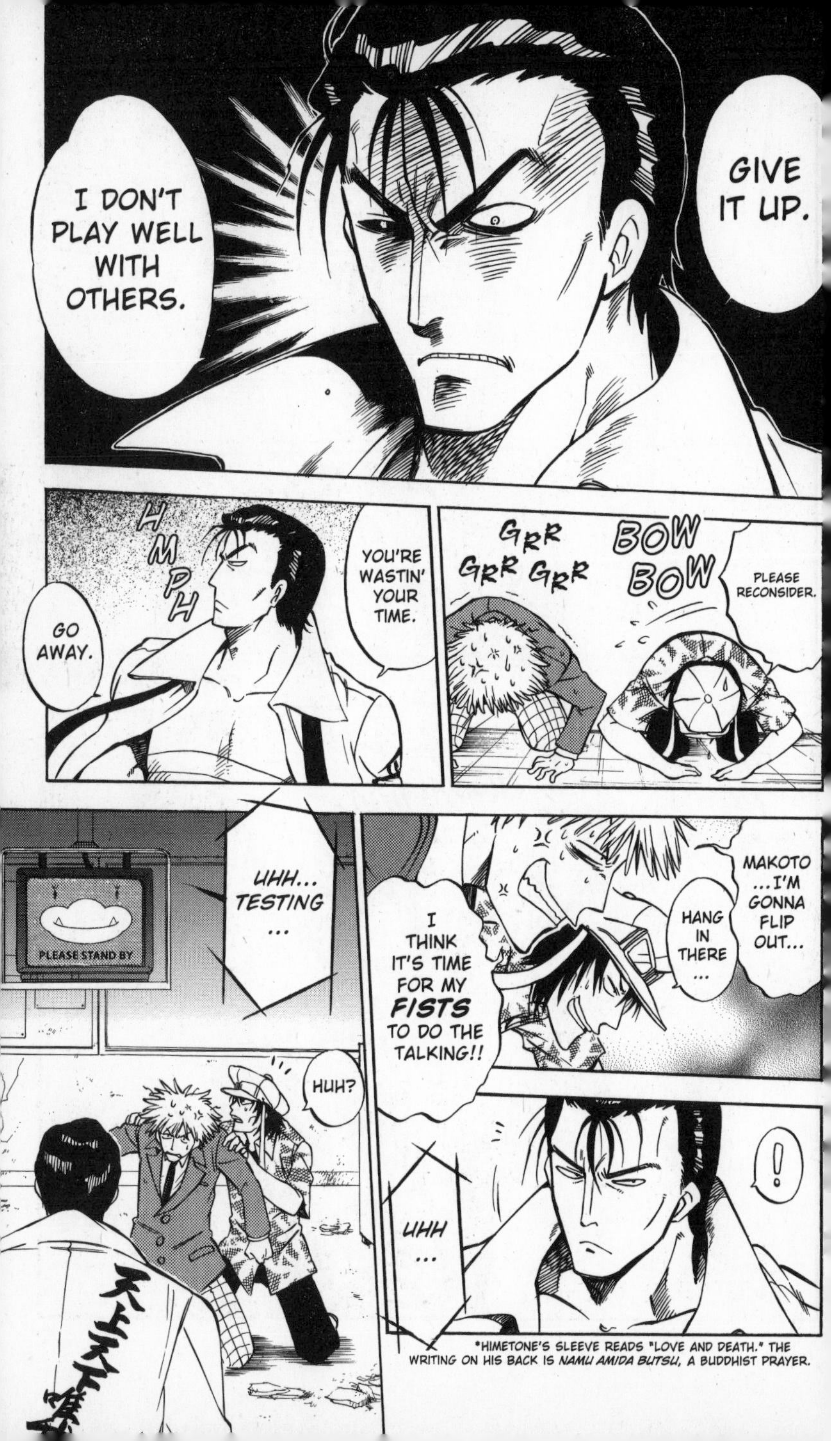
GIVE IT UP.
I DON'T PLAY WELL WITH OTHERS.
PLEASE RECONSIDER.
BOW BOW
GRR GRR GRR
YOU'RE WASTIN' YOUR TIME.
HMPH
GO AWAY.
MAKOTO ...I'M GONNA FLIP OUT...
HANG IN THERE ...
I THINK IT'S TIME FOR MY FISTS TO DO THE TALKING!!
!
UHH ...
UHH... TESTING ...
PLEASE STAND BY
HUH?
天上天下唯

*HIMETONE'S SLEEVE READS "LOVE AND DEATH." THE WRITING ON HIS BACK IS *NAMU AMIDA BUTSU*, A BUDDHIST PRAYER.

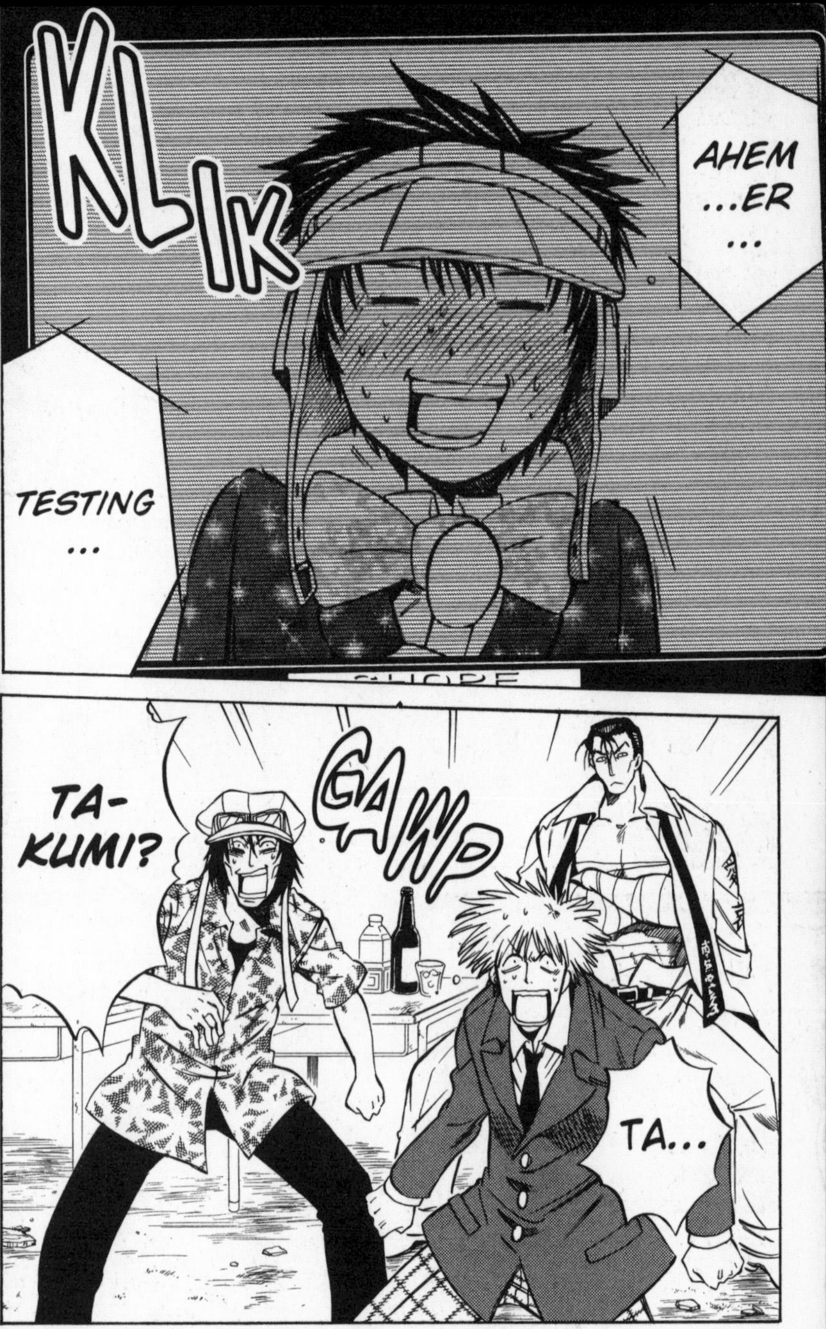
AHEM ...ER ...
KLIK
TESTING ...
GAWP
TA-KUMI?
TA...

READ THIS WAY

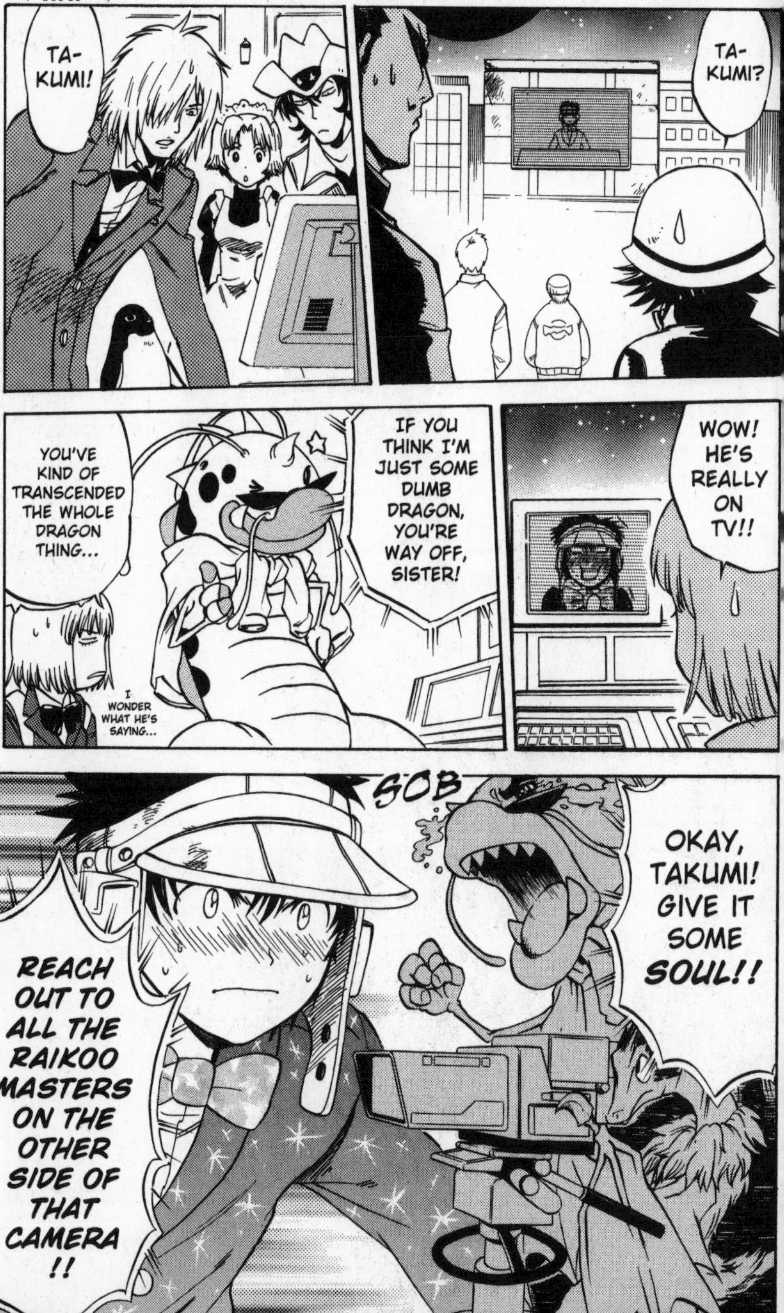
TA-KUMI?
TA-KUMI!
WOW! HE'S REALLY ON TV!!
IF YOU THINK I'M JUST SOME DUMB DRAGON, YOU'RE WAY OFF, SISTER!
YOU'VE KIND OF TRANSCENDED THE WHOLE DRAGON THING...
I WONDER WHAT HE'S SAYING...
SOB
OKAY, TAKUMI! GIVE IT SOME SOUL!!
REACH OUT TO ALL THE RAIKOO MASTERS ON THE OTHER SIDE OF THAT CAMERA!!

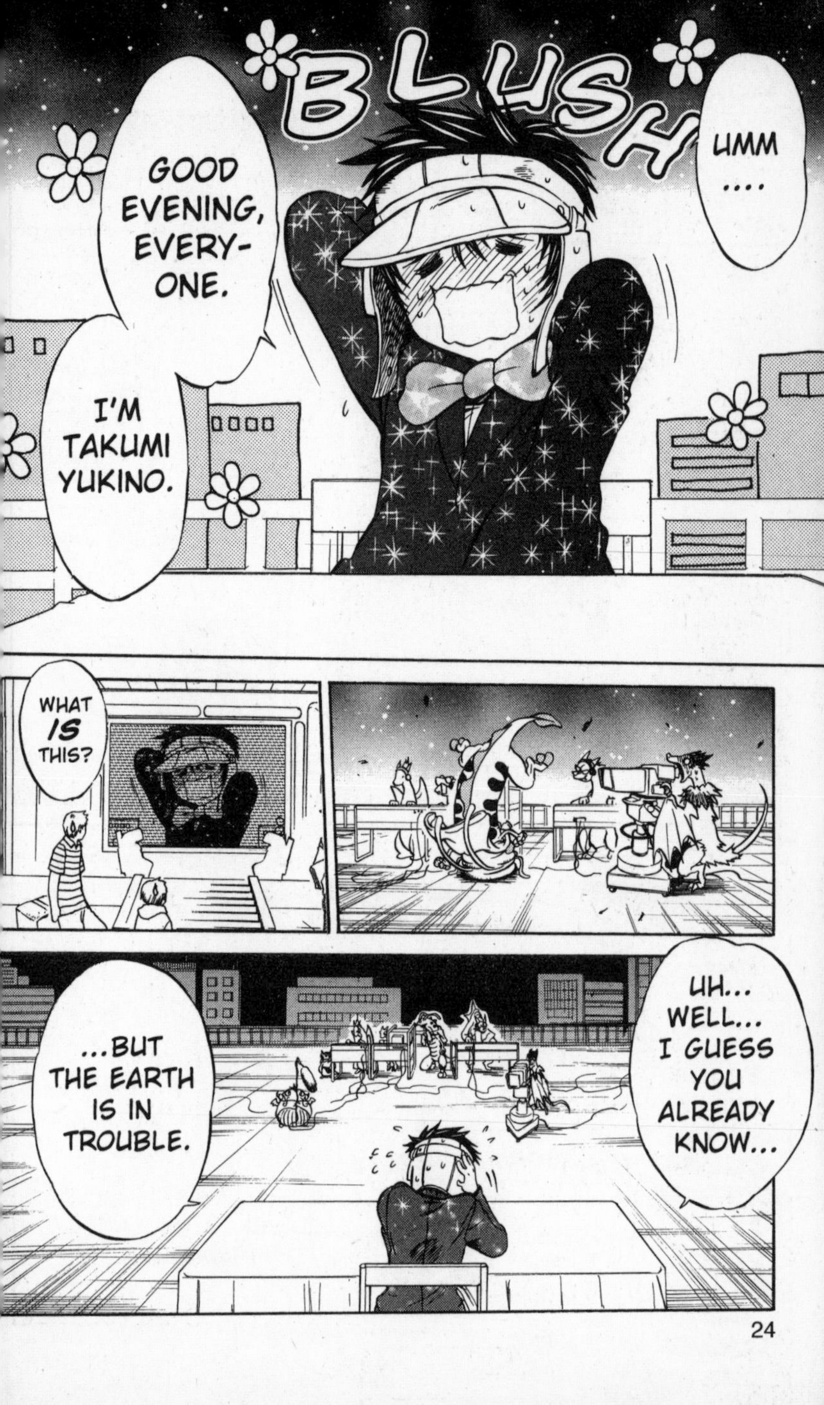
BLUSH
UMM ....
GOOD EVENING, EVERY-ONE.
I'M TAKUMI YUKINO.
WHAT *IS* THIS?
UH... WELL... I GUESS YOU ALREADY KNOW...
...BUT THE EARTH IS IN TROUBLE.

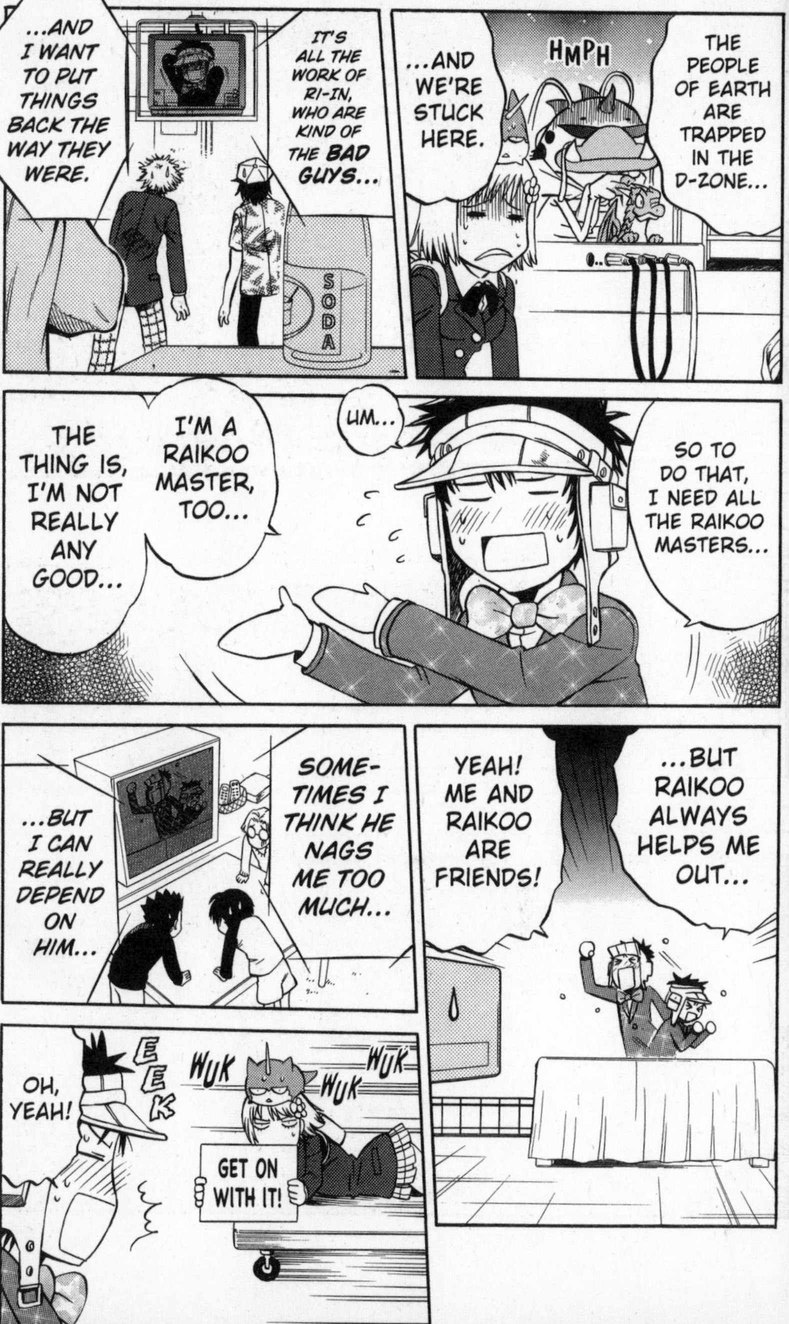
THE PEOPLE OF EARTH ARE TRAPPED IN THE D-ZONE...
HMPH
...AND WE'RE STUCK HERE.
IT'S ALL THE WORK OF RI-IN, WHO ARE KIND OF THE BAD GUYS...
...AND I WANT TO PUT THINGS BACK THE WAY THEY WERE.
SODA
SO TO DO THAT, I NEED ALL THE RAIKOO MASTERS...
UM...
I'M A RAIKOO MASTER, TOO...
THE THING IS, I'M NOT REALLY ANY GOOD...
...BUT RAIKOO ALWAYS HELPS ME OUT...
YEAH! ME AND RAIKOO ARE FRIENDS!
SOMETIMES I THINK HE NAGS ME TOO MUCH...
...BUT I CAN REALLY DEPEND ON HIM...
WUK WUK WUK
GET ON WITH IT!
EEK
OH, YEAH!

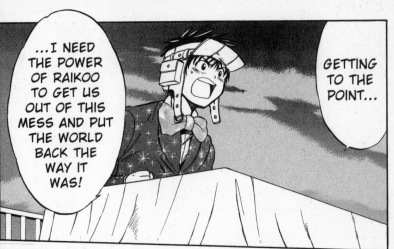

GETTING TO THE POINT...
...I NEED THE POWER OF RAIKOO TO GET US OUT OF THIS MESS AND PUT THE WORLD BACK THE WAY IT WAS!
RI-IN IS AFTER RAIKOO, TOO!

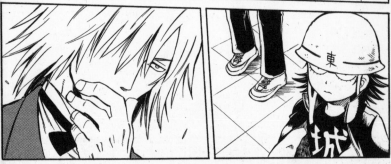

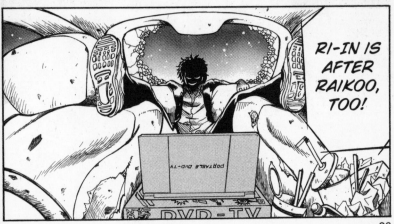

READ THIS WAY

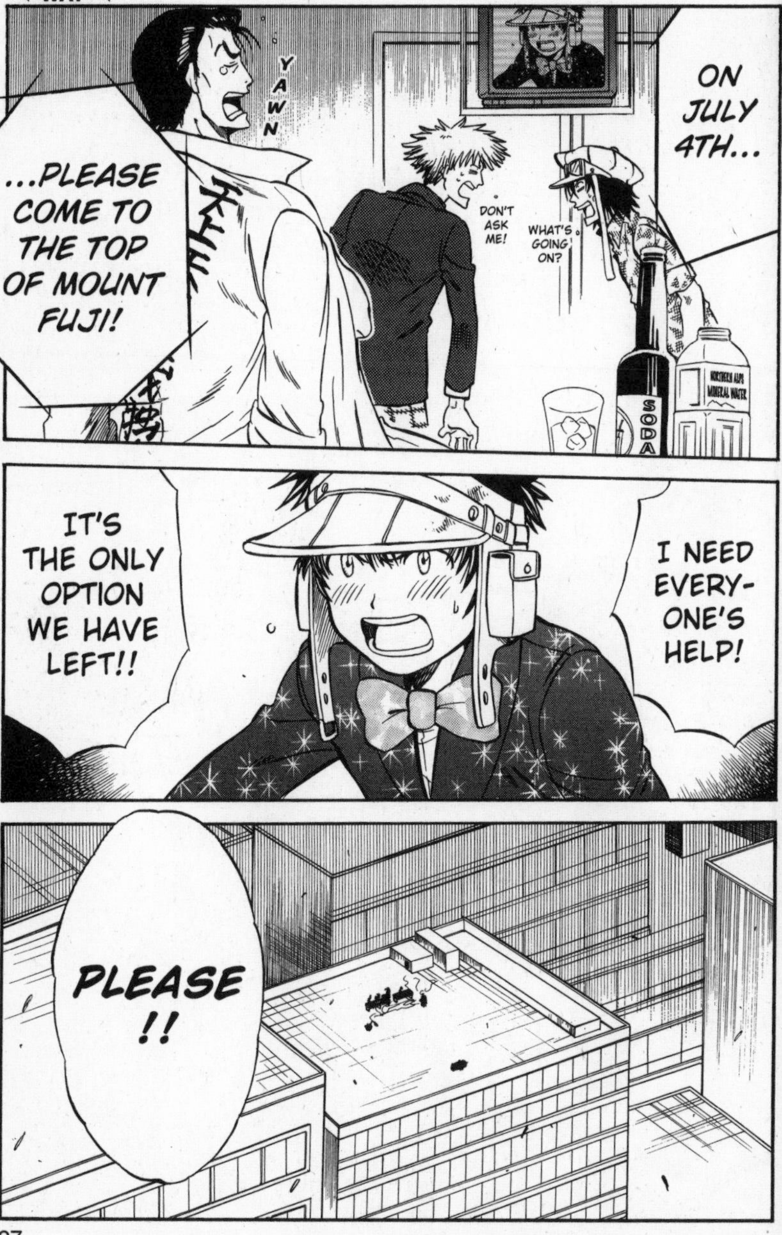
ON JULY 4TH...
WHAT'S GOING ON?
DON'T ASK ME!
YAWN
...PLEASE COME TO THE TOP OF MOUNT FUJI!
NORTHERN ALPS MINERAL WATER
SODA
I NEED EVERY-ONE'S HELP!
IT'S THE ONLY OPTION WE HAVE LEFT!!
PLEASE!!

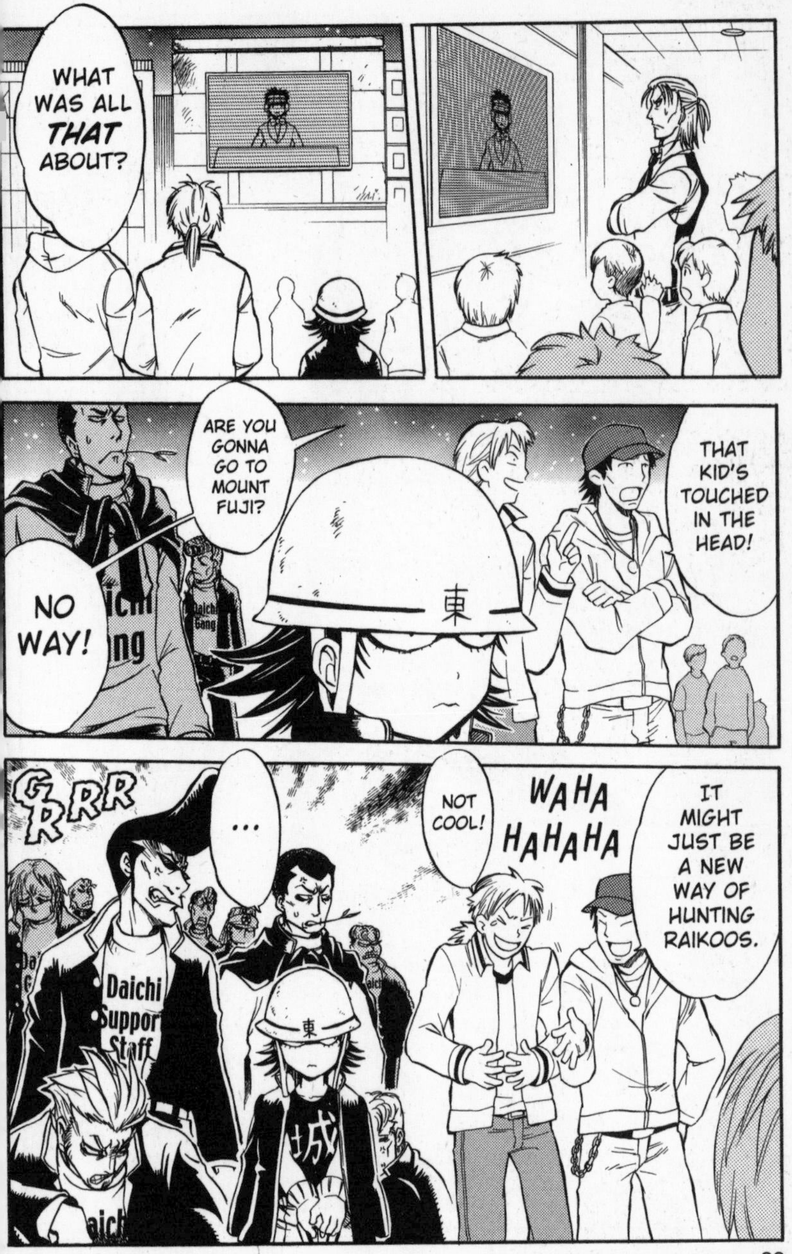
WHAT WAS ALL ***THAT*** ABOUT?
THAT KID'S TOUCHED IN THE HEAD!
ARE YOU GONNA GO TO MOUNT FUJI?
NO WAY!
Daichi Gang
IT MIGHT JUST BE A NEW WAY OF HUNTING RAIKOOS.
WAHA HAHAHA
NOT COOL!
...
GRRR

READ THIS WAY

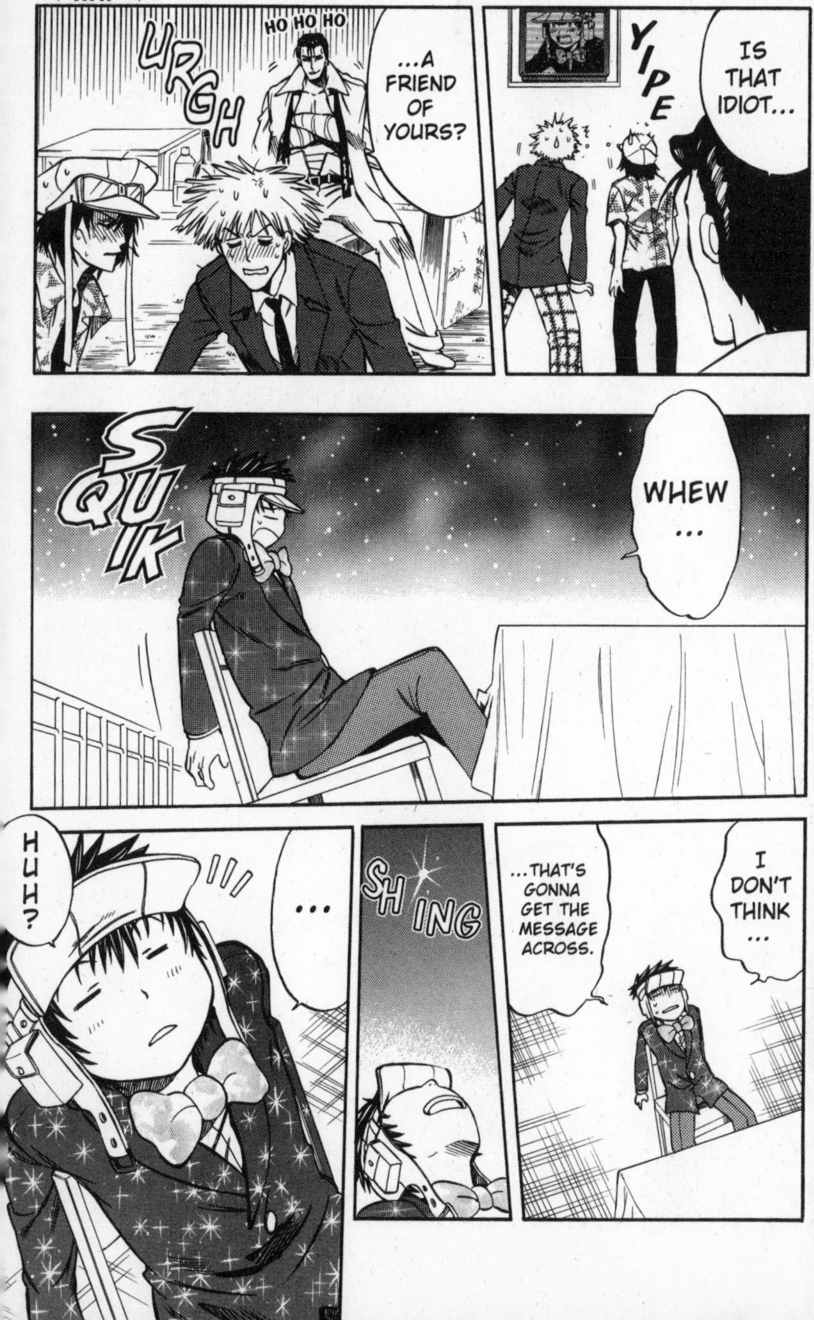
IS THAT IDIOT...
YIPE
...A FRIEND OF YOURS?
HO HO HO
URGH
WHEW...
SQUIK
I DON'T THINK...
...THAT'S GONNA GET THE MESSAGE ACROSS.
SHING
...
HUH?

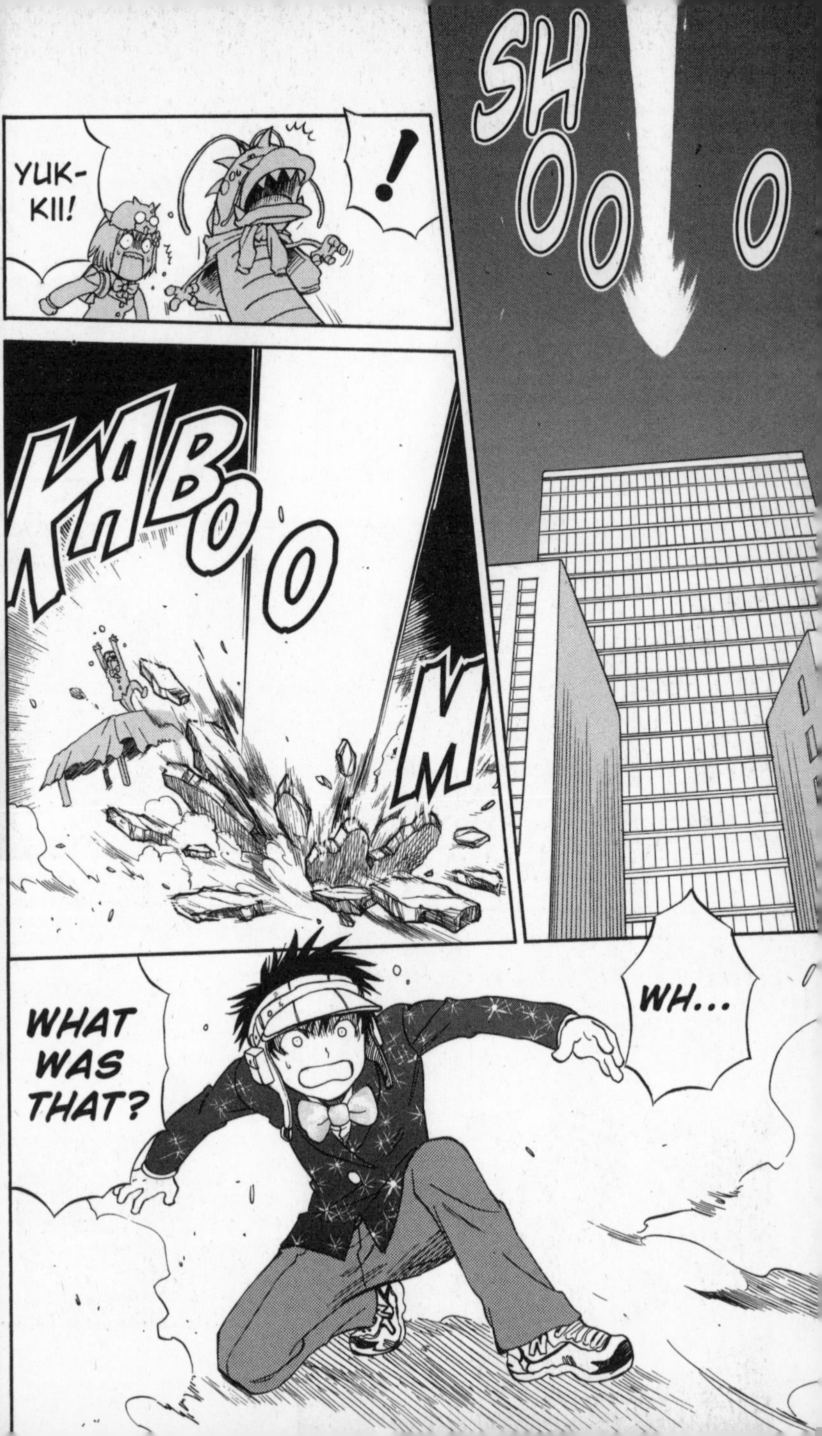
SHOOOO
!
YUK-KII!
KABOOOM
WH...
WHAT WAS THAT?

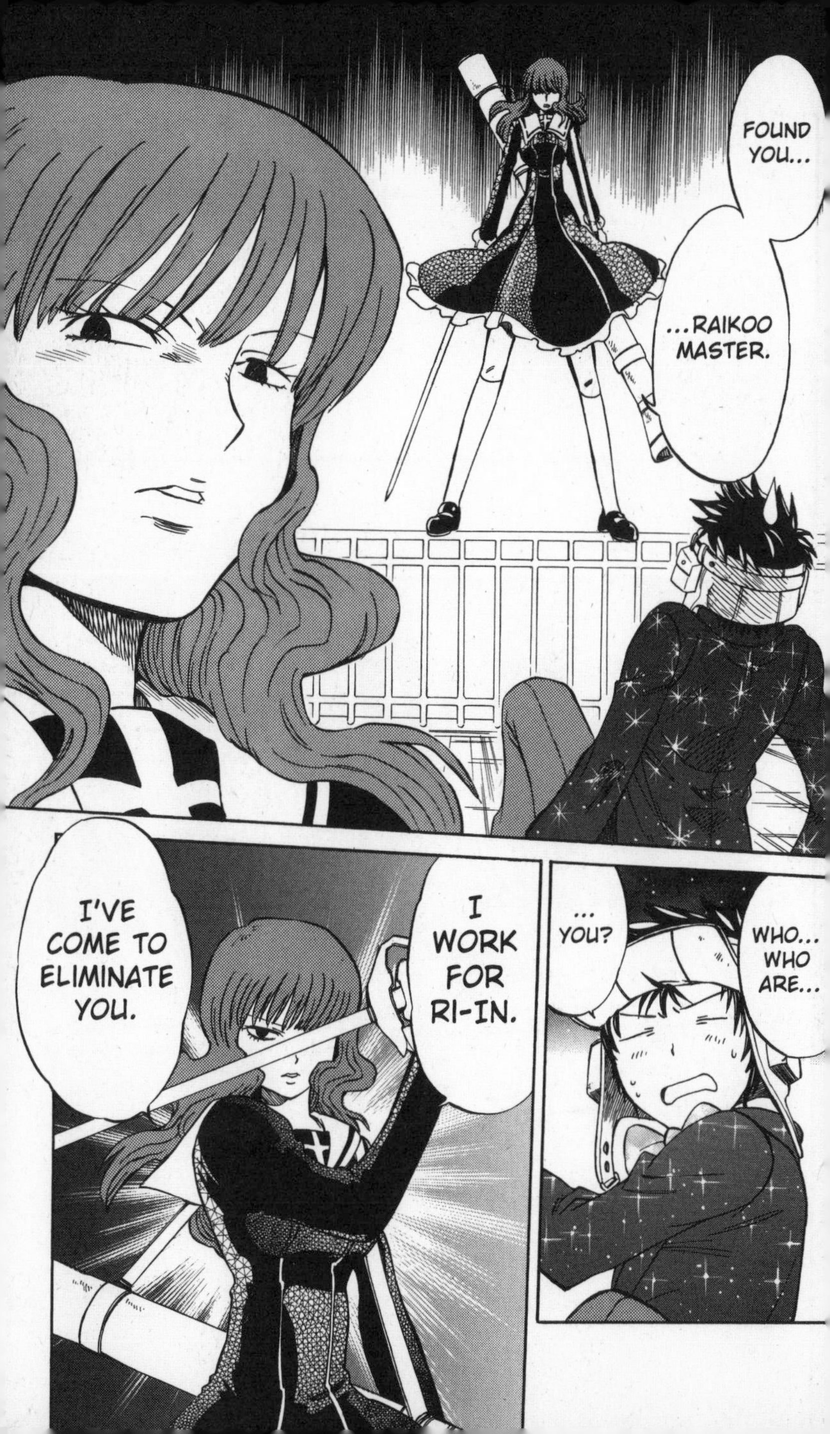
FOUND YOU...
...RAIKOO MASTER.
WHO... WHO ARE...
... YOU?
I WORK FOR RI-IN.
I'VE COME TO ELIMINATE YOU.

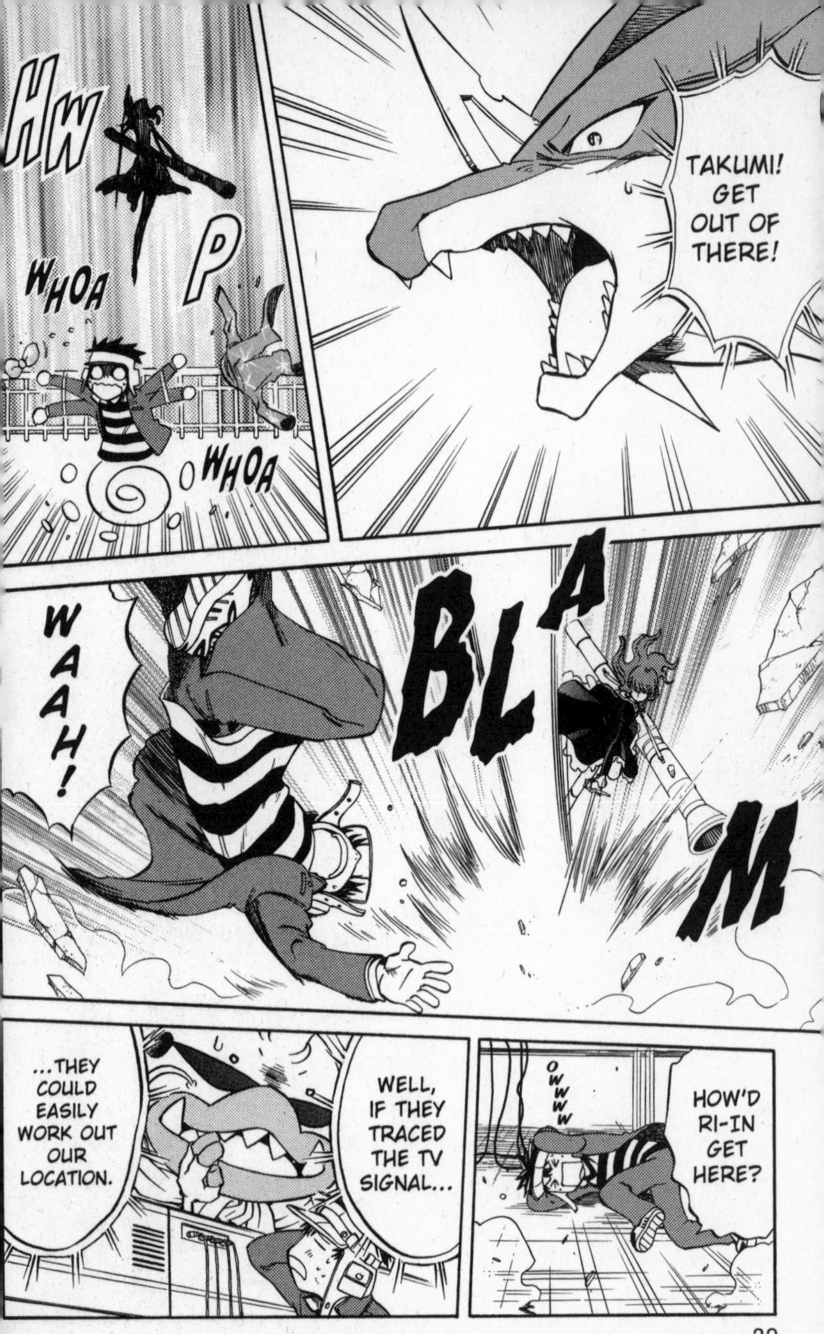
TAKUMI! GET OUT OF THERE!
HWP
WHOA
WHOA
BLAM
WAAAH!
HOW'D RI-IN GET HERE?
OWWWW
WELL, IF THEY TRACED THE TV SIGNAL...
...THEY COULD EASILY WORK OUT OUR LOCATION.

READ THIS WAY

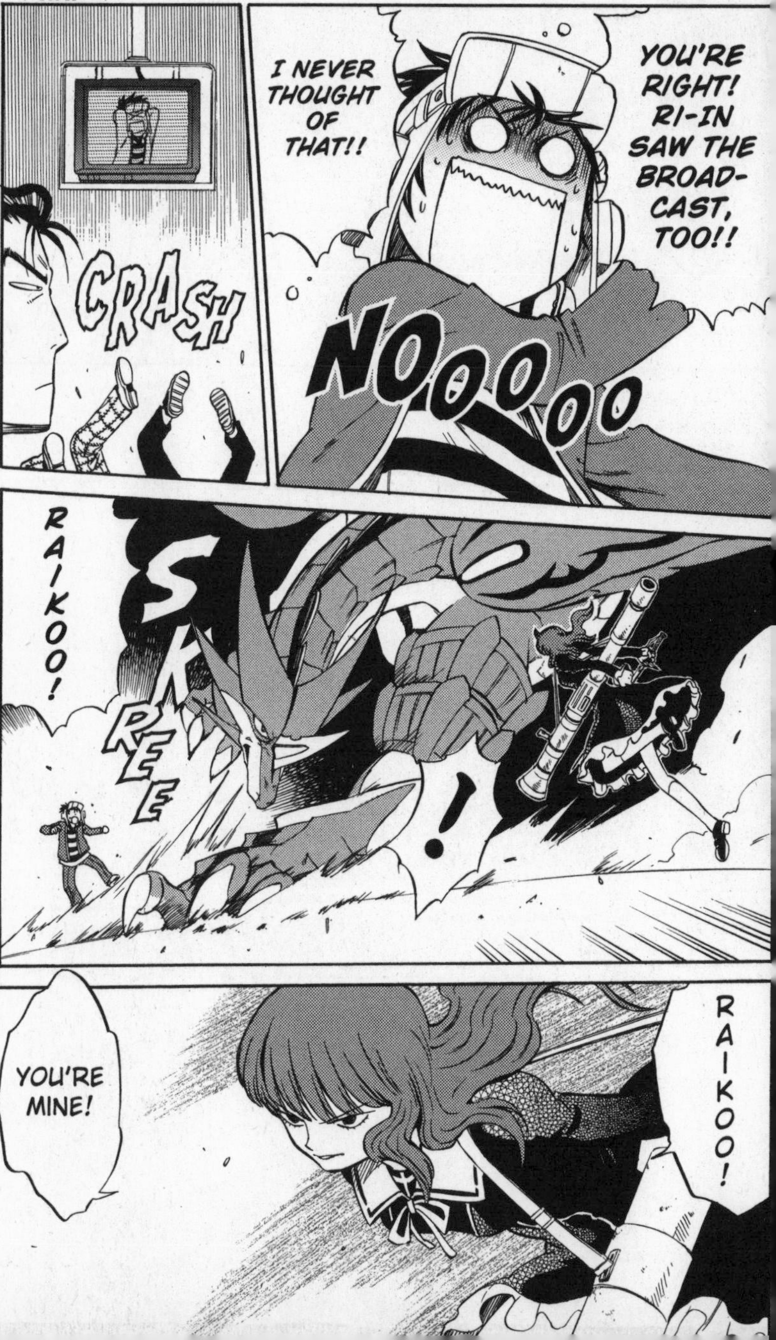

YOU'RE RIGHT! RI-IN SAW THE BROAD-CAST, TOO!!
I NEVER THOUGHT OF THAT!!
NOOOOOO
CRASH
SKREE
RAIKOO!
RAIKOO!
YOU'RE MINE!

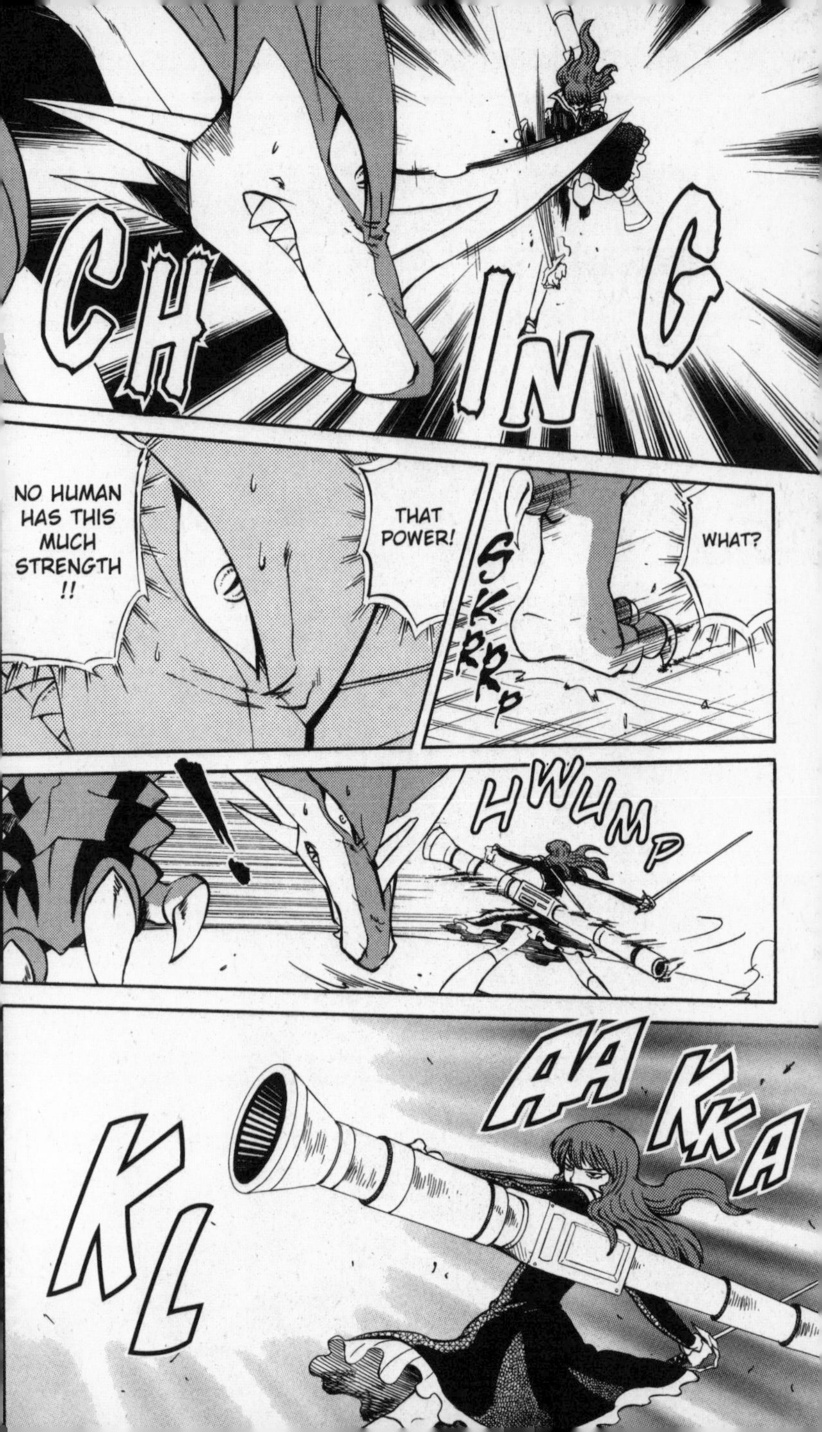
CHING
WHAT?
SKRRRP
THAT POWER!
NO HUMAN HAS THIS MUCH STRENGTH!!
HWUMP
!
AAKKA
KL

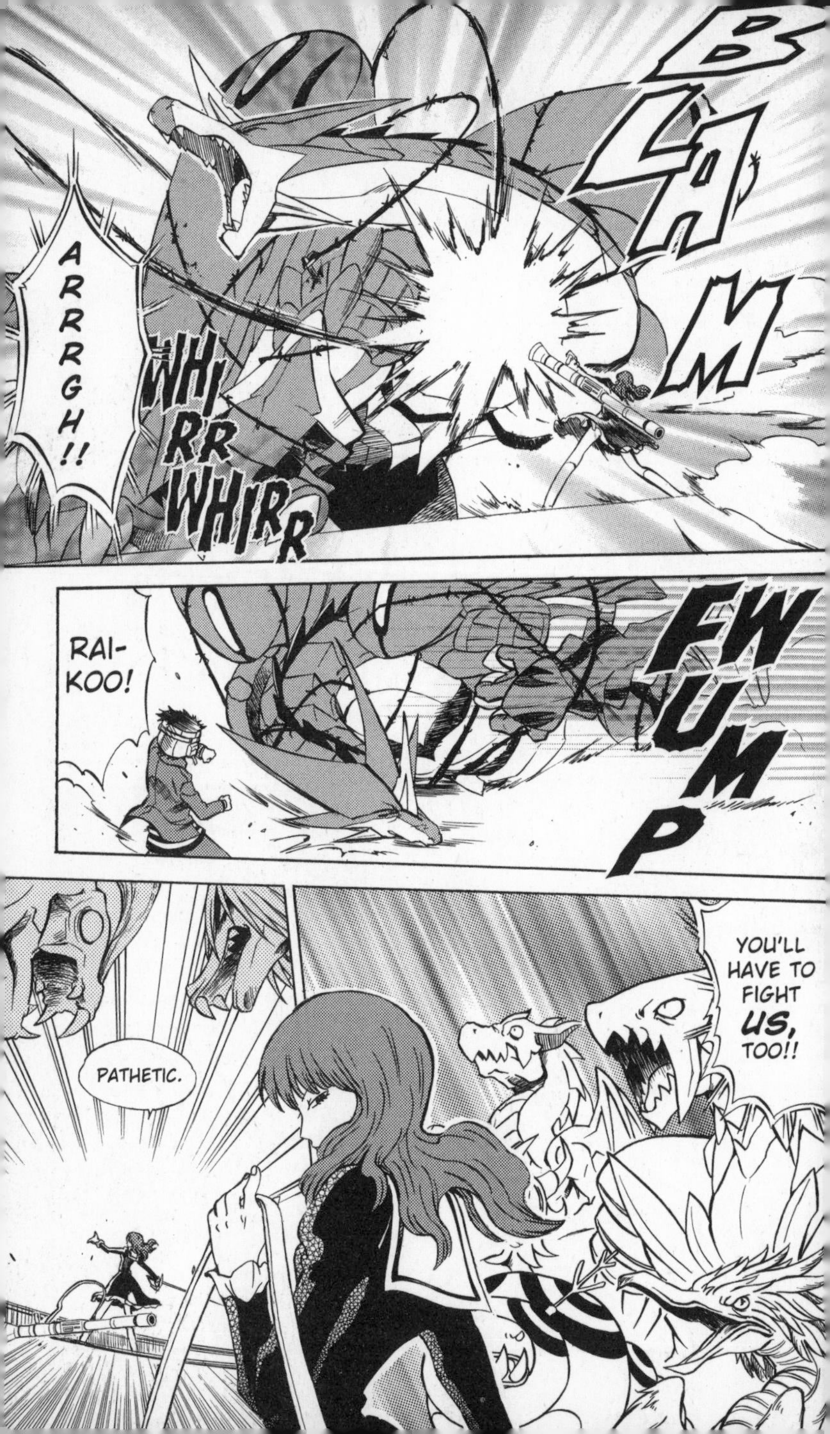
BLAM
WHIRR WHIRR
ARRRGH!!
FWUMP
RAI-KOO!
YOU'LL HAVE TO FIGHT US, TOO!!
PATHETIC.

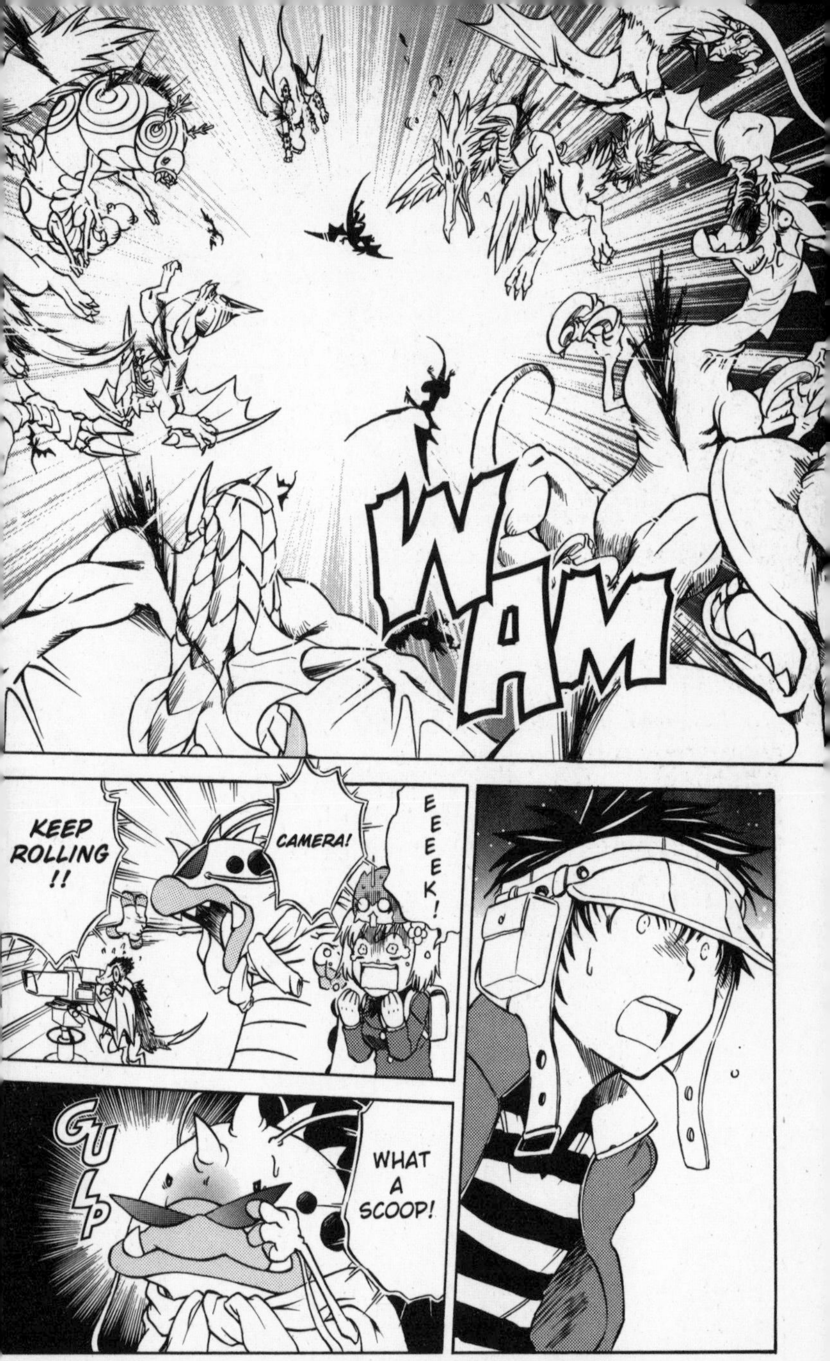
WAM
EEEEK!
CAMERA!
KEEP ROLLING!!
WHAT A SCOOP!
GULP

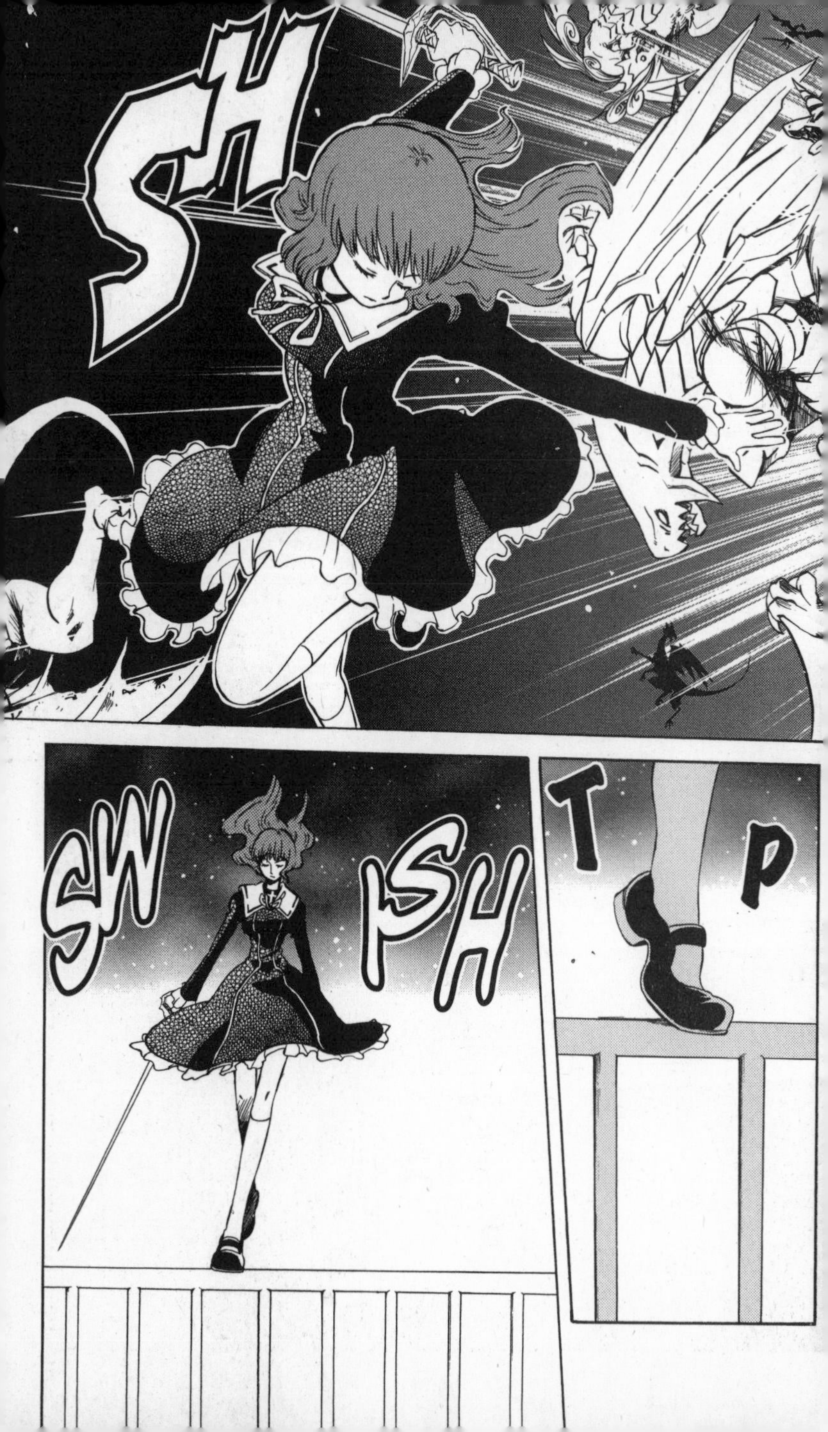
SH
TP
SWISH

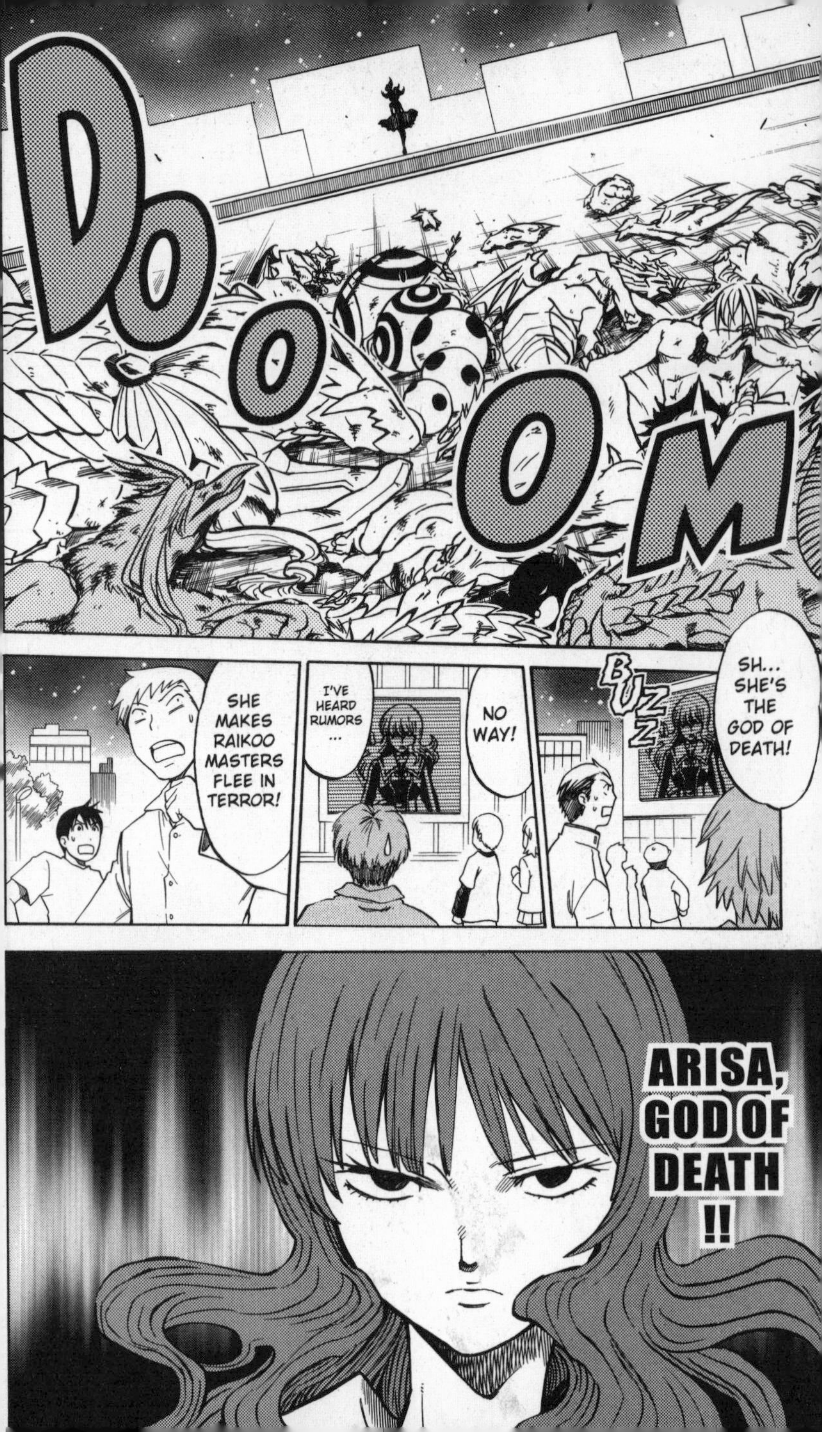
DOOOOM
SH... SHE'S THE GOD OF DEATH!
BUZZ
NO WAY!
I'VE HEARD RUMORS ...
SHE MAKES RAIKOO MASTERS FLEE IN TERROR!
ARISA, GOD OF DEATH !!

READ THIS WAY

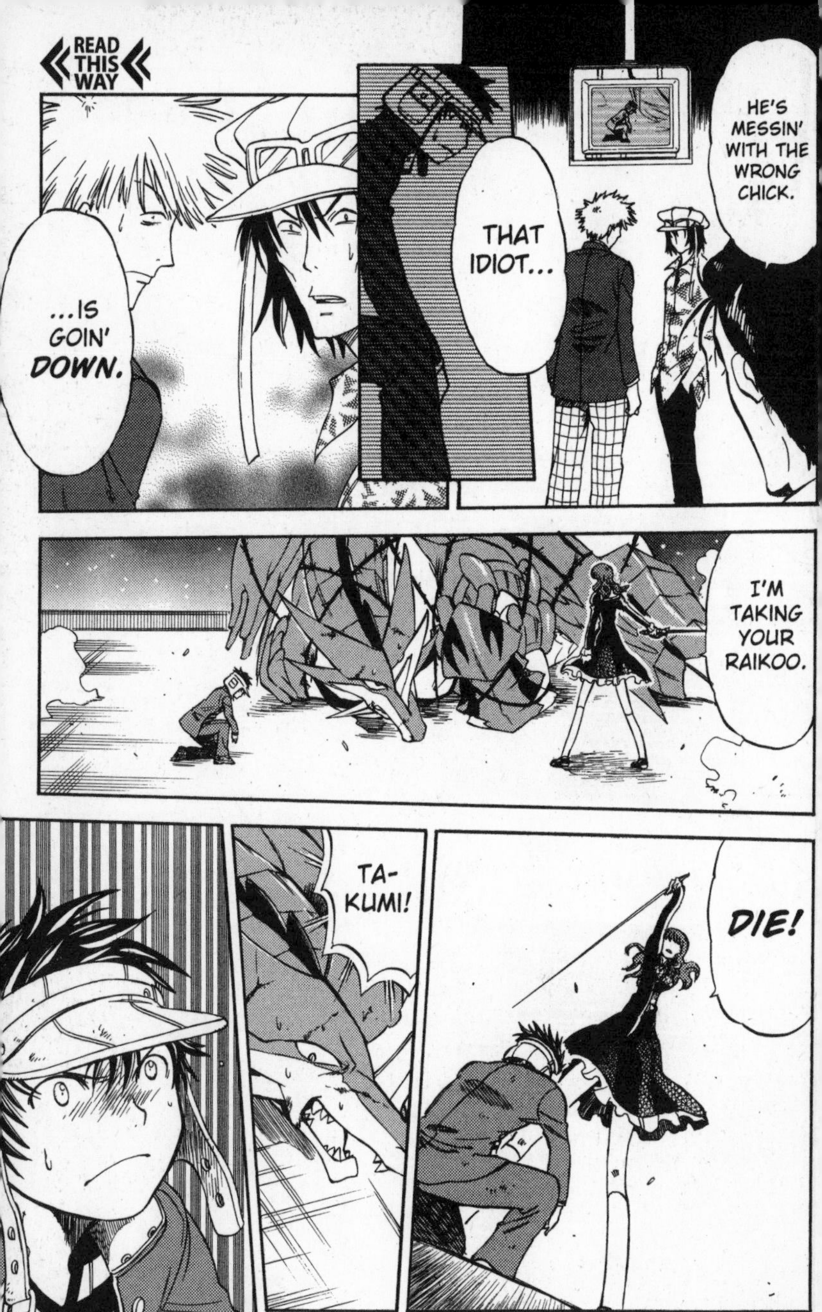
HE'S MESSIN' WITH THE WRONG CHICK.
THAT IDIOT...
...IS GOIN' DOWN.
I'M TAKING YOUR RAIKOO.
DIE!
TA-KUMI!

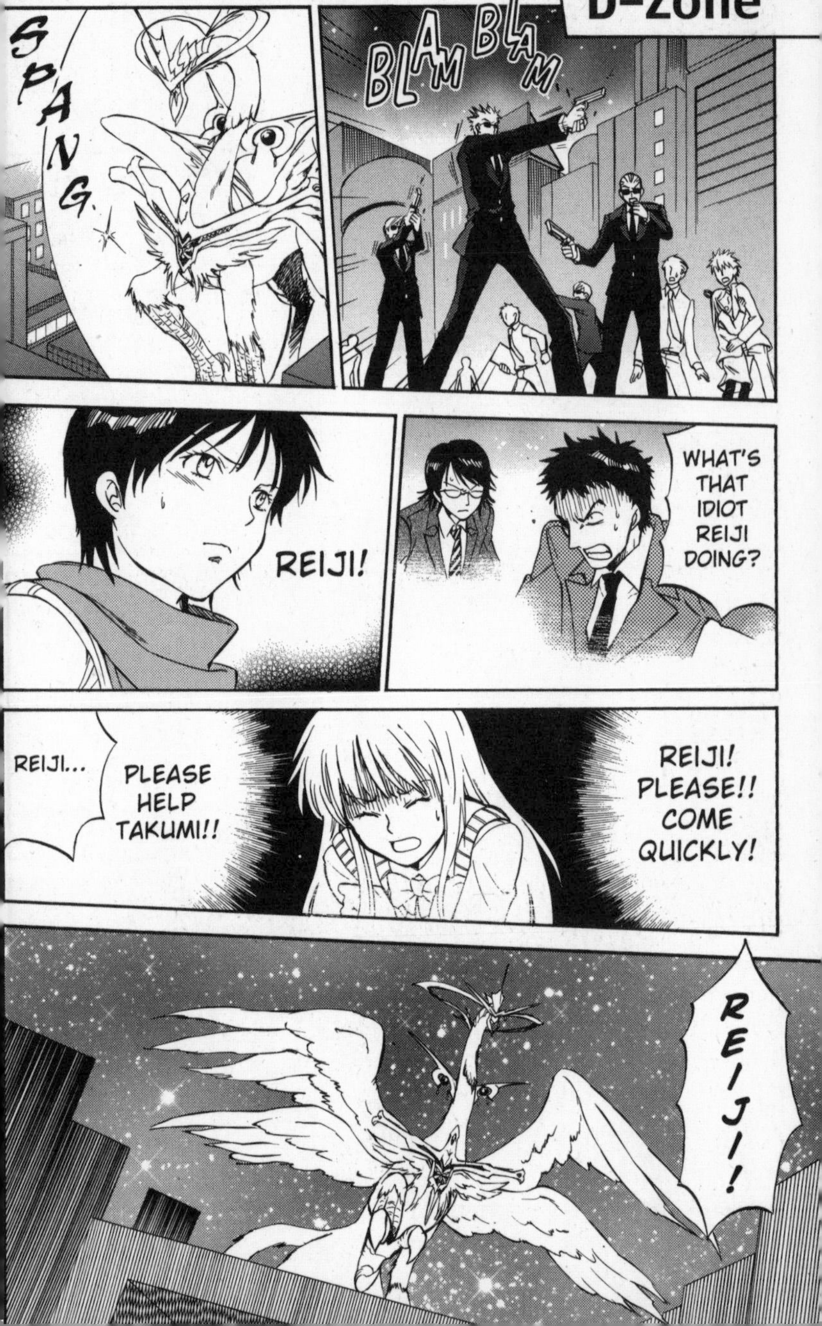
BLAM BLAM
SPANG
WHAT'S THAT IDIOT REIJI DOING?
REIJI!
REIJI! PLEASE!! COME QUICKLY!
PLEASE HELP TAKUMI!!
REIJI...
REIJI!!

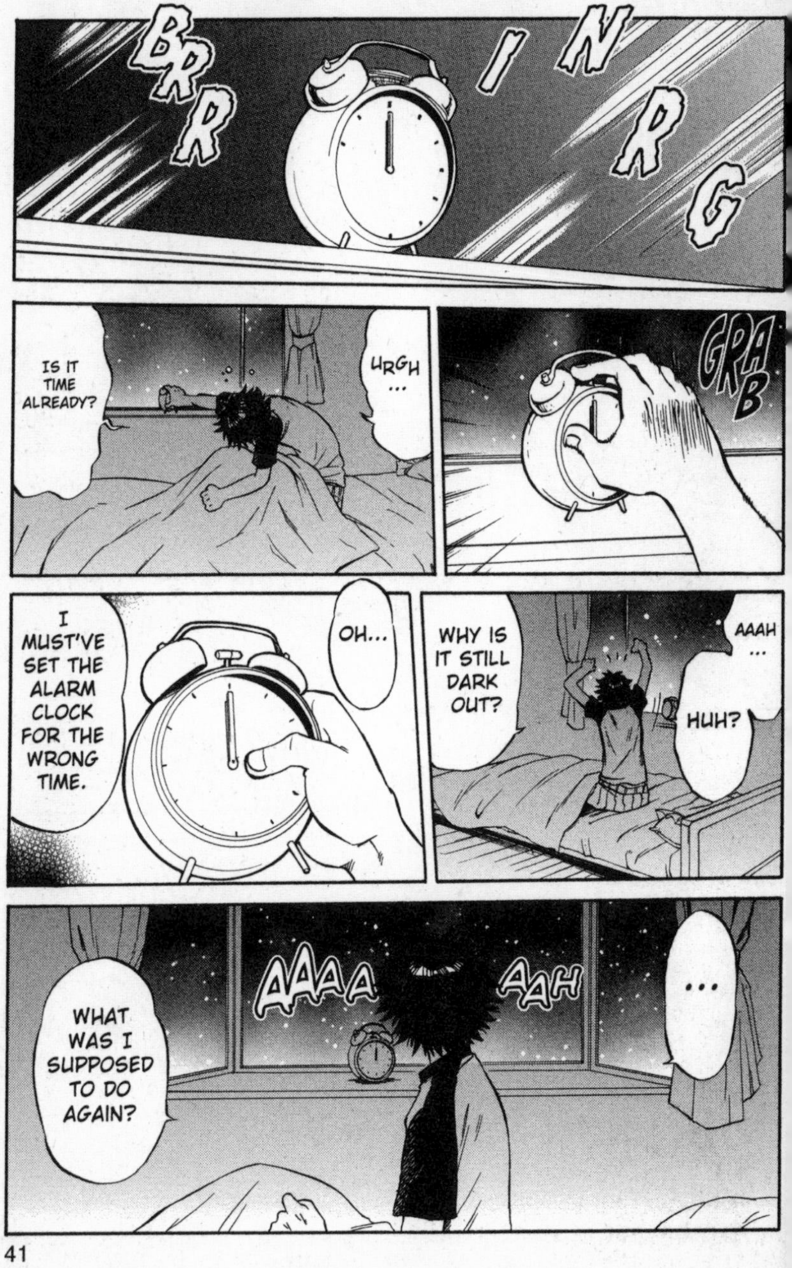

BRRRINRG
GRAB
URGH ...
IS IT TIME ALREADY?
AAAH ...
HUH?
WHY IS IT STILL DARK OUT?
OH...
I MUST'VE SET THE ALARM CLOCK FOR THE WRONG TIME.
...
AAAAAAH
WHAT WAS I SUPPOSED TO DO AGAIN?

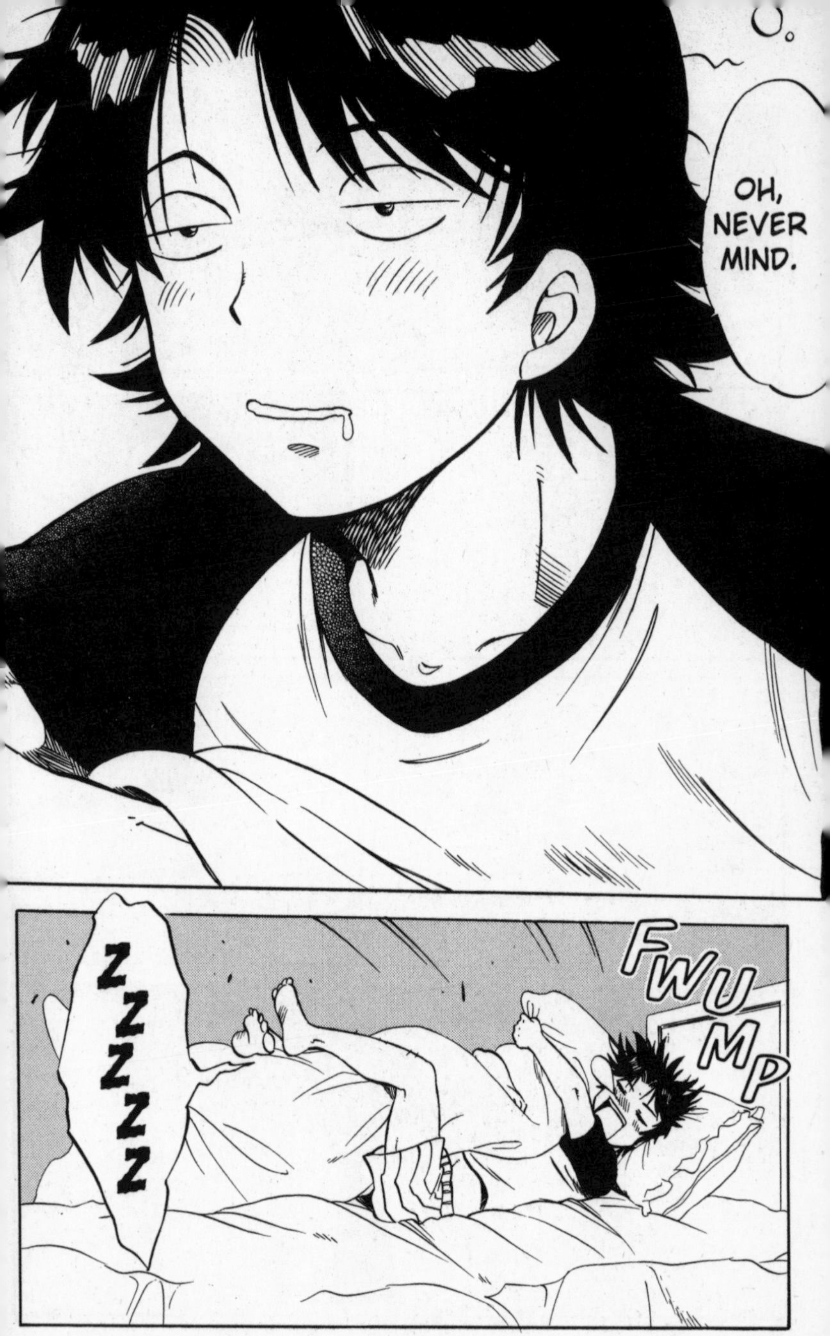
OH, NEVER MIND.
FWUMP
ZZZZZ

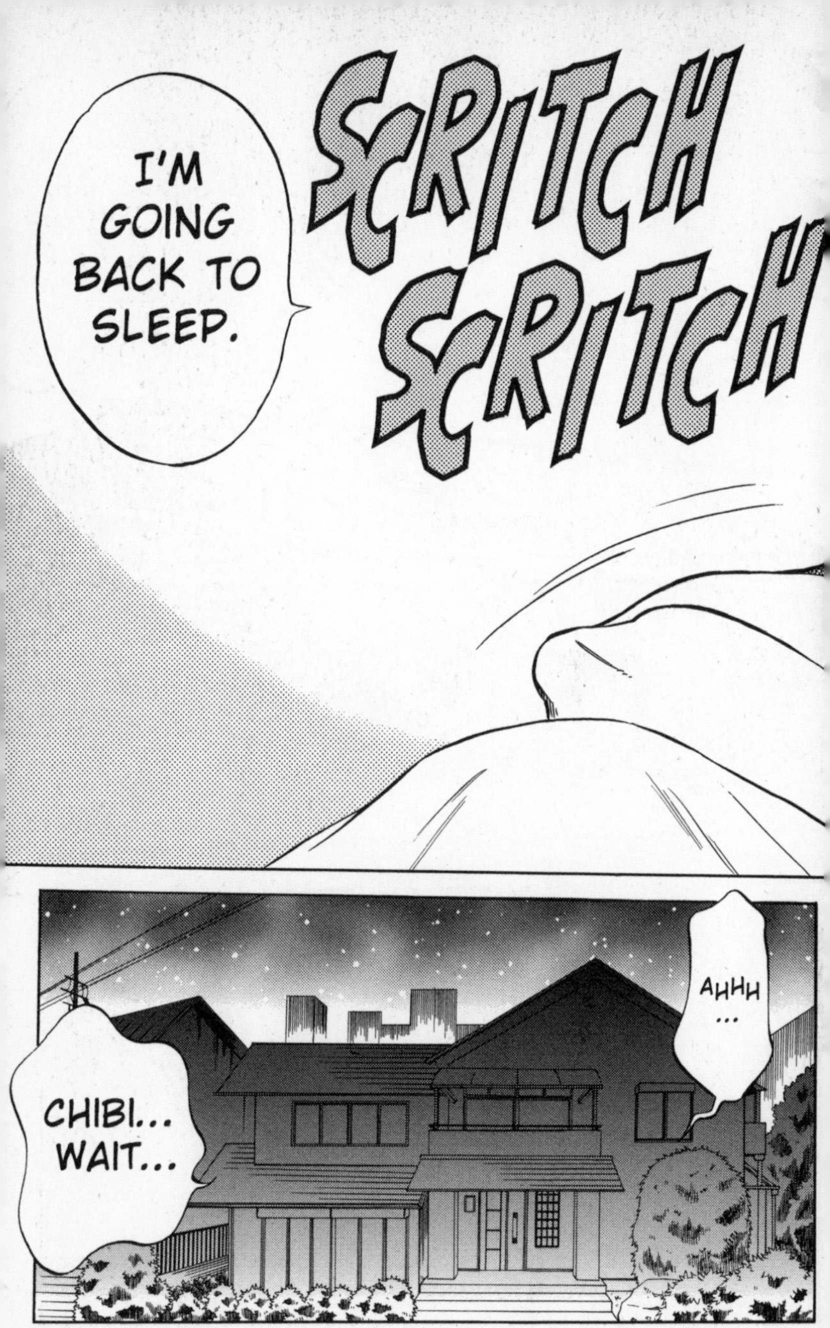
SCRITCH
SCRITCH
I'M GOING BACK TO SLEEP.
AHHH ...
CHIBI... WAIT...

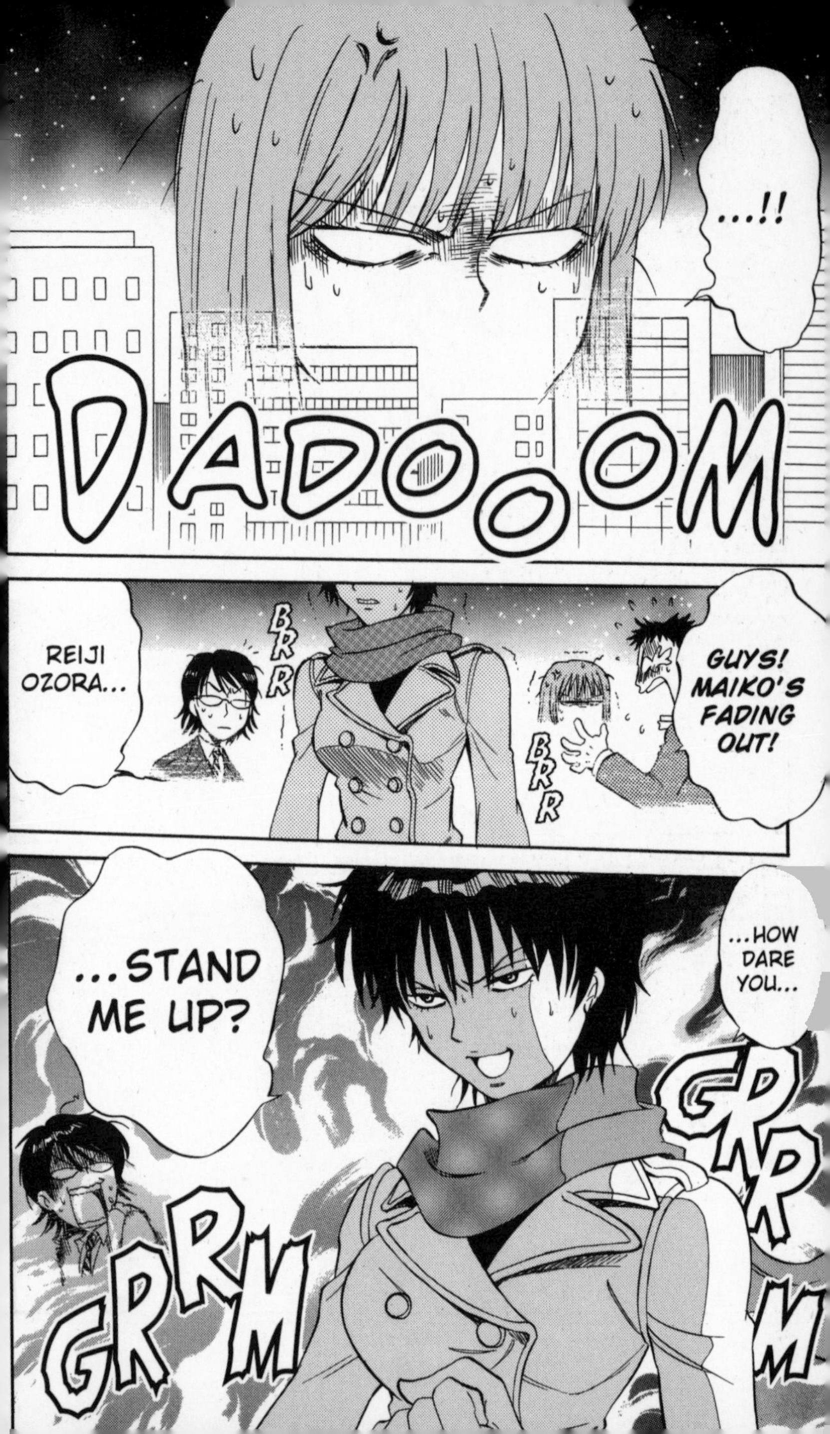
...!!
DADOOOOM
GUYS! MAIKO'S FADING OUT!
BRR
BRR
REIJI OZORA...
...HOW DARE YOU...
...STAND ME UP?
GRRM
GRRM

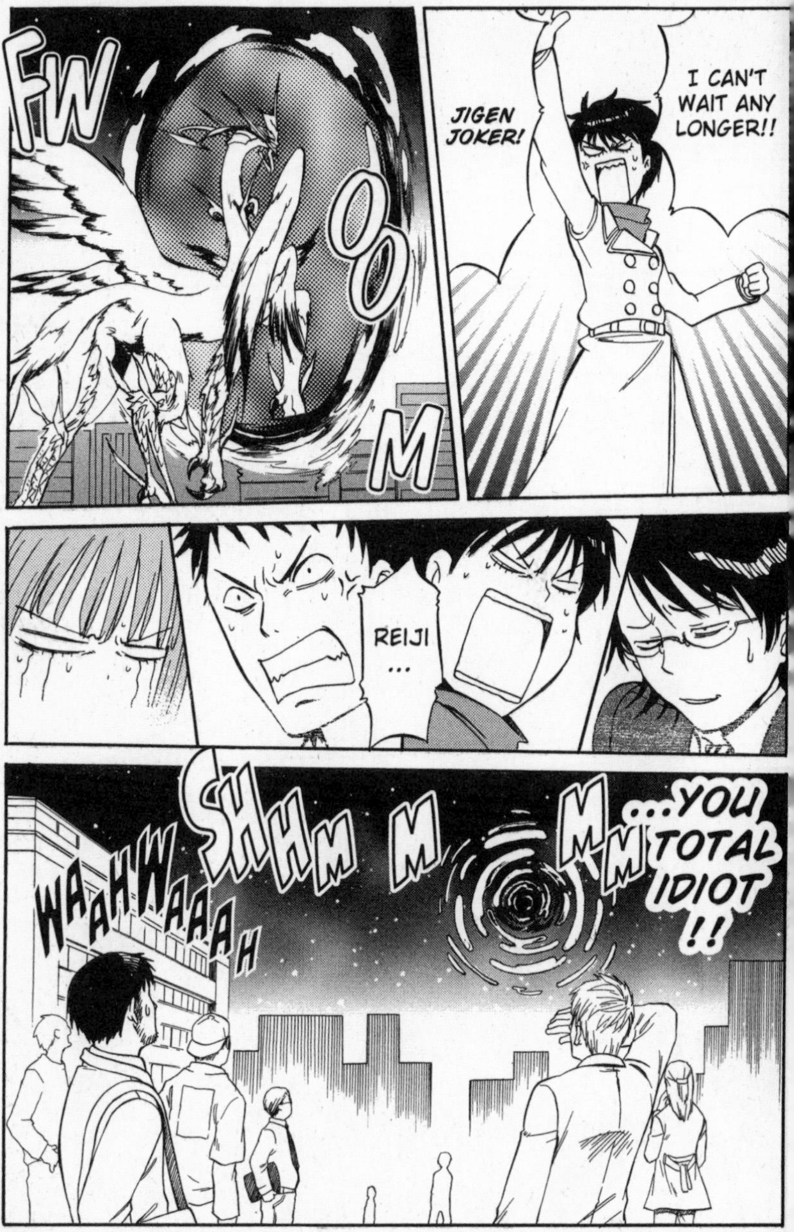
I CAN'T WAIT ANY LONGER!!
JIGEN JOKER!
FWOOOM
REIJI ...
...YOU TOTAL IDIOT!!
SHHM M M M
WAAHWAAAAH

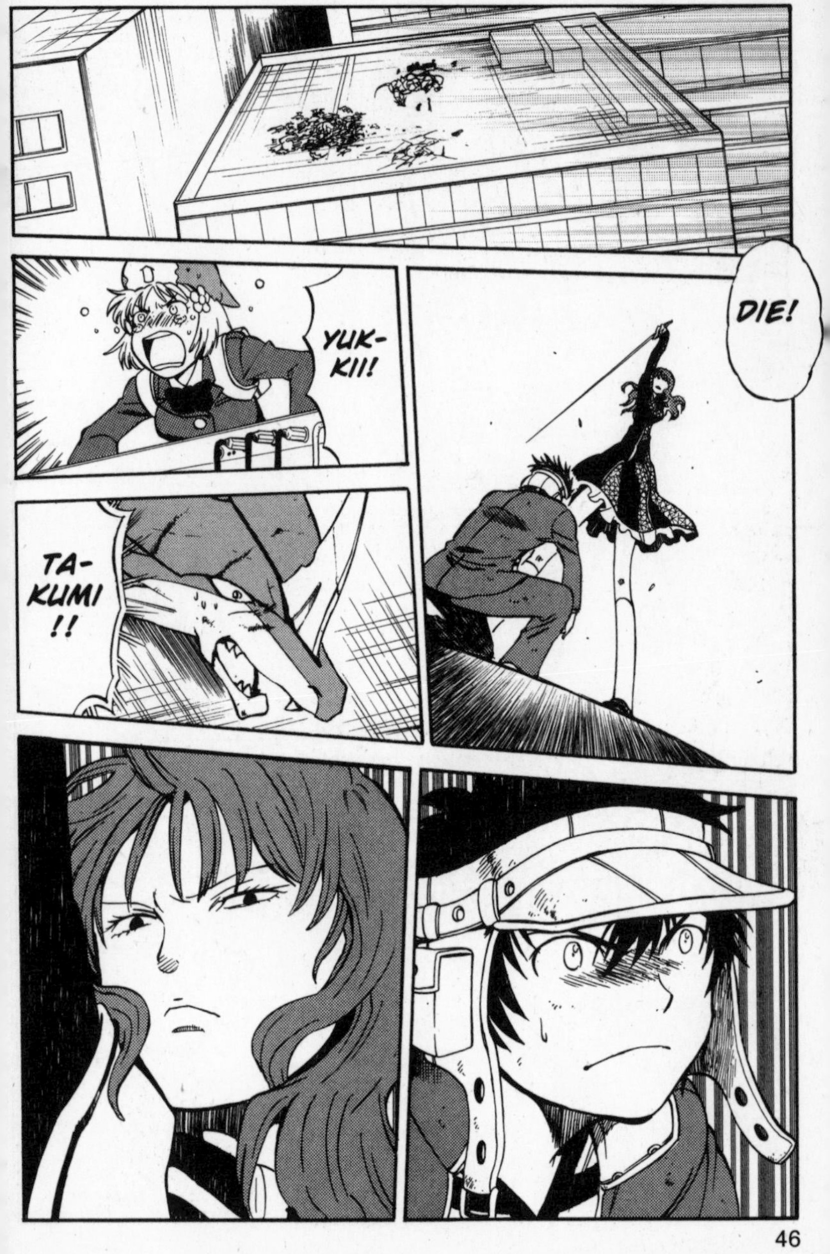
DIE!
YUK-KII!
TA-KUMI !!

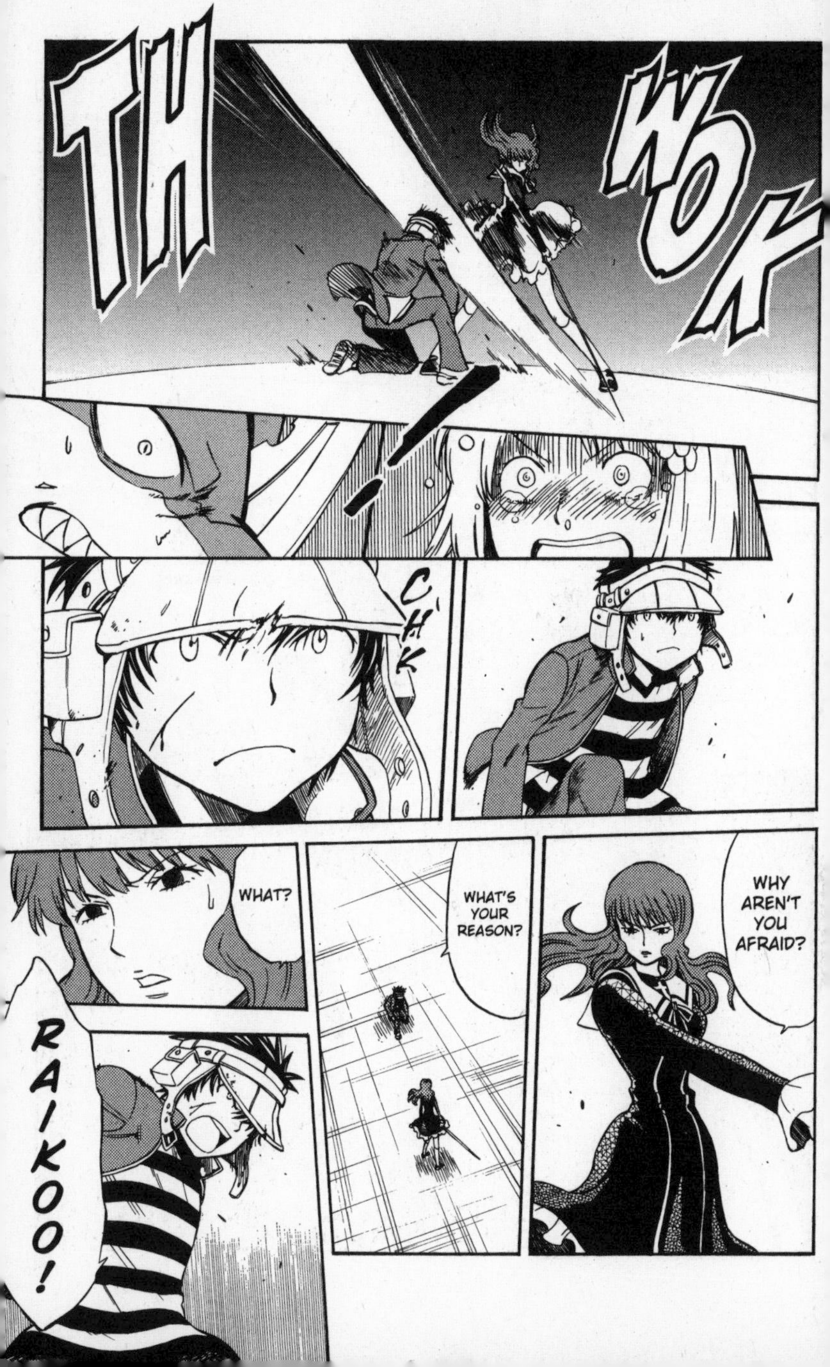
THWOK
CHK
WHY AREN'T YOU AFRAID?
WHAT'S YOUR REASON?
WHAT?
RAIKOOO!

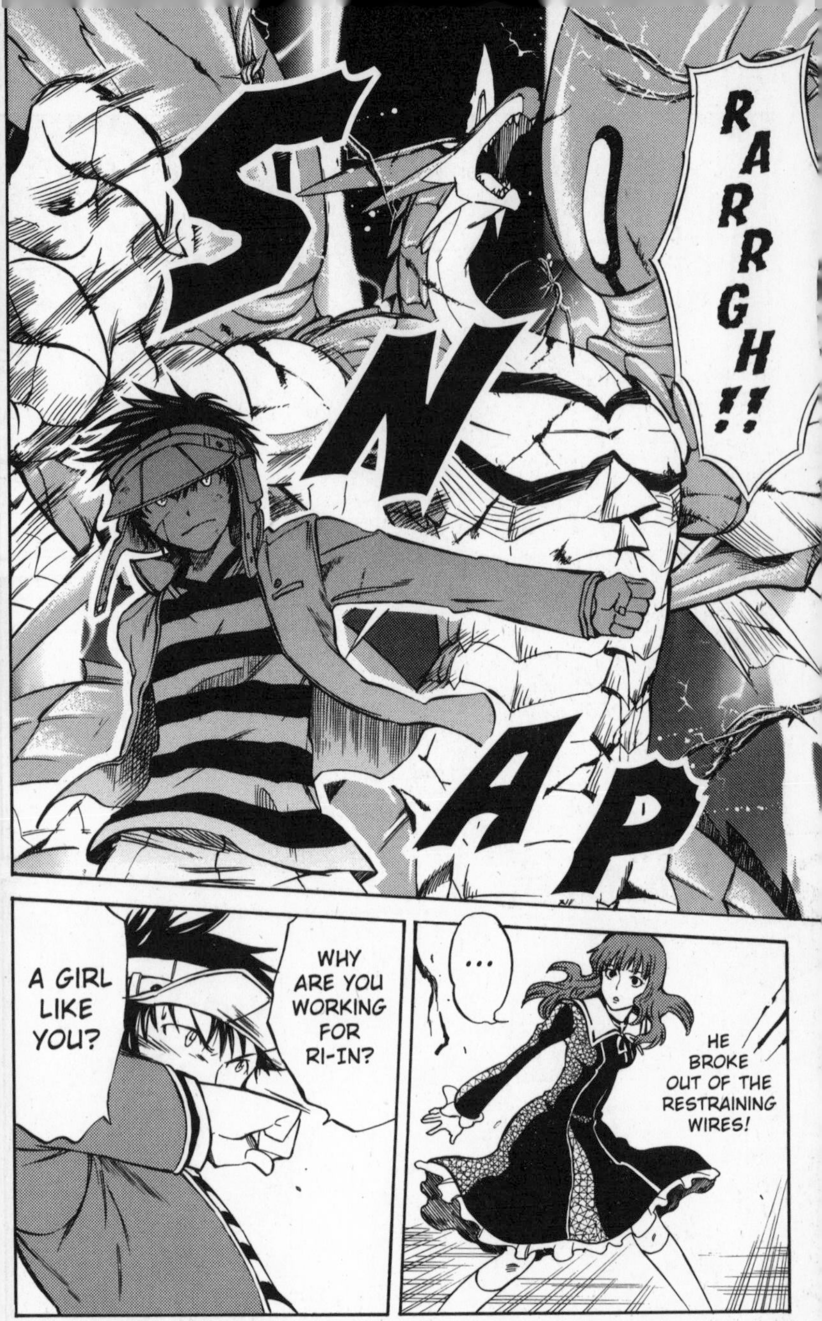
RARRGH!!
SNAP
...
HE BROKE OUT OF THE RESTRAINING WIRES!
WHY ARE YOU WORKING FOR RI-IN?
A GIRL LIKE YOU?

READ THIS WAY

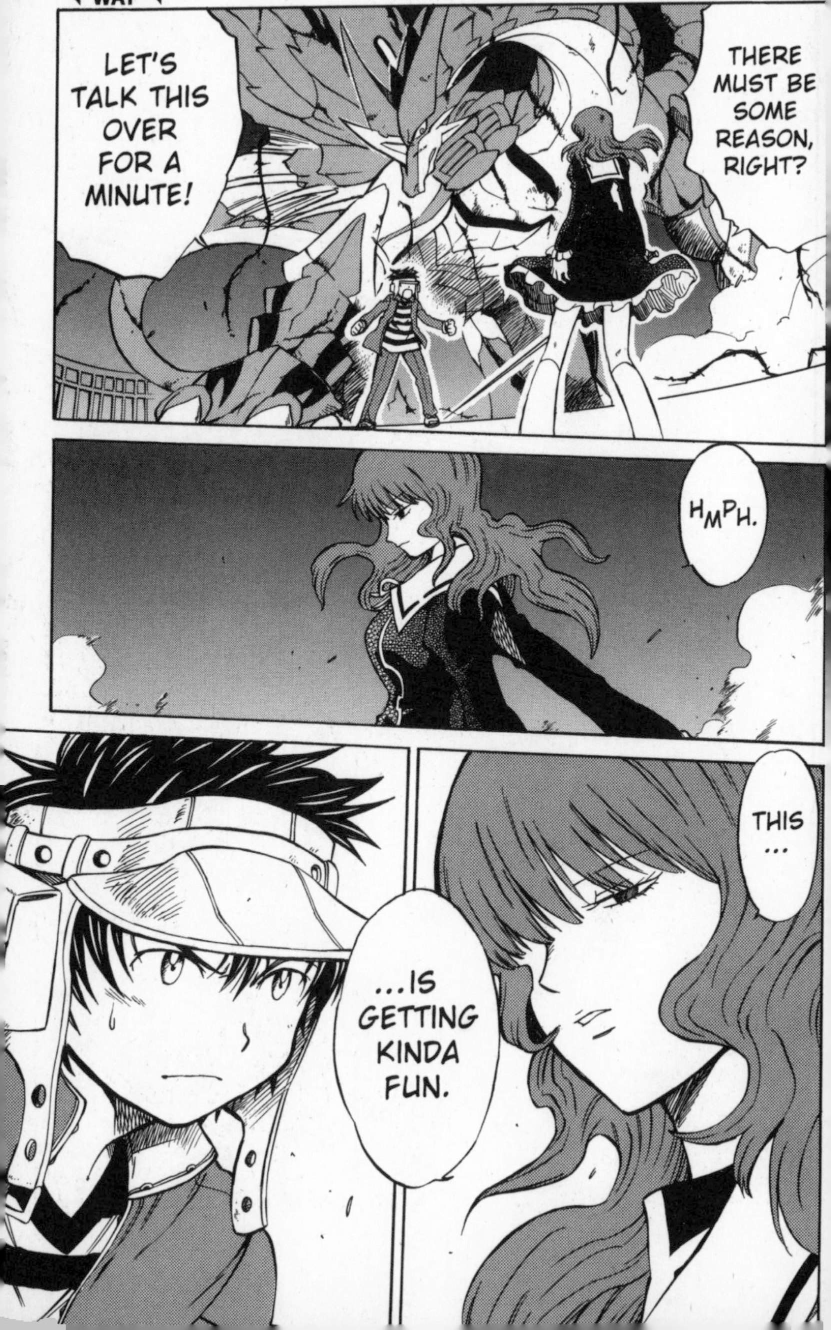
THERE MUST BE SOME REASON, RIGHT?
LET'S TALK THIS OVER FOR A MINUTE!
HMPH.
THIS...
...IS GETTING KINDA FUN.

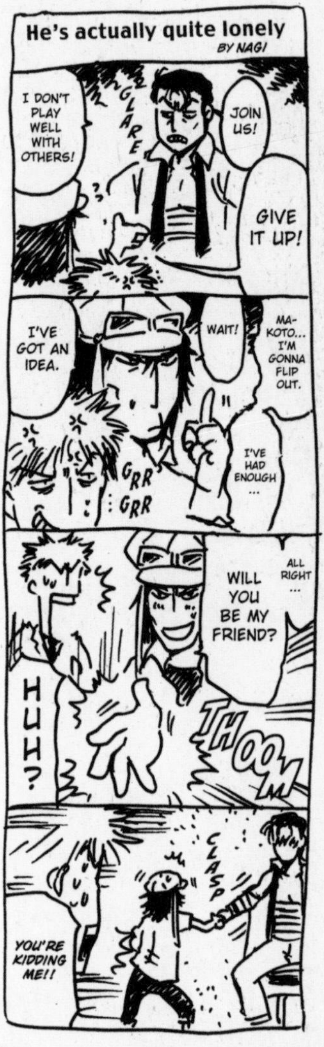
He's actually quite lonely
BY NAGI
JOIN US!
GIVE IT UP!
GLARE
I DON'T PLAY WELL WITH OTHERS!
MA-KOTO... I'M GONNA FLIP OUT.
WAIT!
I'VE HAD ENOUGH...
I'VE GOT AN IDEA.
GRR GRR
ALL RIGHT...
WILL YOU BE MY FRIEND?
THOOM
HUH?
CLASP
YOU'RE KIDDING ME!!

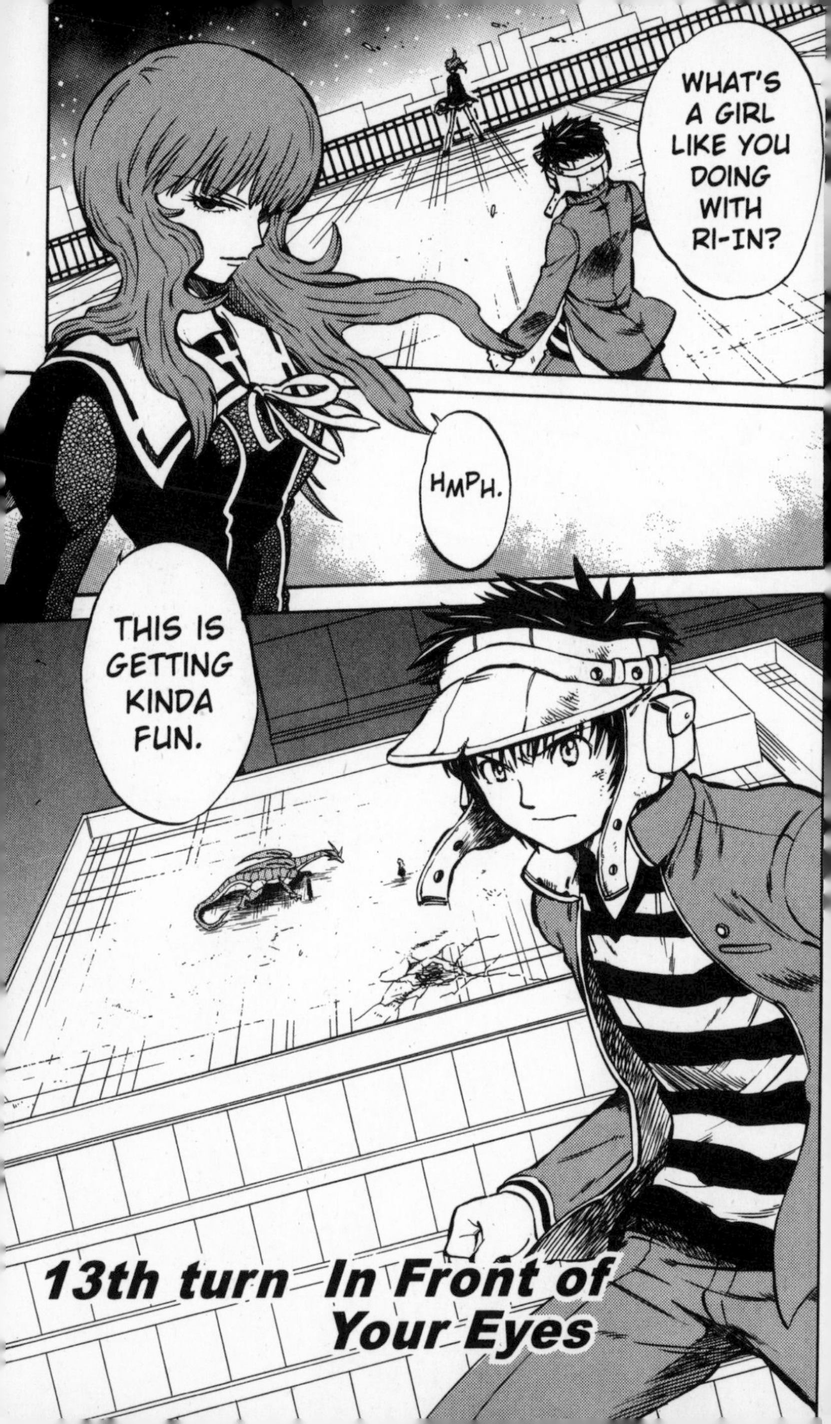
WHAT'S A GIRL LIKE YOU DOING WITH RI-IN?
HMPH.
THIS IS GETTING KINDA FUN.
13th turn In Front of Your Eyes

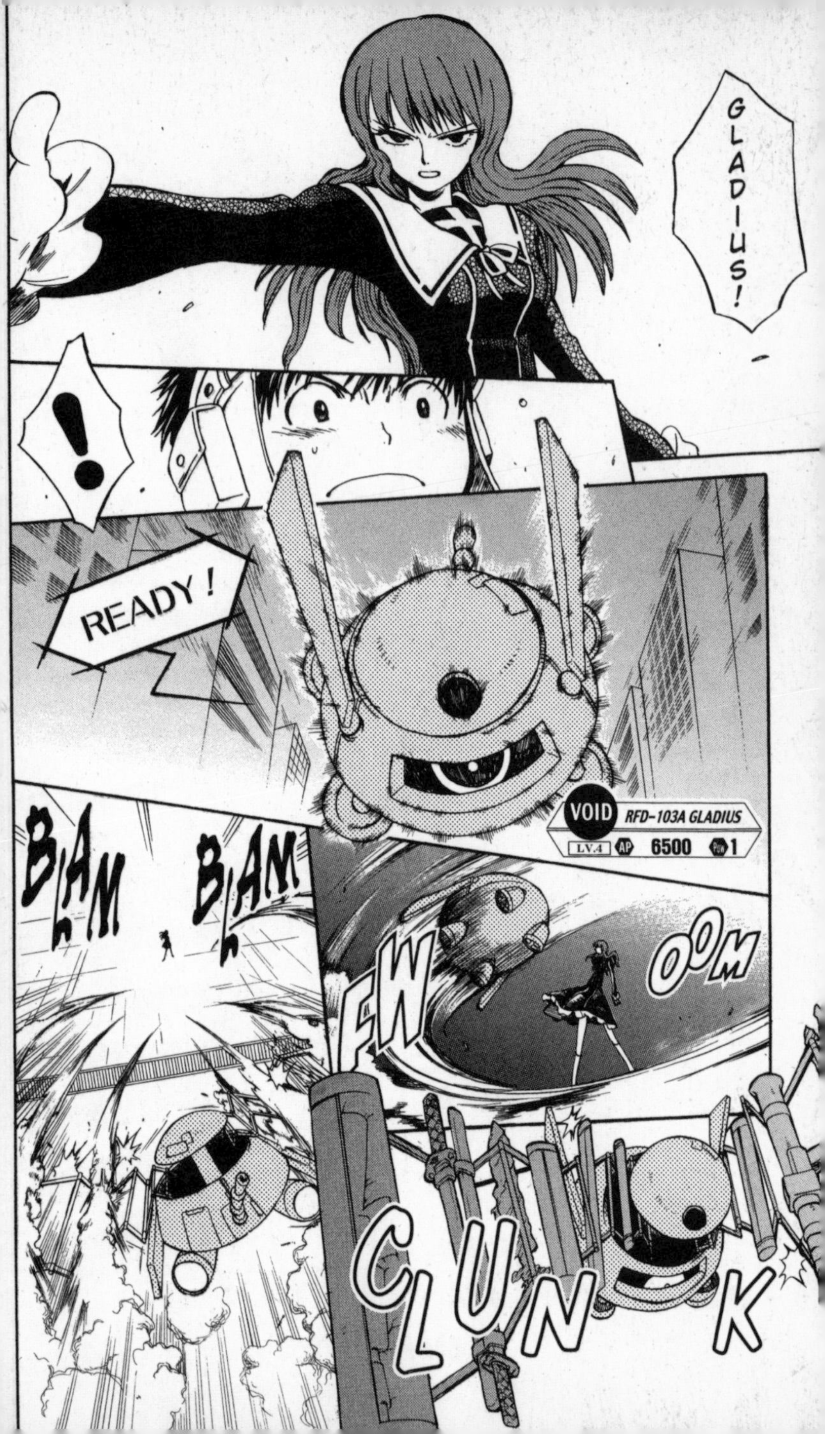
GLADIUS!
!
READY!
VOID RFD-103A GLADIUS
LV.4 AP 6500 1
FWOOM
CLUNK
BLAM BLAM

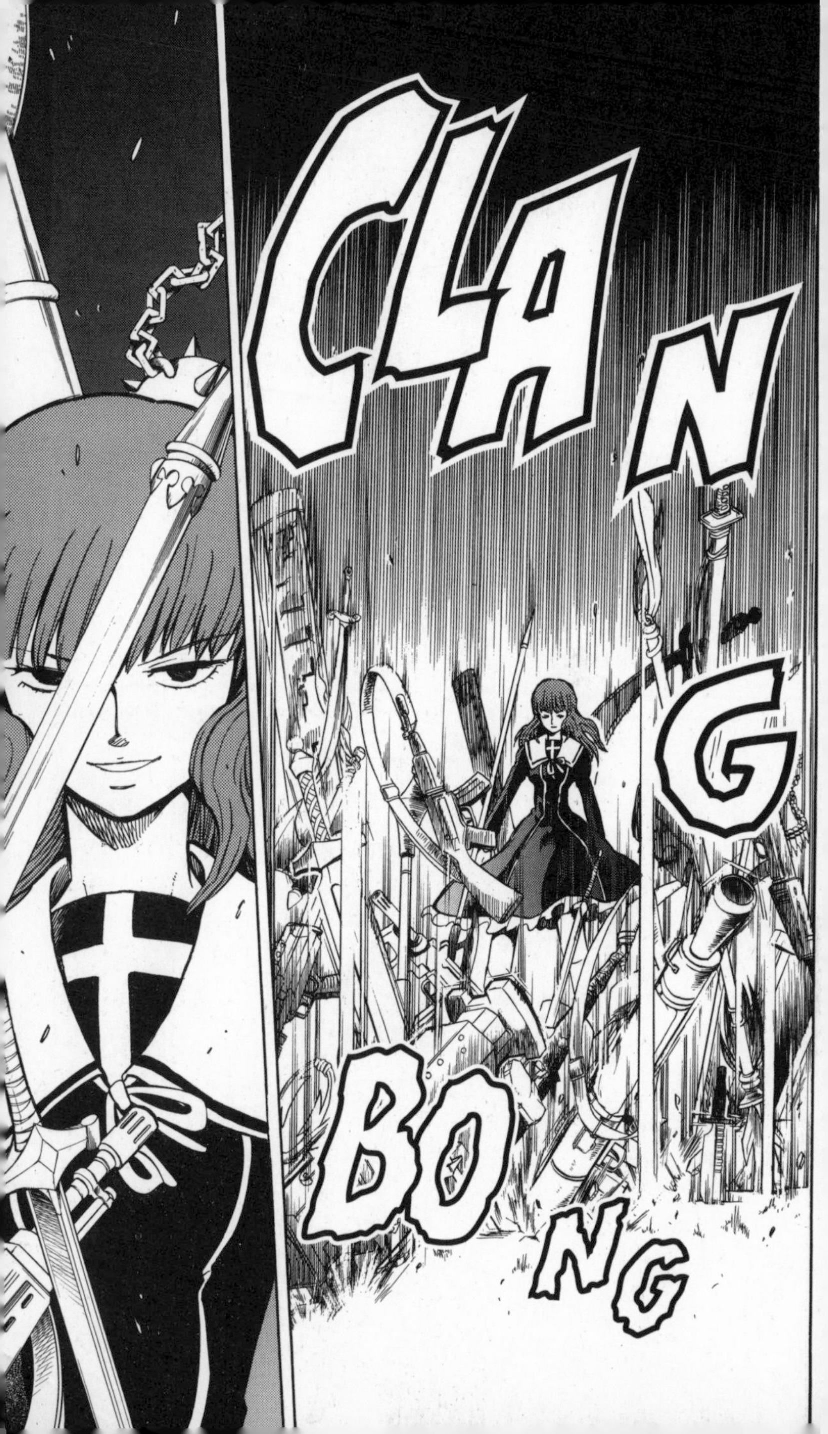
CLANG
BONG

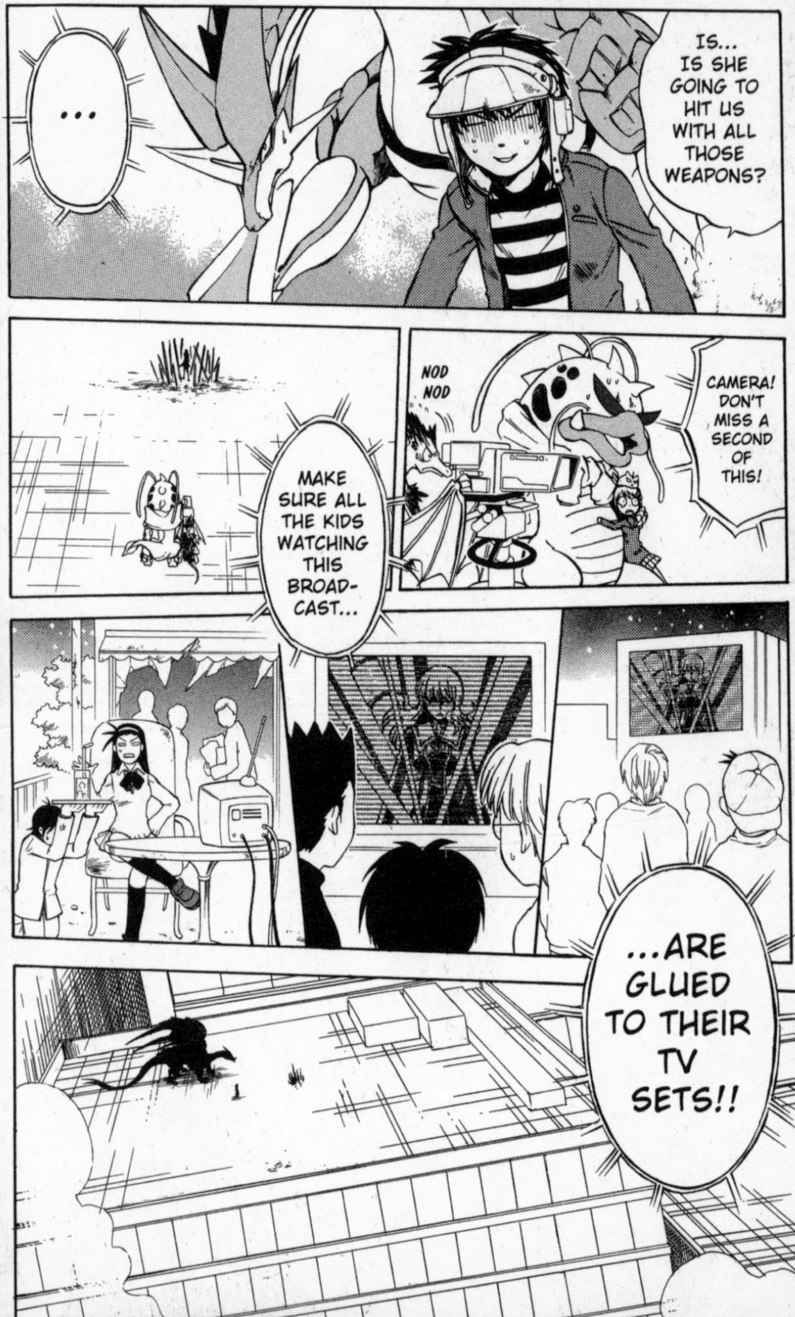
IS... IS SHE GOING TO HIT US WITH ALL THOSE WEAPONS?
...
CAMERA! DON'T MISS A SECOND OF THIS!
NOD NOD
MAKE SURE ALL THE KIDS WATCHING THIS BROAD-CAST...
...ARE GLUED TO THEIR TV SETS!!

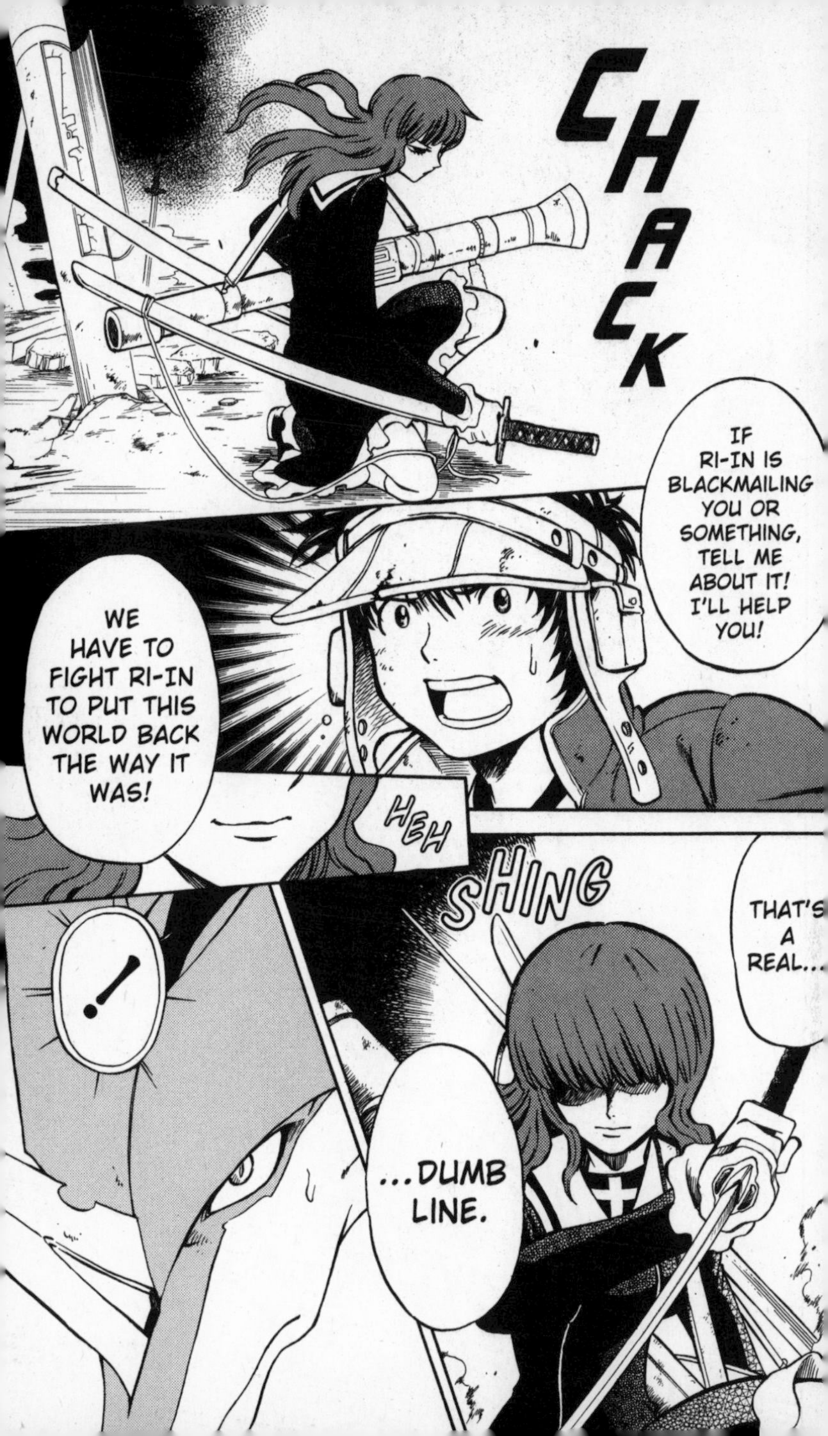
CHACK
IF RI-IN IS BLACKMAILING YOU OR SOMETHING, TELL ME ABOUT IT! I'LL HELP YOU!
WE HAVE TO FIGHT RI-IN TO PUT THIS WORLD BACK THE WAY IT WAS!
HEH
SHING
THAT'S A REAL...
!
...DUMB LINE.

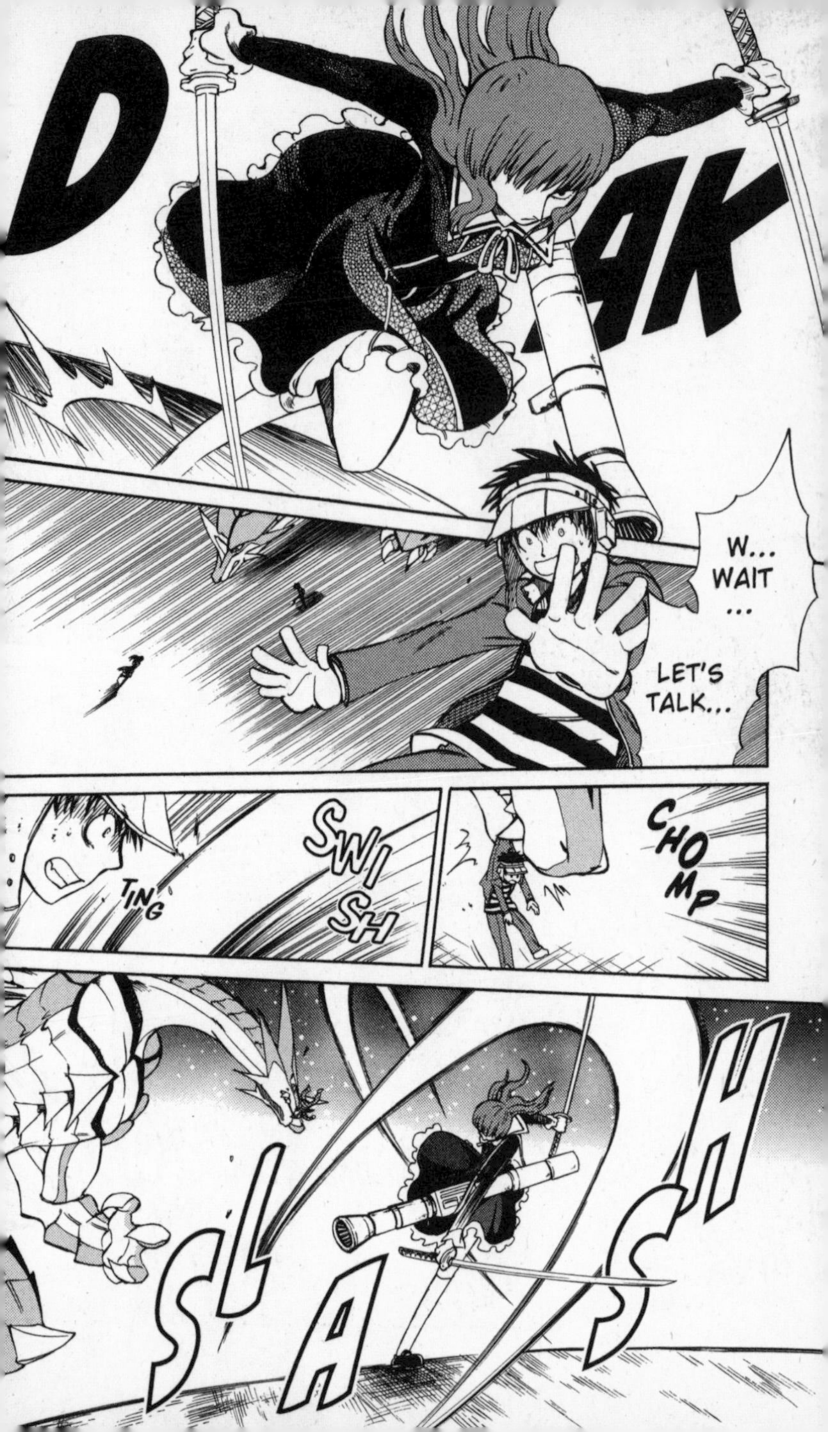
D
AK
W... WAIT ...
LET'S TALK...
CHOMP
SWISH
TING
SLASH

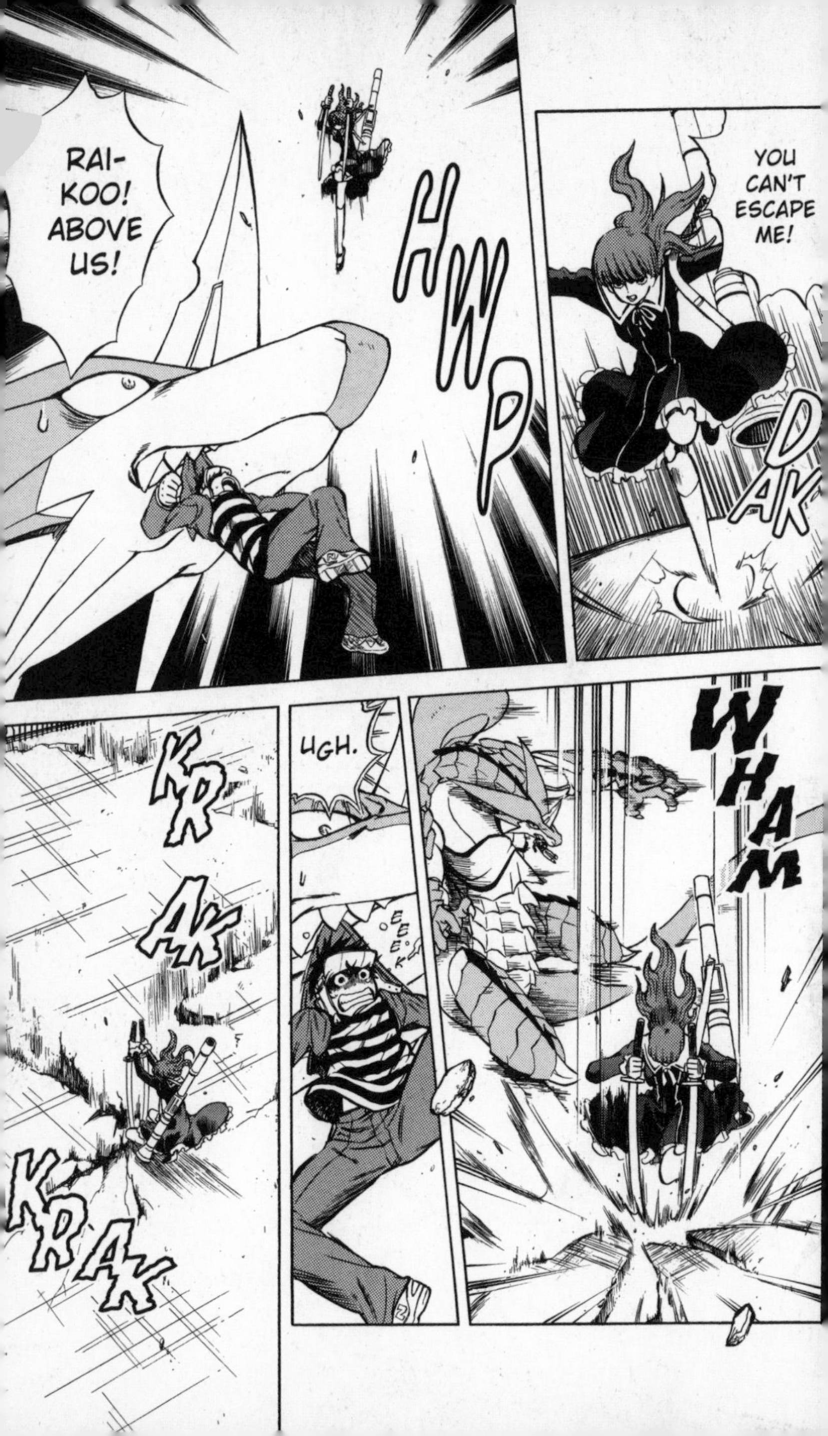
YOU CAN'T ESCAPE ME!
DAK
HWP
RAI-KOO! ABOVE US!
WHAM
UGH.
EEEK
KRAK
KRAK

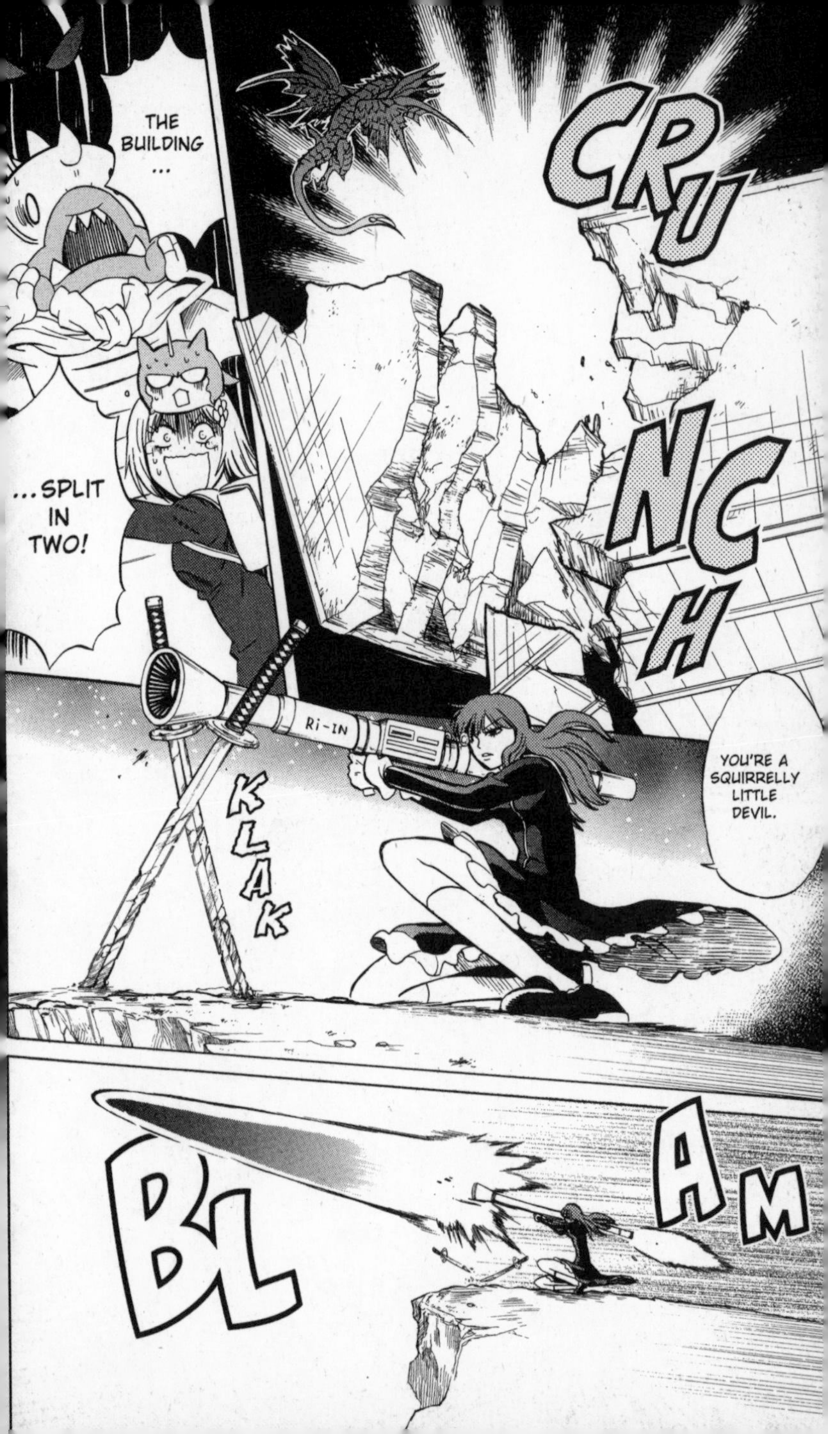
CRUNCH
YOU'RE A SQUIRRELLY LITTLE DEVIL.
Ri-IN
KLAK
THE BUILDING ...
...SPLIT IN TWO!
BLAM

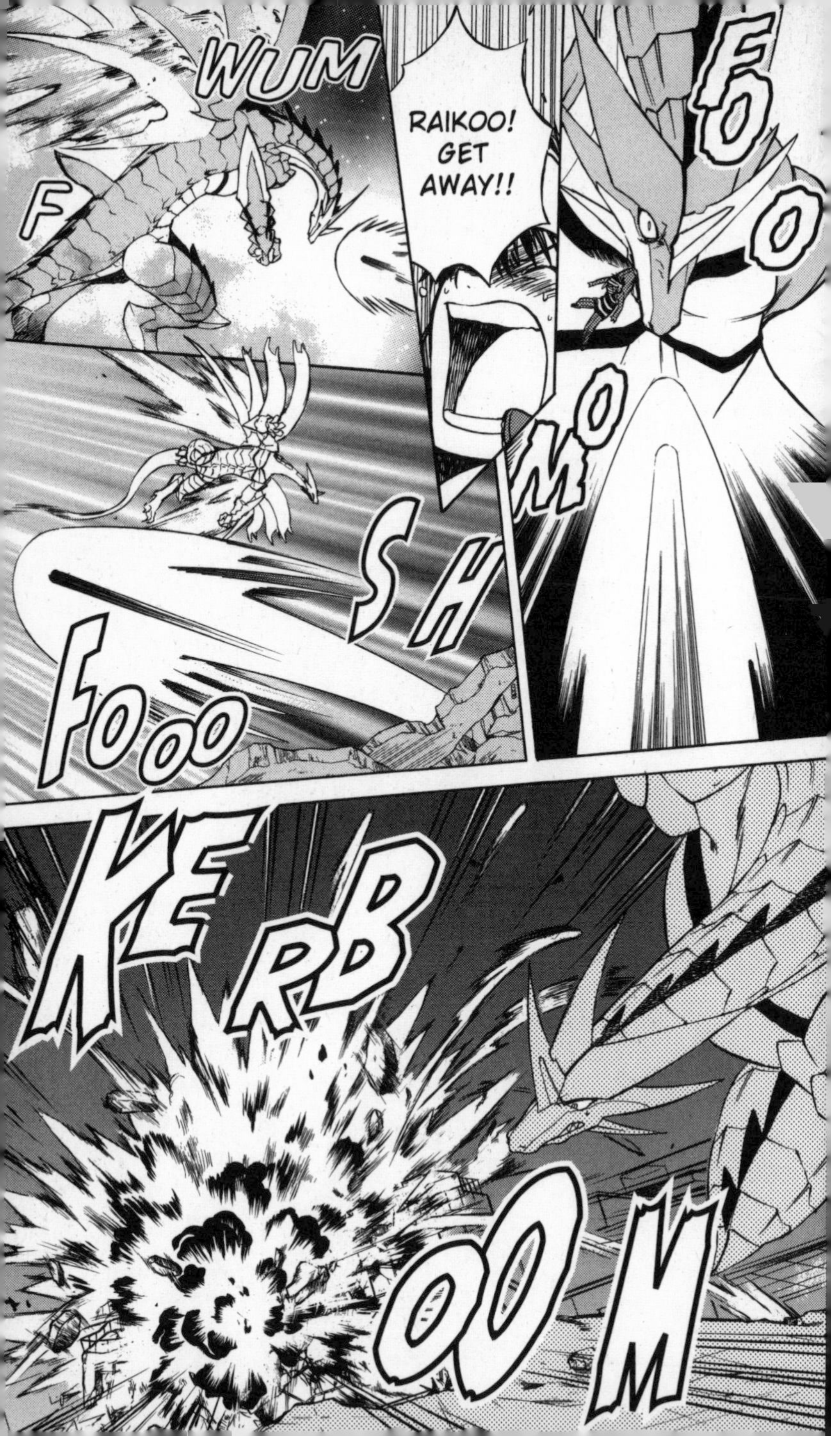
FOOOM
RAIKOO! GET AWAY!!
FWUM
FOOOSH
KERBOOOM

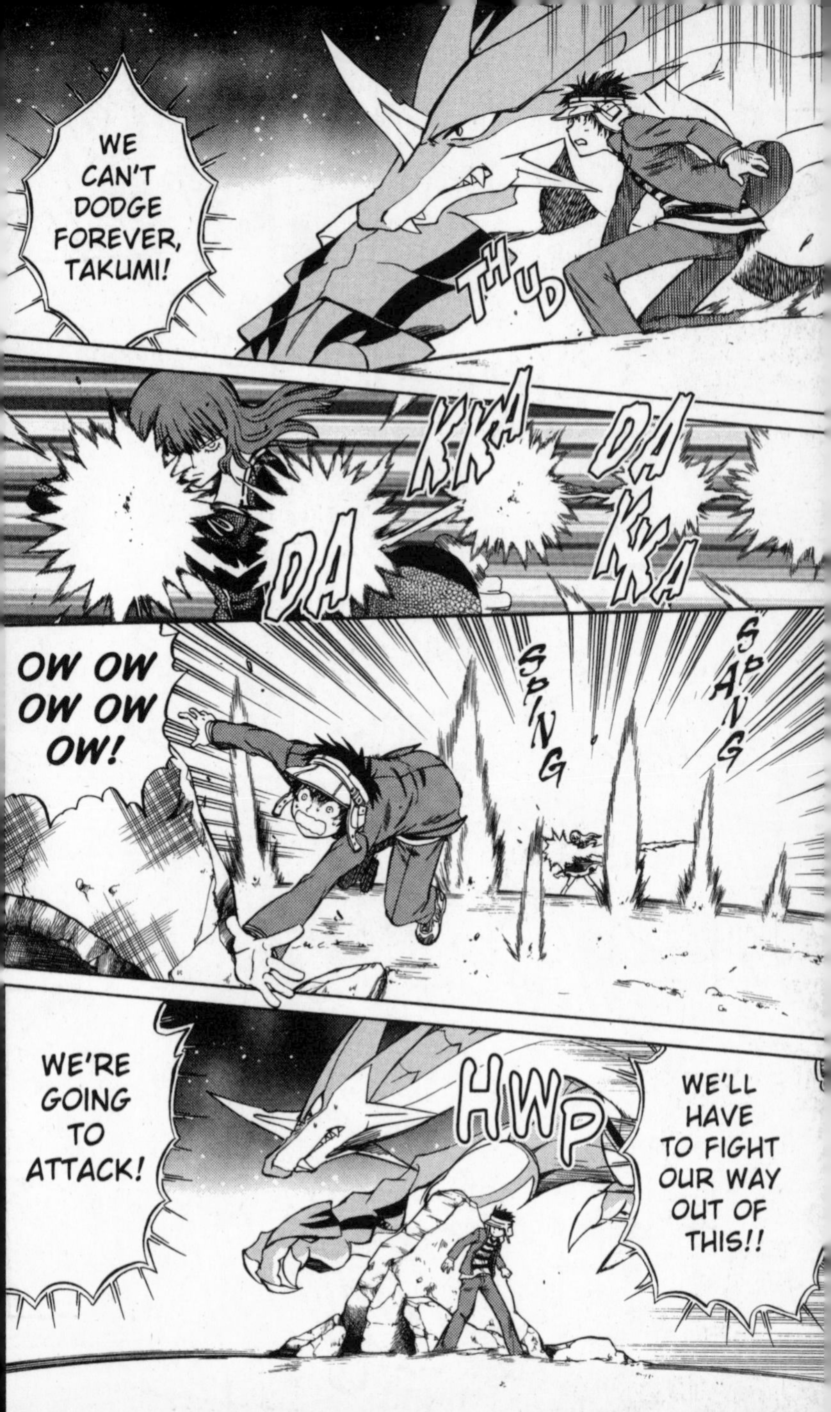
WE CAN'T DODGE FOREVER, TAKUMI!
THUD
DA
KKA
KKA
DA
SPANG
SPING
OW OW OW OW OW!
WE'LL HAVE TO FIGHT OUR WAY OUT OF THIS!!
HWP
WE'RE GOING TO ATTACK!

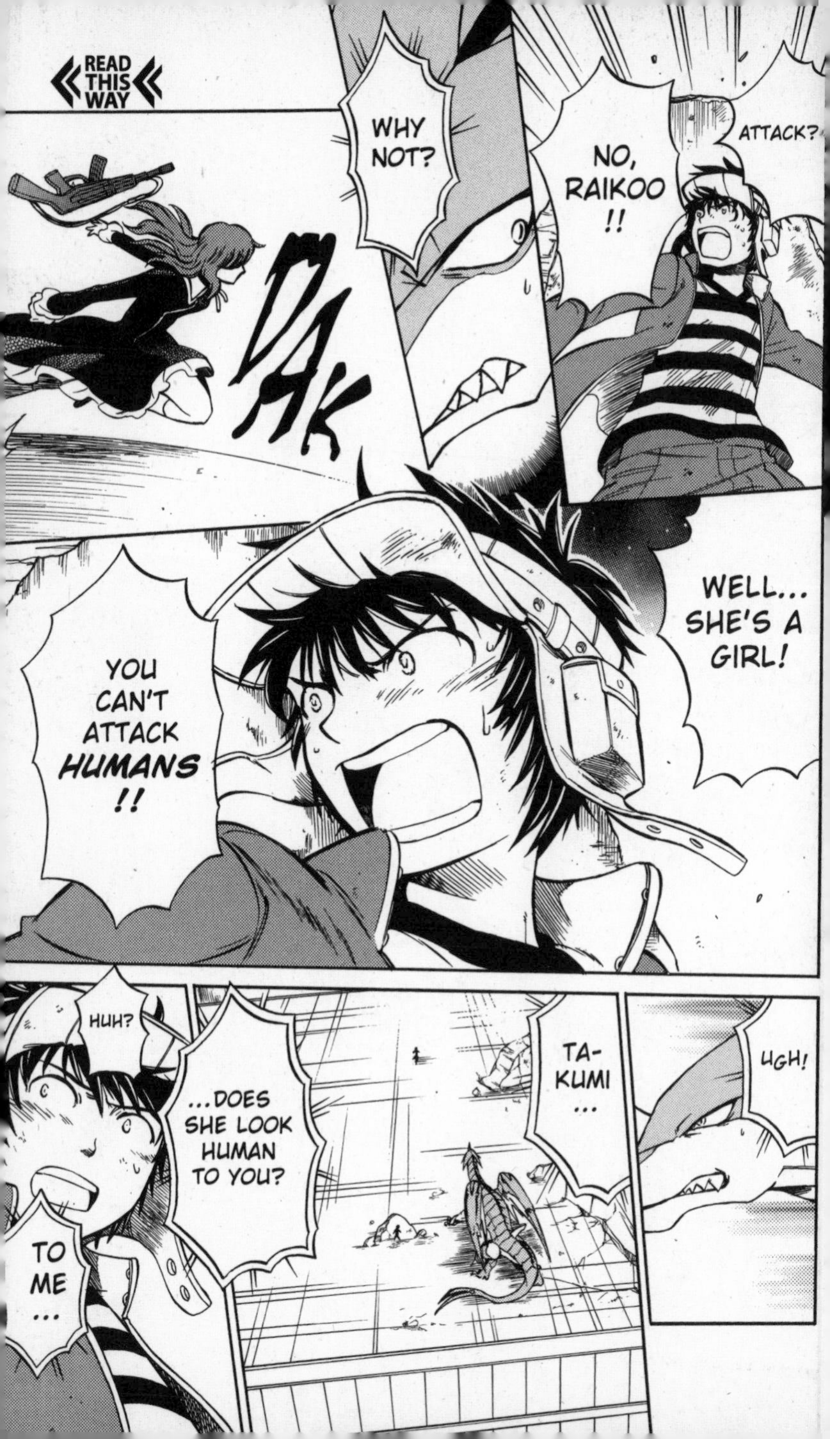
READ THIS WAY
ATTACK?
NO, RAIKOO!!
WHY NOT?
DAK
WELL... SHE'S A GIRL!
YOU CAN'T ATTACK *HUMANS*!!
UGH!
TA-KUMI...
...DOES SHE LOOK HUMAN TO YOU?
HUH?
TO ME...

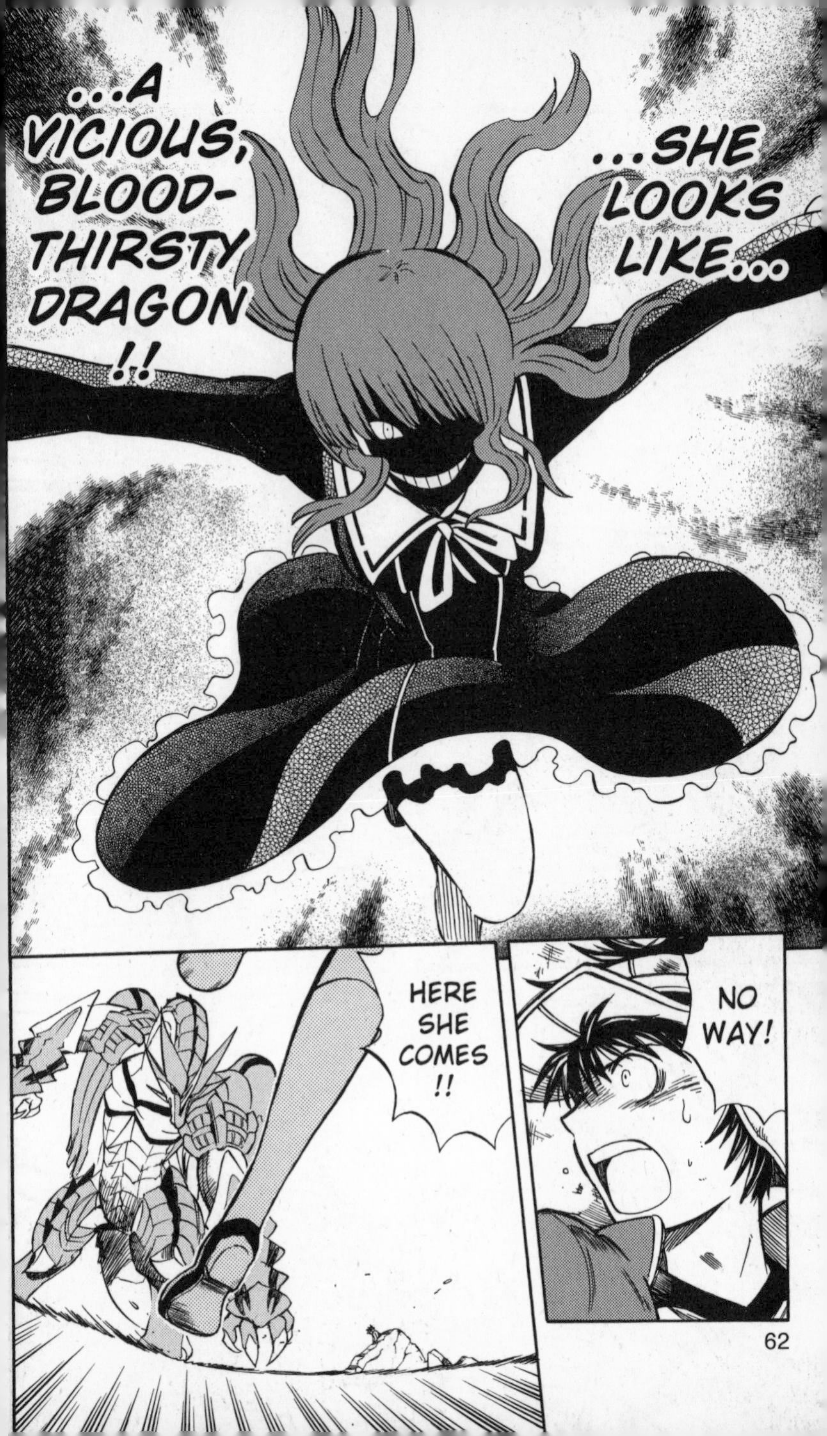
...SHE LOOKS LIKE...
...A VICIOUS, BLOOD-THIRSTY DRAGON!!
NO WAY!
HERE SHE COMES!!

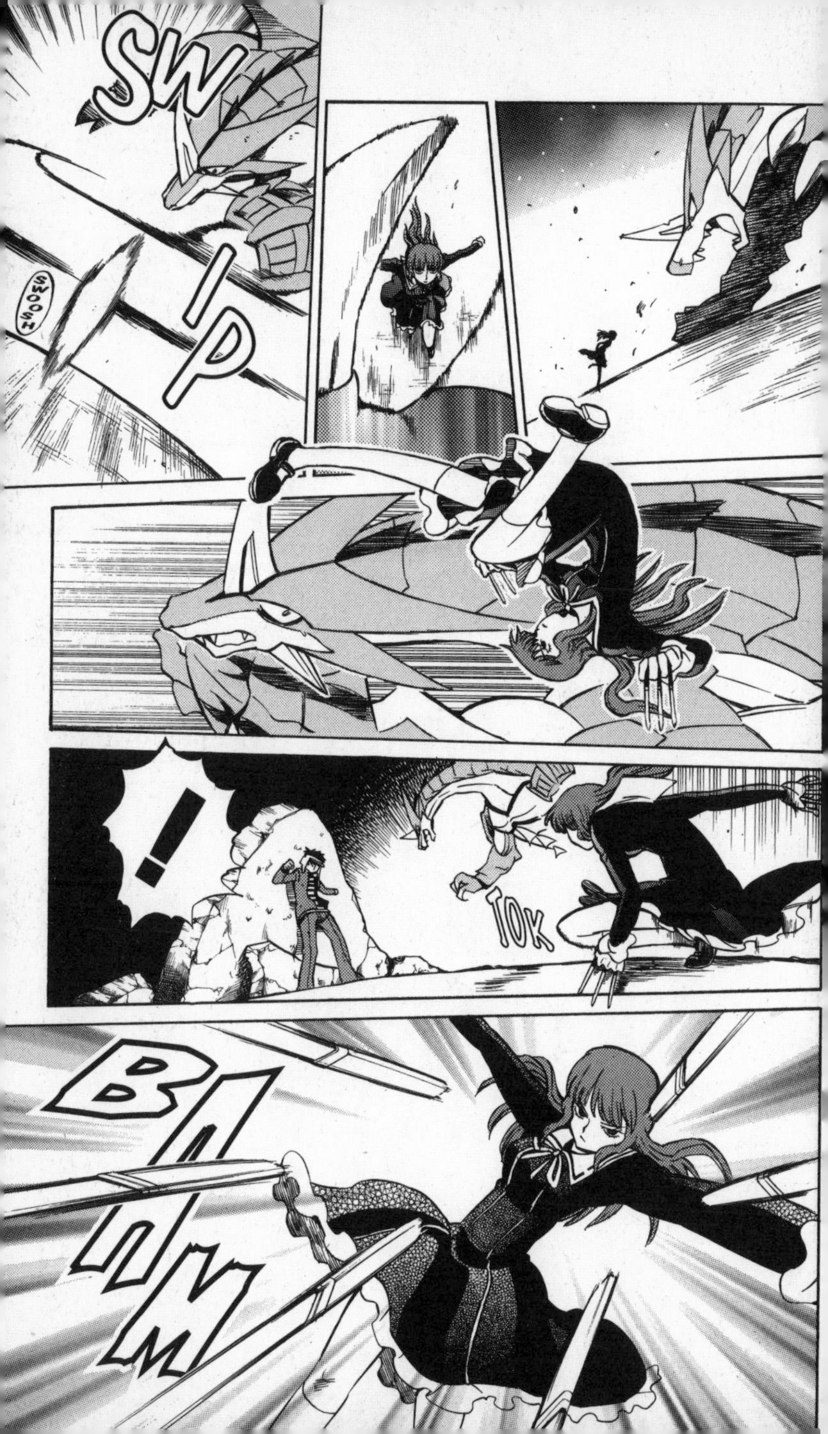
SWIP
SWOOSH
TOK
!
BAM

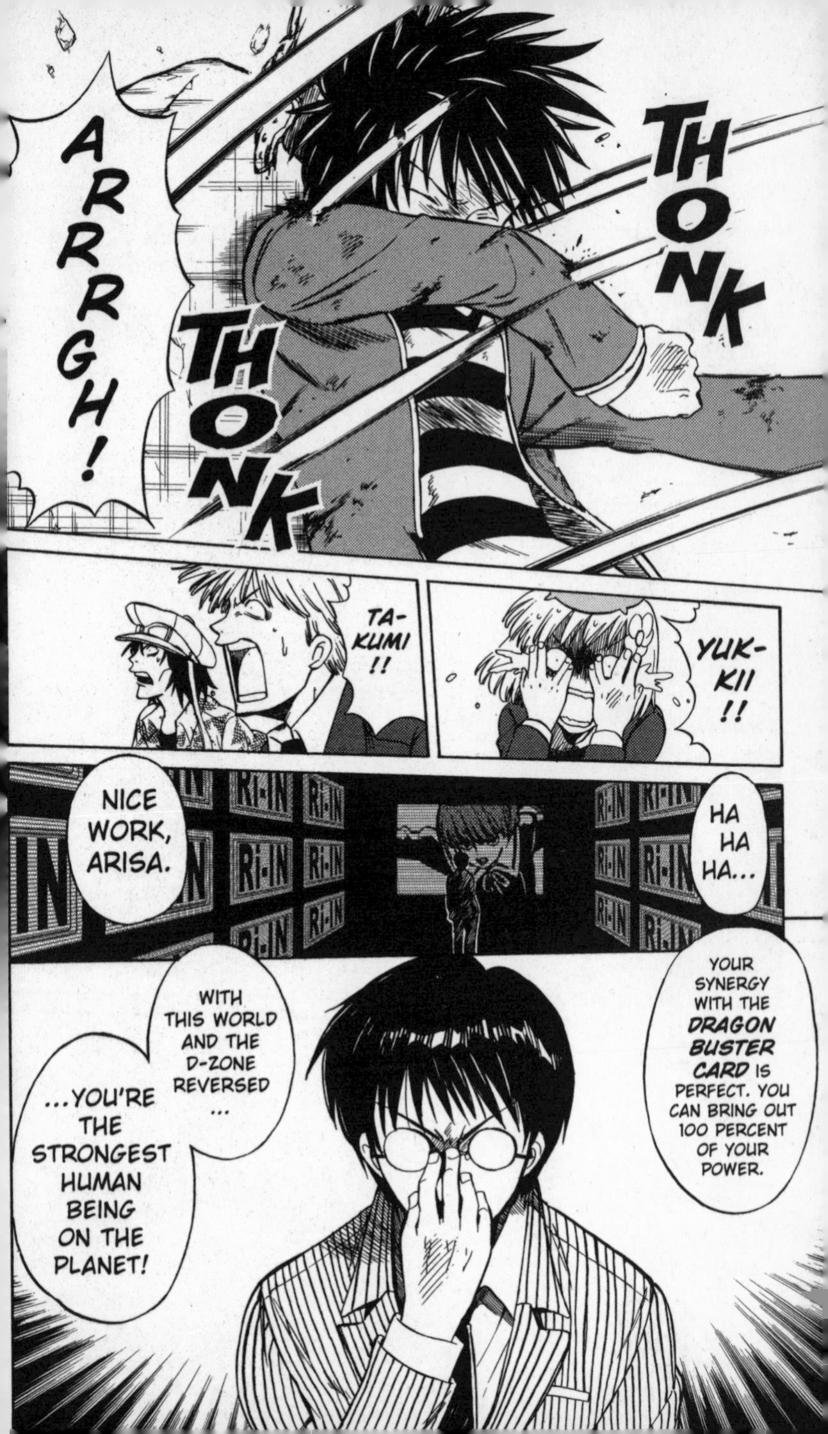

THONK
ARRRGH!
THONK
TA-KUMI!!
YUK-KII!!
RI-IN
NICE WORK, ARISA.
HA HA HA...
YOUR SYNERGY WITH THE DRAGON BUSTER CARD IS PERFECT. YOU CAN BRING OUT 100 PERCENT OF YOUR POWER.
WITH THIS WORLD AND THE D-ZONE REVERSED...
...YOU'RE THE STRONGEST HUMAN BEING ON THE PLANET!

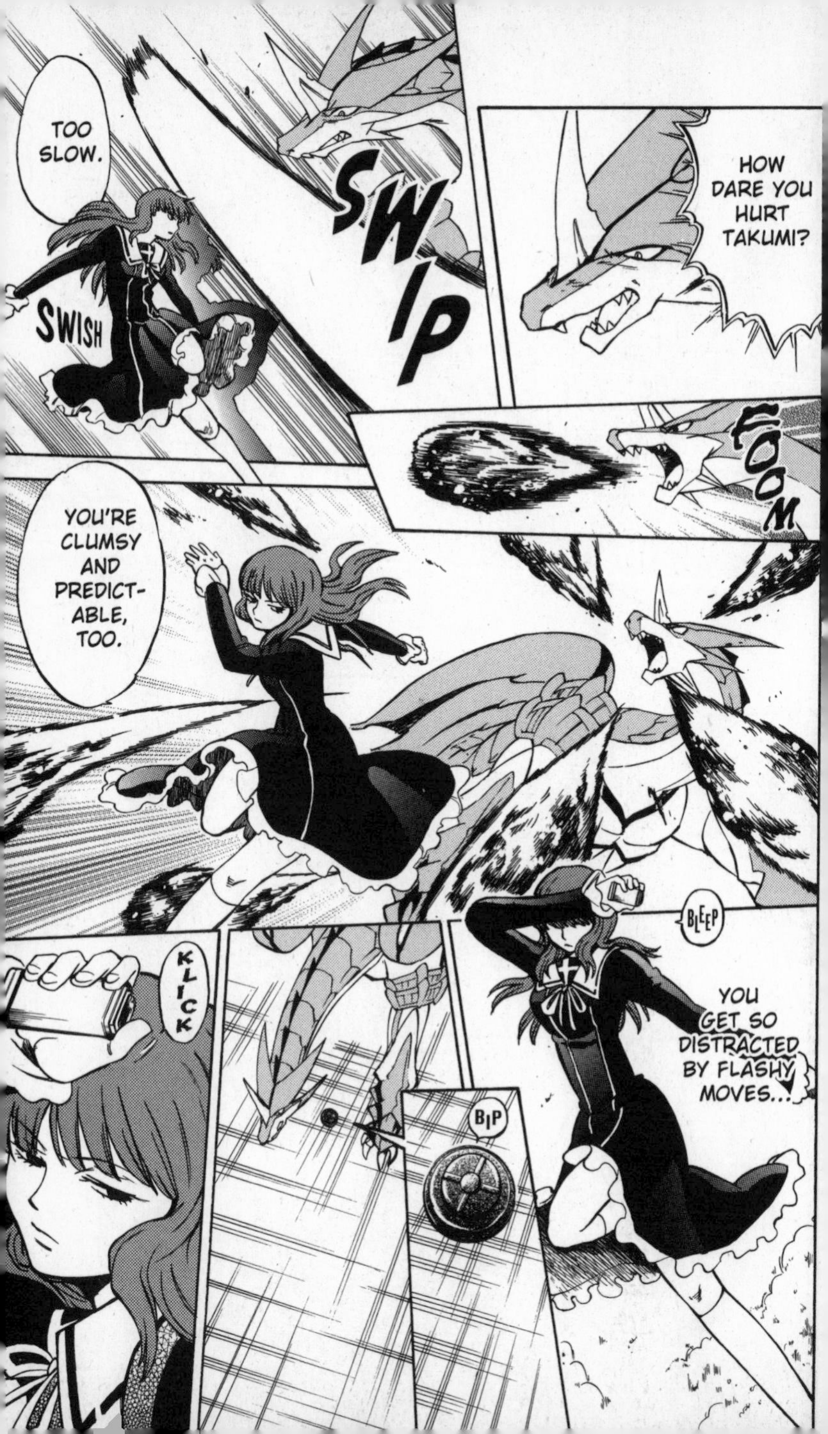
HOW DARE YOU HURT TAKUMI?
FOOM
SWIP
TOO SLOW.
SWISH
YOU'RE CLUMSY AND PREDICT-ABLE, TOO.
BLEEP
YOU GET SO DISTRACTED BY FLASHY MOVES...
BIP
KLICK

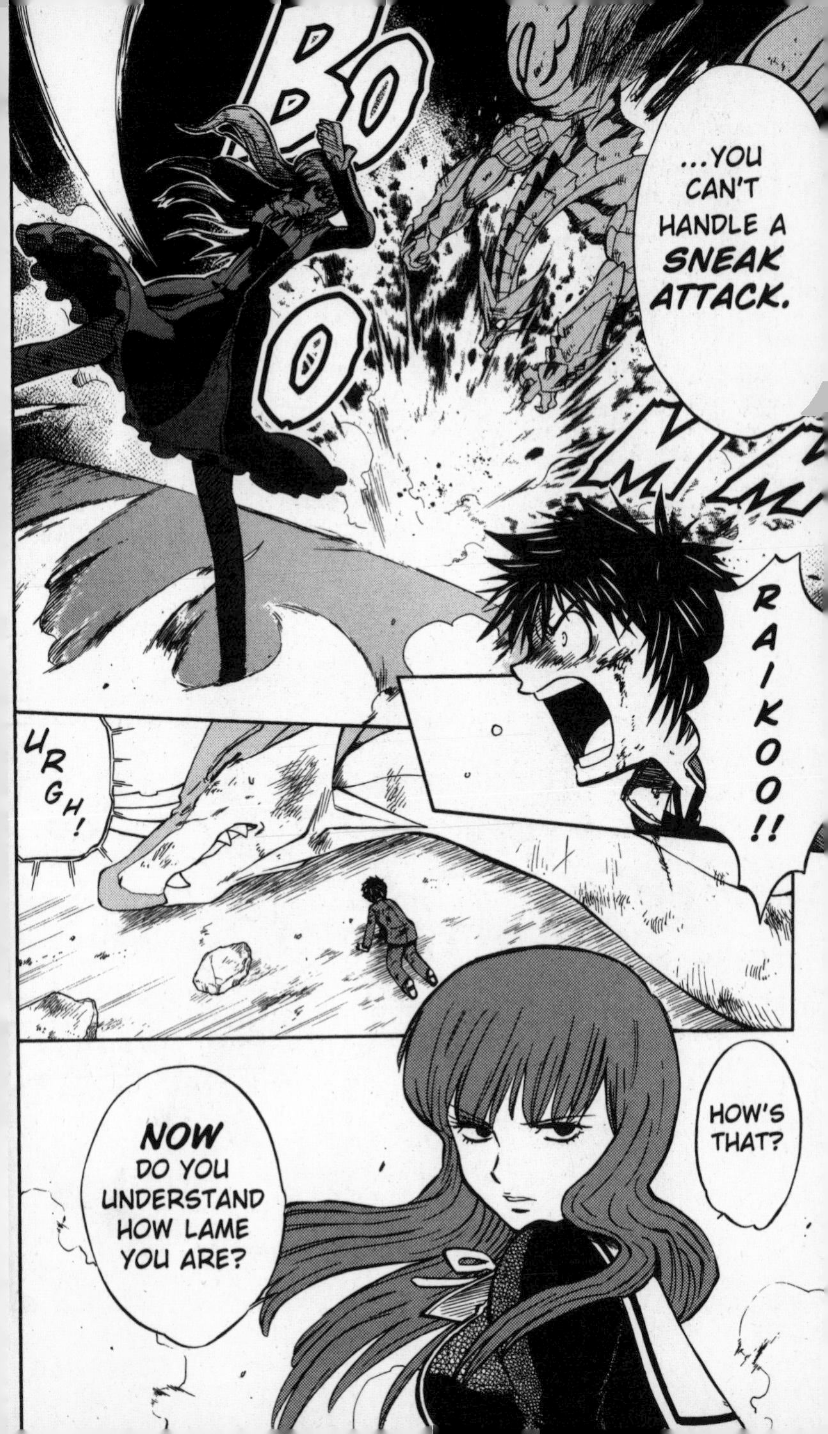
...YOU CAN'T HANDLE A SNEAK ATTACK.
RAIKOO!!
URGH!
HOW'S THAT?
NOW DO YOU UNDERSTAND HOW LAME YOU ARE?

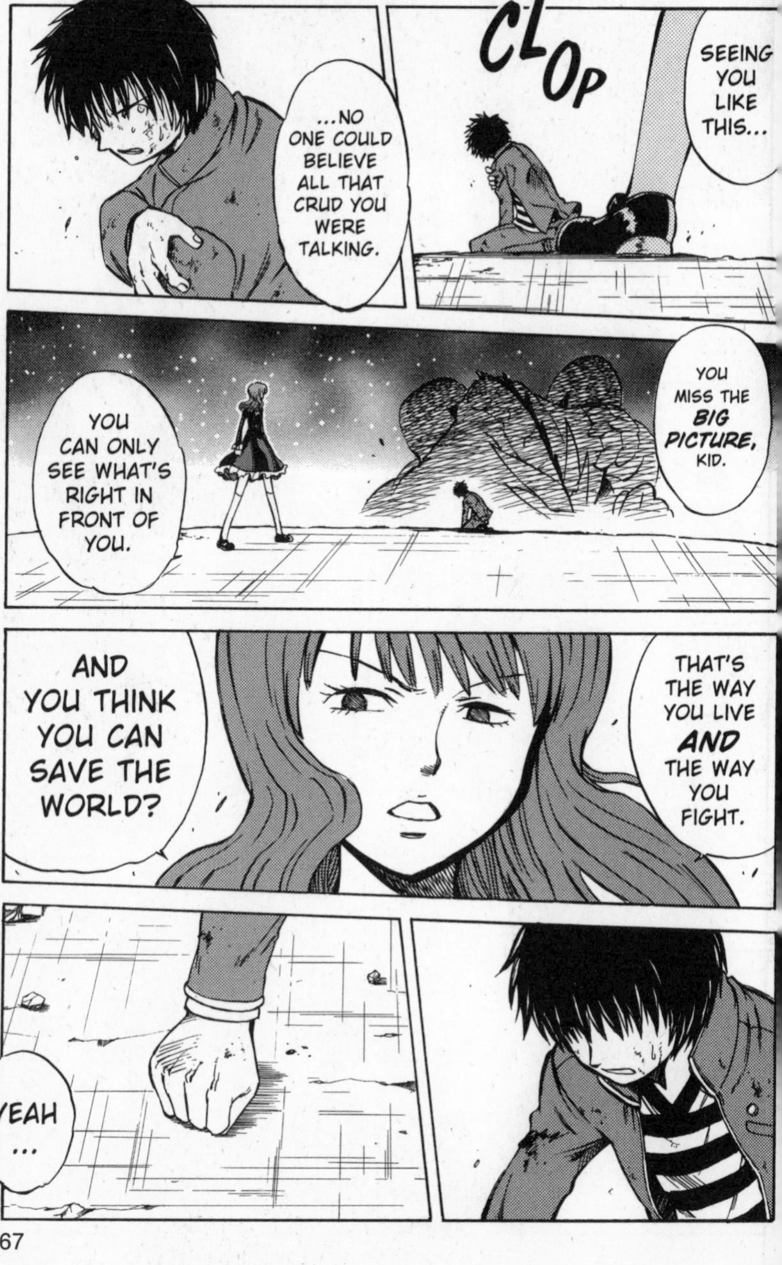
CLOP
SEEING YOU LIKE THIS...
...NO ONE COULD BELIEVE ALL THAT CRUD YOU WERE TALKING.
YOU MISS THE BIG PICTURE, KID.
YOU CAN ONLY SEE WHAT'S RIGHT IN FRONT OF YOU.
THAT'S THE WAY YOU LIVE AND THE WAY YOU FIGHT.
AND YOU THINK YOU CAN SAVE THE WORLD?
YEAH ...

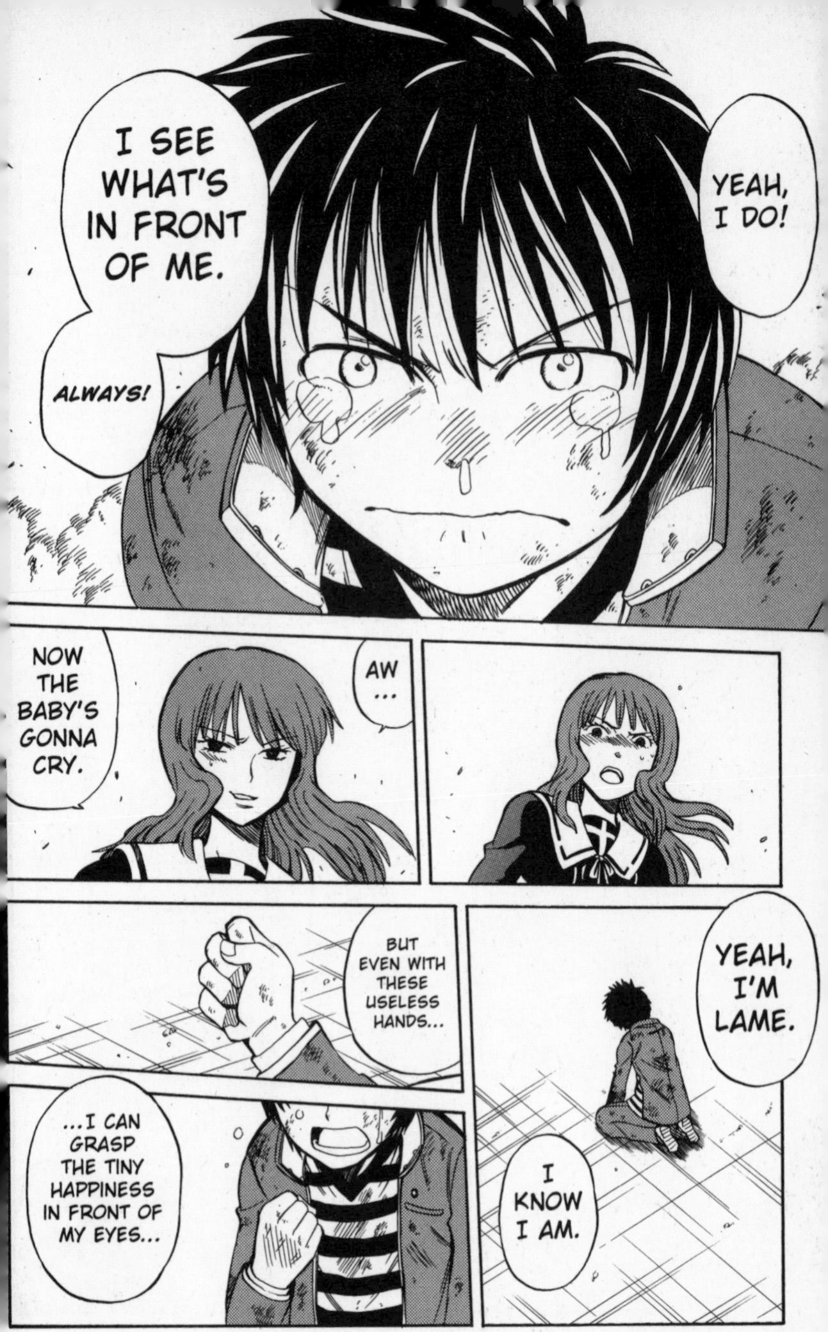
YEAH, I DO!
I SEE WHAT'S IN FRONT OF ME.
ALWAYS!
AW...
NOW THE BABY'S GONNA CRY.
YEAH, I'M LAME.
I KNOW I AM.
BUT EVEN WITH THESE USELESS HANDS...
...I CAN GRASP THE TINY HAPPINESS IN FRONT OF MY EYES...

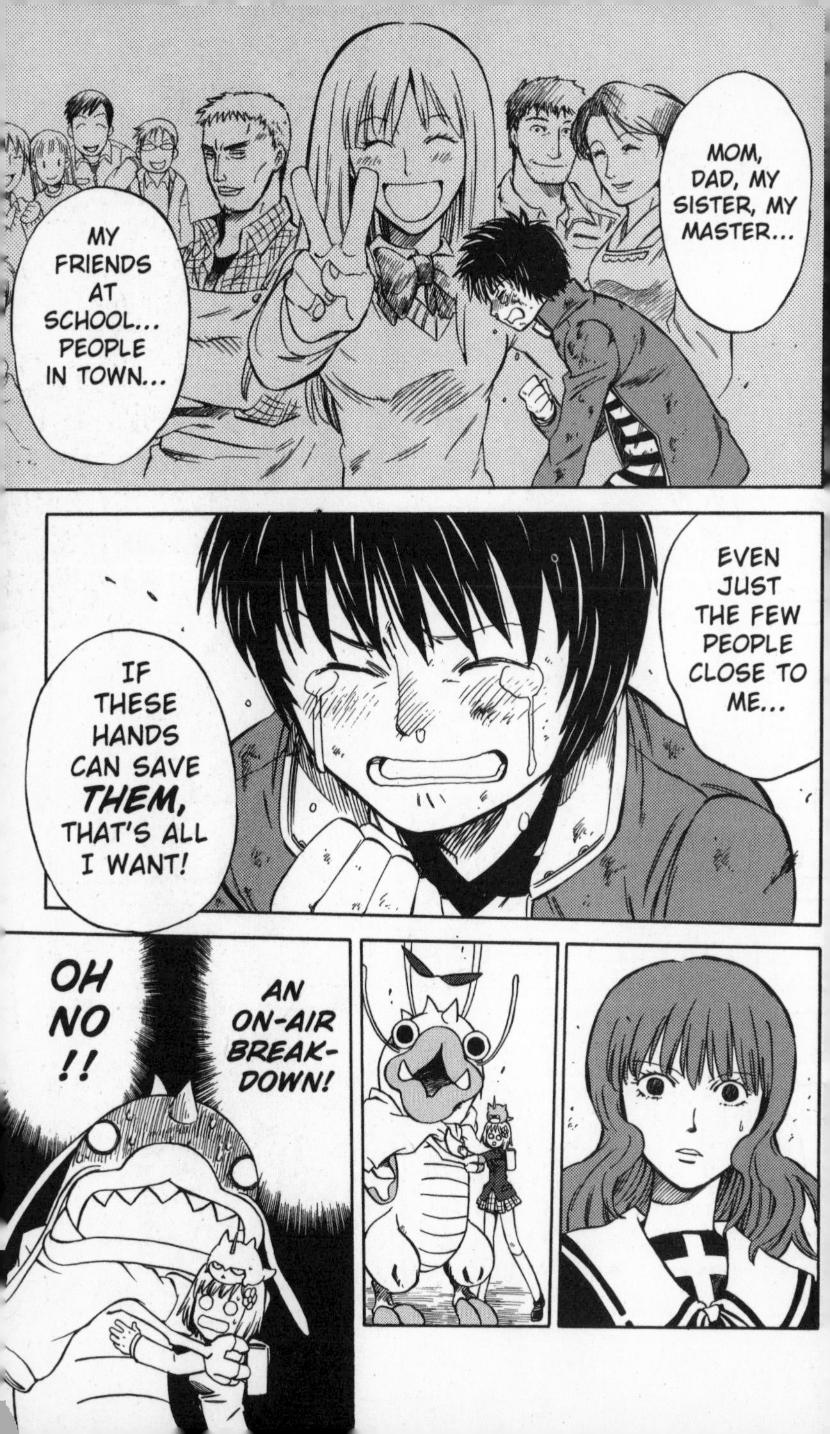
MOM, DAD, MY SISTER, MY MASTER...
MY FRIENDS AT SCHOOL... PEOPLE IN TOWN...
EVEN JUST THE FEW PEOPLE CLOSE TO ME...
IF THESE HANDS CAN SAVE *THEM,* THAT'S ALL I WANT!
AN ON-AIR BREAK-DOWN!
OH NO !!

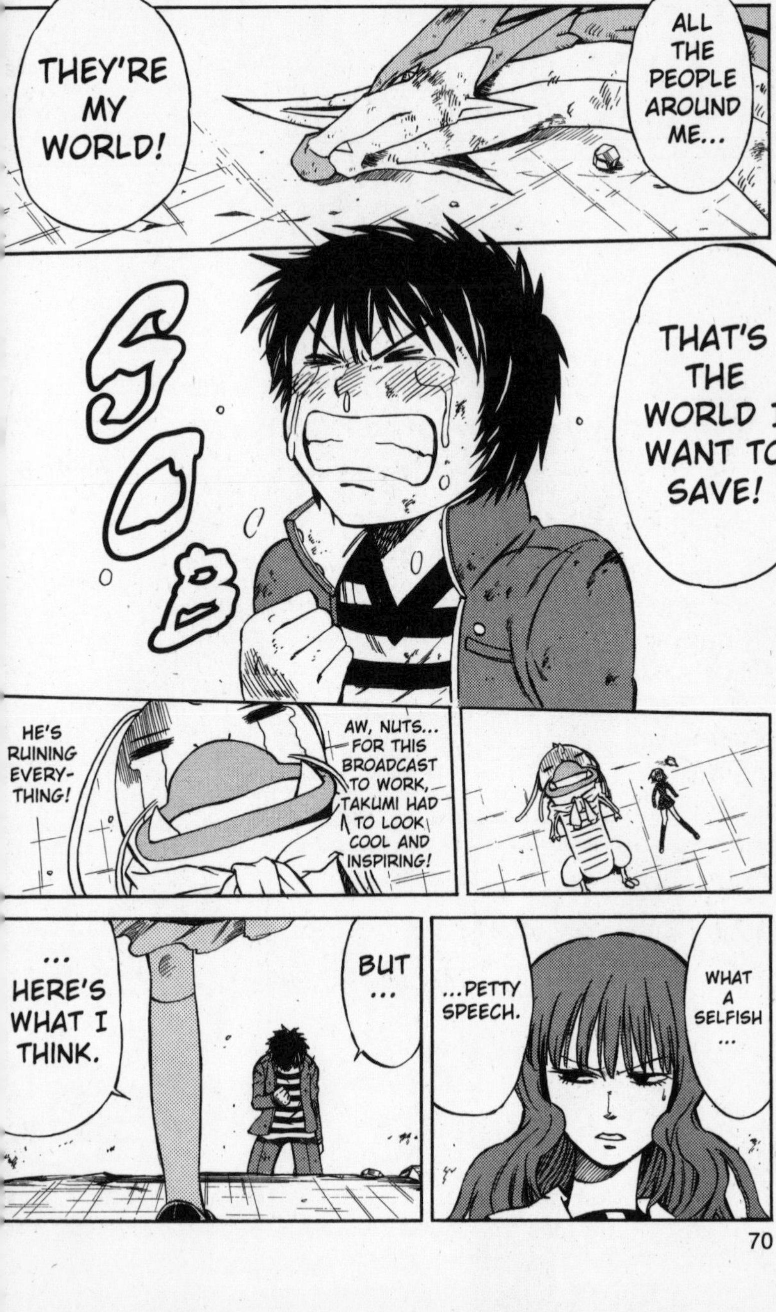
ALL THE PEOPLE AROUND ME...
THEY'RE MY WORLD!
THAT'S THE WORLD I WANT TO SAVE!
SOB
AW, NUTS... FOR THIS BROADCAST TO WORK, TAKUMI HAD TO LOOK COOL AND INSPIRING!
HE'S RUINING EVERY-THING!
WHAT A SELFISH...
...PETTY SPEECH.
BUT...
... HERE'S WHAT I THINK.

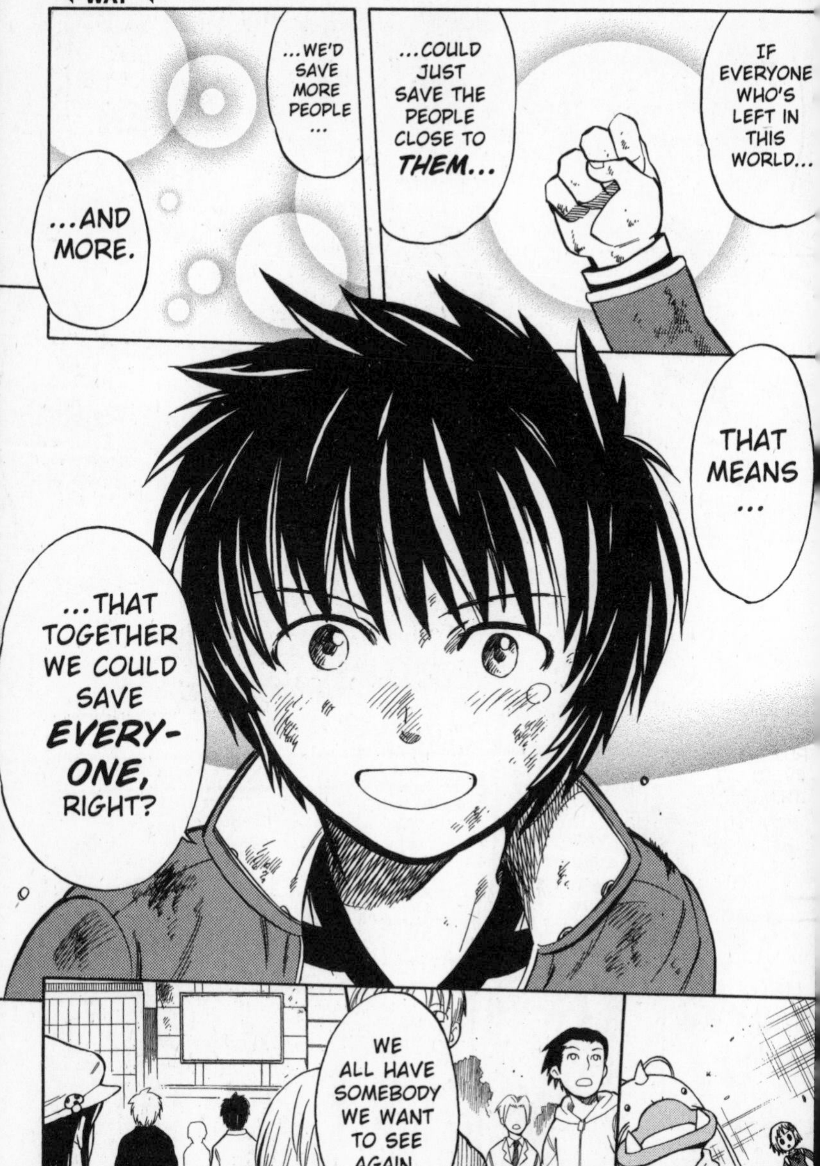
IF EVERYONE WHO'S LEFT IN THIS WORLD...
...COULD JUST SAVE THE PEOPLE CLOSE TO *THEM*...
...WE'D SAVE MORE PEOPLE...
...AND MORE.
THAT MEANS...
...THAT TOGETHER WE COULD SAVE *EVERY-ONE,* RIGHT?
WE ALL HAVE SOMEBODY WE WANT TO SEE AGAIN.

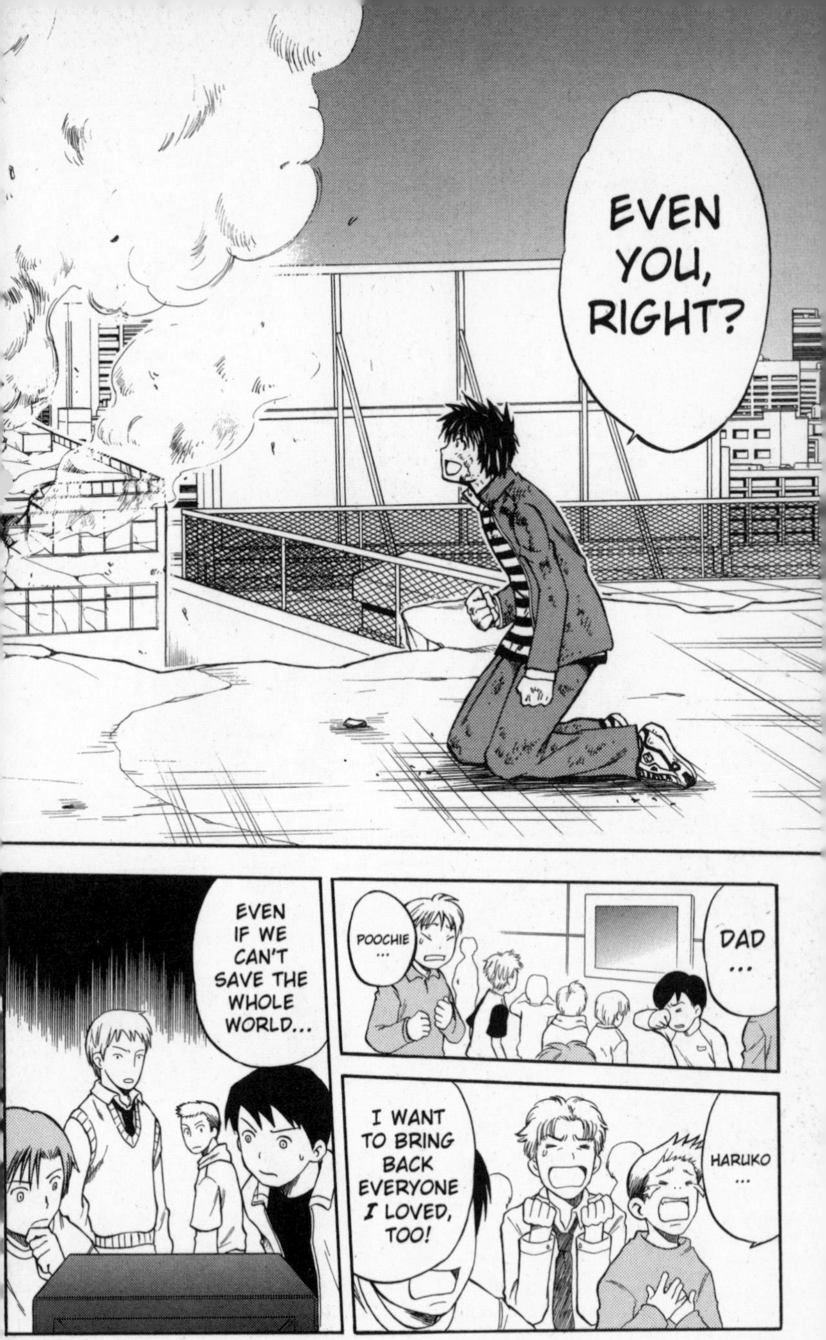
EVEN YOU, RIGHT?
DAD...
POOCHIE...
HARUKO...
I WANT TO BRING BACK EVERYONE *I* LOVED, TOO!
EVEN IF WE CAN'T SAVE THE WHOLE WORLD...

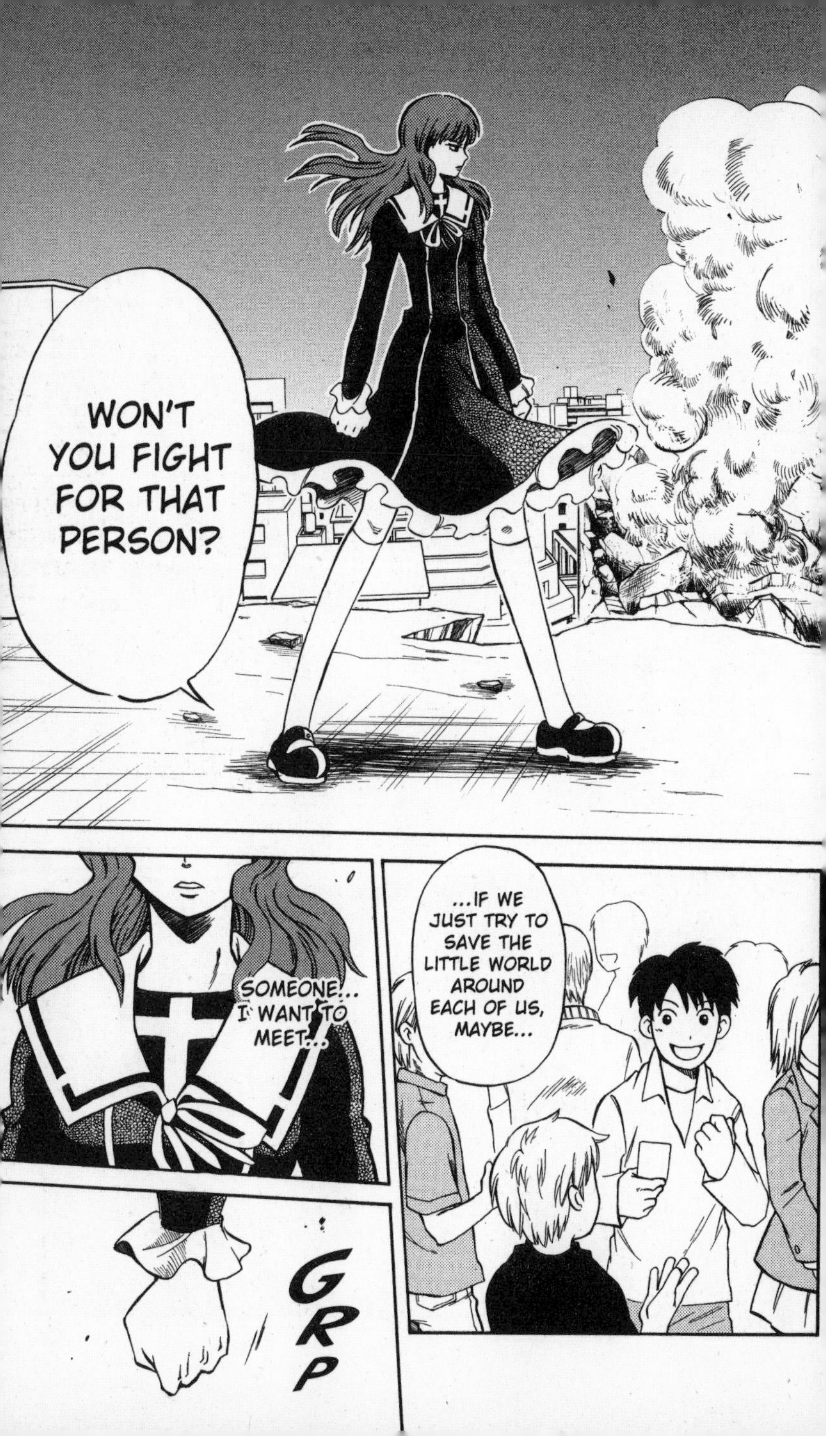
WON'T YOU FIGHT FOR THAT PERSON?
...IF WE JUST TRY TO SAVE THE LITTLE WORLD AROUND EACH OF US, MAYBE...
SOMEONE... I WANT TO MEET...
GRP

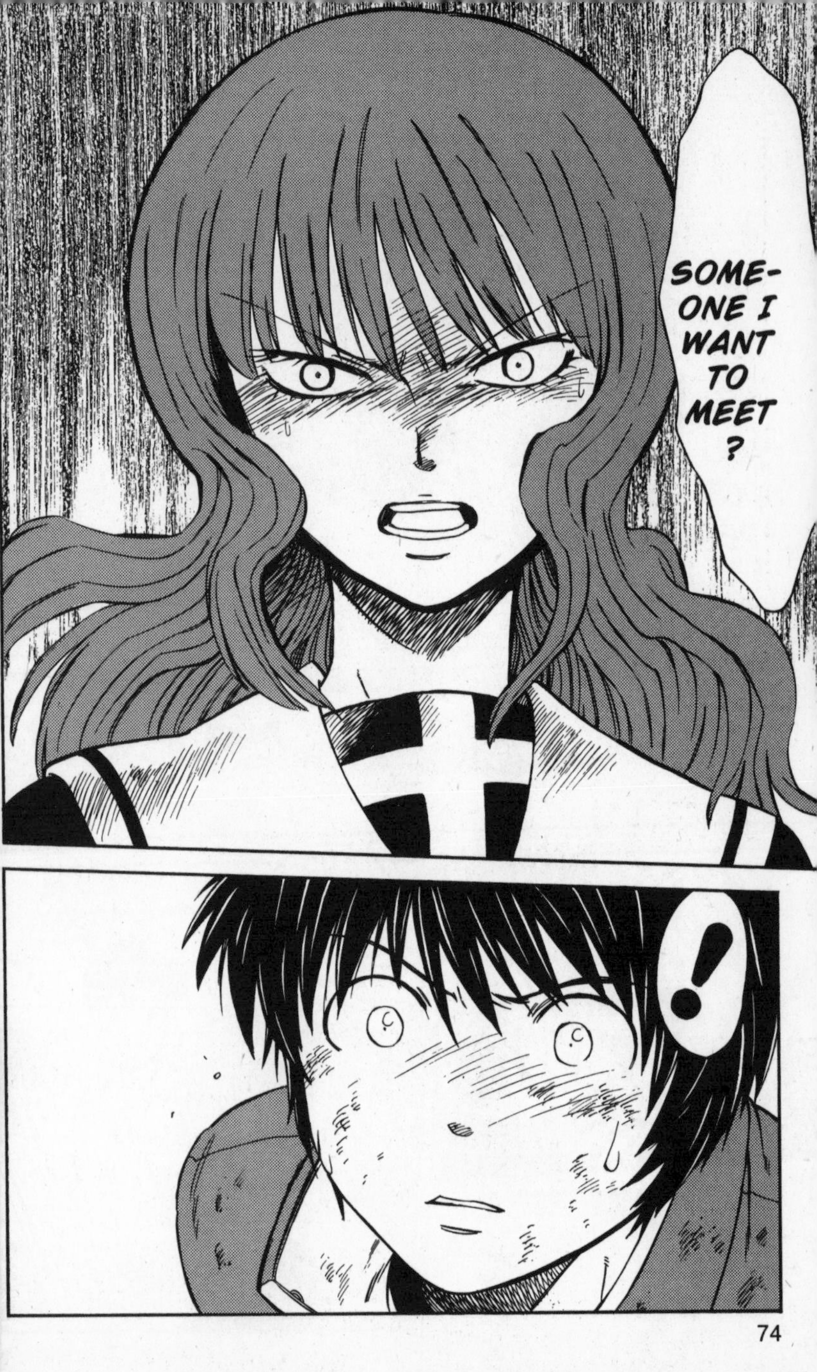
SOME-ONE I WANT TO MEET?
!

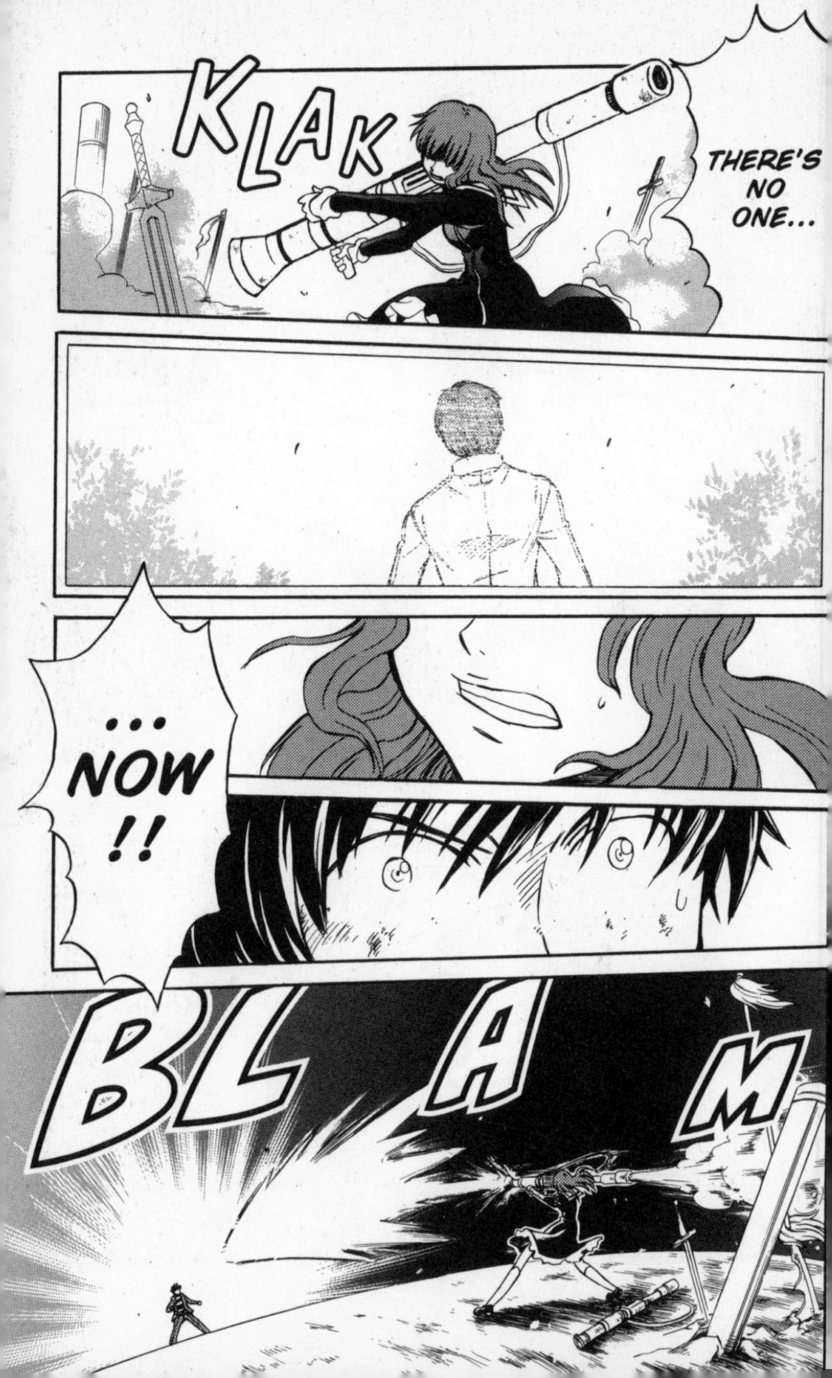
THERE'S NO ONE...
KLAK
...NOW!!
BLAM

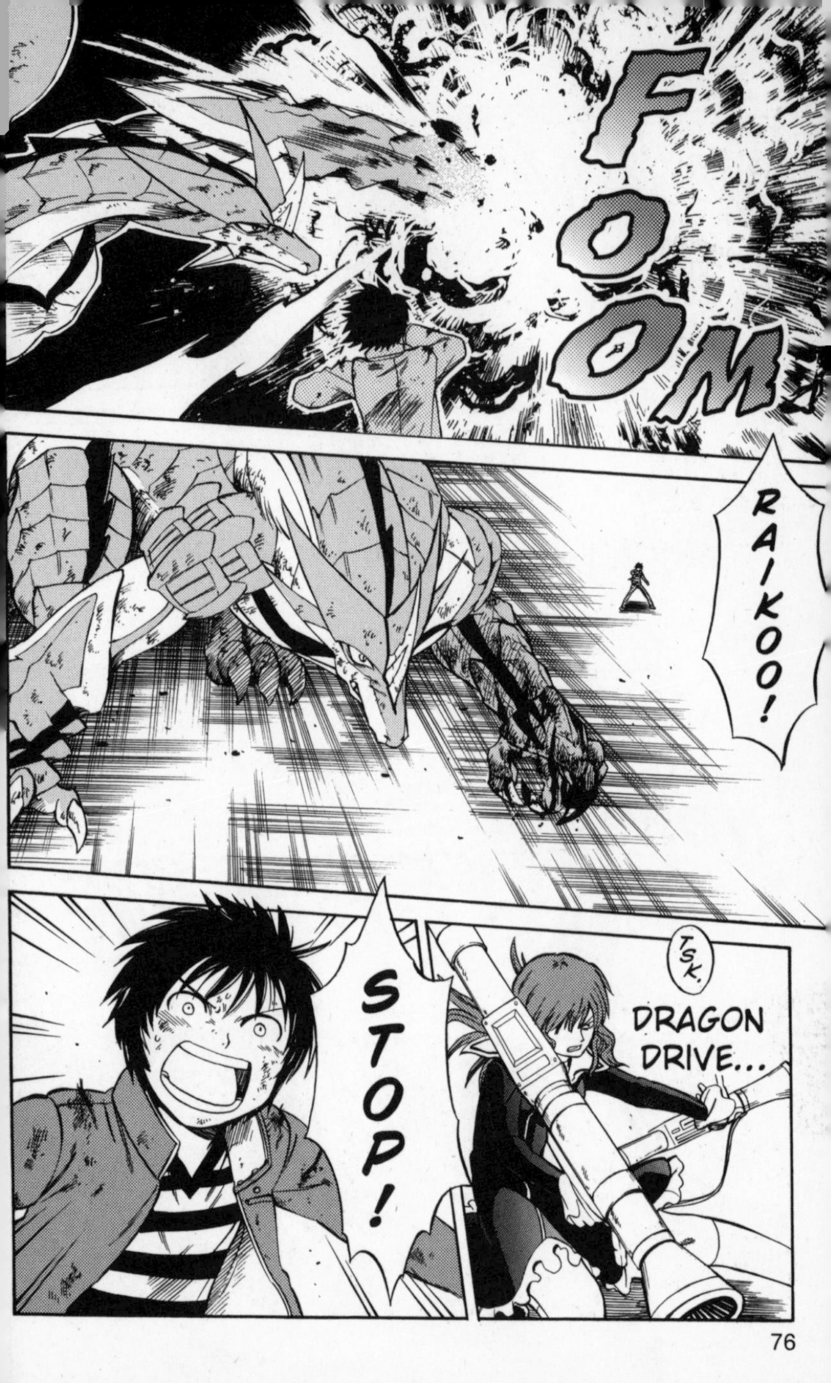
FOOM
RAIKOOO!
TSK.
DRAGON DRIVE...
STOP!

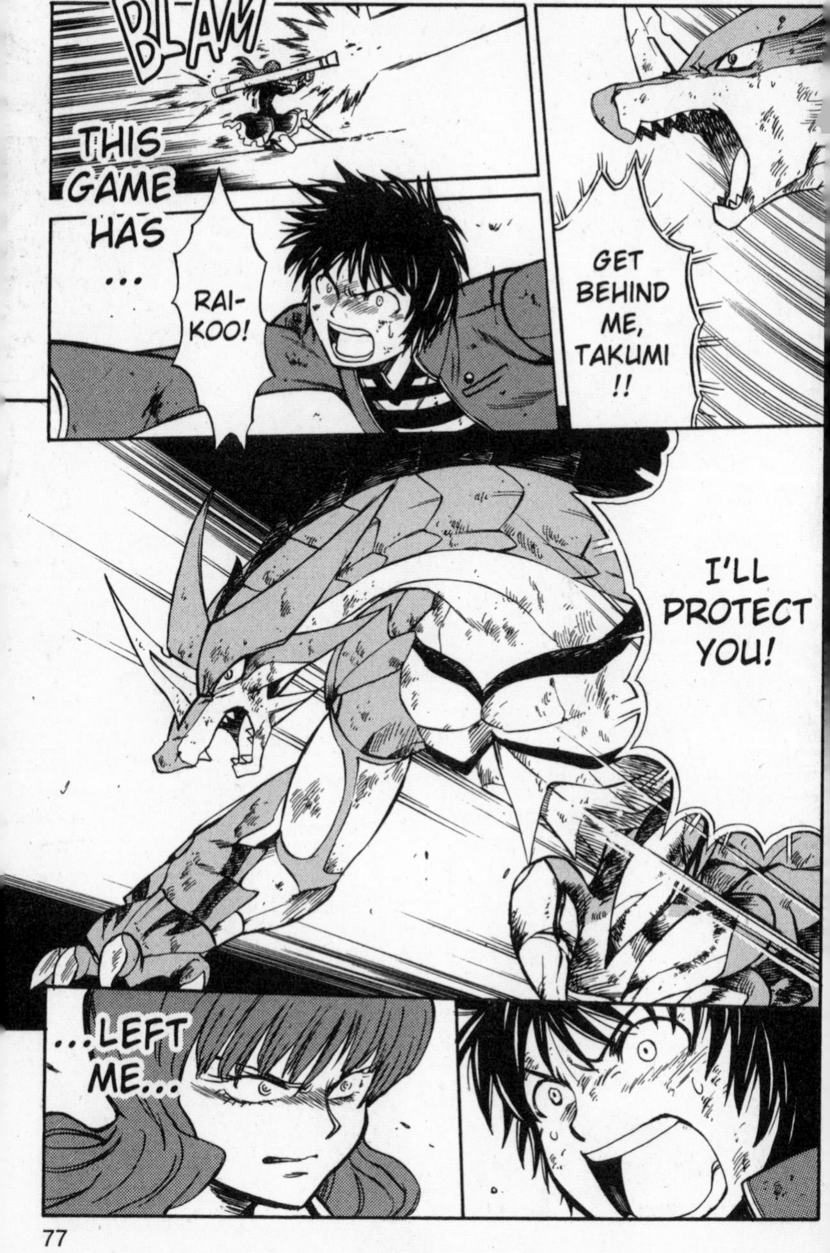
GET BEHIND ME, TAKUMI!!
BLAM
THIS GAME HAS ...
RAI-KOO!
I'LL PROTECT YOU!
...LEFT ME...

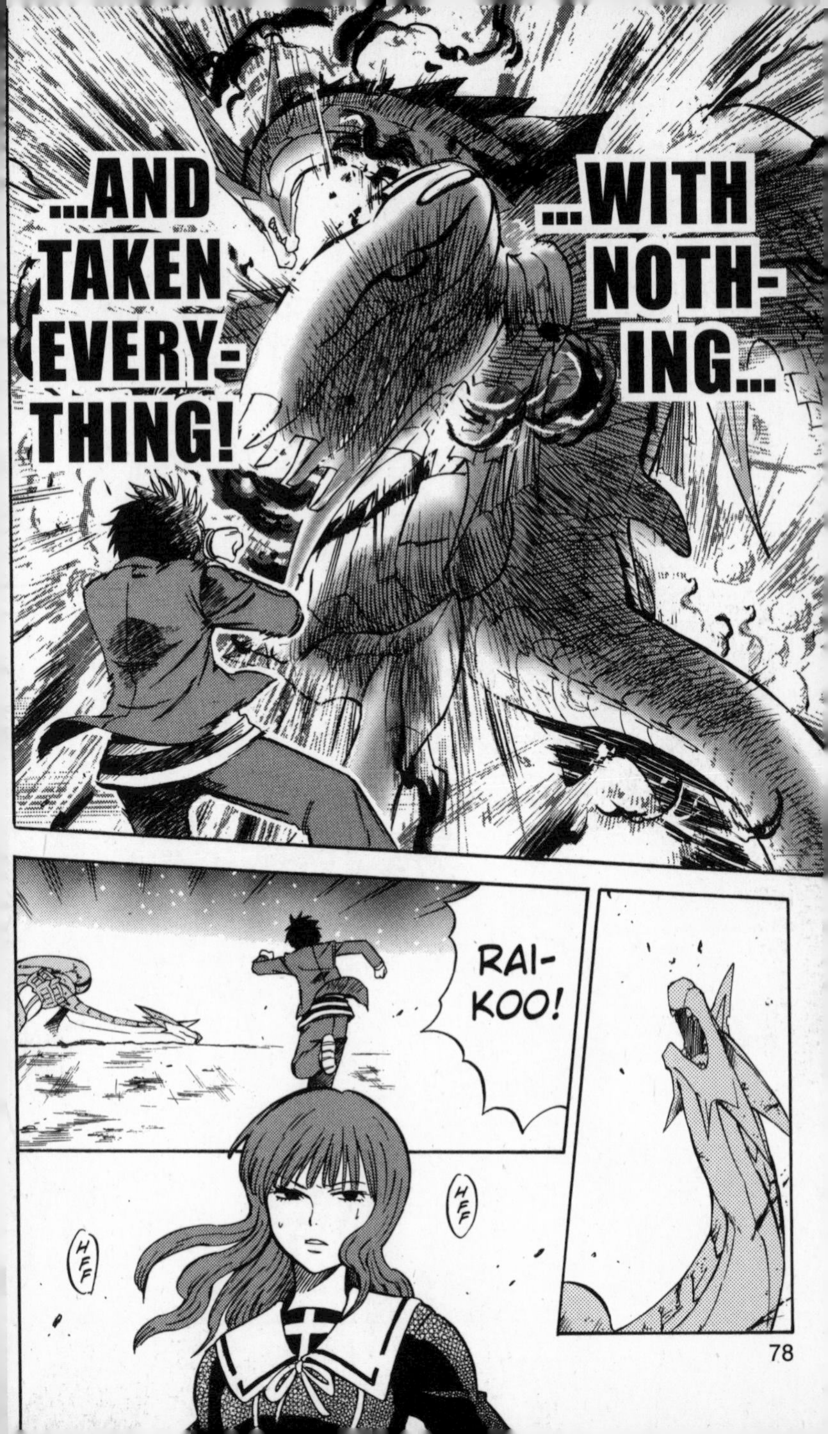
...WITH NOTH-ING...
...AND TAKEN EVERY-THING!
RAI-KOO!
HFF
HFF

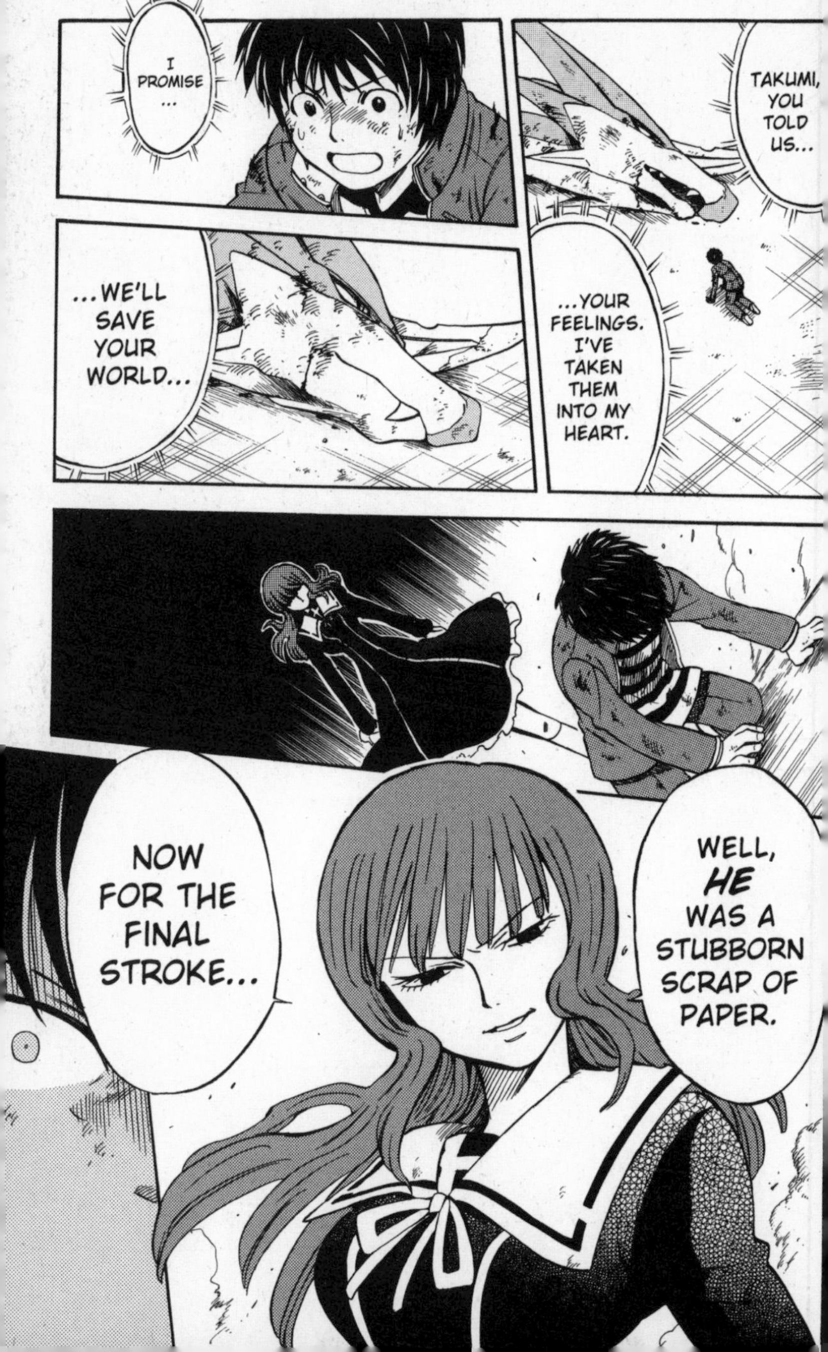
TAKUMI, YOU TOLD US...
I PROMISE ...
...YOUR FEELINGS. I'VE TAKEN THEM INTO MY HEART.
...WE'LL SAVE YOUR WORLD...
WELL, *HE* WAS A STUBBORN SCRAP OF PAPER.
NOW FOR THE FINAL STROKE...

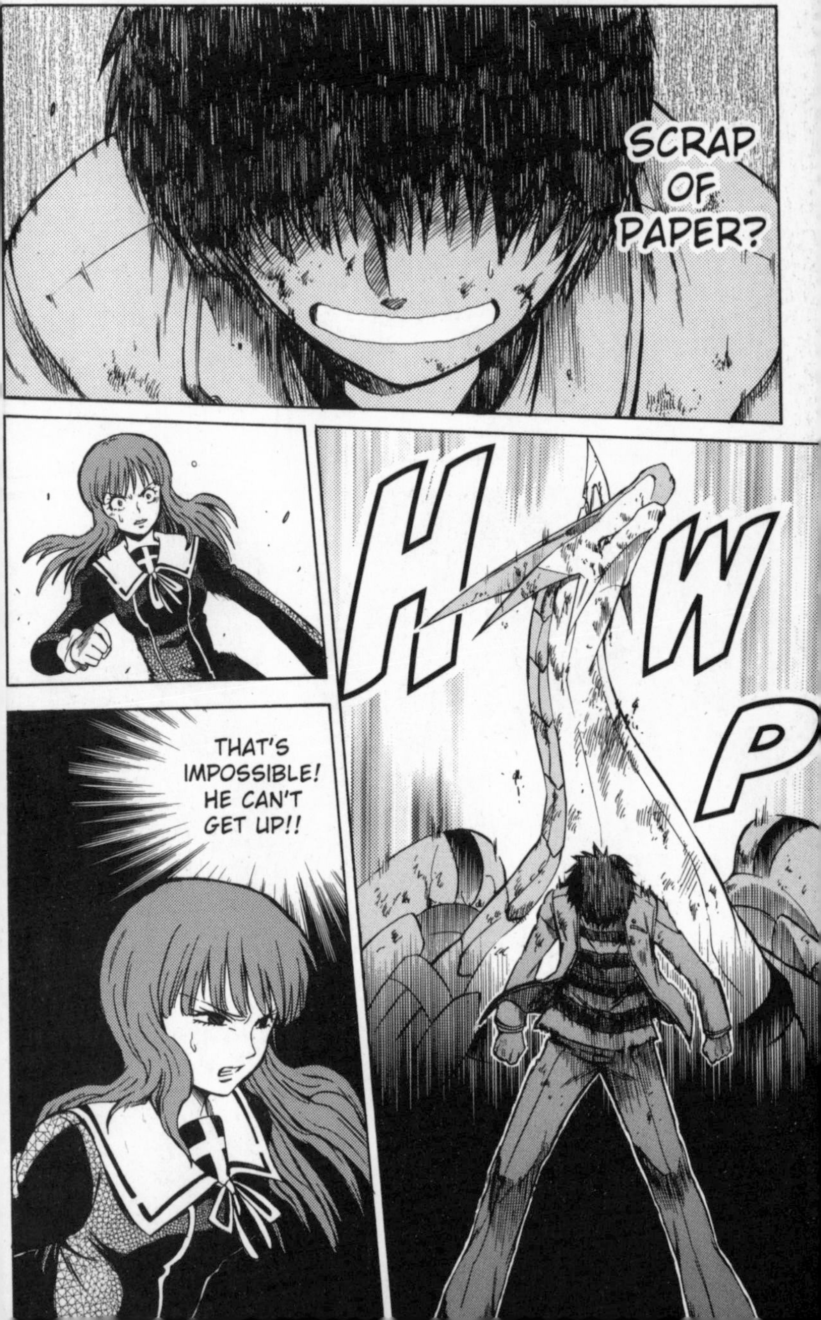
SCRAP OF PAPER?
HWP
THAT'S IMPOSSIBLE! HE CAN'T GET UP!!

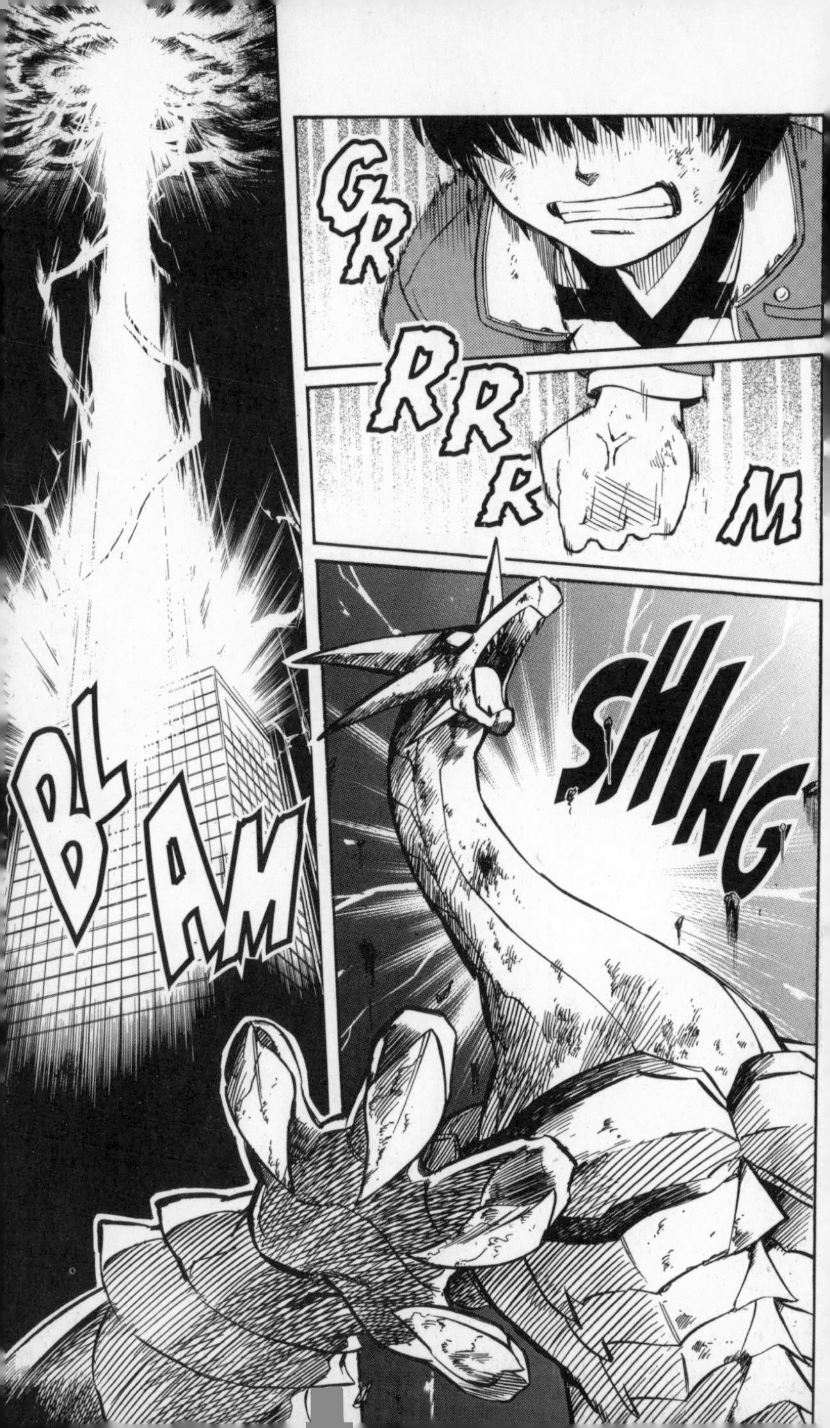
GRRRRM
SHING
BLAM

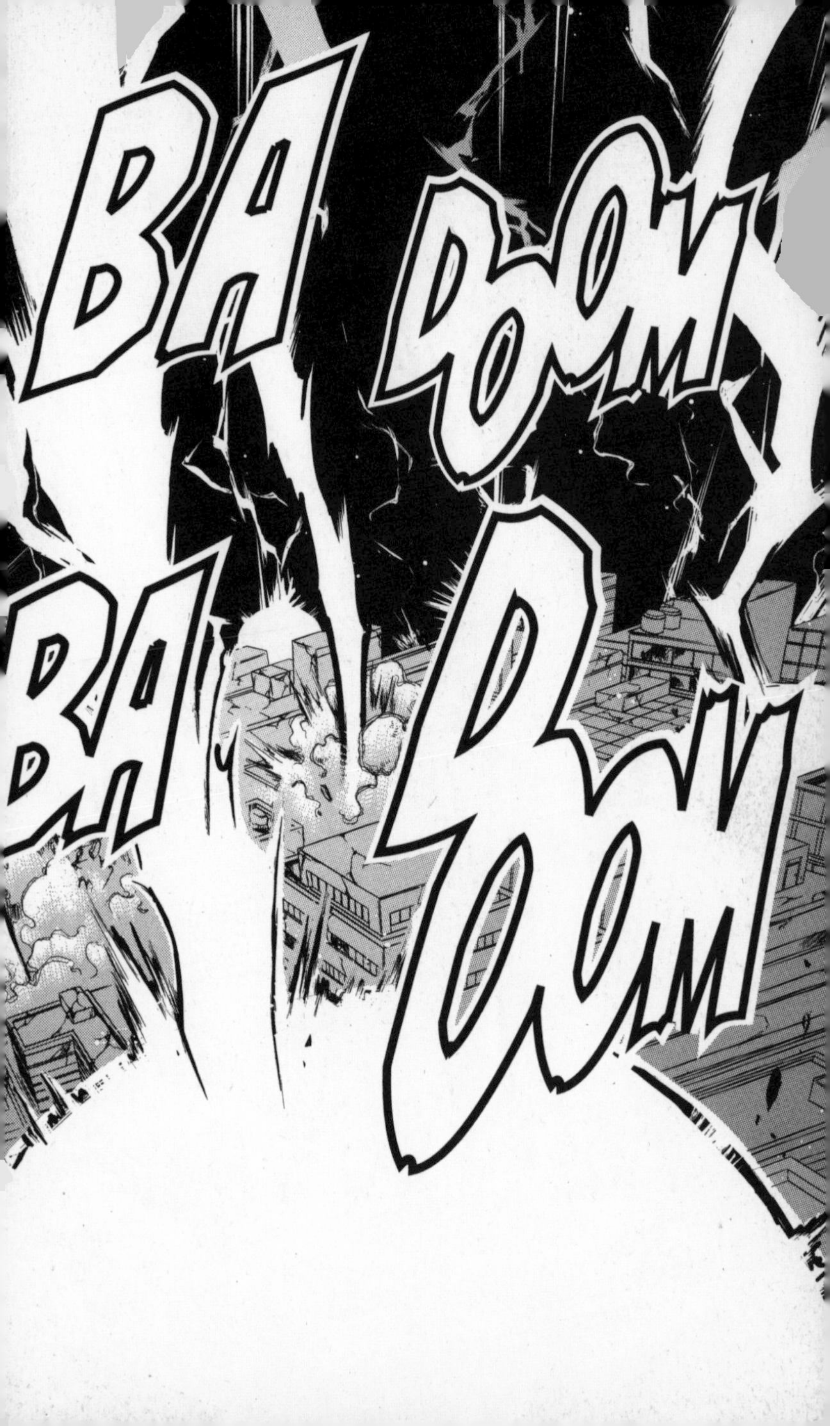
BA DOOM
BA DOOM

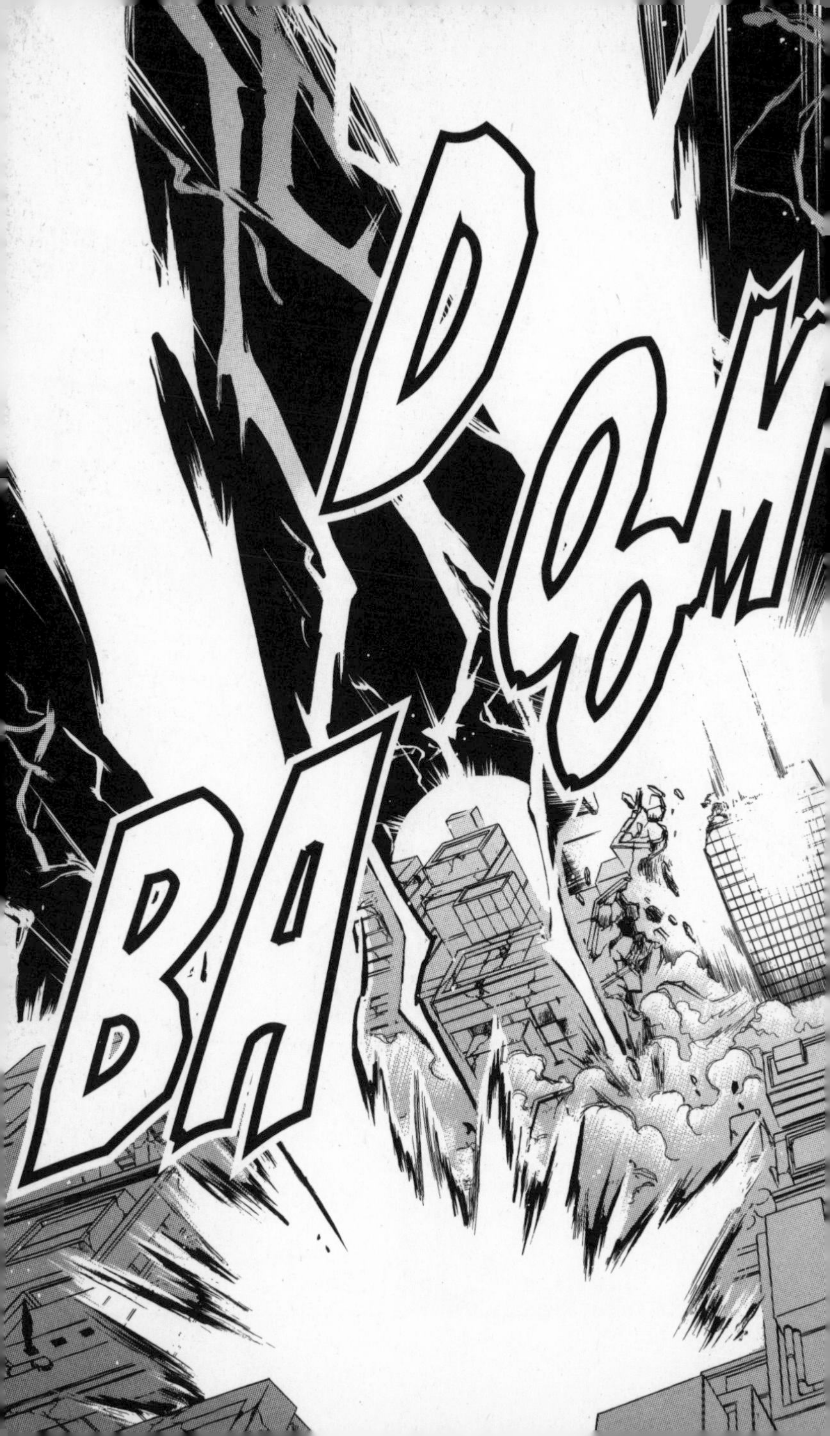
BADOOM

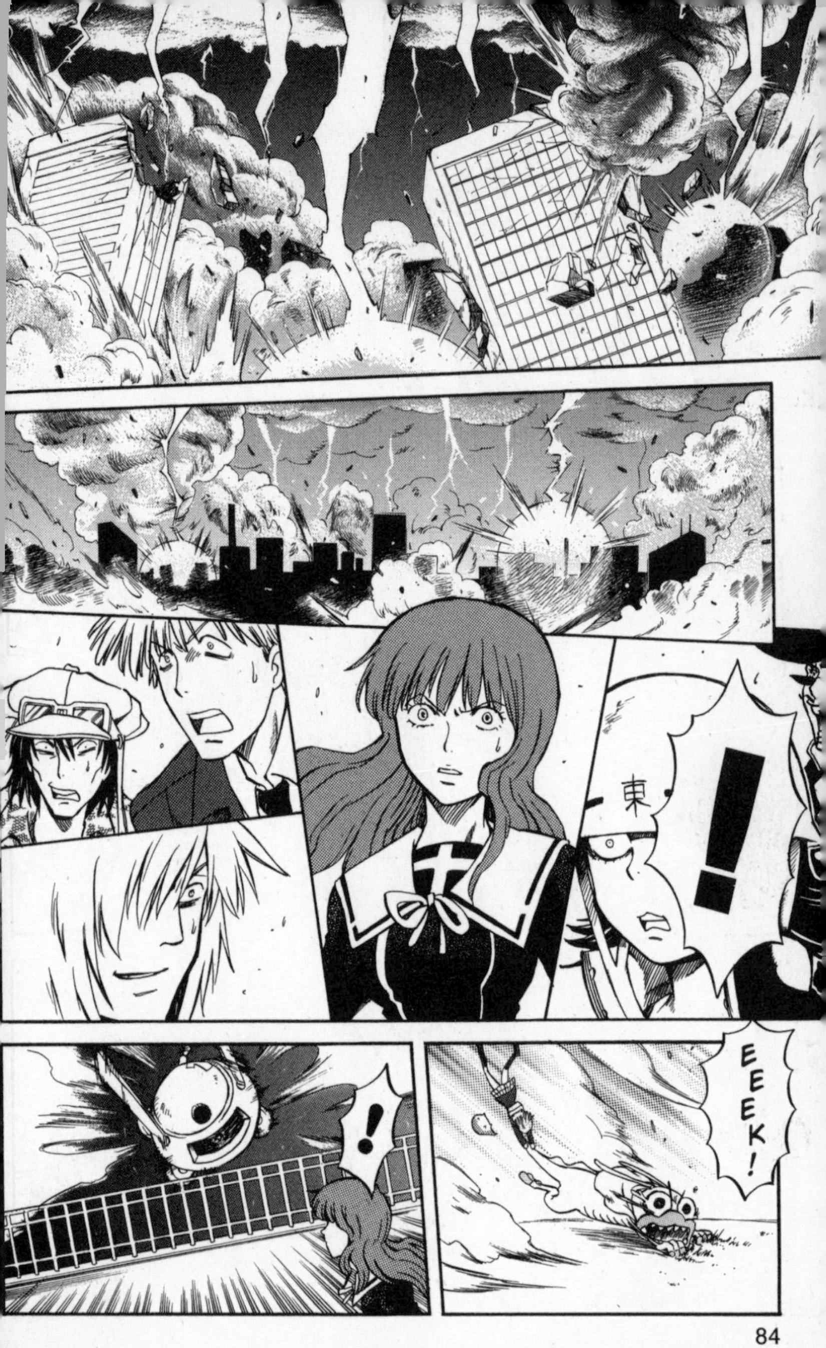
東
!
!
EEEK!

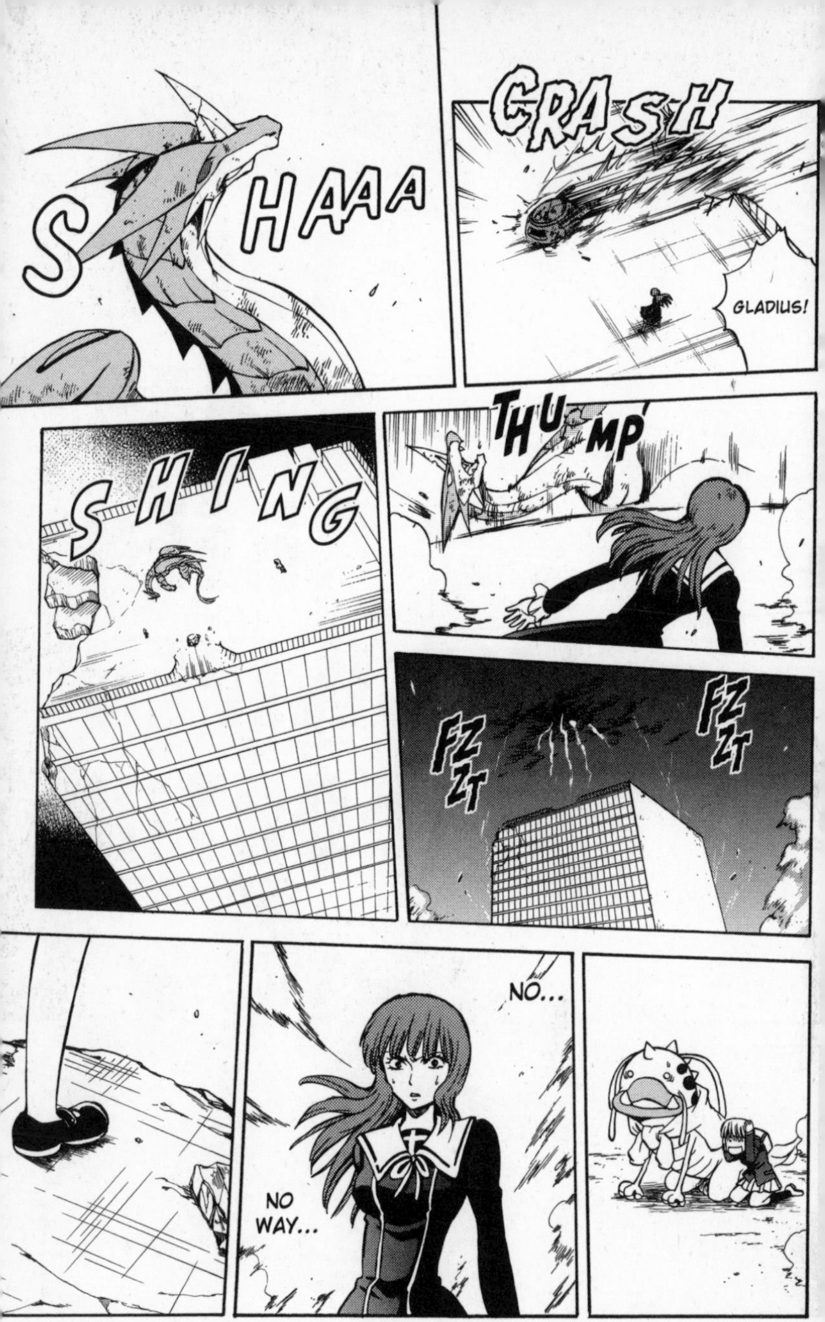
CRASH
GLADIUS!
SHAAA
THUMP
FZZT
FZZT
SHING
NO...
NO WAY...

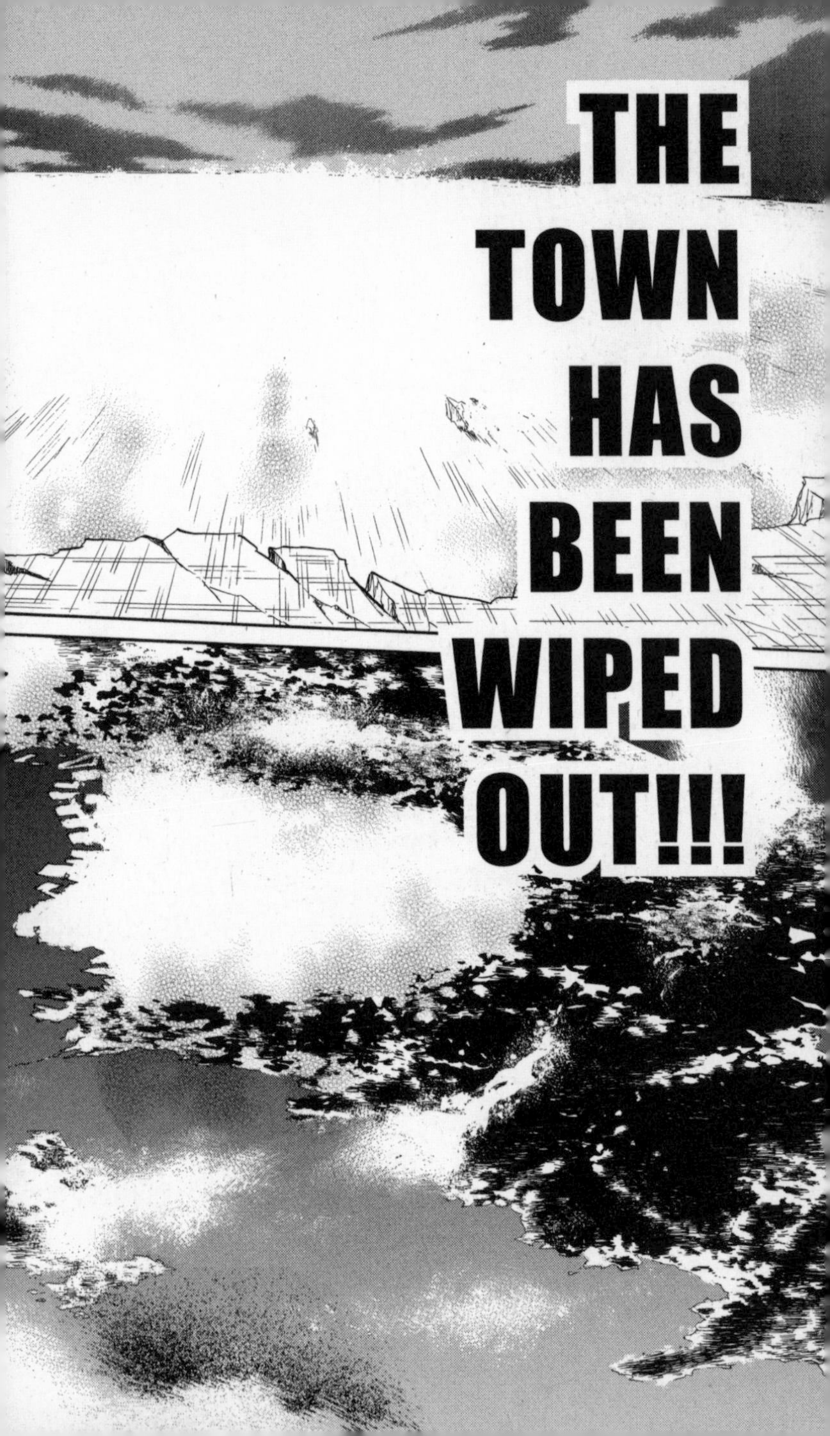
THE TOWN HAS BEEN WIPED OUT!!!

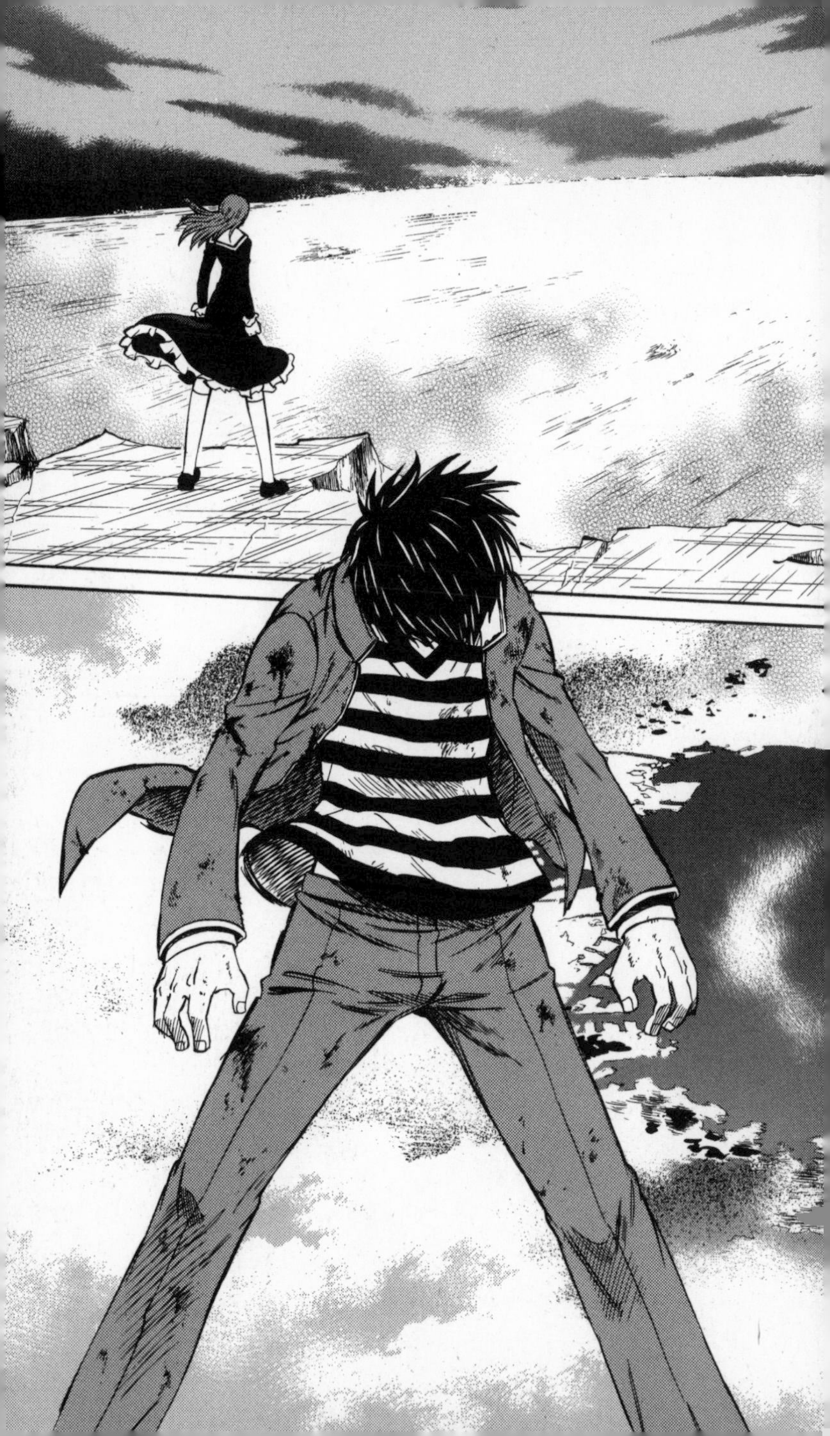

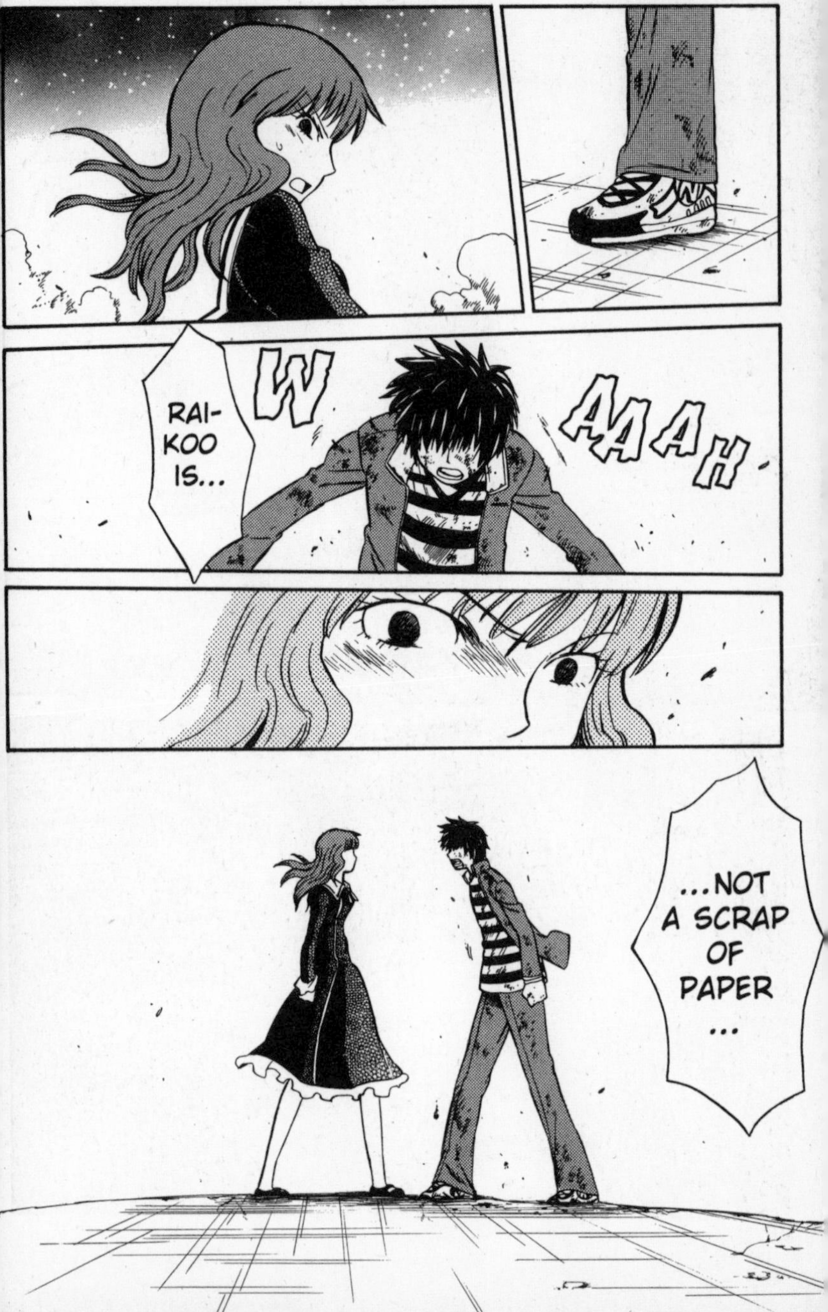
RAI-KOO IS...
WAAAH
...NOT A SCRAP OF PAPER...

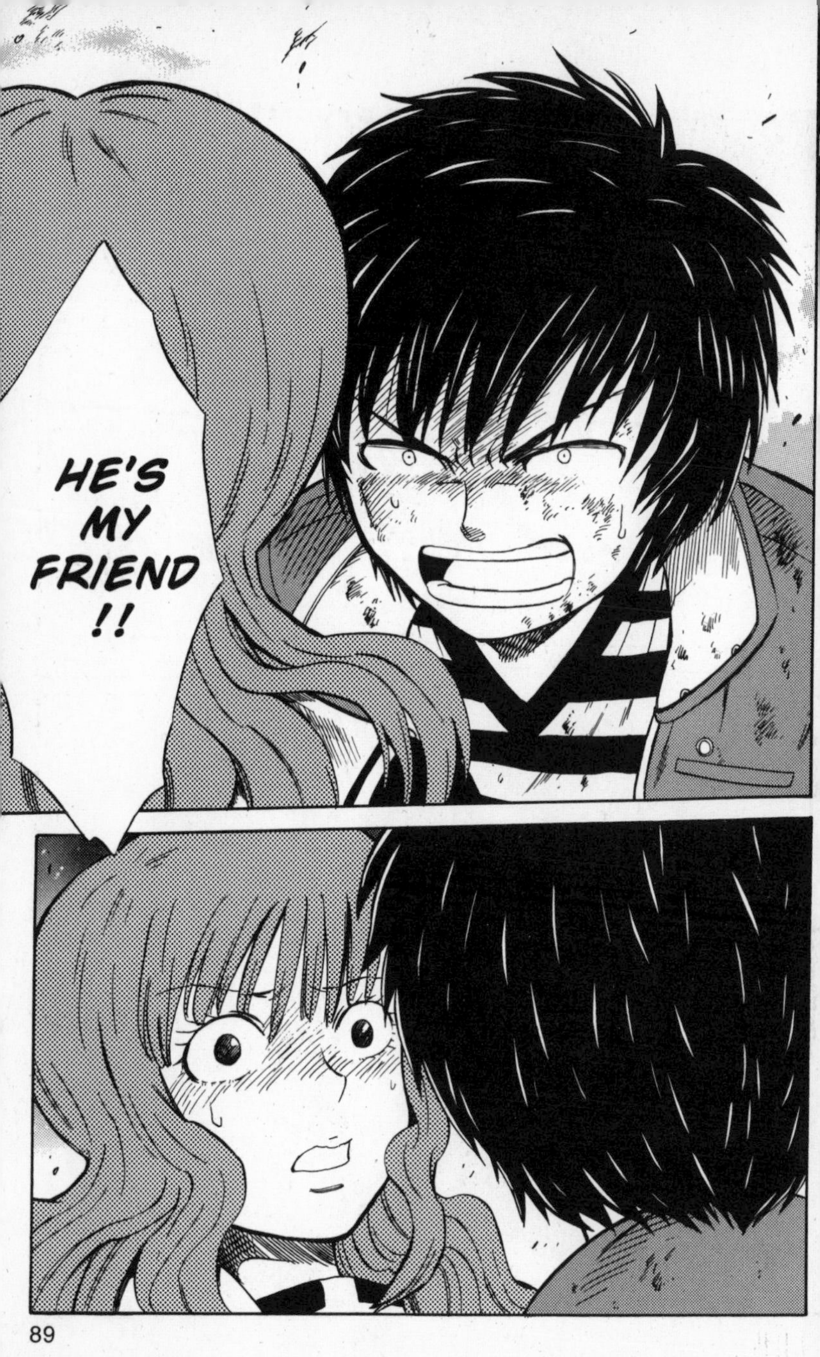
HE'S MY FRIEND!!

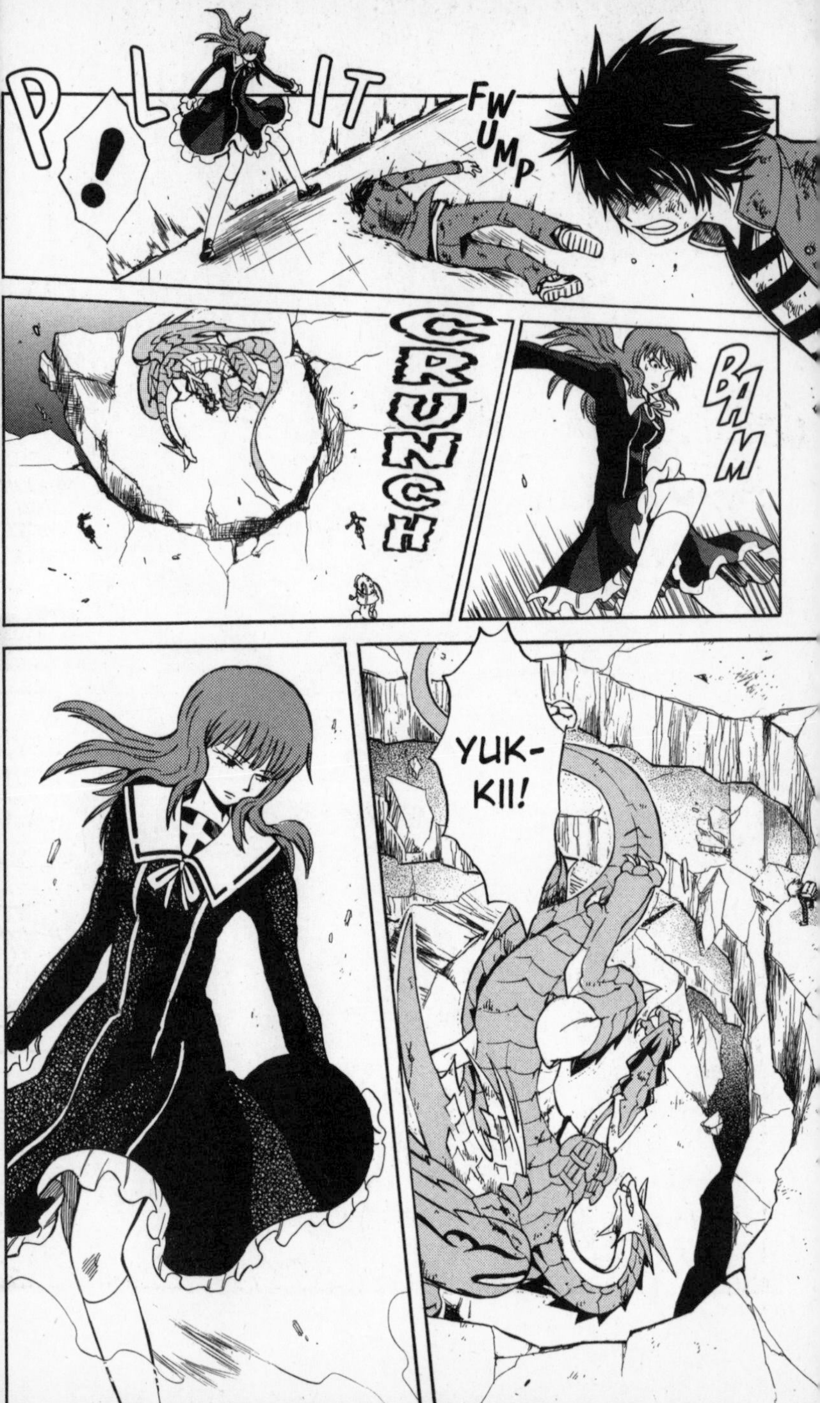
FWUMP
PLIT
!
BAMM
CRUNCH
YUK-KII!

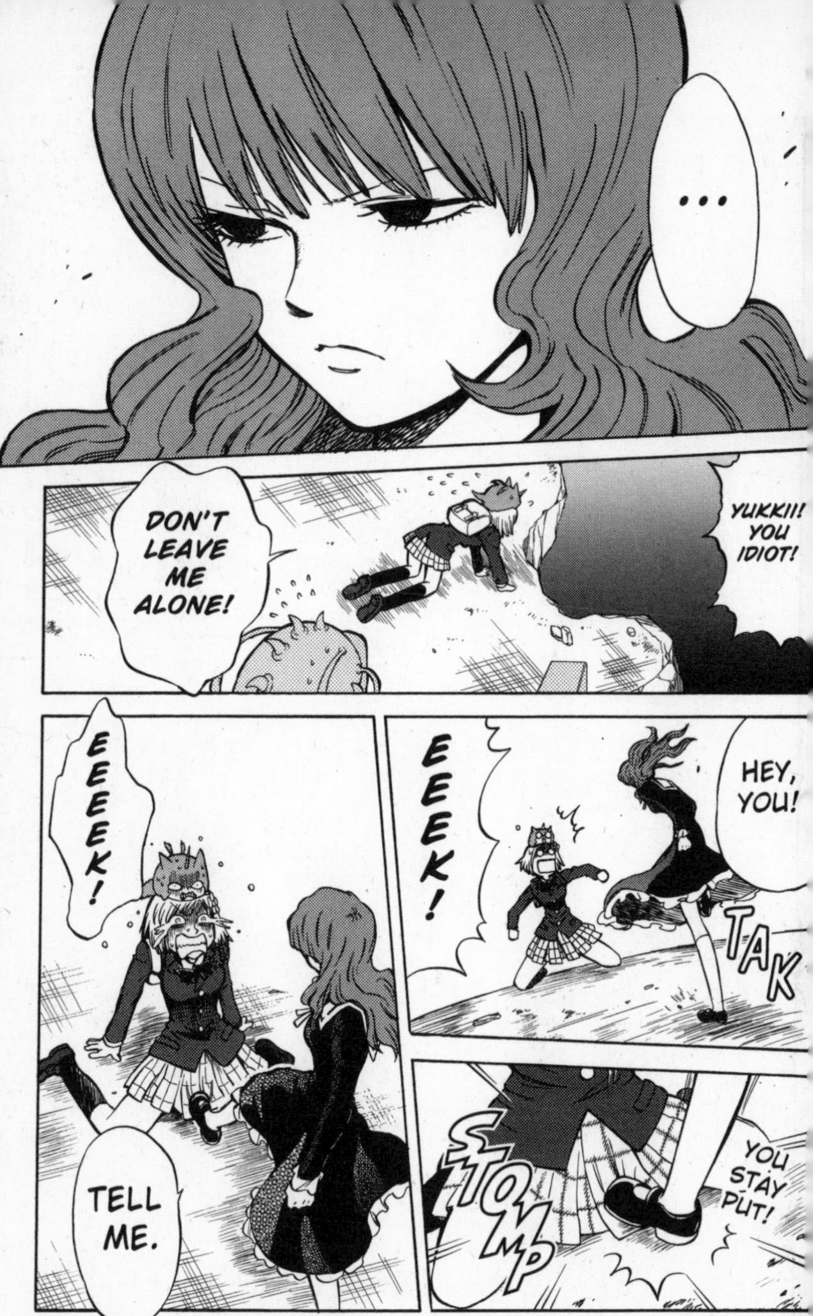
...
YUKKII! YOU IDIOT!
DON'T LEAVE ME ALONE!
HEY, YOU!
TAK
EEEEK!
YOU STAY PUT!
STOMP
EEEEEK!
TELL ME.

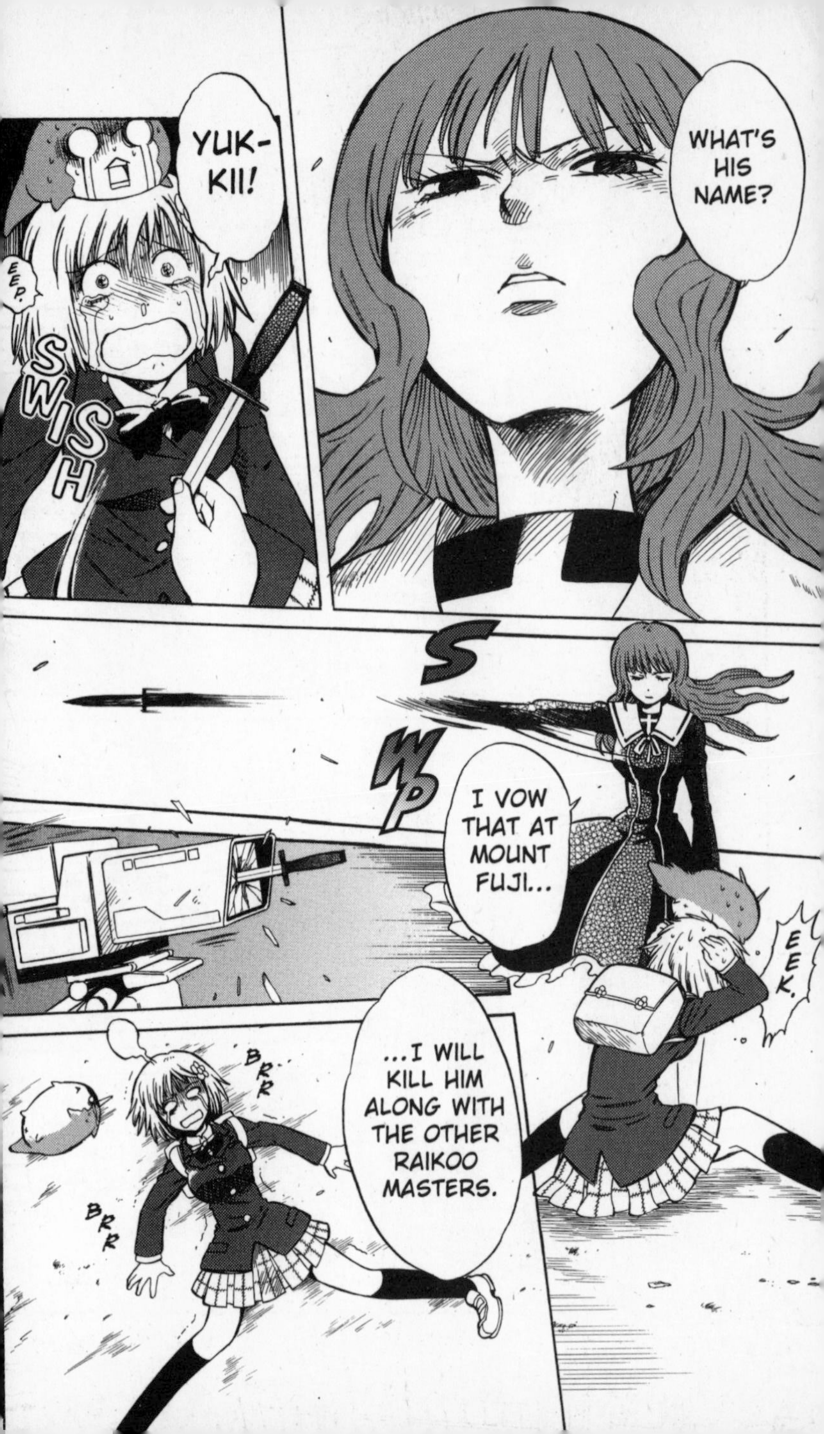
WHAT'S HIS NAME?
YUK-KII!
EEP.
SWISH
SWP
I VOW THAT AT MOUNT FUJI...
EEK.
...I WILL KILL HIM ALONG WITH THE OTHER RAIKOO MASTERS.
BRR
BRR

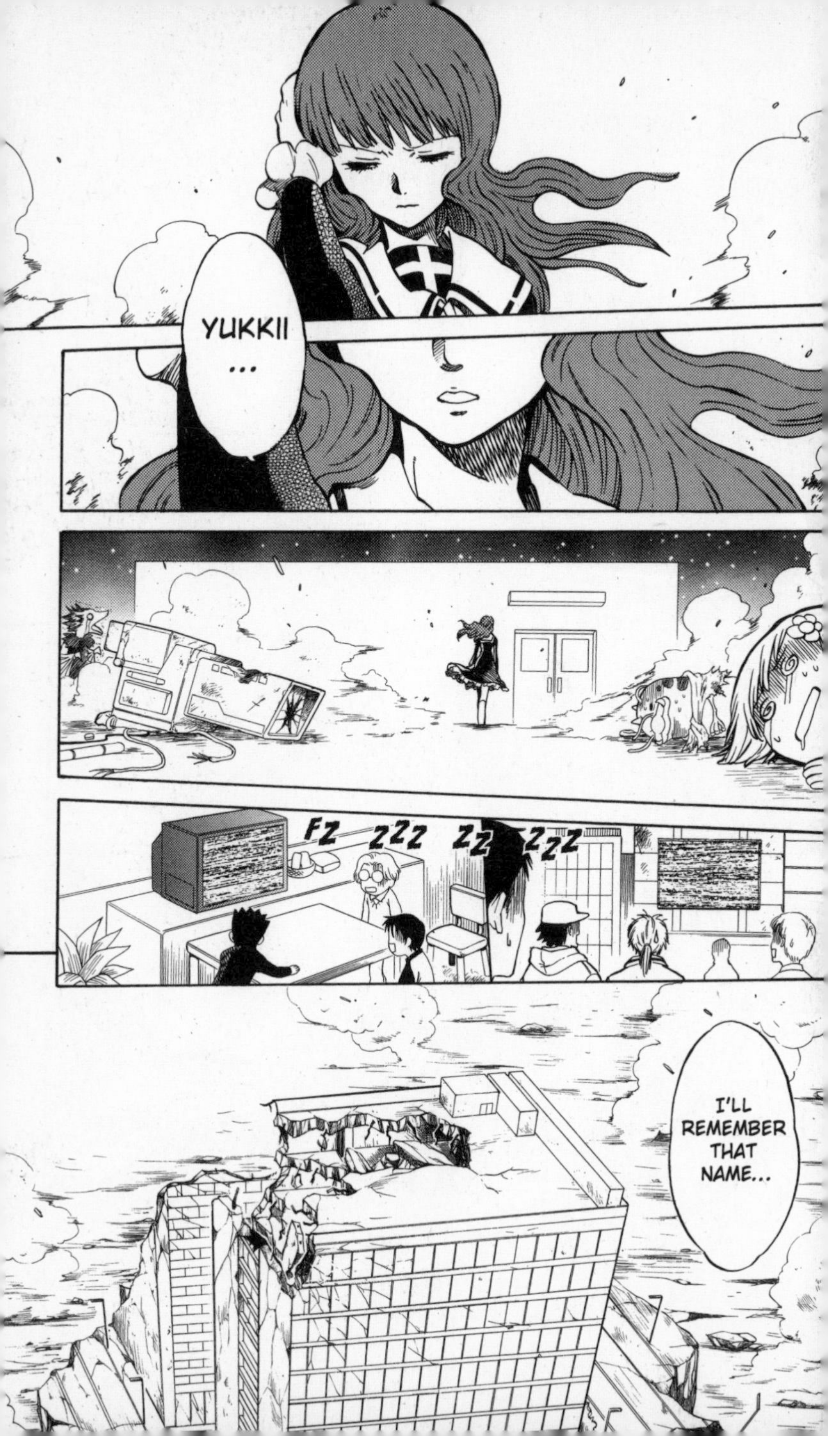
YUKKII ...
FZ
ZZZ
ZZ
ZZZ
I'LL REMEMBER THAT NAME...

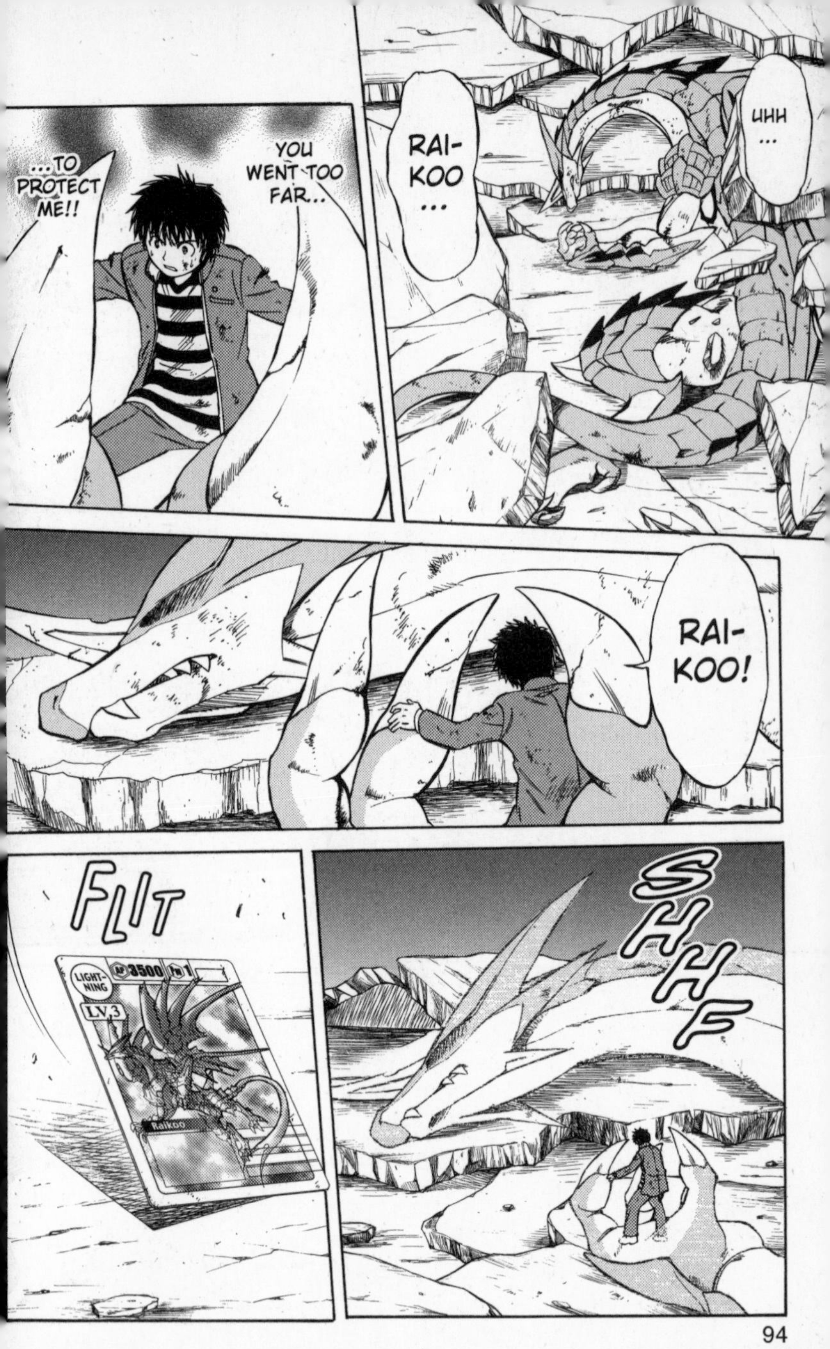
UHH ...
RAI-KOO ...
YOU WENT TOO FAR...
...TO PROTECT ME!!
RAI-KOO!
SHHF
FLIT
LIGHTNING
3500
1
LV.3
Raikoo

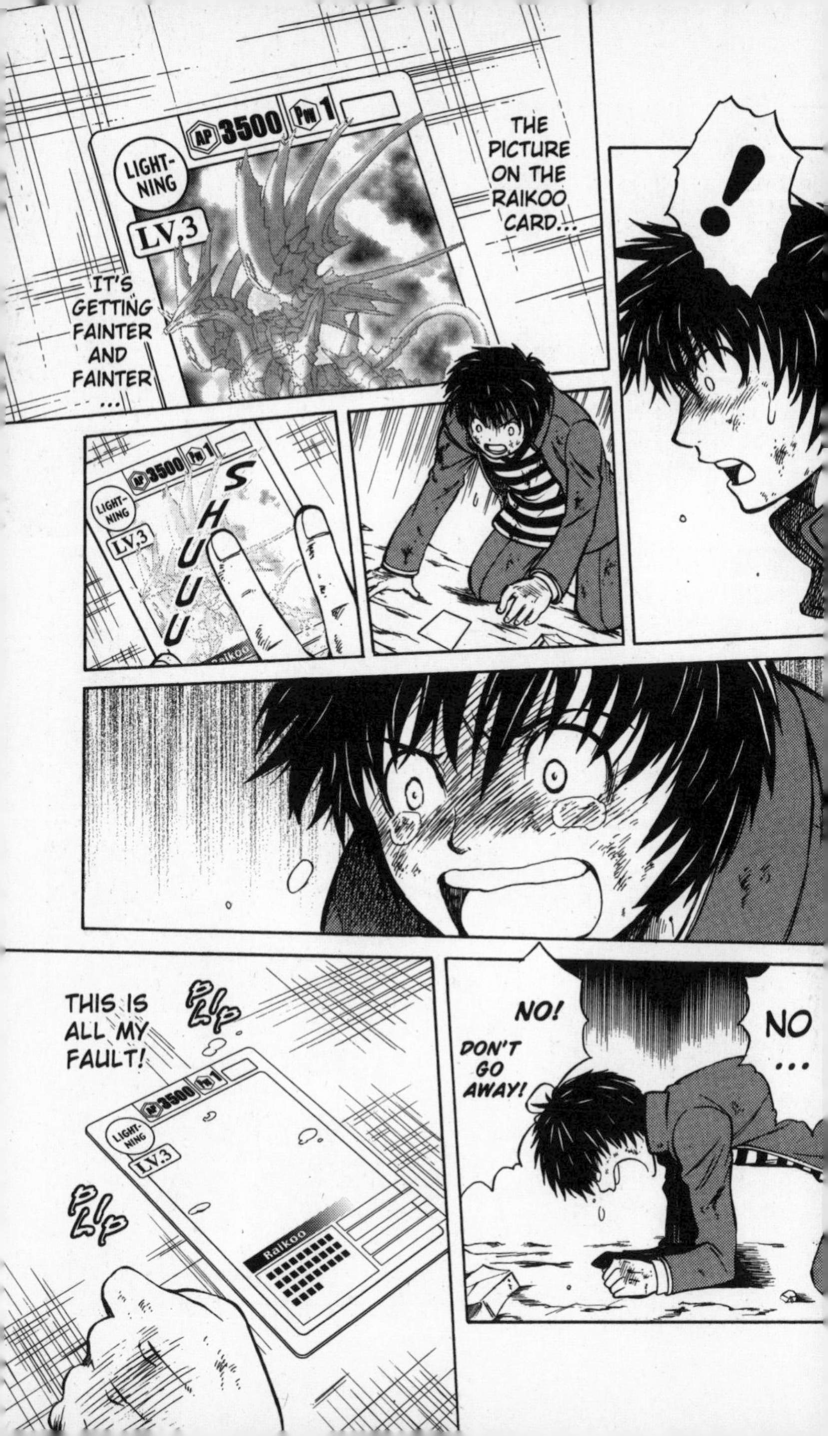
!
THE PICTURE ON THE RAIKOO CARD...
IT'S GETTING FAINTER AND FAINTER...
LIGHT-NING
LV.3
AP 3500
PW 1
SHUUUU
NO...
NO!
DON'T GO AWAY!
THIS IS ALL MY FAULT!
PLIP
PLIP
Raikoo

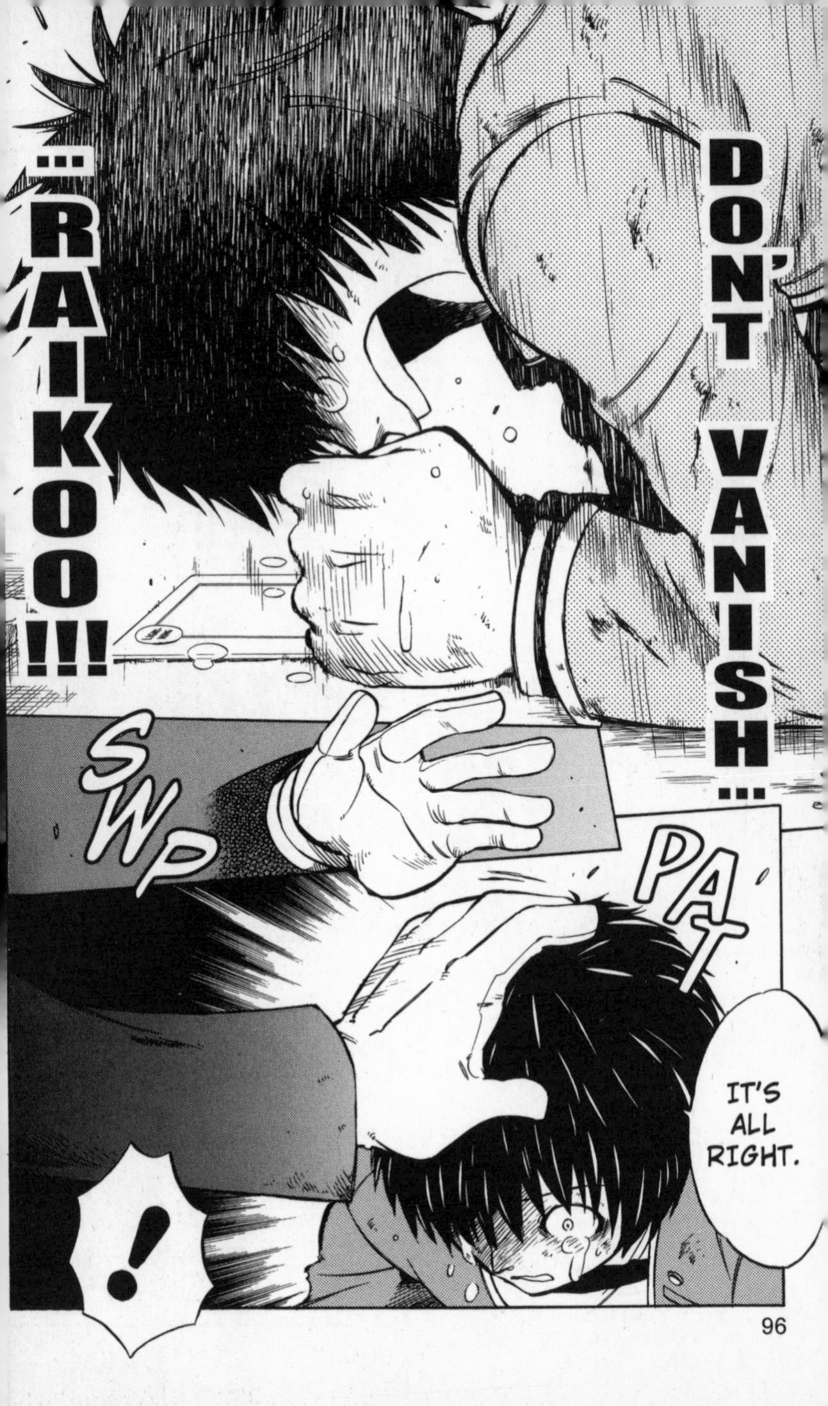
DON'T VANISH...
...RAIKOOO!!!
SWP
PAT
IT'S ALL RIGHT.
!

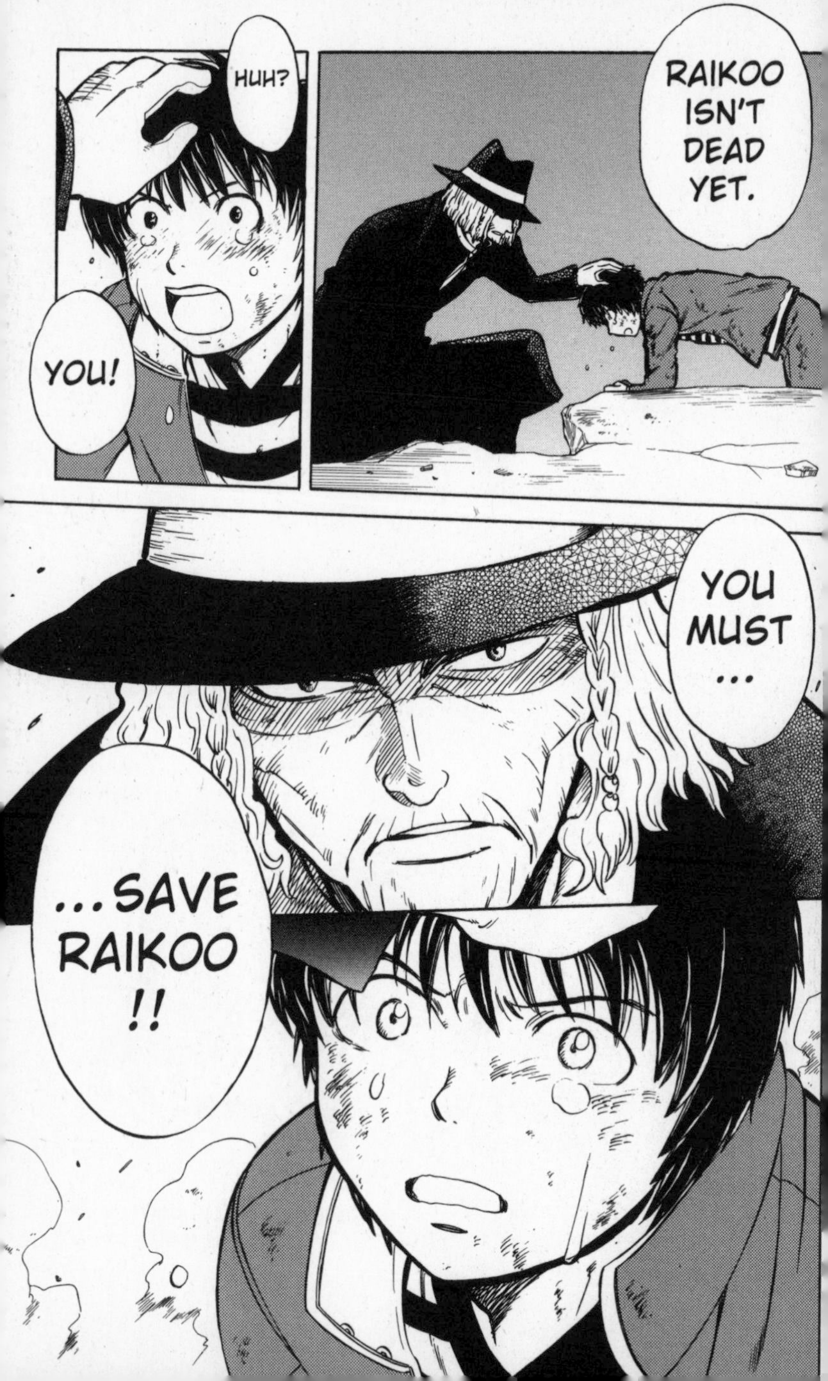
RAIKOO ISN'T DEAD YET.
HUH?
YOU!
YOU MUST ...
...SAVE RAIKOO !!

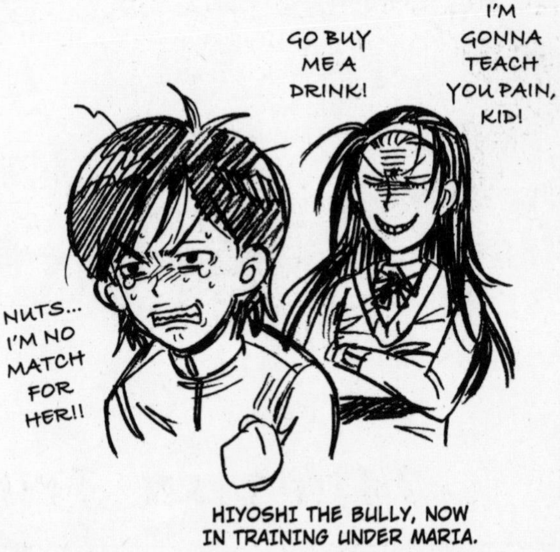
I'M GONNA TEACH YOU PAIN, KID!
GO BUY ME A DRINK!
NUTS... I'M NO MATCH FOR HER!!

HIYOSHI THE BULLY, NOW IN TRAINING UNDER MARIA.

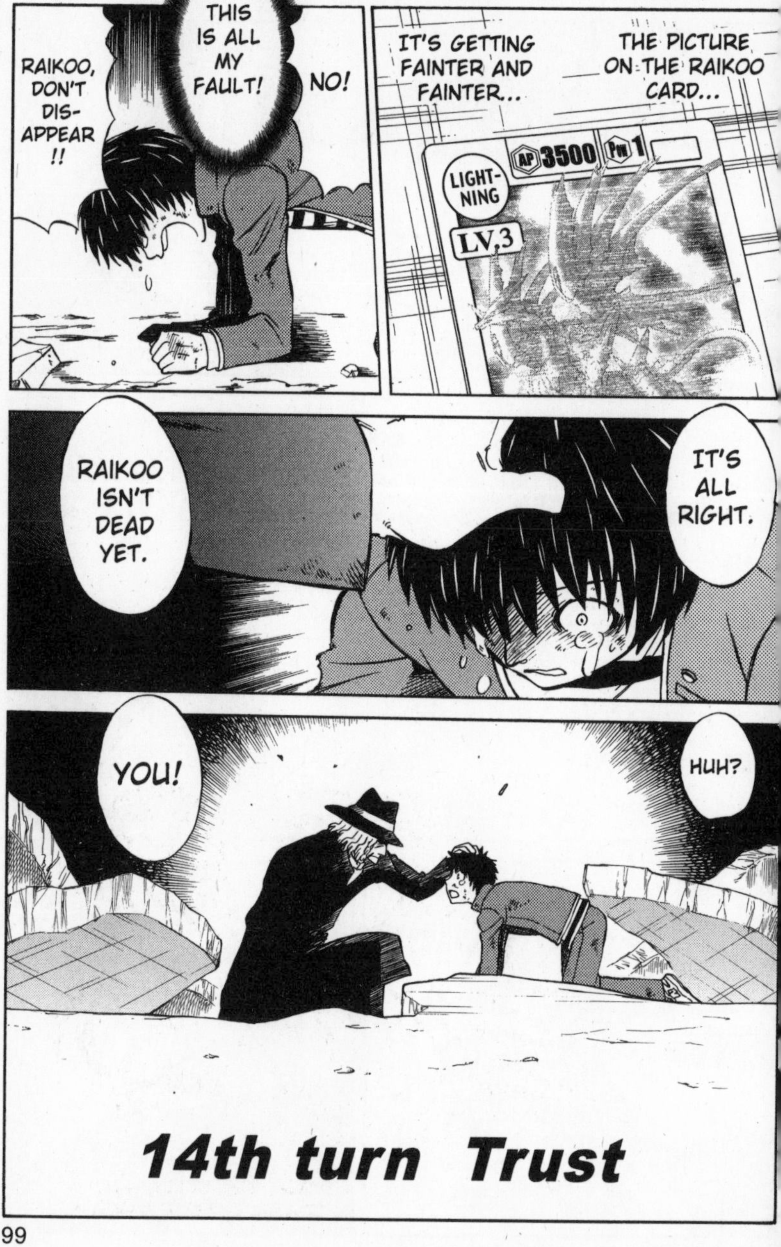
THE PICTURE ON THE RAIKOO CARD...
IT'S GETTING FAINTER AND FAINTER...
AP 3500
PW 1
LIGHTNING
LV.3
NO!
THIS IS ALL MY FAULT!
RAIKOO, DON'T DISAPPEAR!!
IT'S ALL RIGHT.
RAIKOO ISN'T DEAD YET.
HUH?
YOU!
14th turn Trust

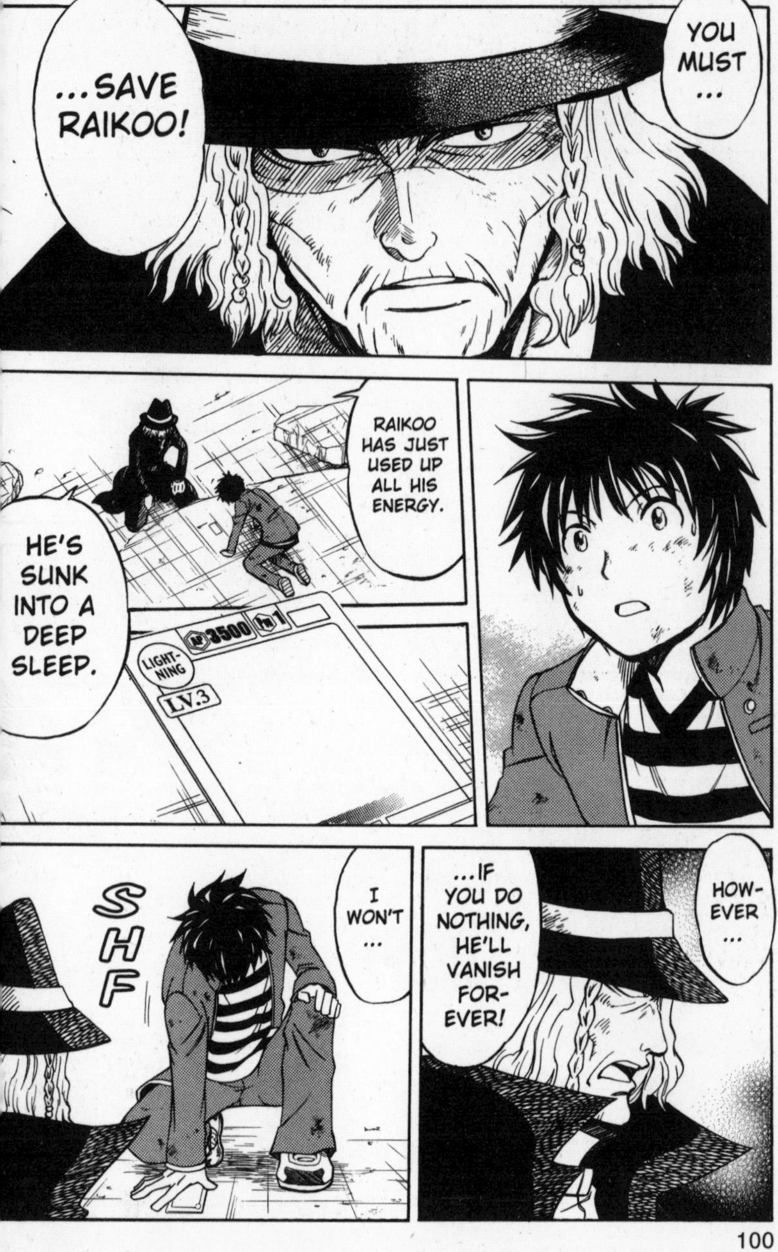
YOU MUST ...
...SAVE RAIKOO!
RAIKOO HAS JUST USED UP ALL HIS ENERGY.
HE'S SUNK INTO A DEEP SLEEP.
LIGHT-NING
3500
LV.3
HOW-EVER ...
...IF YOU DO NOTHING, HE'LL VANISH FOR-EVER!
I WON'T ...
SHF

READ THIS WAY

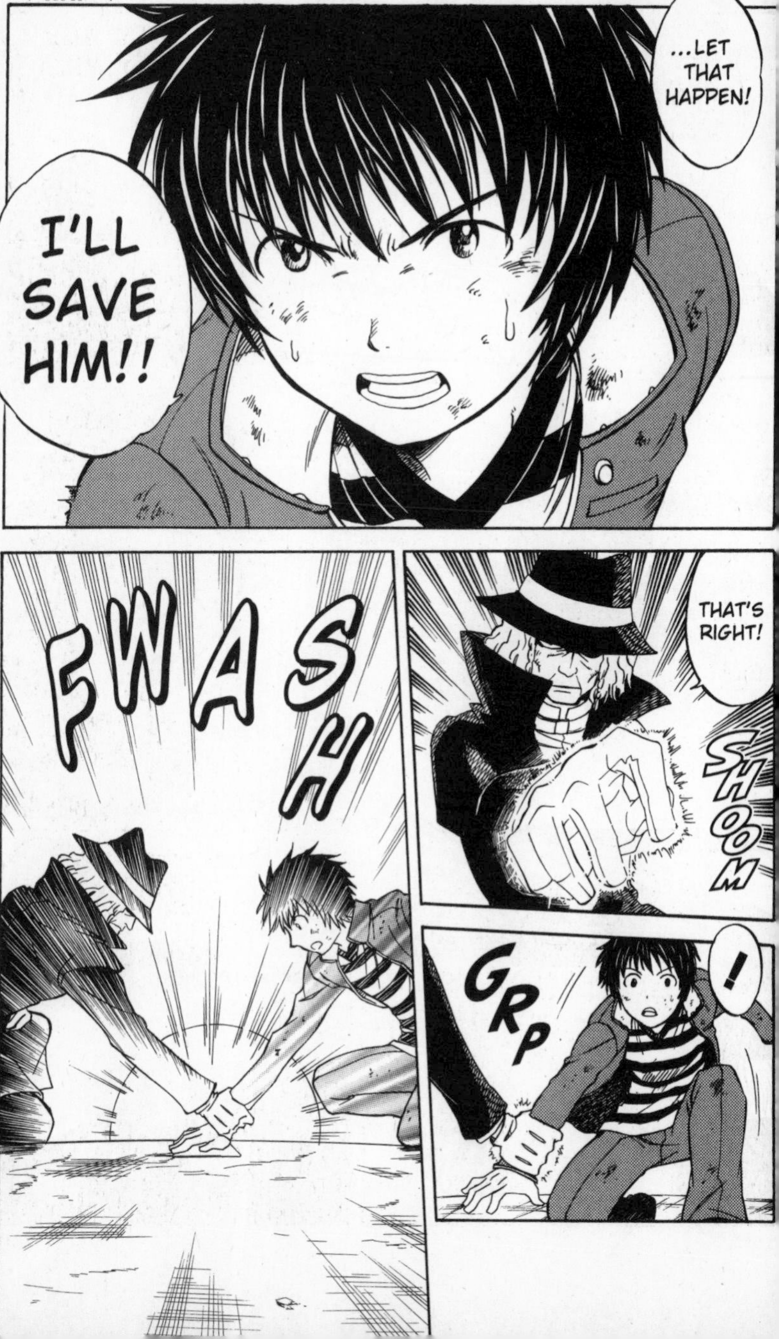
...LET THAT HAPPEN!
I'LL SAVE HIM!!
THAT'S RIGHT!
SHOOM
!
GRP
FWASH

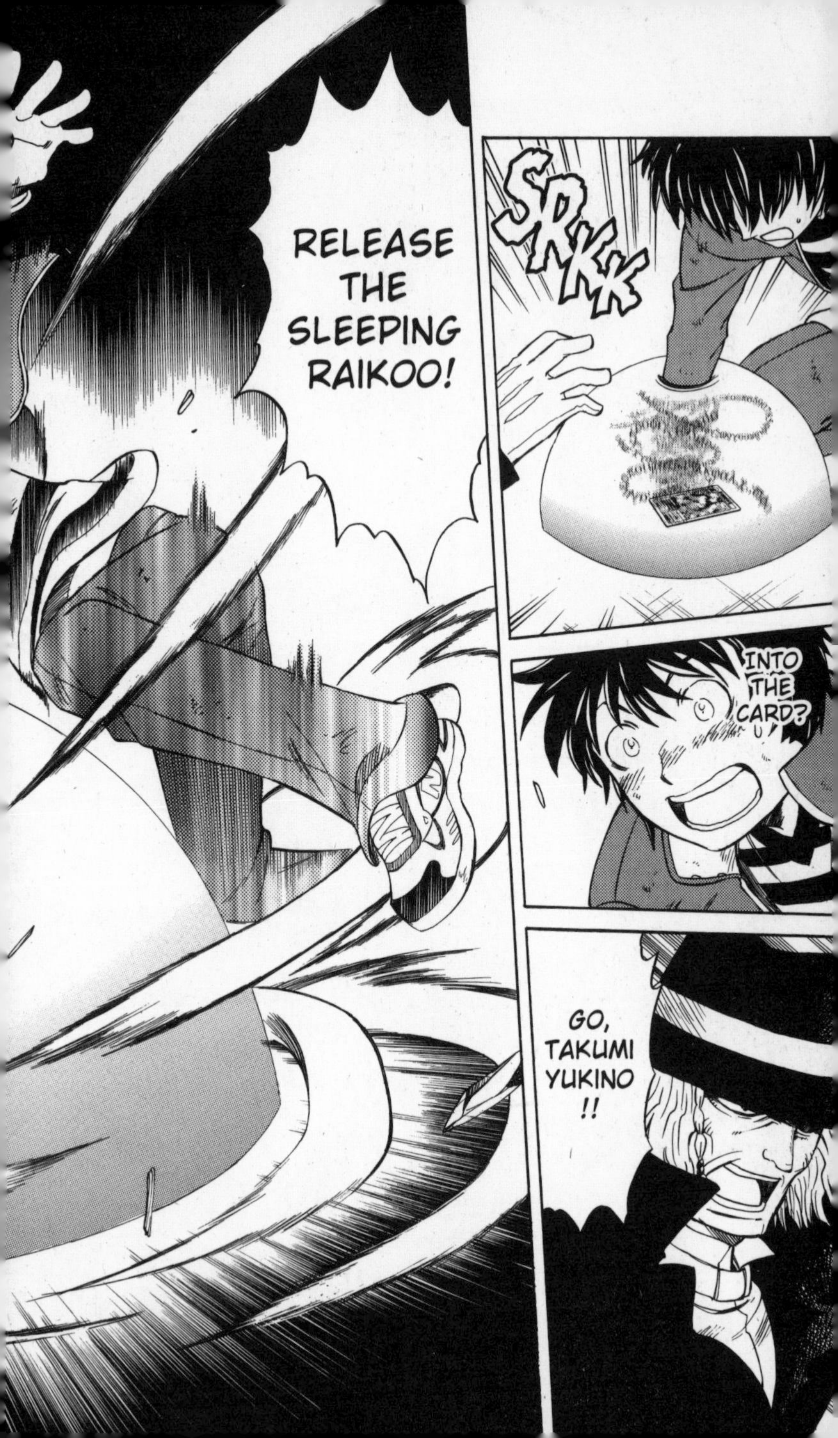

SRKK
INTO THE CARD?
GO, TAKUMI YUKINO !!
RELEASE THE SLEEPING RAIKOO!

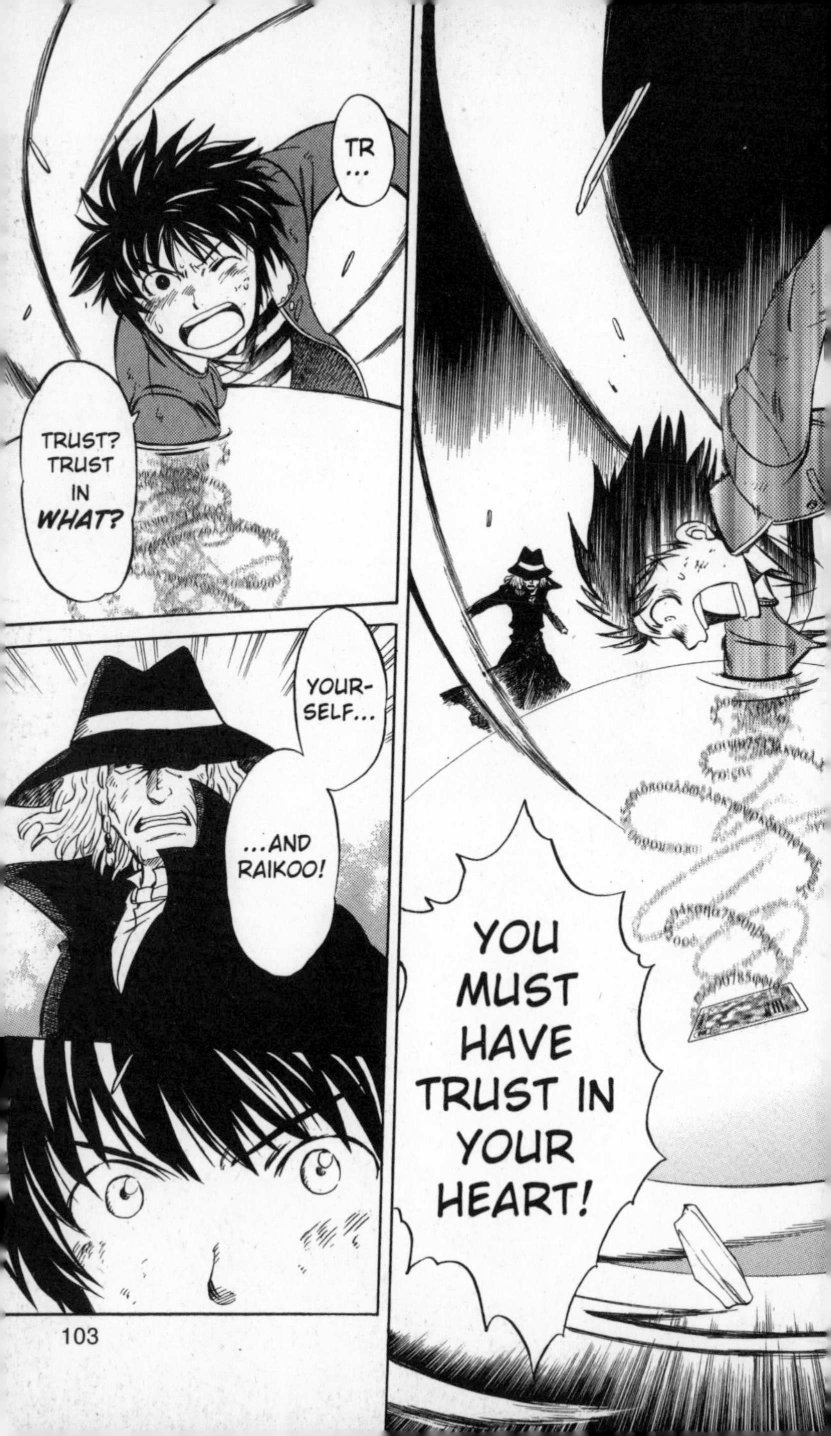
YOU MUST HAVE TRUST IN YOUR HEART!
TR...
TRUST? TRUST IN *WHAT?*
YOURSELF...
...AND RAIKOO!

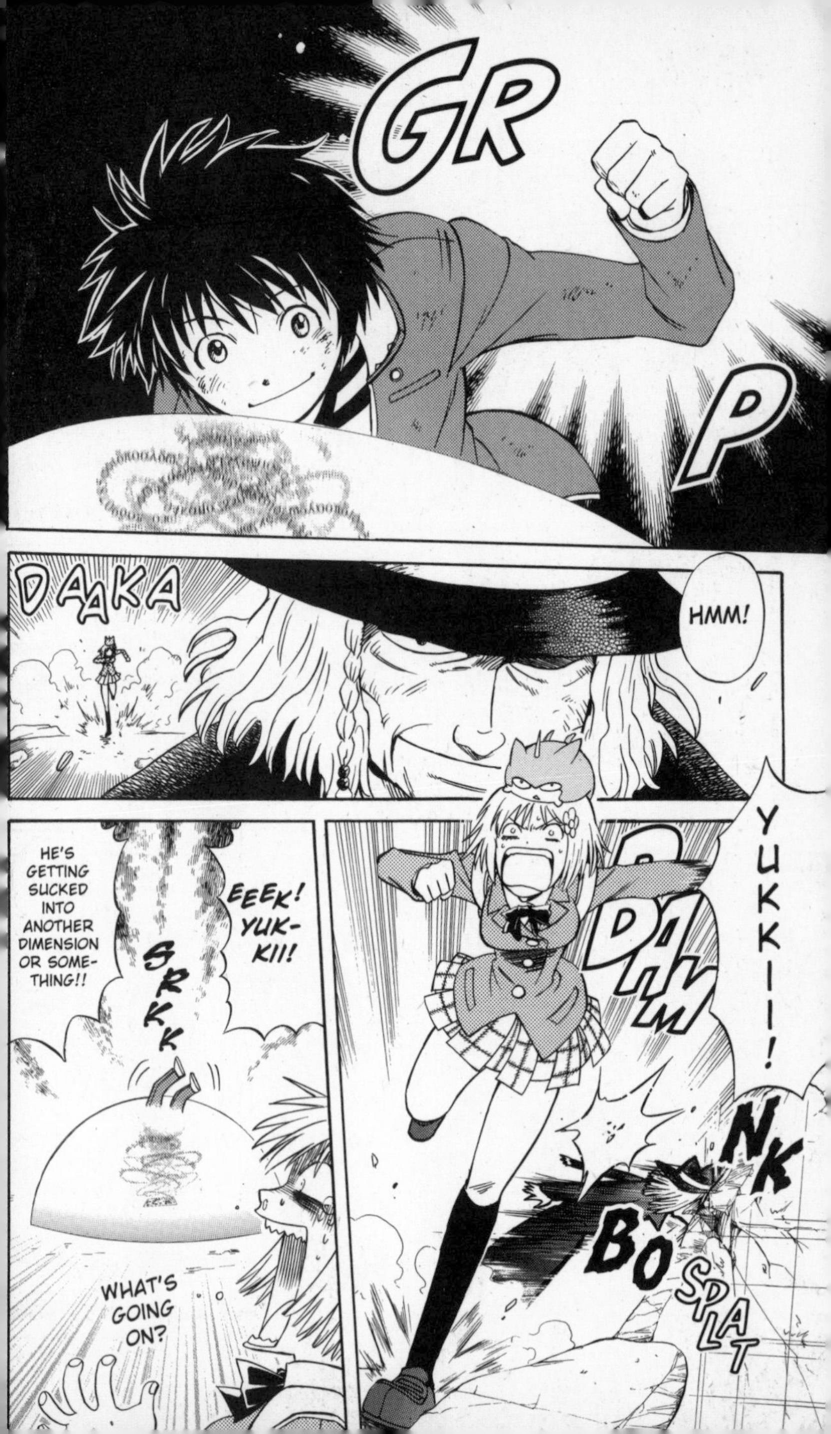
GR
P
HMM!
DAAKA
YUKKII!
DAM
NK
BO
SPLAT
HE'S GETTING SUCKED INTO ANOTHER DIMENSION OR SOMETHING!!
EEEK! YUKKII!
SRKKK
WHAT'S GOING ON?

READ THIS WAY

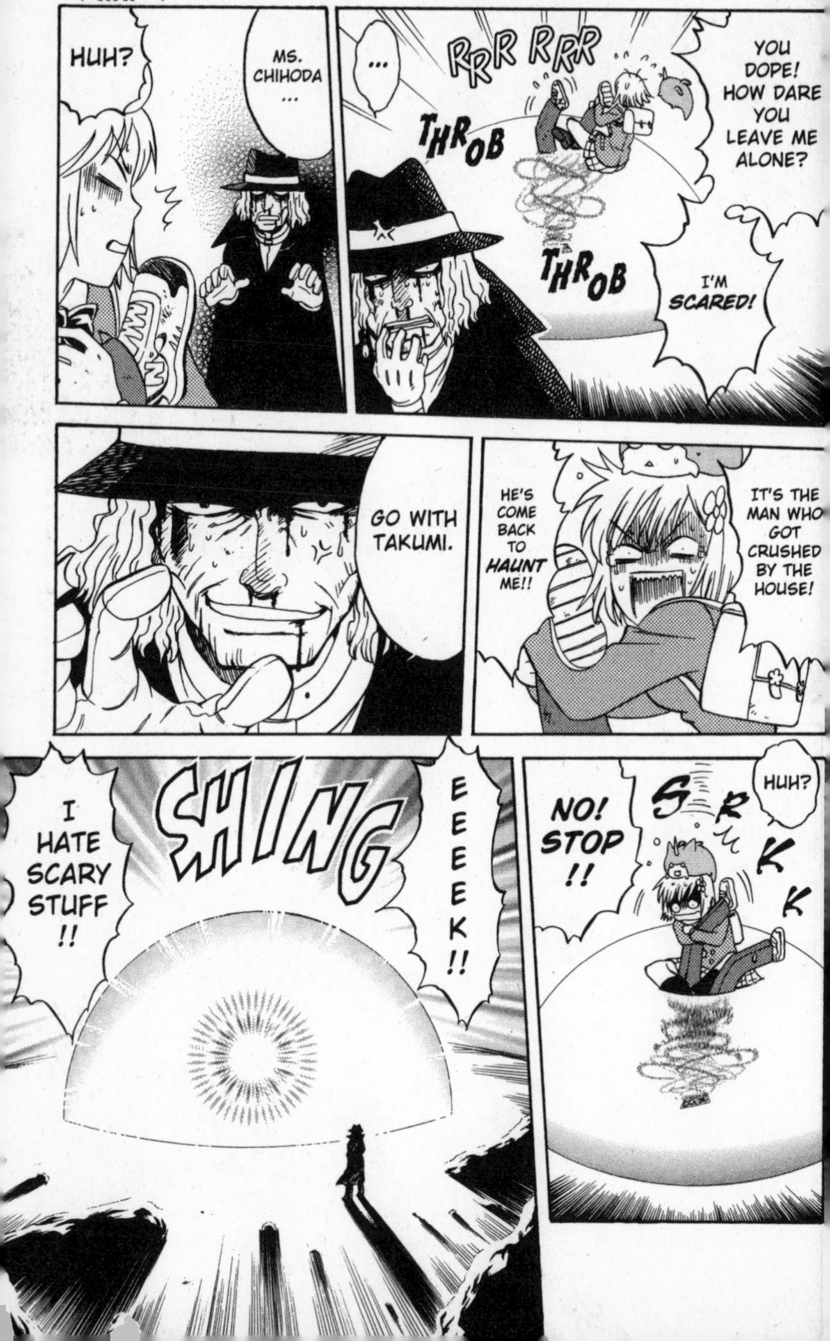
YOU DOPE! HOW DARE YOU LEAVE ME ALONE?
RRR RRR
...
THROB
THROB
I'M *SCARED!*
MS. CHIHODA ...
HUH?
IT'S THE MAN WHO GOT CRUSHED BY THE HOUSE!
HE'S COME BACK TO *HAUNT* ME!!
GO WITH TAKUMI.
HUH?
SRKK
NO! STOP!!
EEEEEK!!
SHING
I HATE SCARY STUFF!!

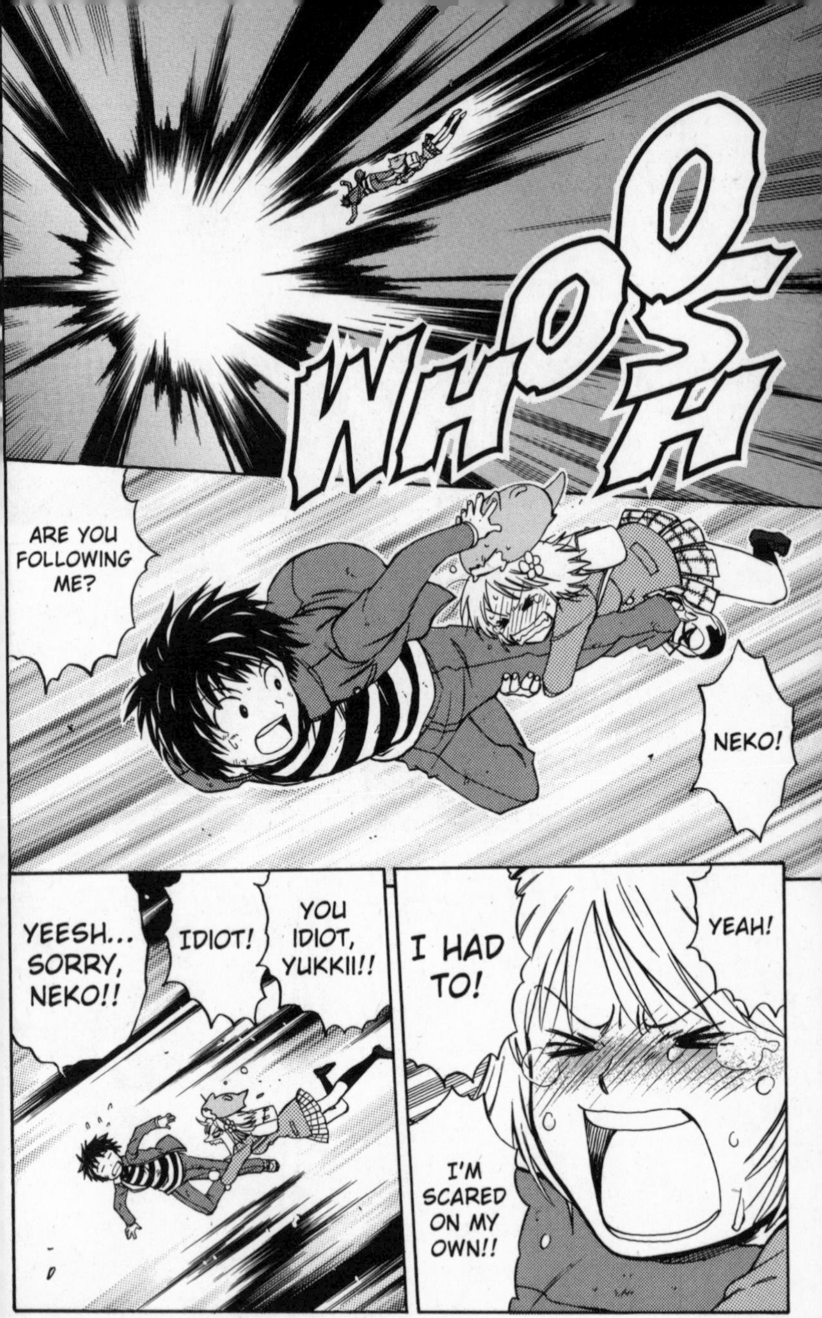
WHOOSH
NEKO!
ARE YOU FOLLOWING ME?
YEAH!
I HAD TO!
I'M SCARED ON MY OWN!!
YOU IDIOT, YUKKI!!
IDIOT!
YEESH... SORRY, NEKO!!

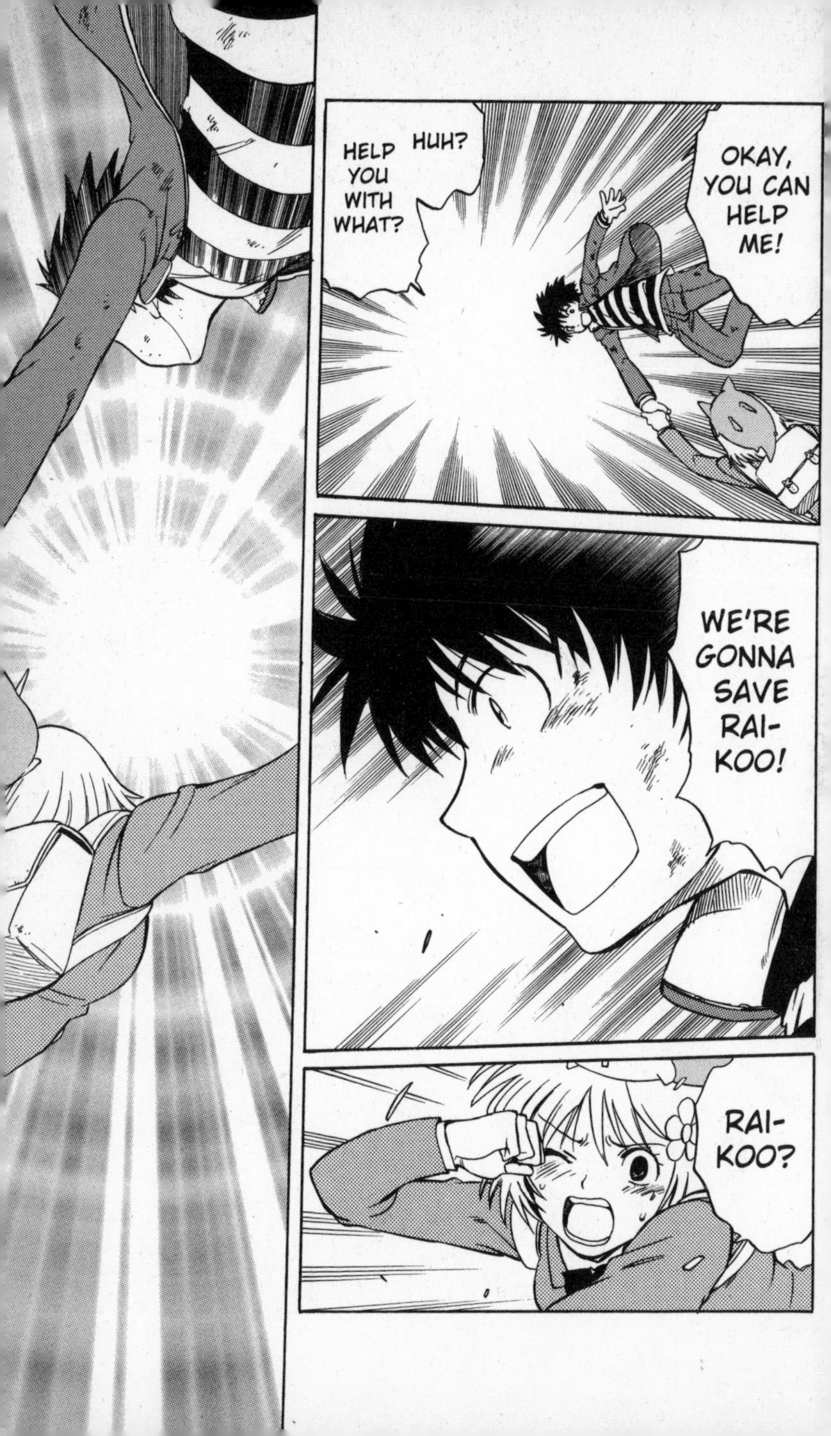
OKAY, YOU CAN HELP ME!
HUH?
HELP YOU WITH WHAT?
WE'RE GONNA SAVE RAI-KOO!
RAI-KOO?

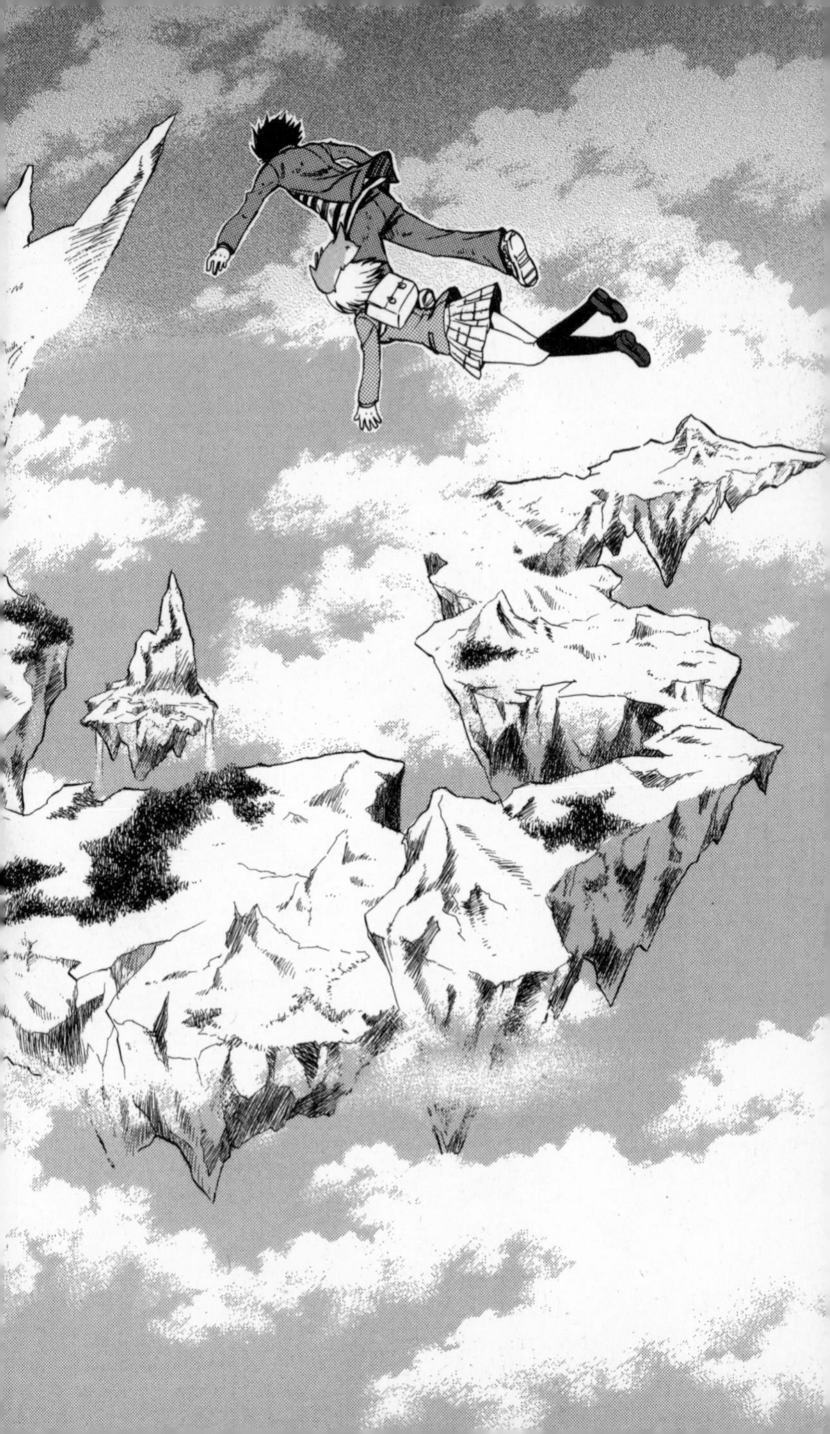

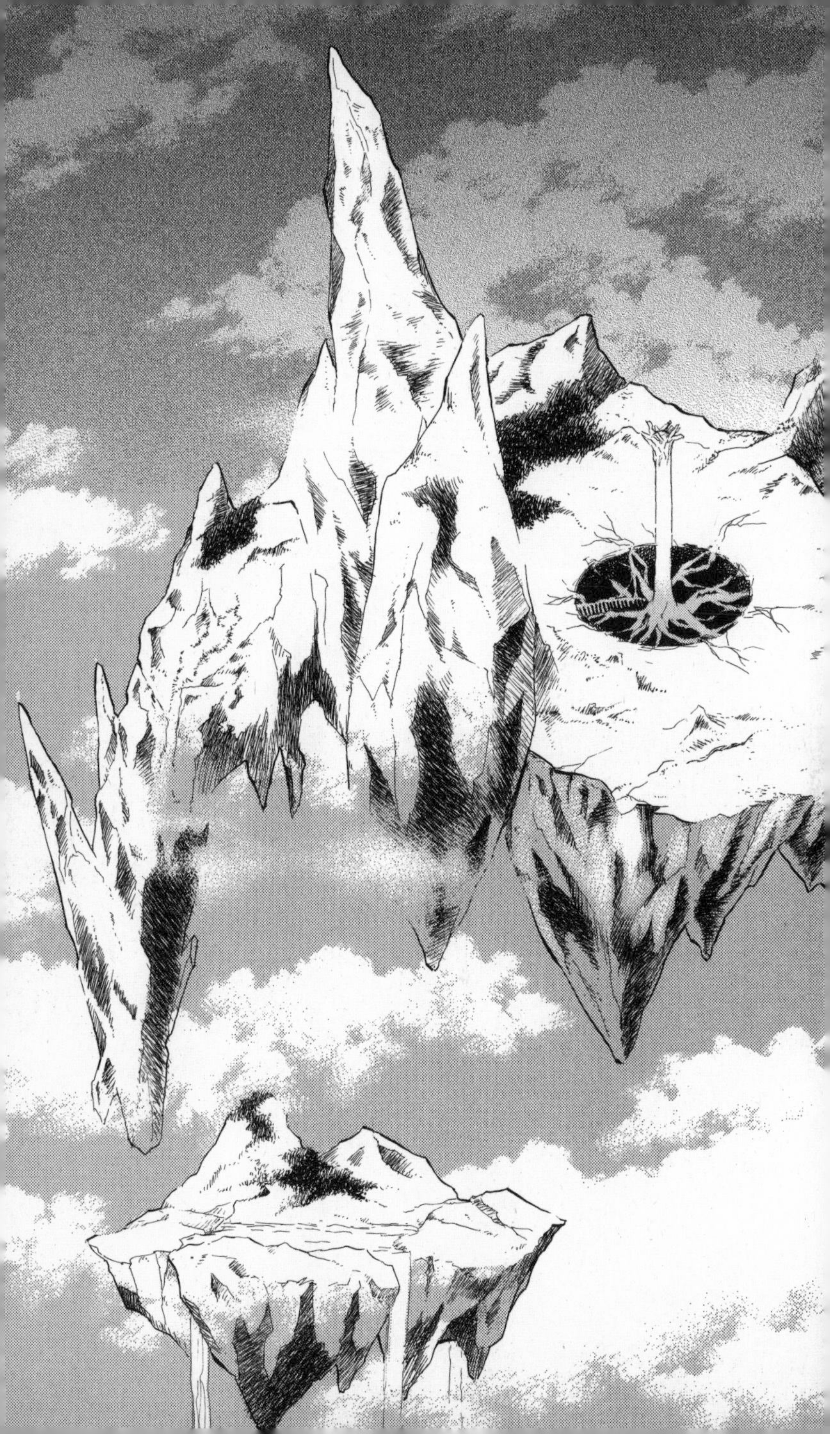

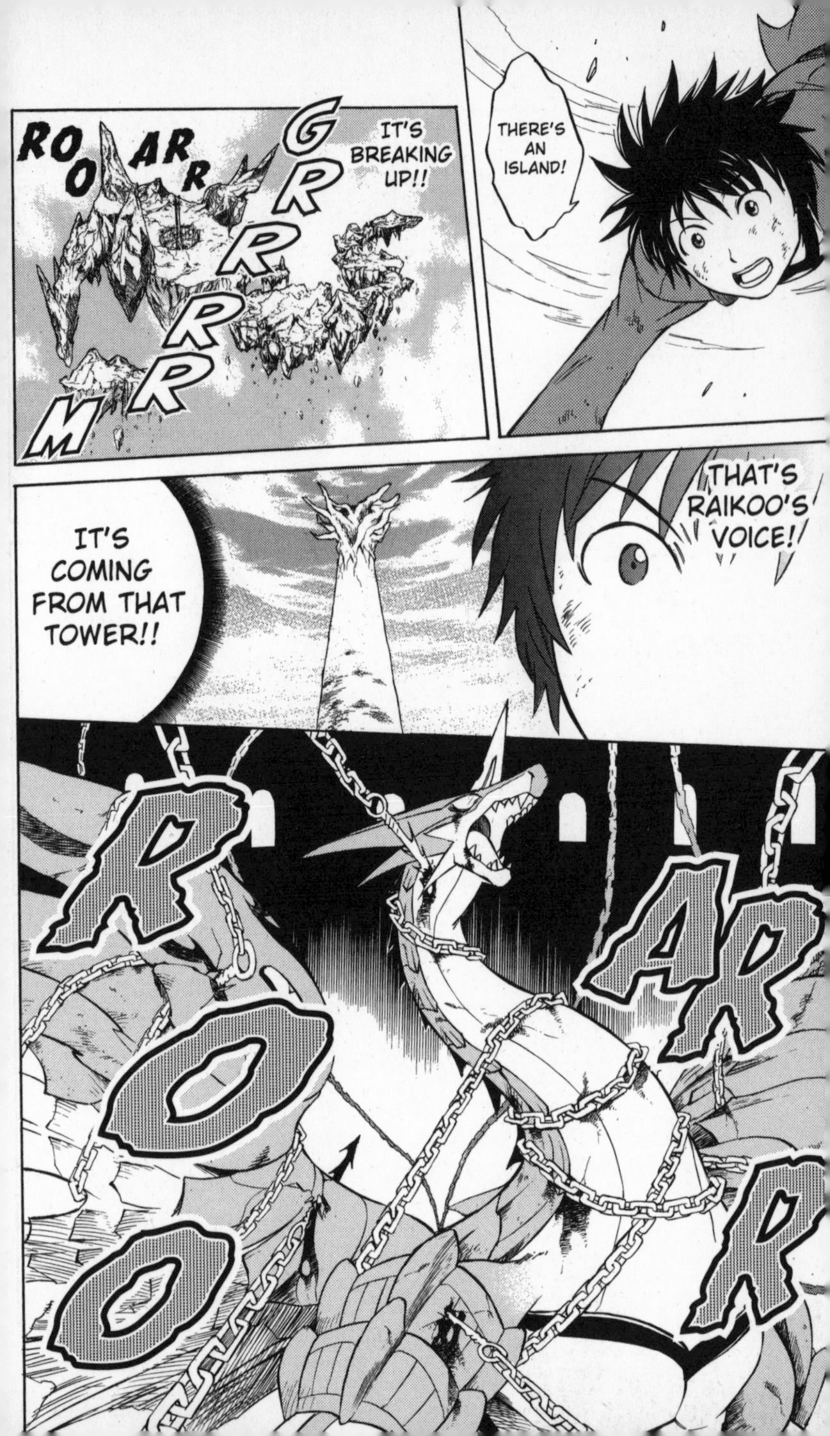
THERE'S AN ISLAND!
IT'S BREAKING UP!!
ROOARR
GRRRRM
THAT'S RAIKOO'S VOICE!
IT'S COMING FROM THAT TOWER!!
ROOARR

READ THIS WAY

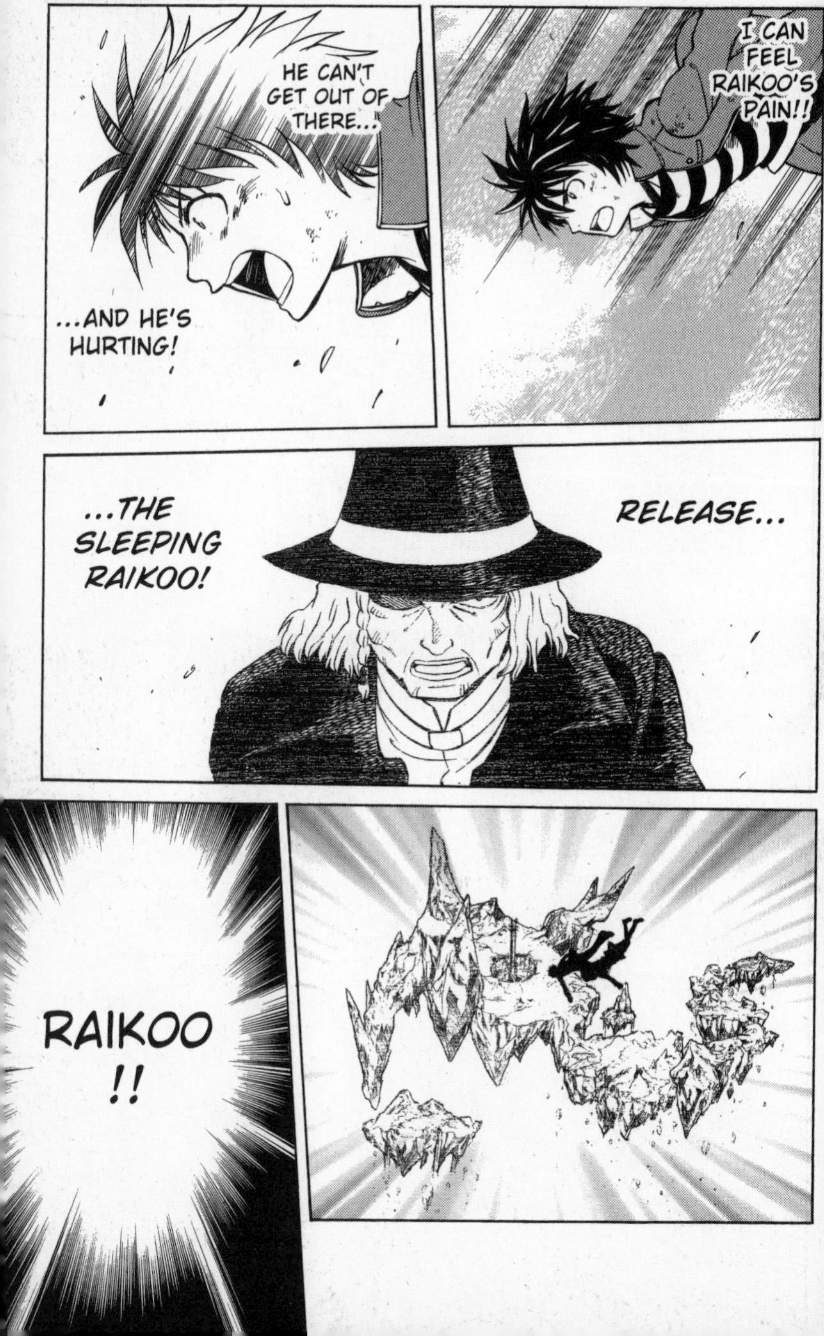
I CAN FEEL RAIKOO'S PAIN!!
HE CAN'T GET OUT OF THERE...
...AND HE'S HURTING!
RELEASE...
...THE SLEEPING RAIKOO!
RAIKOO !!

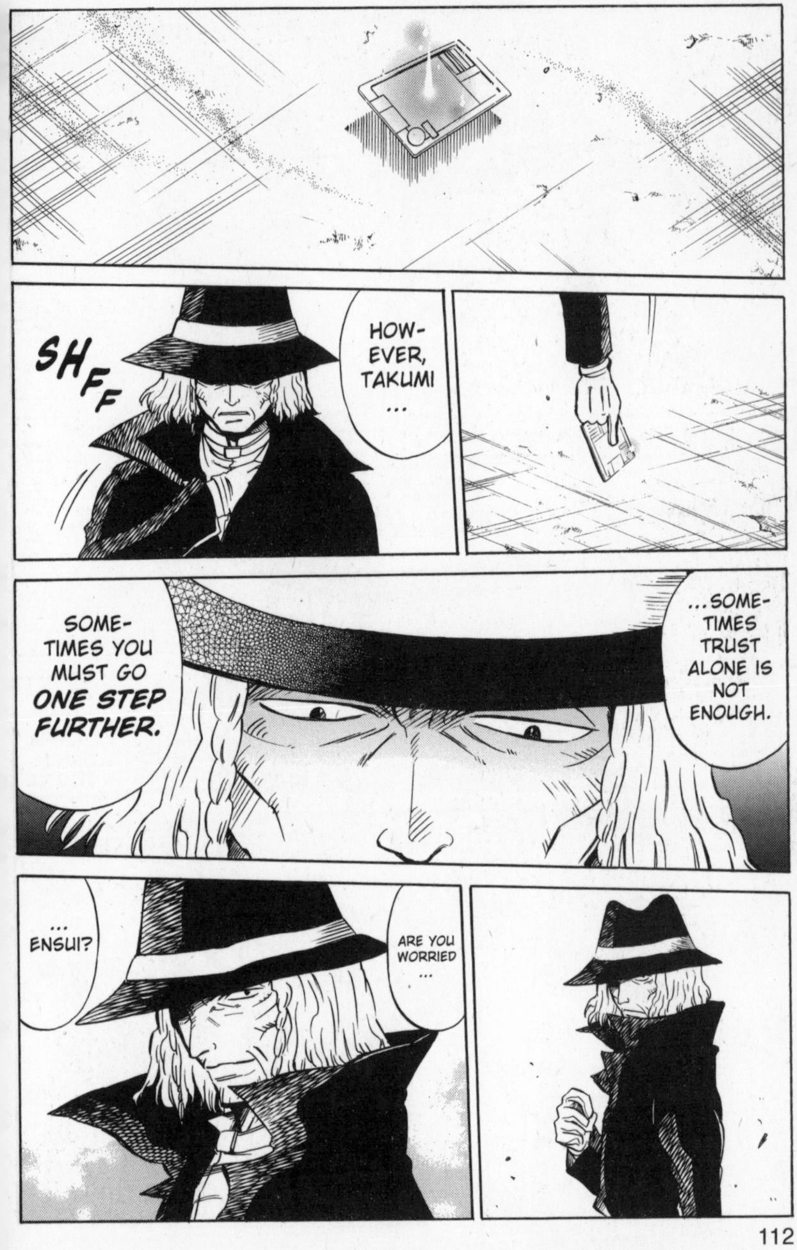
HOW-EVER, TAKUMI ...
SHFF
...SOME-TIMES TRUST ALONE IS NOT ENOUGH.
SOME-TIMES YOU MUST GO **ONE STEP FURTHER.**
ARE YOU WORRIED ...
... ENSUI?

READ THIS WAY

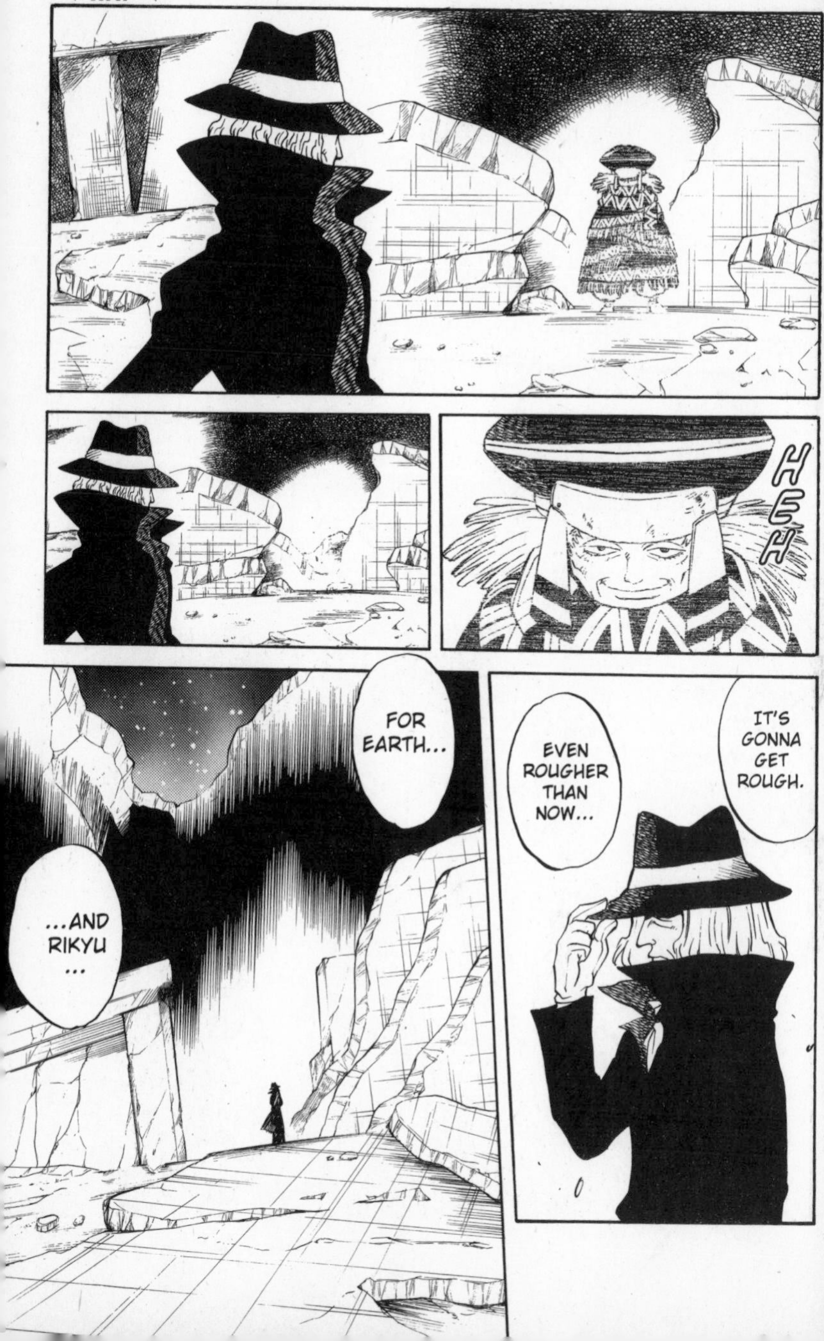
HEH
IT'S GONNA GET ROUGH.
EVEN ROUGHER THAN NOW...
FOR EARTH...
...AND RIKYU ...

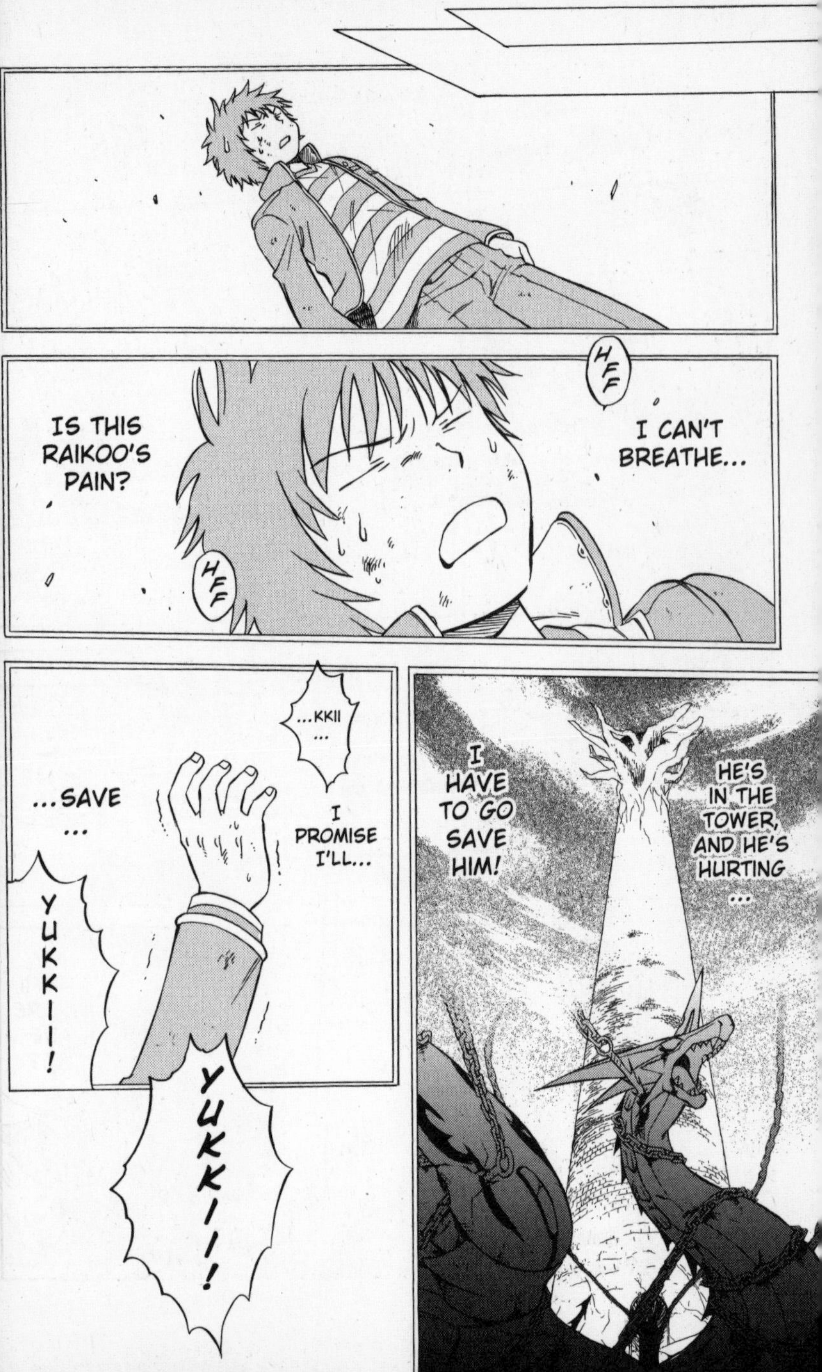
HEFF
I CAN'T BREATHE...
IS THIS RAIKOO'S PAIN?
HEFF
HE'S IN THE TOWER, AND HE'S HURTING...
I HAVE TO GO SAVE HIM!
...KKII...
I PROMISE I'LL...
...SAVE...
YUKKII!
YUKKII!!

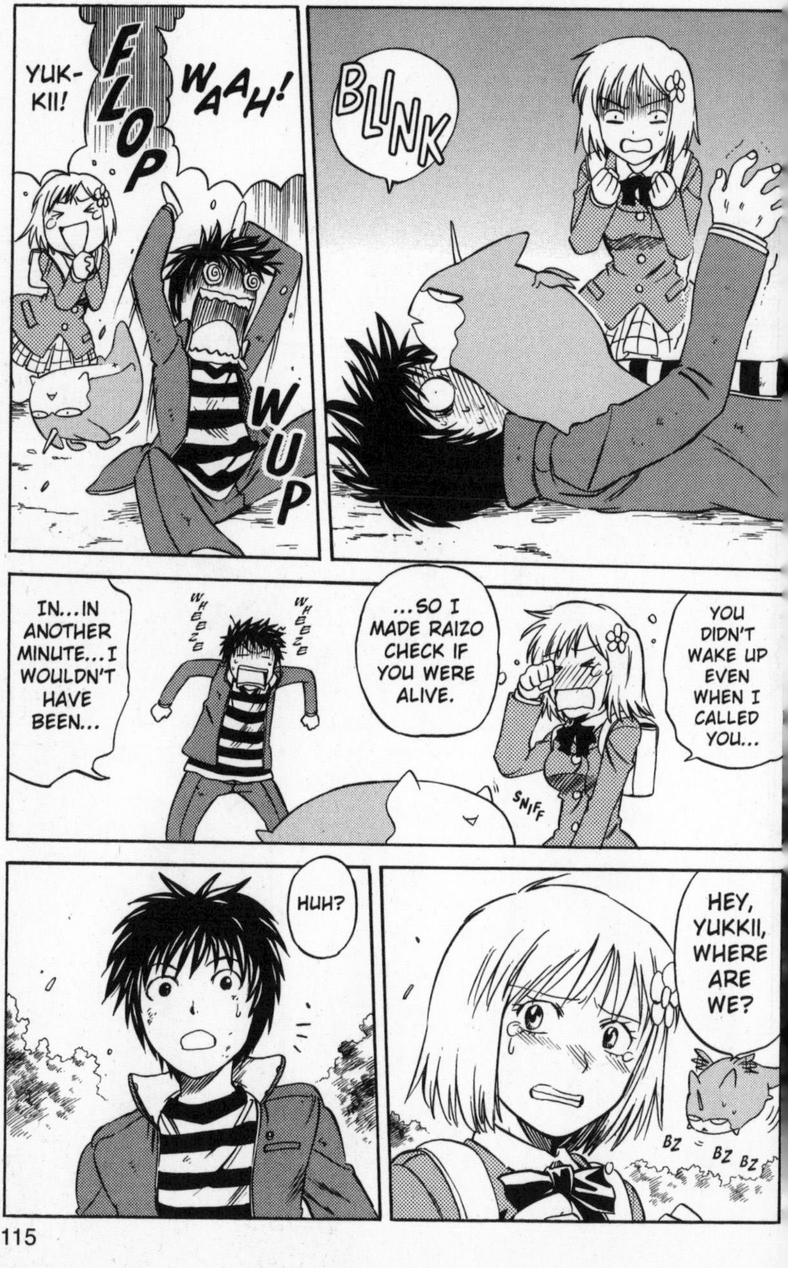
BLINK
WAAH!
FLOP
YUK-KII!
WUP
YOU DIDN'T WAKE UP EVEN WHEN I CALLED YOU...
SNIFF
...SO I MADE RAIZO CHECK IF YOU WERE ALIVE.
WHEEZE
WHEEZE
IN...IN ANOTHER MINUTE...I WOULDN'T HAVE BEEN...
HEY, YUKKII, WHERE ARE WE?
BZ BZ BZ
HUH?

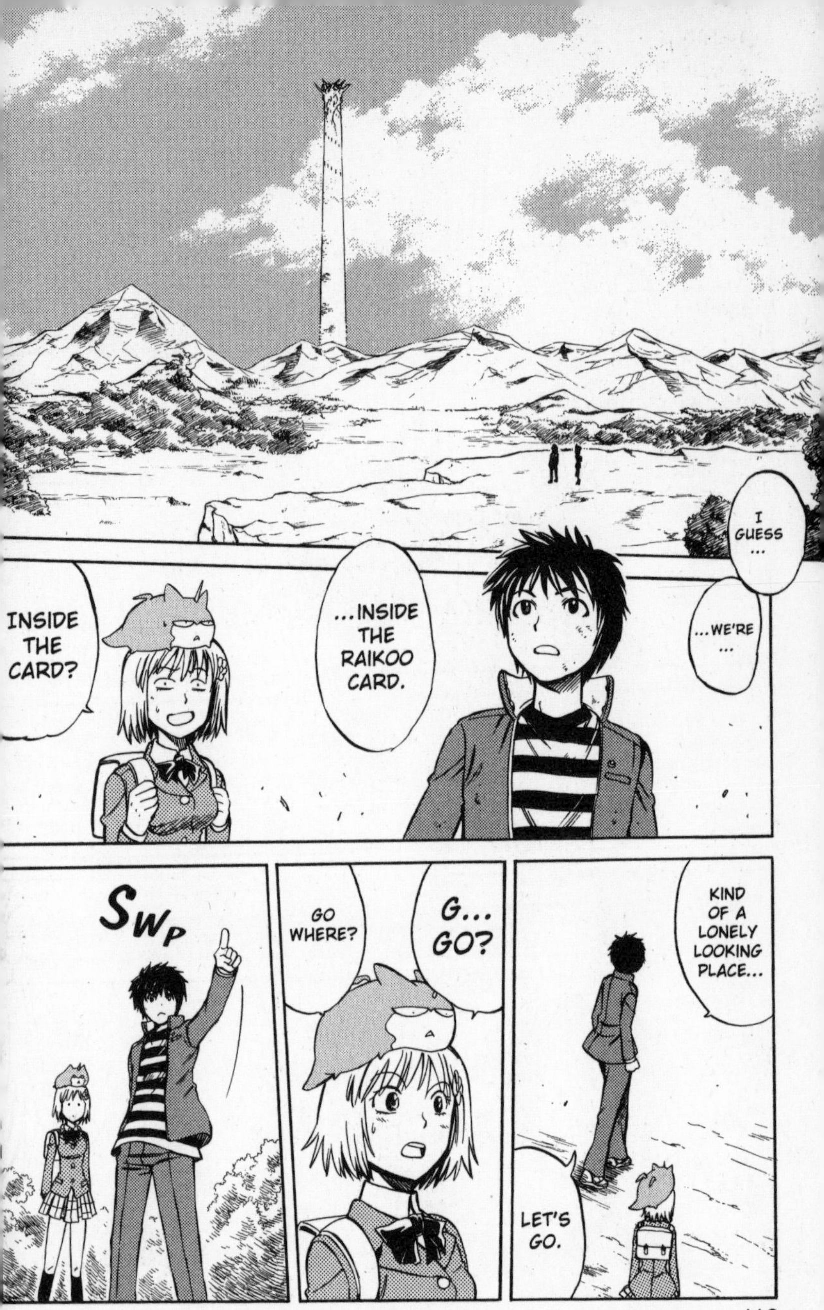
I GUESS...
...WE'RE...
...INSIDE THE RAIKOO CARD.
INSIDE THE CARD?
KIND OF A LONELY LOOKING PLACE...
LET'S GO.
G... GO?
GO WHERE?
SWP

READ THIS WAY

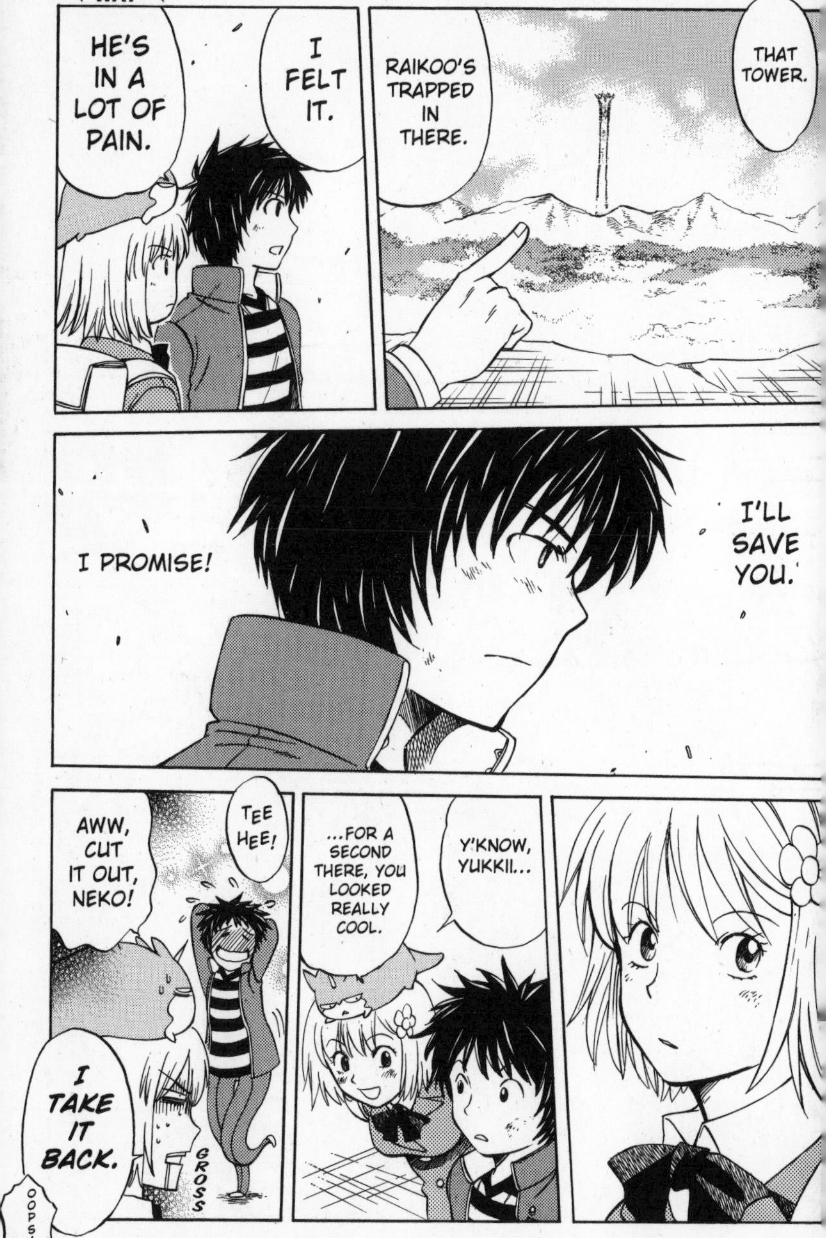
THAT TOWER.
RAIKOO'S TRAPPED IN THERE.
I FELT IT.
HE'S IN A LOT OF PAIN.
I'LL SAVE YOU.
I PROMISE!
Y'KNOW, YUKKII...
...FOR A SECOND THERE, YOU LOOKED REALLY COOL.
TEE HEE!
AWW, CUT IT OUT, NEKO!
I TAKE IT BACK.
GROSS
OOPS!

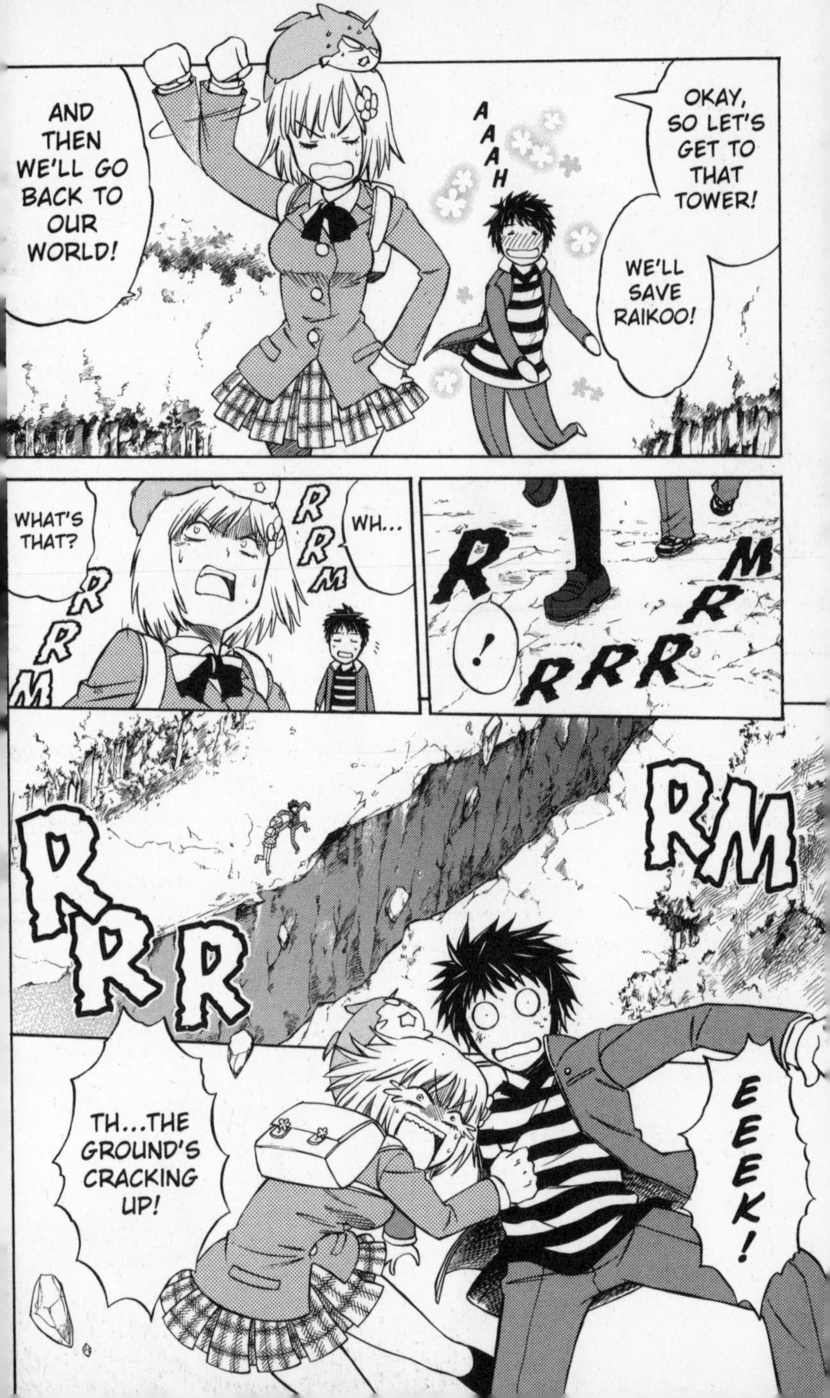

OKAY, SO LET'S GET TO THAT TOWER!
WE'LL SAVE RAIKOO!
AAAH
AND THEN WE'LL GO BACK TO OUR WORLD!
R
MRRRRR
!
WH...
RRM
WHAT'S THAT?
RRRM
RM
RRR
EEEEK!
TH...THE GROUND'S CRACKING UP!

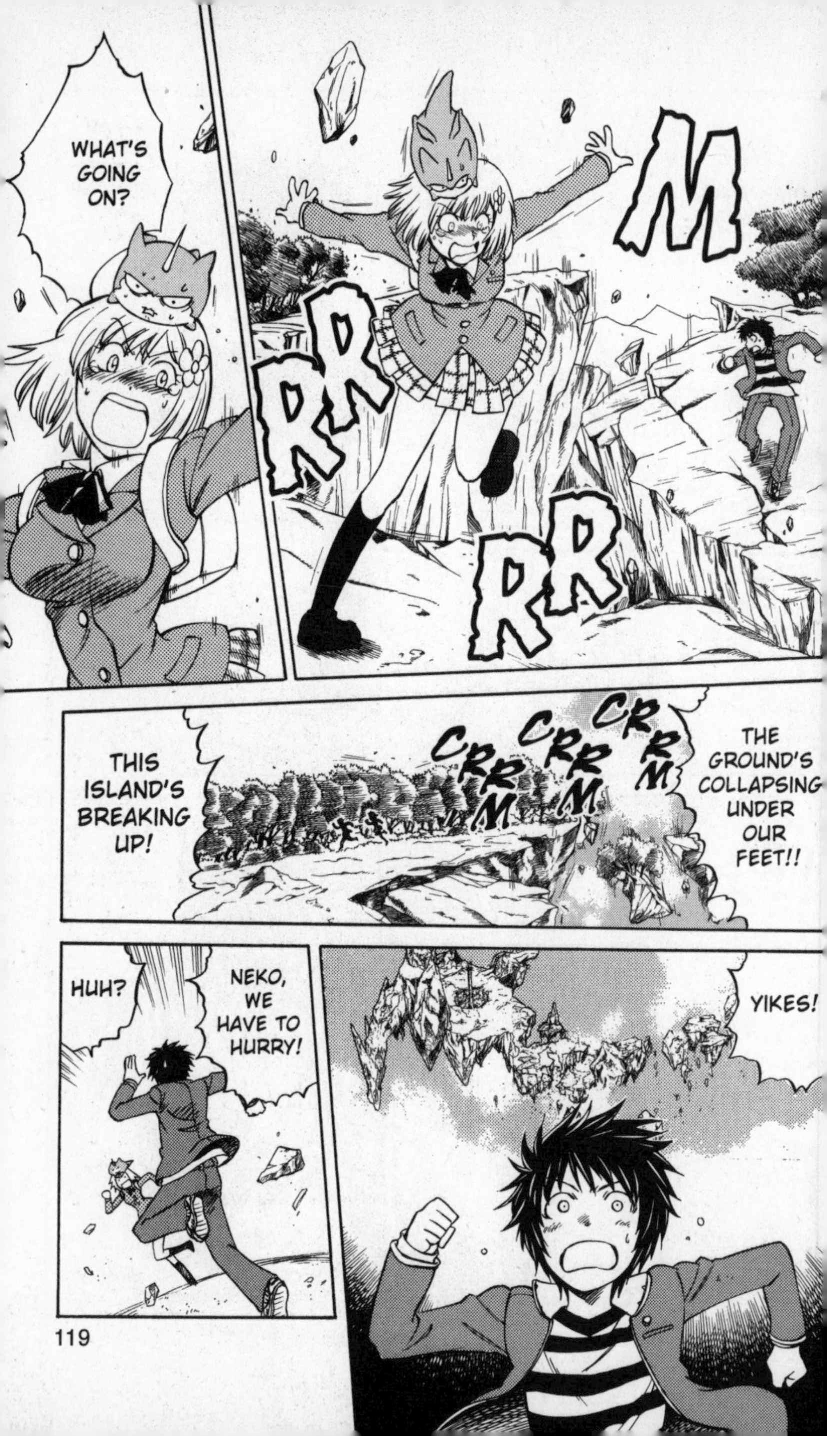
RRRM
WHAT'S GOING ON?
THE GROUND'S COLLAPSING UNDER OUR FEET!!
CRRRM
CRRRM
CRRRM
THIS ISLAND'S BREAKING UP!
YIKES!
NEKO, WE HAVE TO HURRY!
HUH?

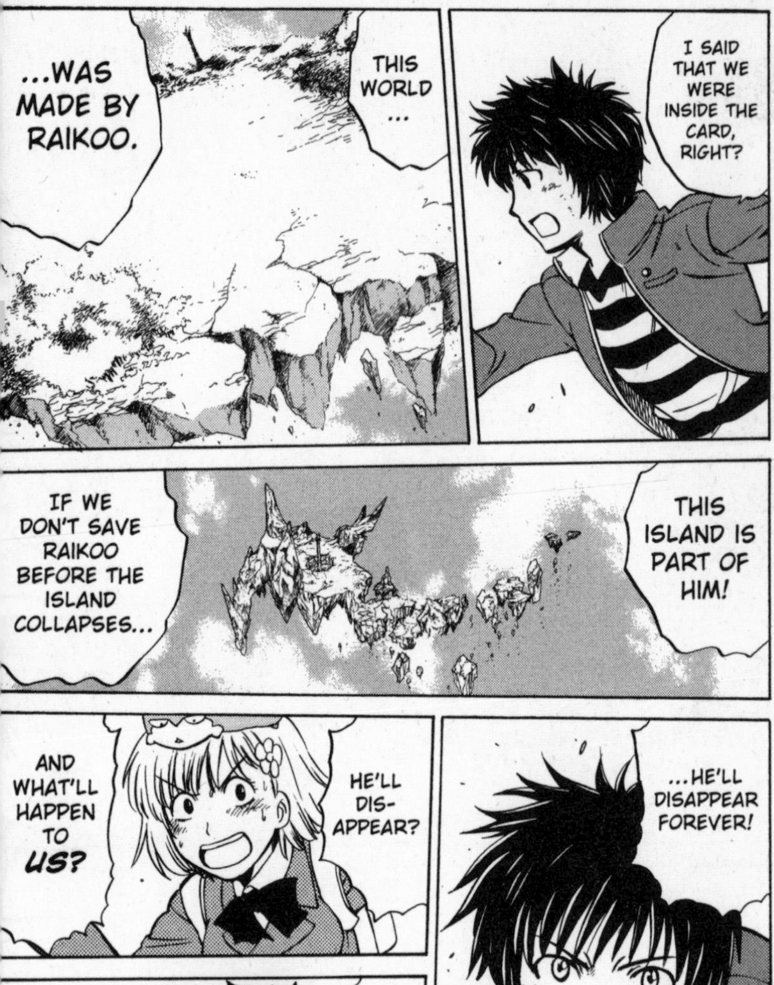
I SAID THAT WE WERE INSIDE THE CARD, RIGHT?
THIS WORLD ...
...WAS MADE BY RAIKOO.
THIS ISLAND IS PART OF HIM!
IF WE DON'T SAVE RAIKOO BEFORE THE ISLAND COLLAPSES...
...HE'LL DISAPPEAR FOREVER!
HE'LL DIS-APPEAR?
AND WHAT'LL HAPPEN TO *US?*
!

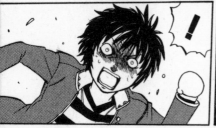

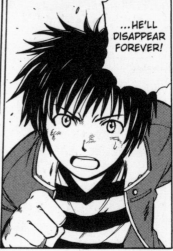

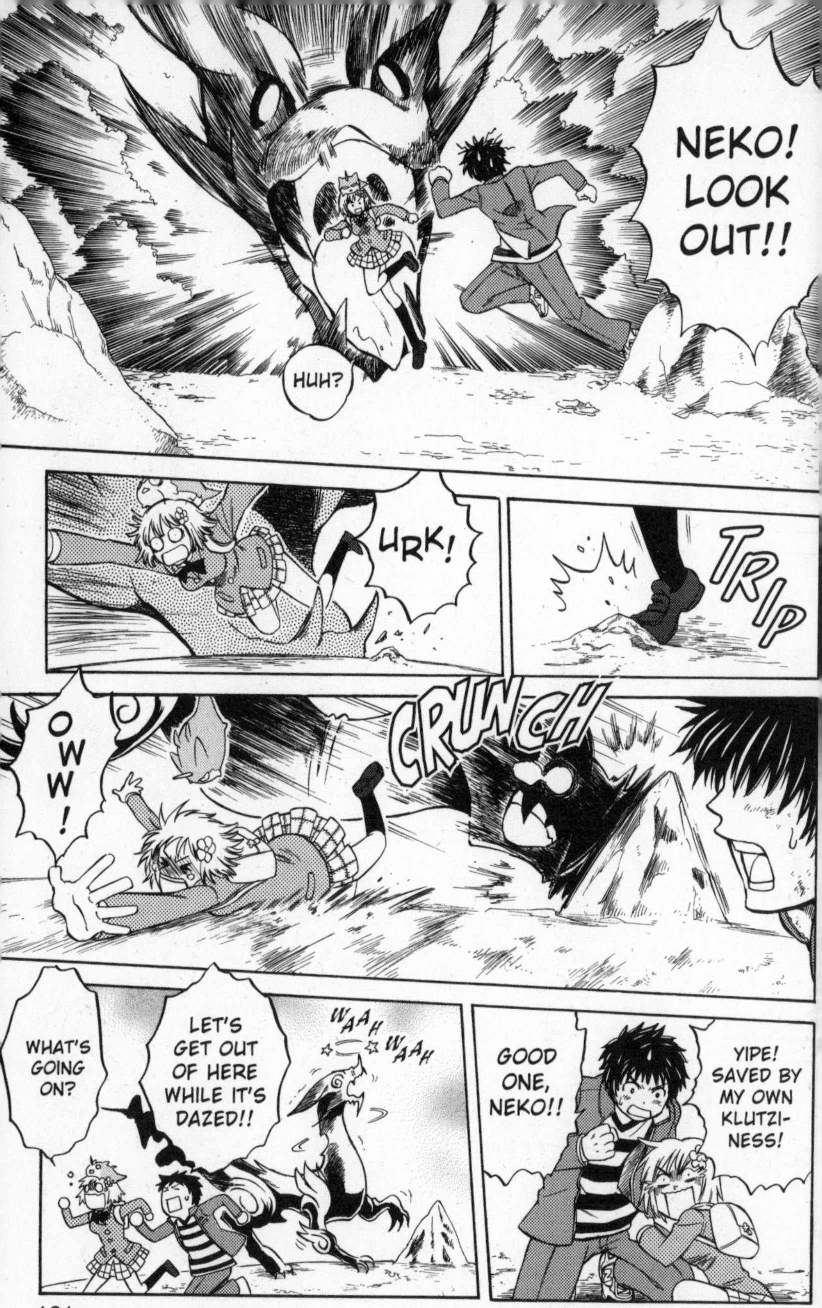

NEKO! LOOK OUT!!
HUH?
TRIP
URK!
CRUNCH
OWW!
YIPE! SAVED BY MY OWN KLUTZINESS!
GOOD ONE, NEKO!!
WAAH WAAH
LET'S GET OUT OF HERE WHILE IT'S DAZED!!
WHAT'S GOING ON?

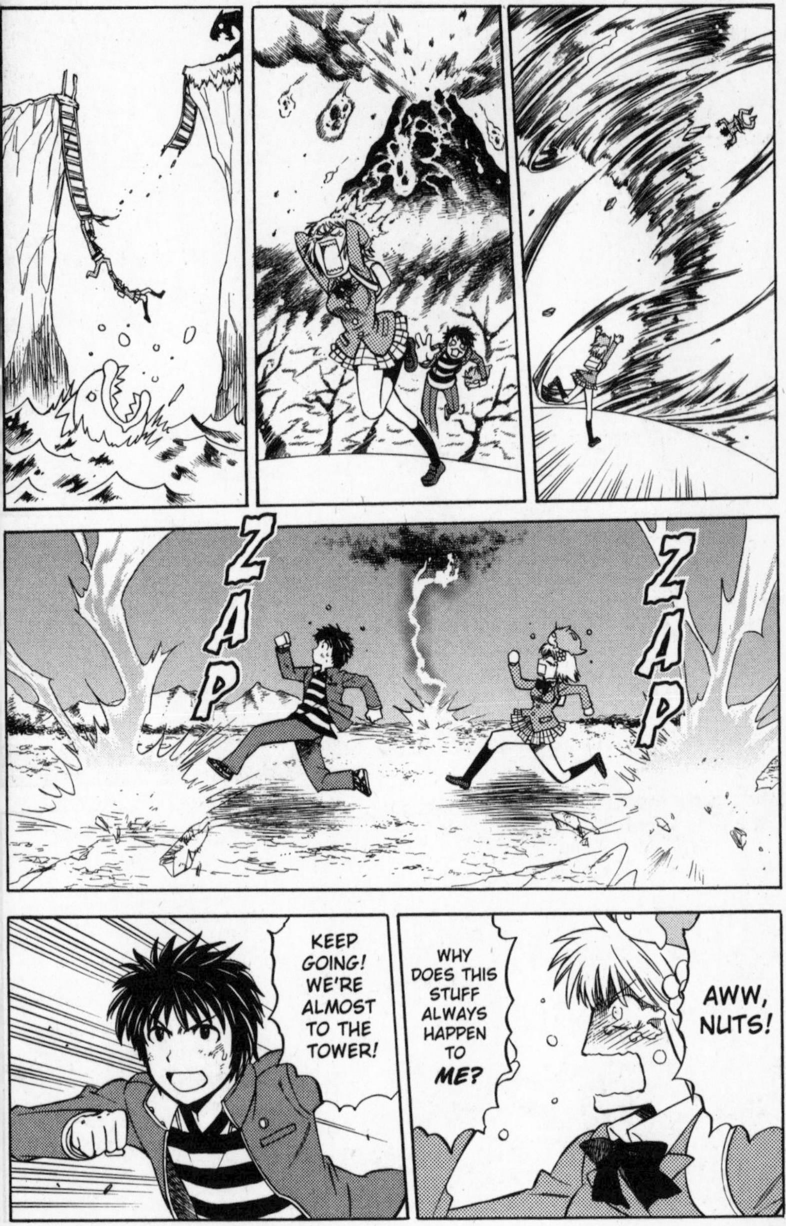
ZAP
ZAP
AWW, NUTS!
WHY DOES THIS STUFF ALWAYS HAPPEN TO *ME*?
KEEP GOING! WE'RE ALMOST TO THE TOWER!

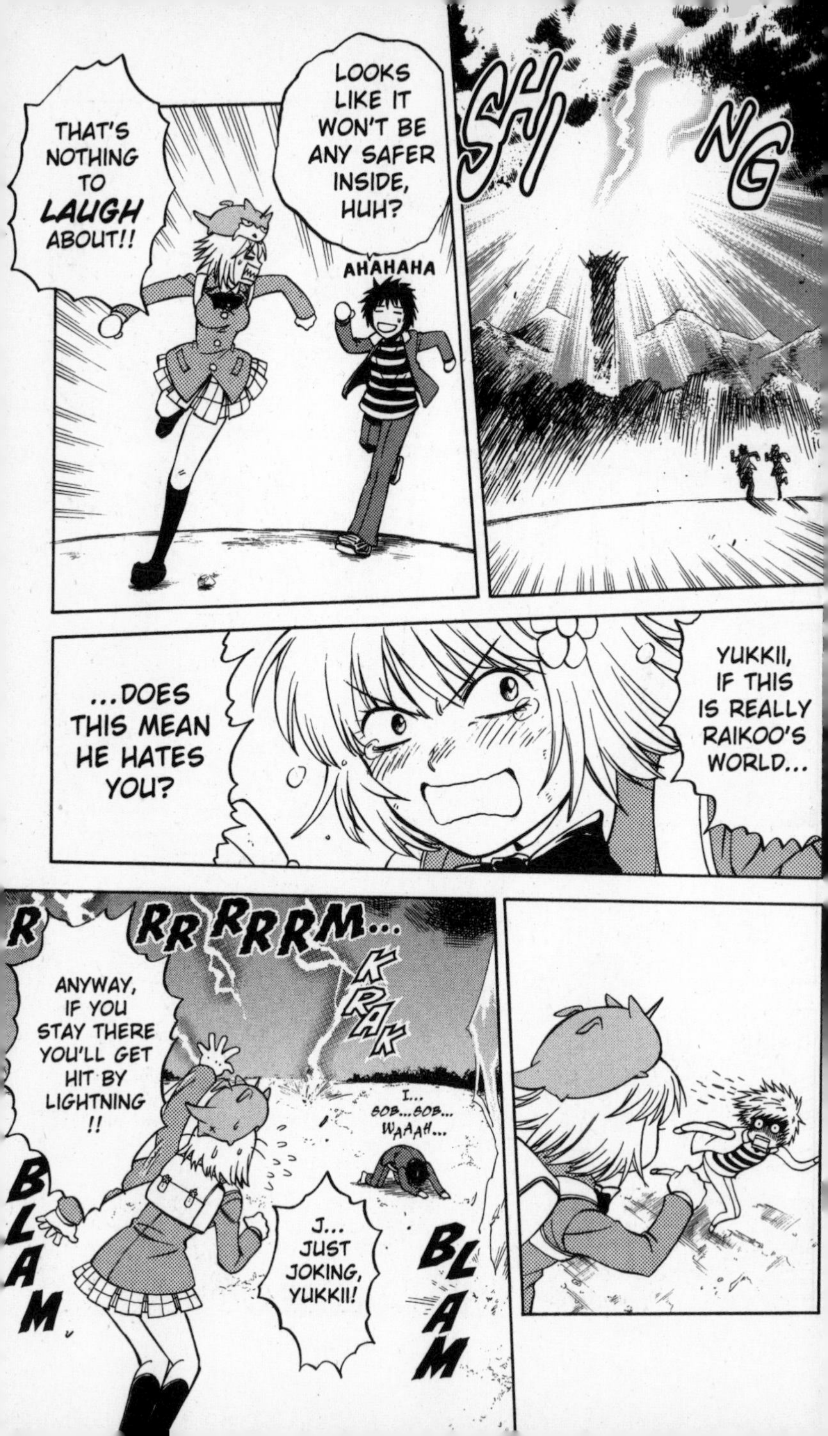
SHING
LOOKS LIKE IT WON'T BE ANY SAFER INSIDE, HUH?
AHAHAHA
THAT'S NOTHING TO LAUGH ABOUT!!
YUKKII, IF THIS IS REALLY RAIKOO'S WORLD...
...DOES THIS MEAN HE HATES YOU?
R RR RRRM...
KRAK
I... SOB...SOB... WAAAH...
ANYWAY, IF YOU STAY THERE YOU'LL GET HIT BY LIGHTNING !!
BLAM
J... JUST JOKING, YUKKII!
BLAM

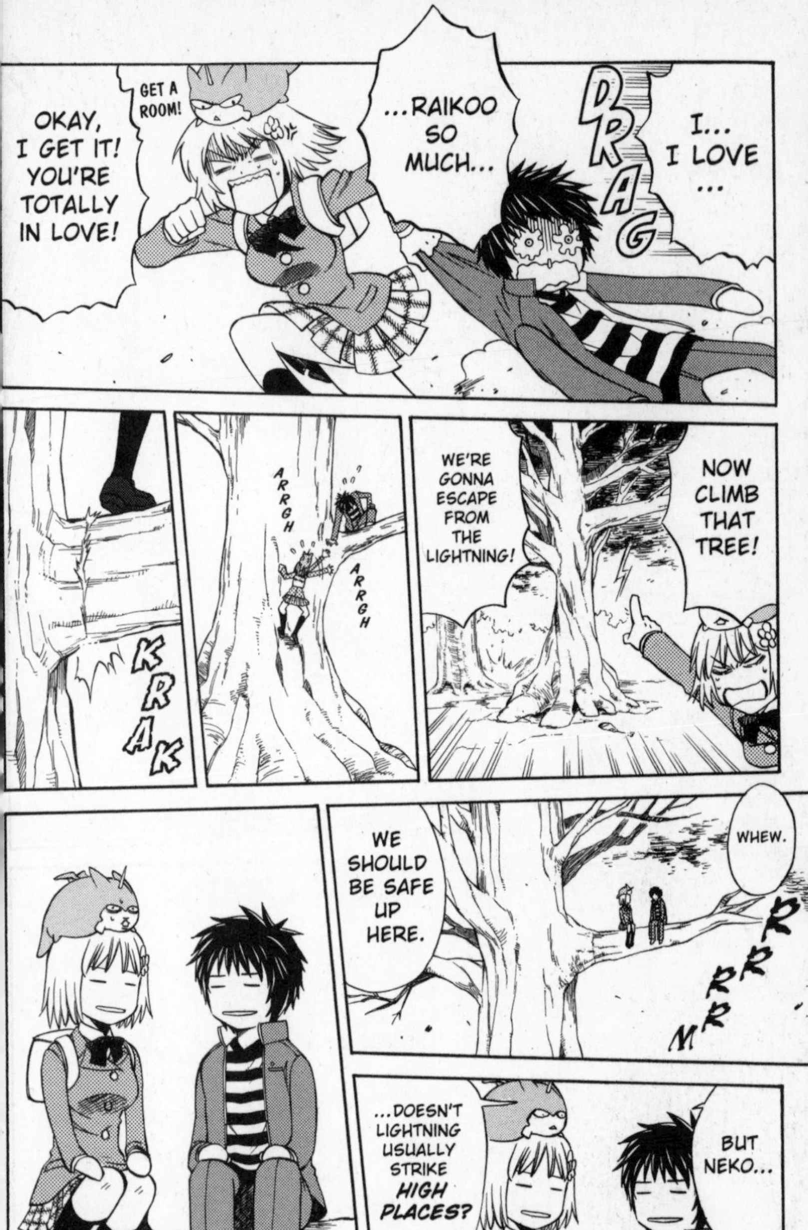
I... I LOVE ...
DRAG
...RAIKOO SO MUCH...
GET A ROOM!
OKAY, I GET IT! YOU'RE TOTALLY IN LOVE!
NOW CLIMB THAT TREE!
WE'RE GONNA ESCAPE FROM THE LIGHTNING!
ARRGH
ARRGH
KRAK
WHEW.
MRRRRR
WE SHOULD BE SAFE UP HERE.
BUT NEKO...
...DOESN'T LIGHTNING USUALLY STRIKE *HIGH PLACES?*

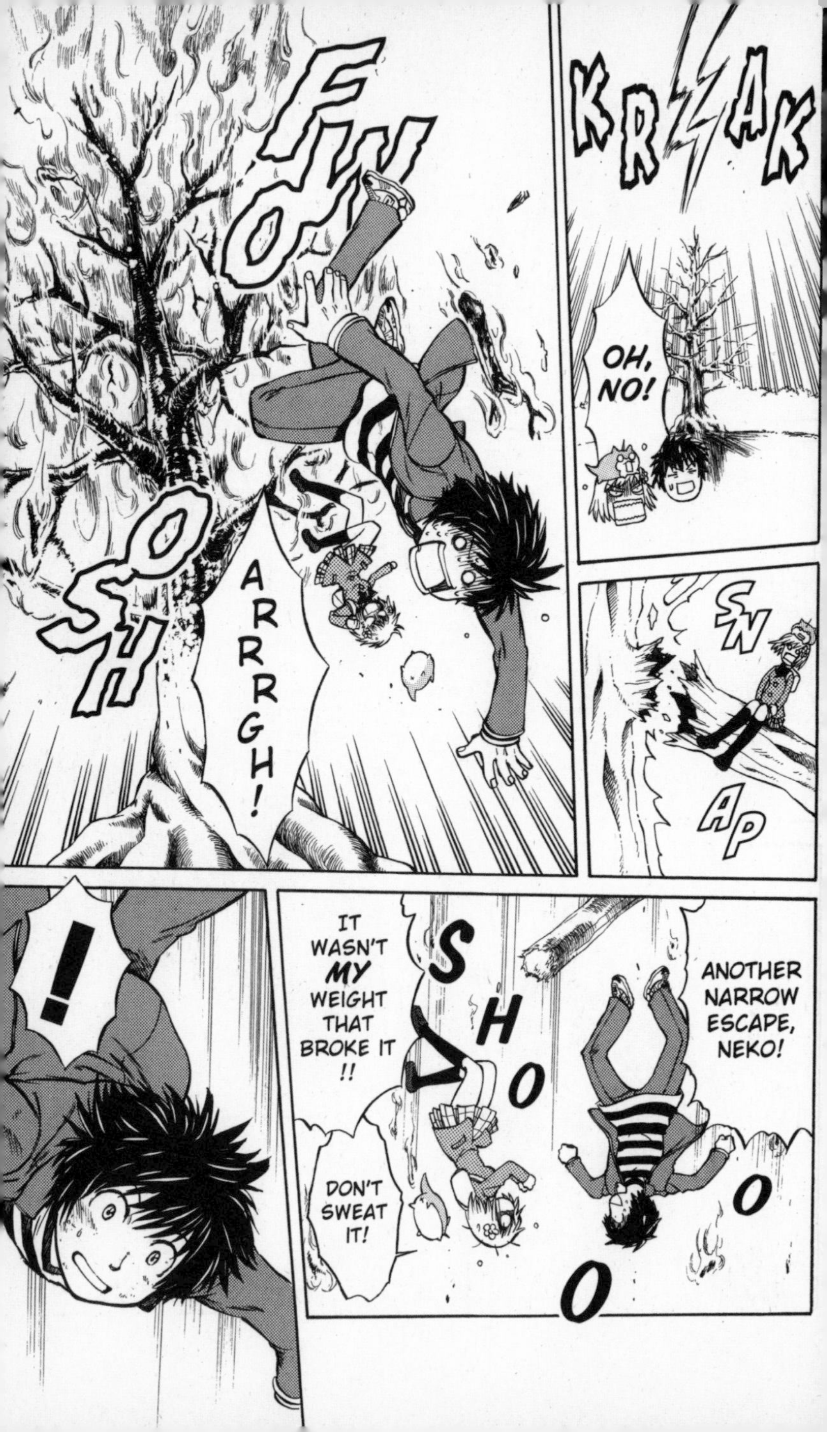
KRZAK
OH, NO!
SNAP
FWOOSH
ARRRGH!
ANOTHER NARROW ESCAPE, NEKO!
SHOOO
IT WASN'T **MY** WEIGHT THAT BROKE IT!!
DON'T SWEAT IT!
!

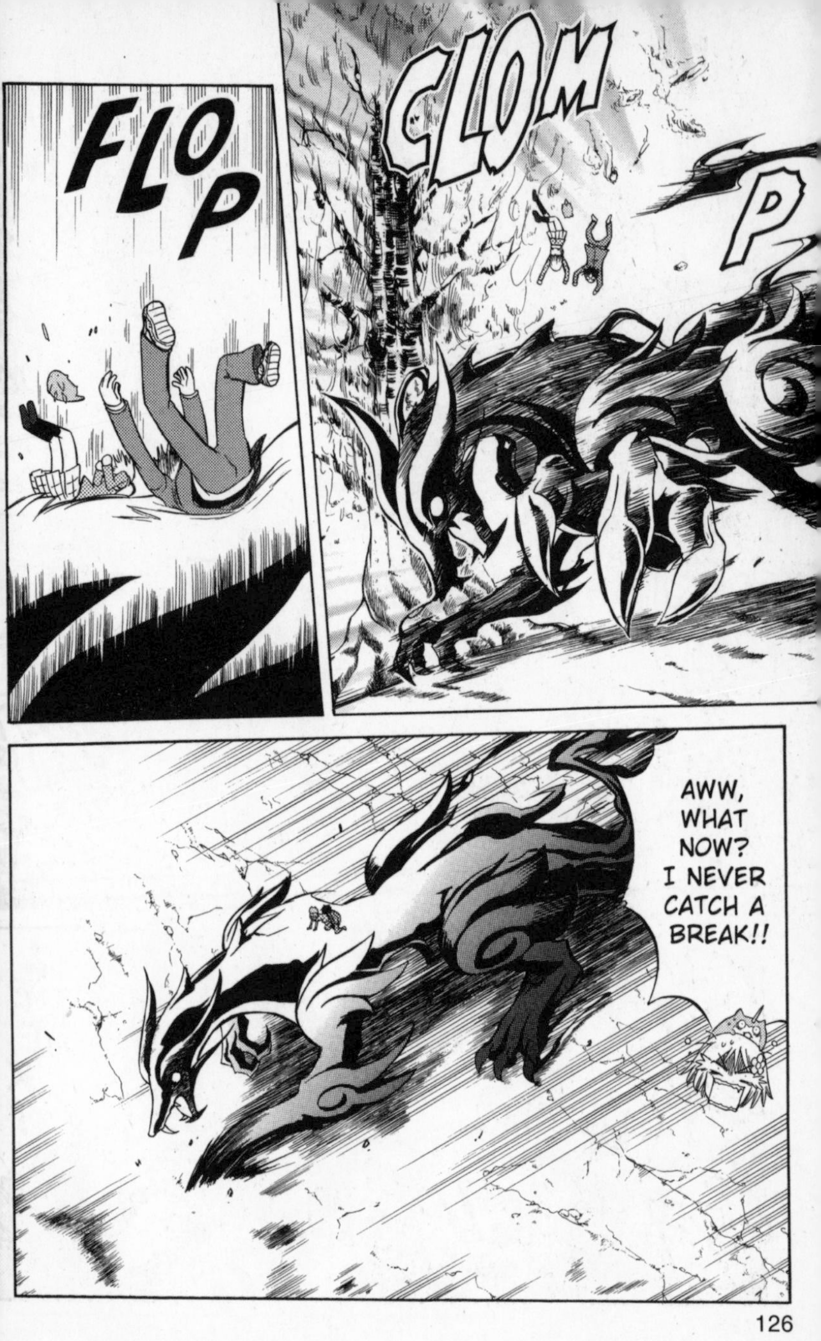
CLOM
P
FLOP
AWW, WHAT NOW? I NEVER CATCH A BREAK!!

READ THIS WAY

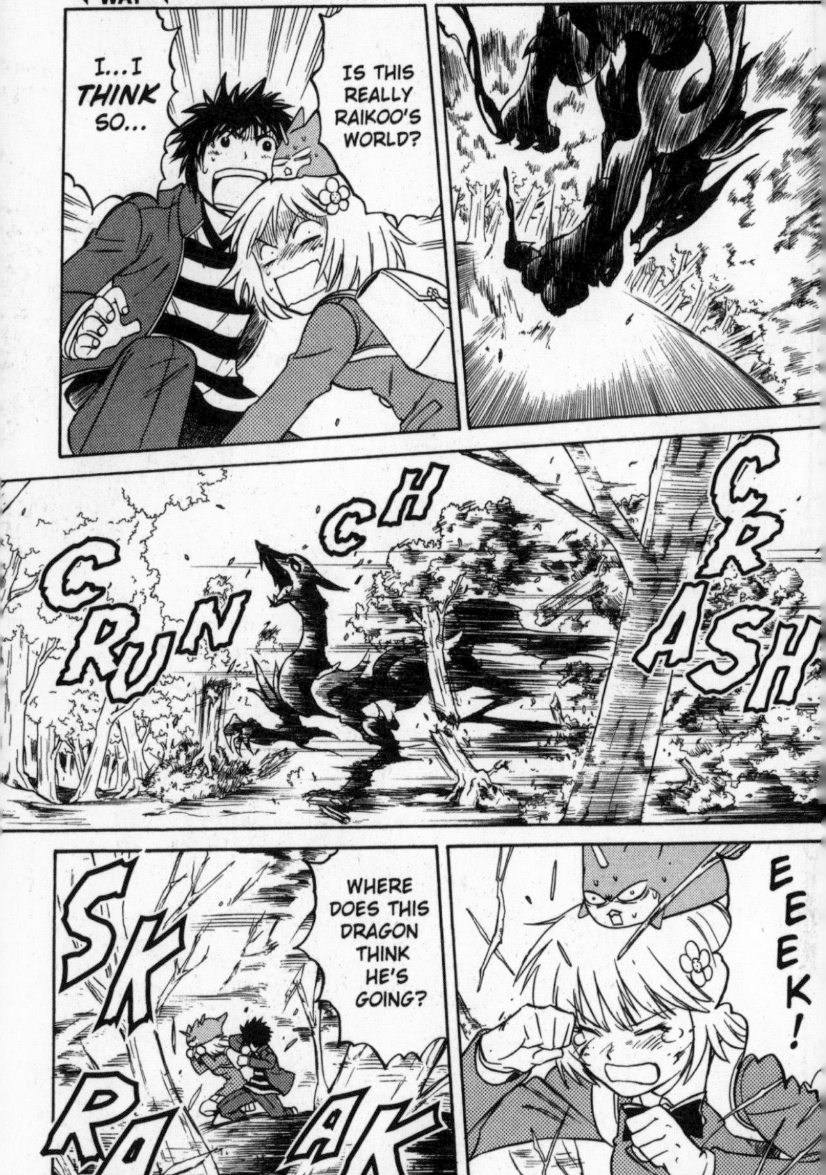

IS THIS REALLY RAIKOO'S WORLD?
I...I THINK SO...
CRASH
CRUNCH
EEEK!
WHERE DOES THIS DRAGON THINK HE'S GOING?
SKRAAK

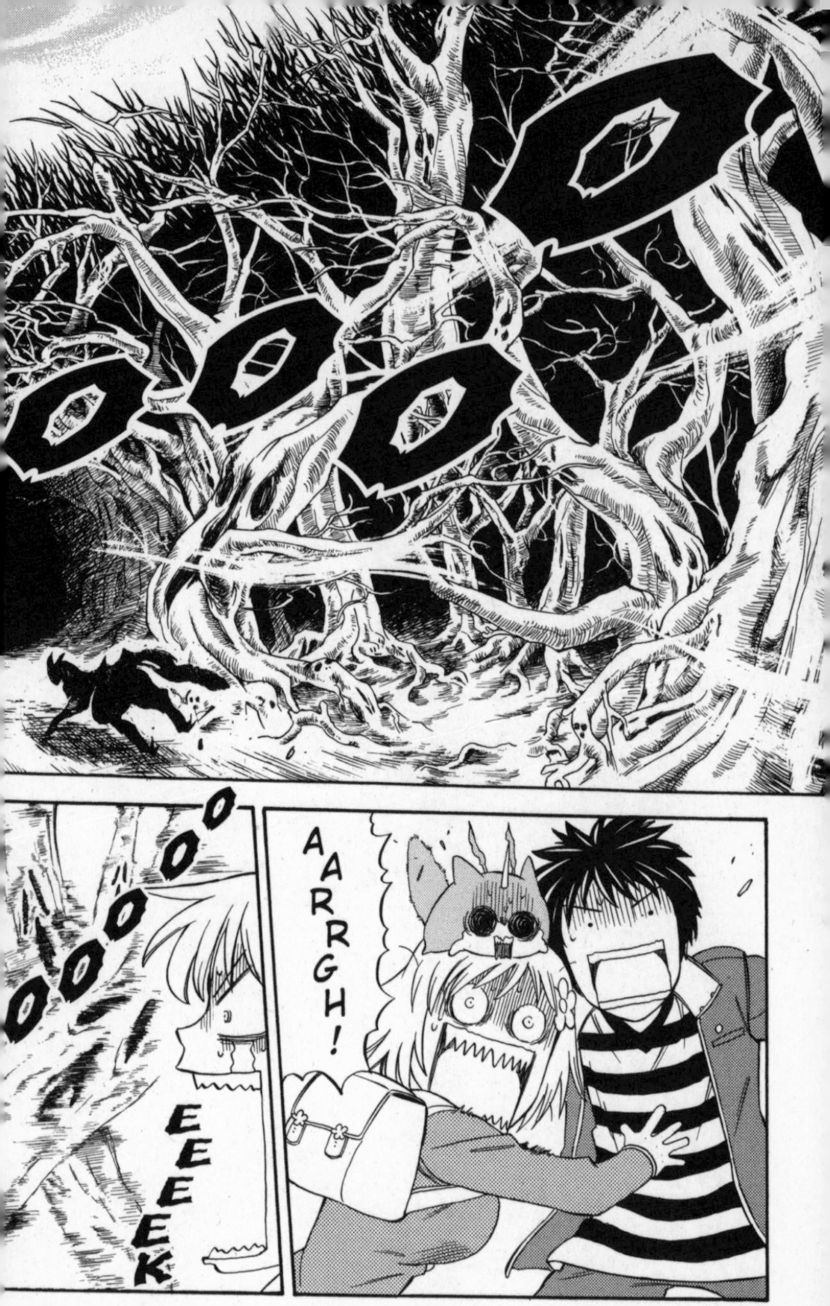
OOOOO
AARRGH!
OOOOOO
EEEEK

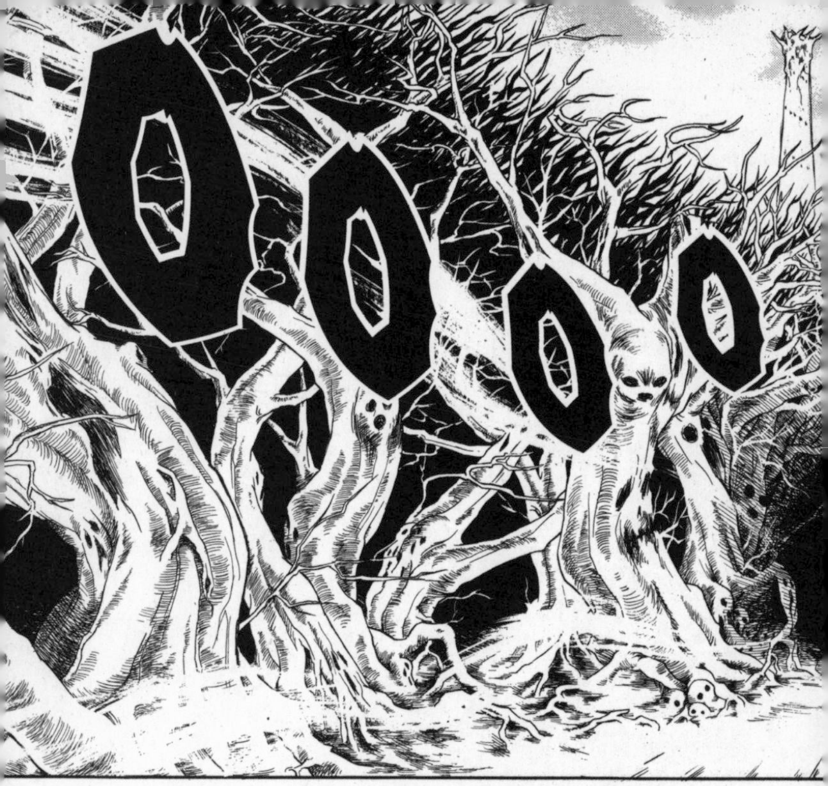
OOOO

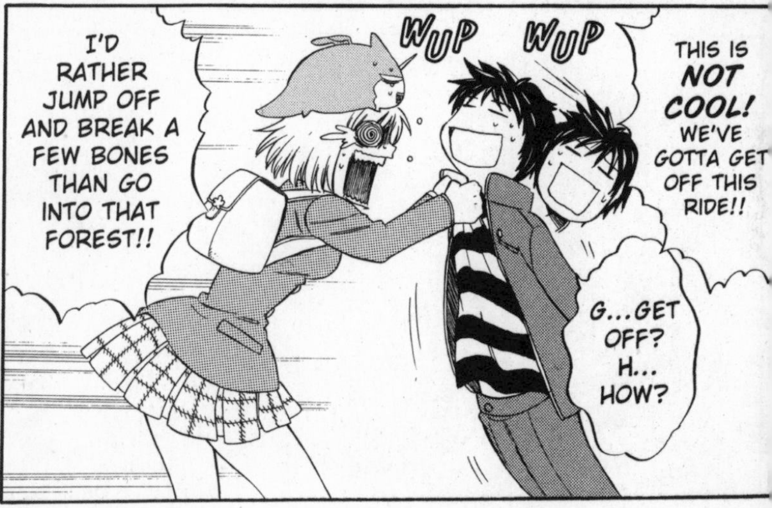
THIS IS **NOT COOL!** WE'VE GOTTA GET OFF THIS RIDE!!
WUP WUP
I'D RATHER JUMP OFF AND BREAK A FEW BONES THAN GO INTO THAT FOREST!!
G...GET OFF? H... HOW?

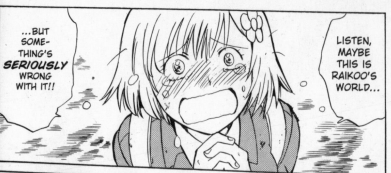

LISTEN, MAYBE THIS IS RAIKOO'S WORLD...
...BUT SOME-THING'S **SERIOUSLY** WRONG WITH IT!!
WE'VE HAD SOME LUCKY ESCAPES SO FAR...
...BUT NEXT TIME WE COULD **DIE!!**
...
!
OH.
I GET IT!

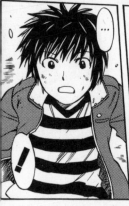

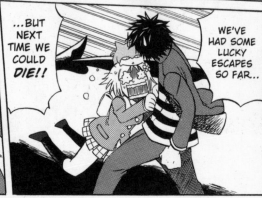

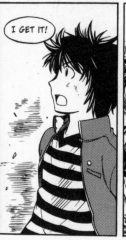

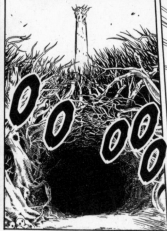

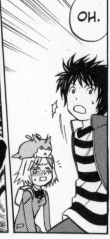

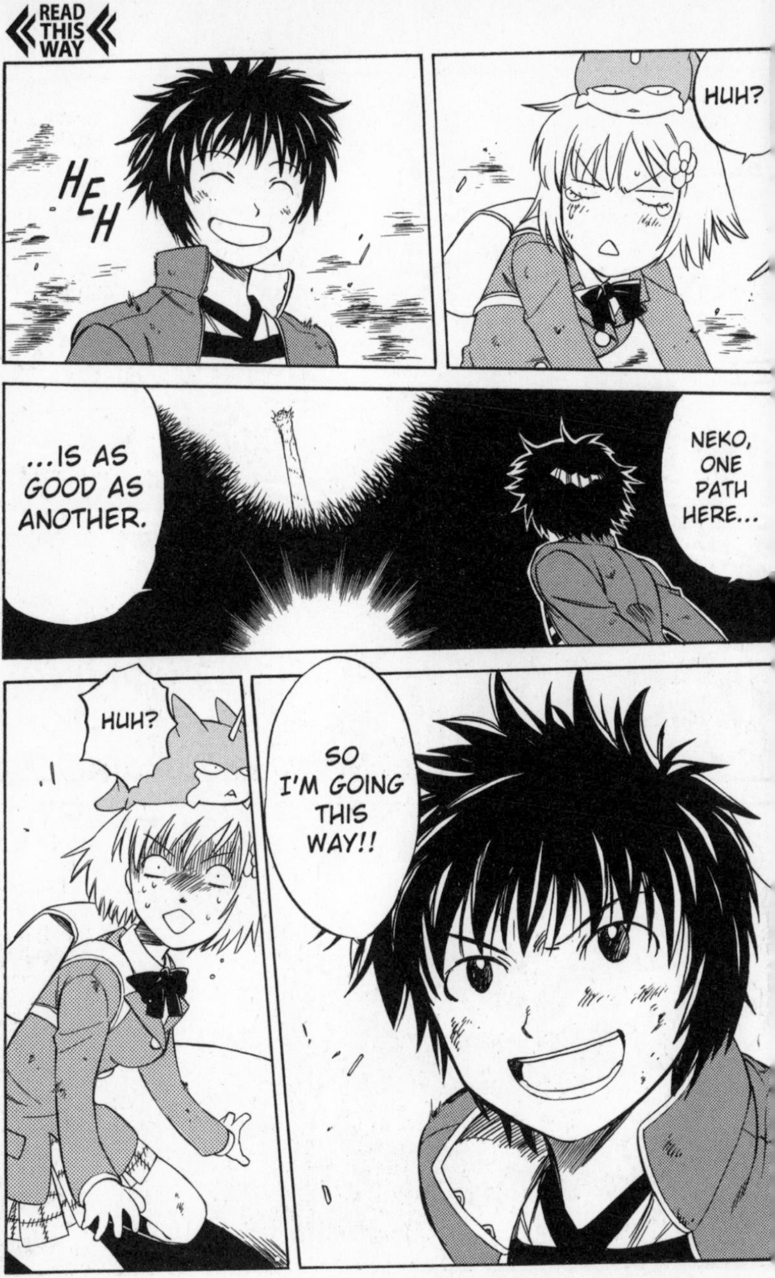
READ THIS WAY
HUH?
HEH
NEKO, ONE PATH HERE...
...IS AS GOOD AS ANOTHER.
SO I'M GOING THIS WAY!!
HUH?

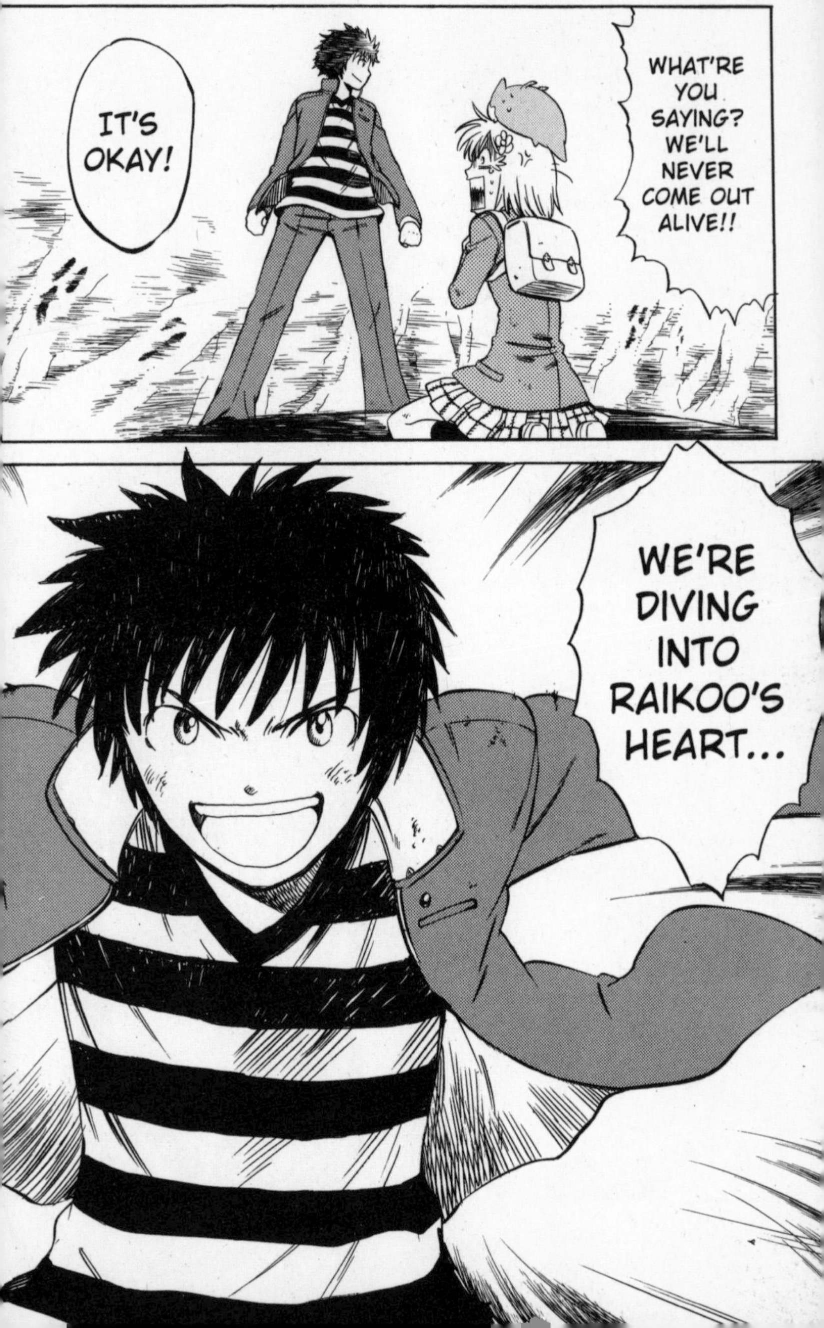
WHAT'RE YOU SAYING? WE'LL NEVER COME OUT ALIVE!!
IT'S OKAY!
WE'RE DIVING INTO RAIKOO'S HEART...

READ THIS WAY

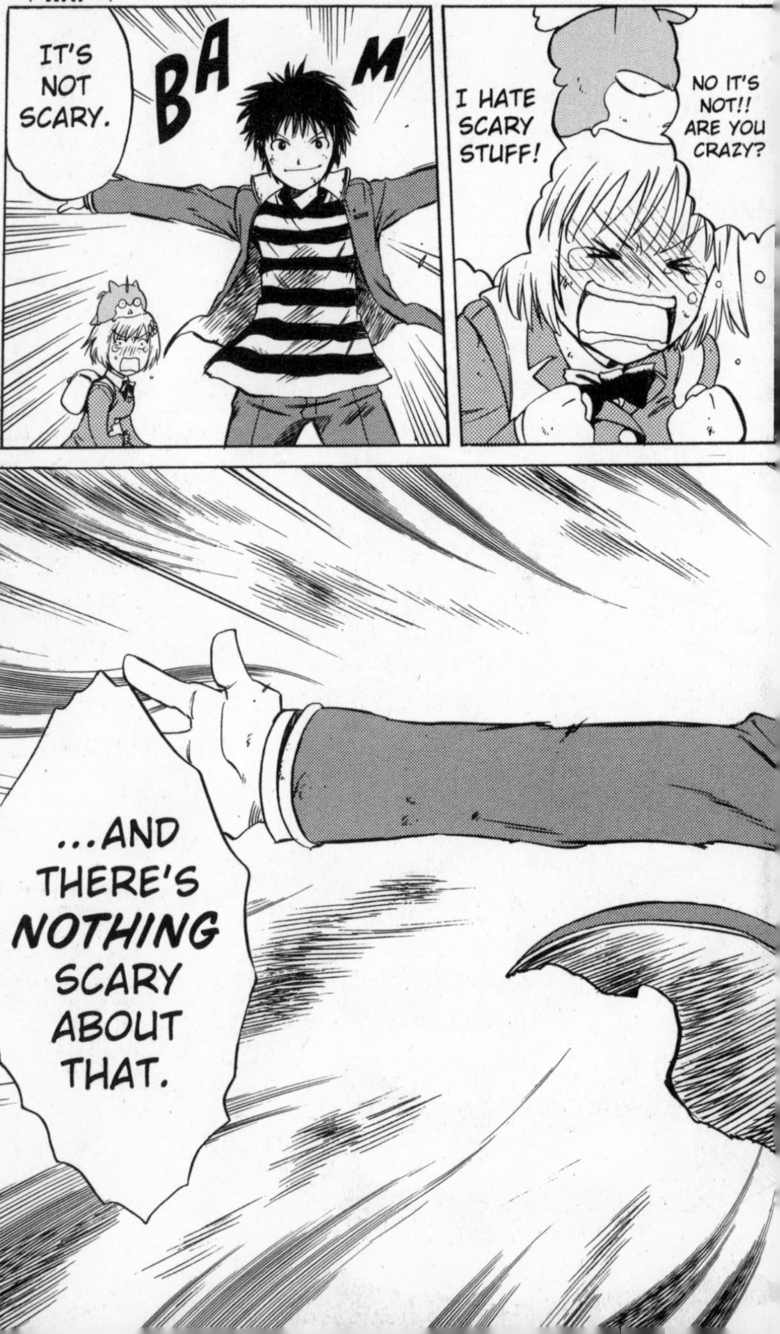
NO IT'S NOT!! ARE YOU CRAZY?
I HATE SCARY STUFF!
BAM
IT'S NOT SCARY.
...AND THERE'S NOTHING SCARY ABOUT THAT.

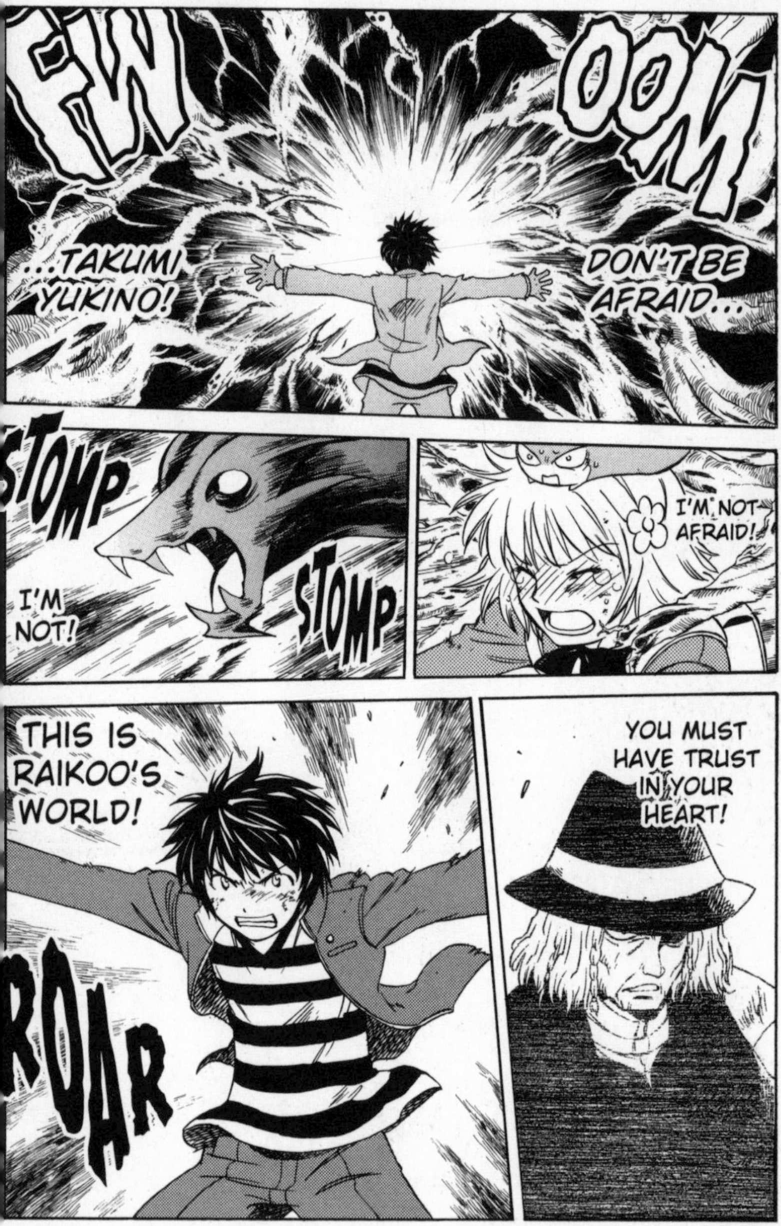
OOM
FW
DON'T BE AFRAID...
...TAKUMI YUKINO!
I'M NOT AFRAID!
STOMP
STOMP
I'M NOT!
YOU MUST HAVE TRUST IN YOUR HEART!
THIS IS RAIKOO'S WORLD!
ROAR

READ THIS WAY

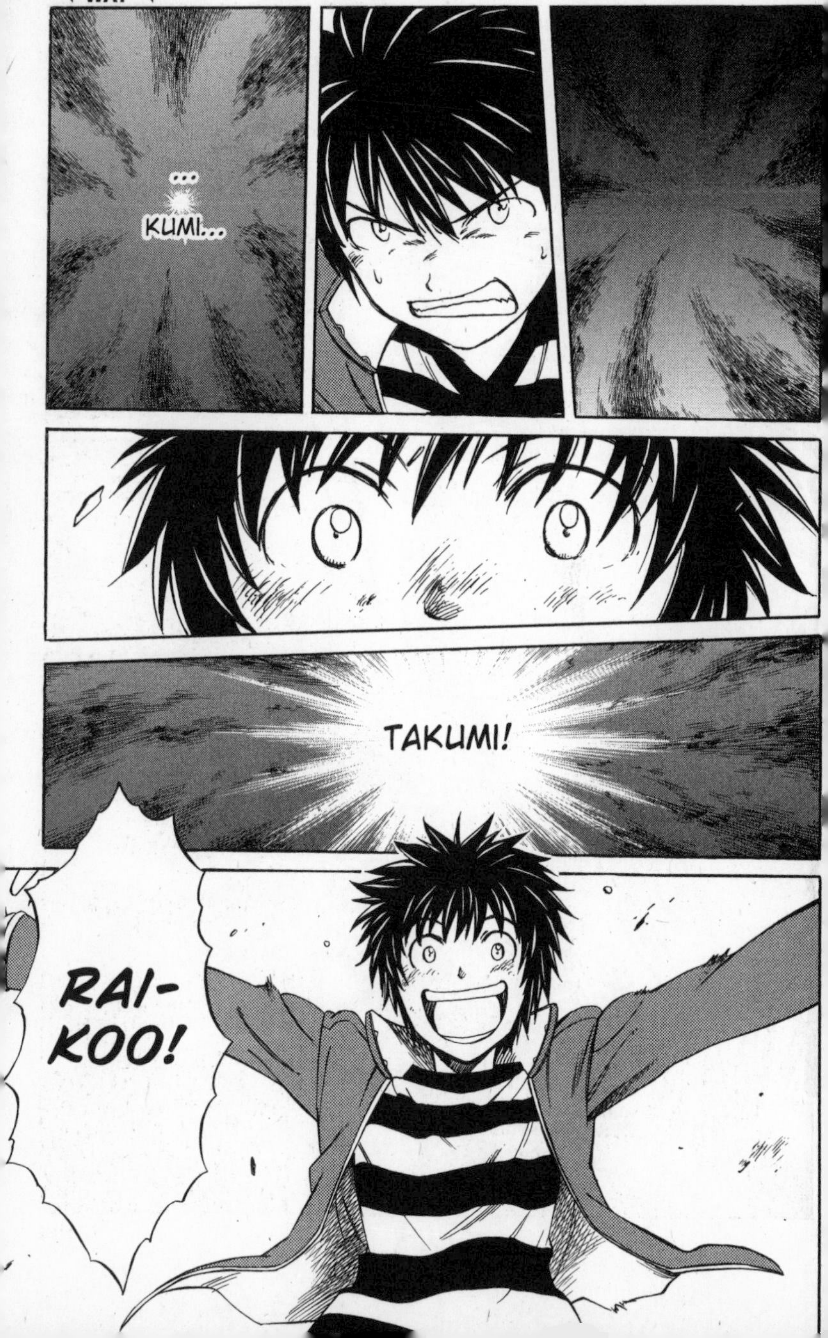
...
KUMI...
TAKUMI!
RAI-KOO!

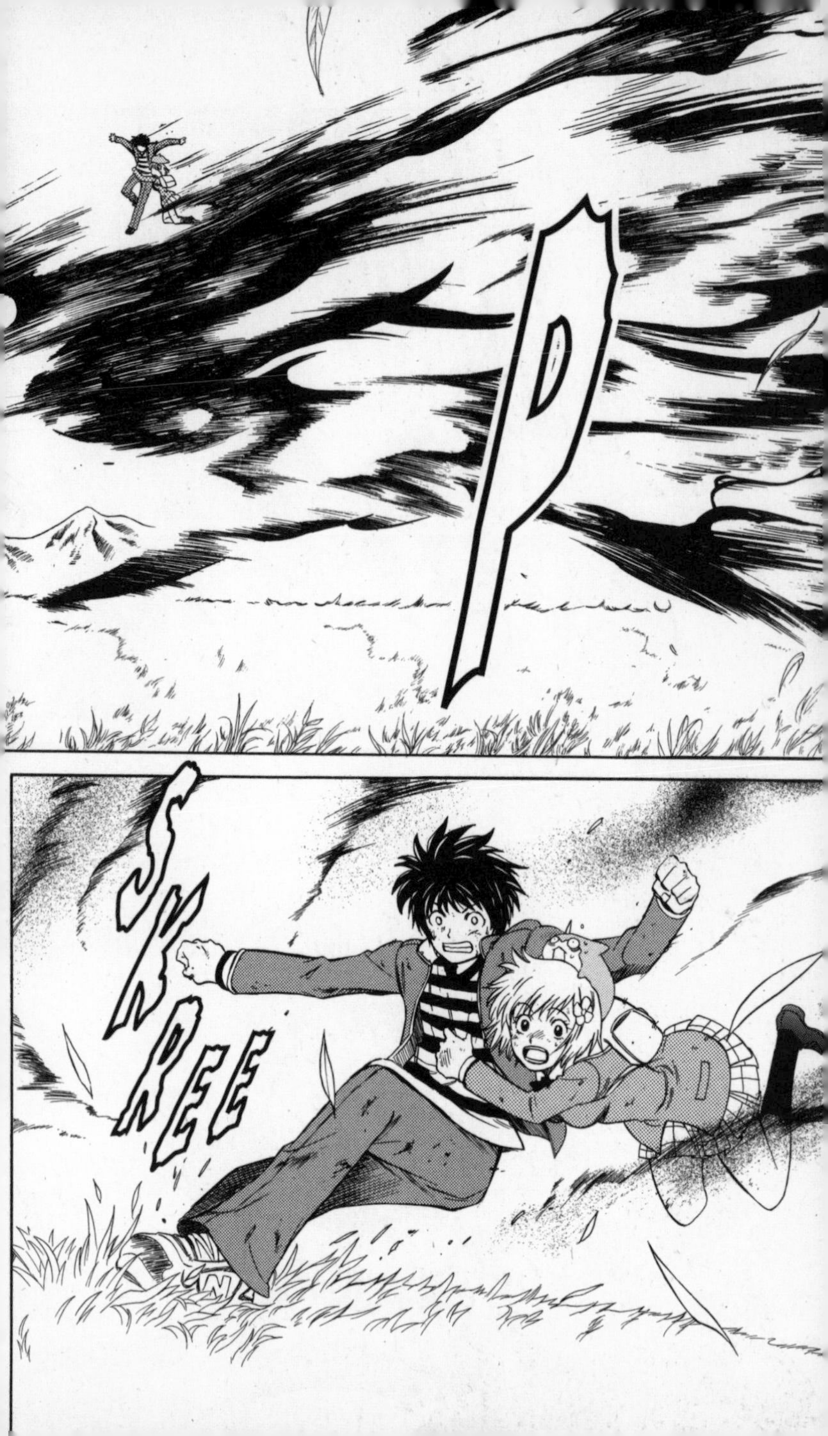
P
SKREE

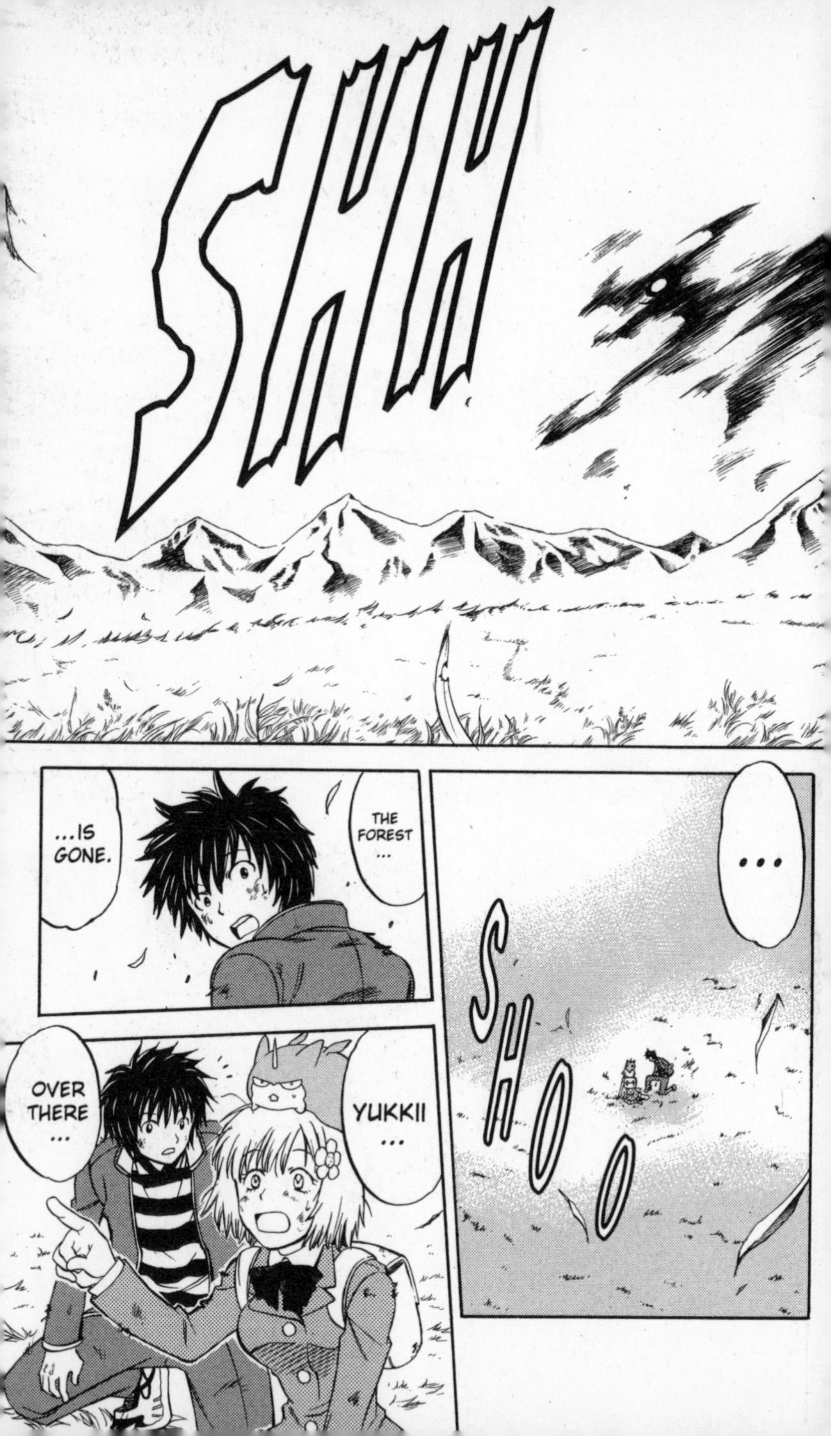
SHH
...
SHOOO
THE FOREST ...
...IS GONE.
YUKKII ...
OVER THERE ...

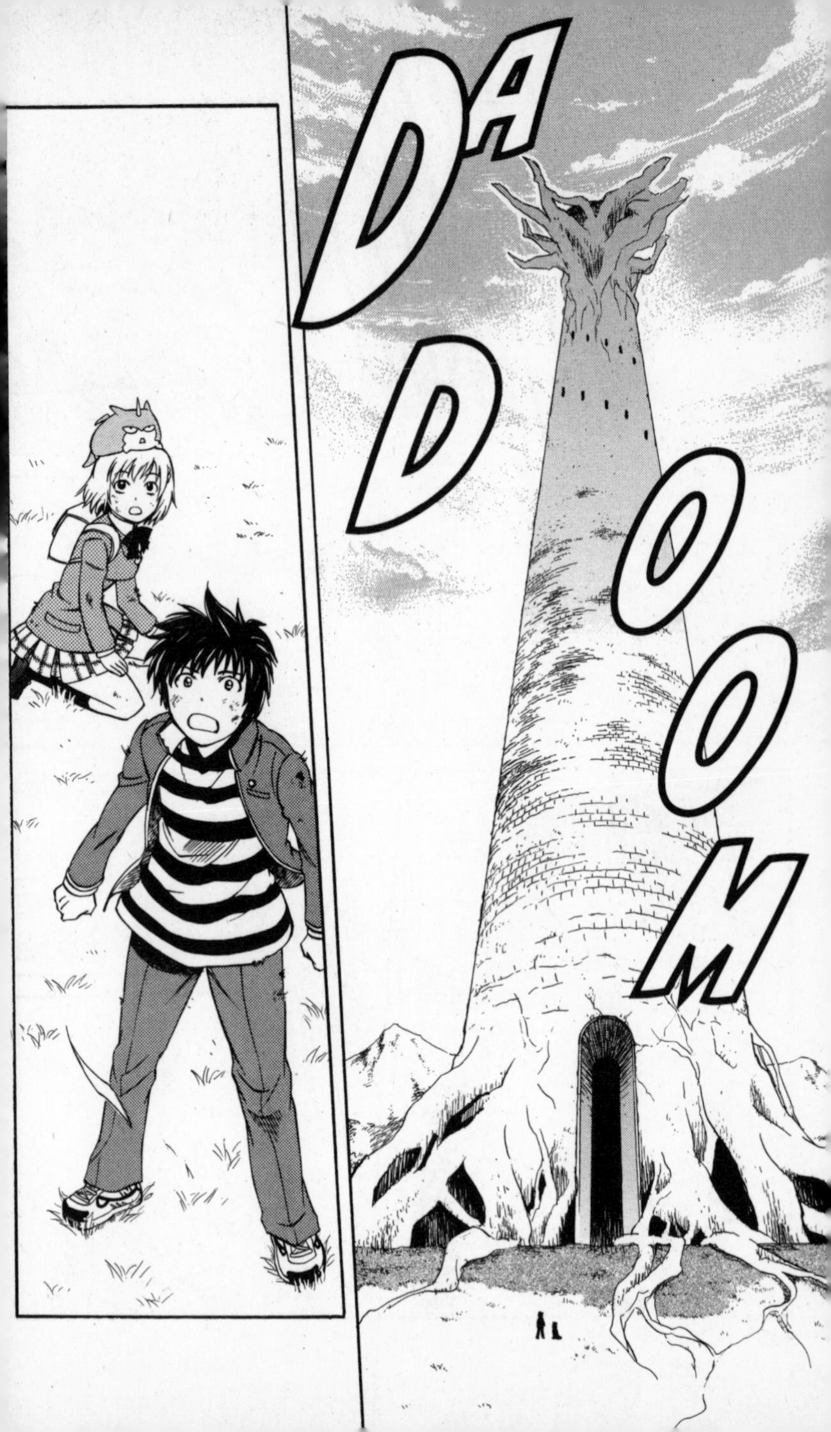
DADOOM

READ THIS WAY

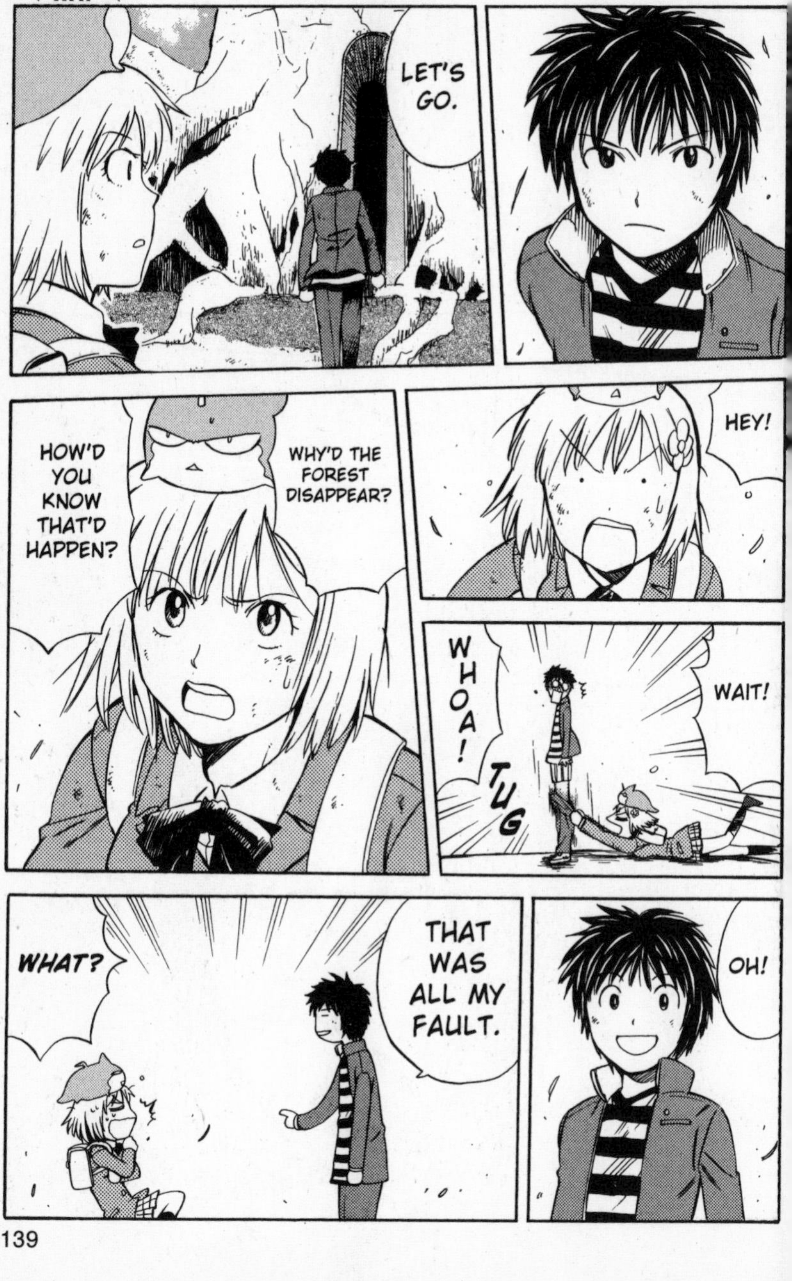
LET'S GO.
HEY!
WAIT!
WHOA!
TUG
WHY'D THE FOREST DISAPPEAR?
HOW'D YOU KNOW THAT'D HAPPEN?
OH!
THAT WAS ALL MY FAULT.
WHAT?

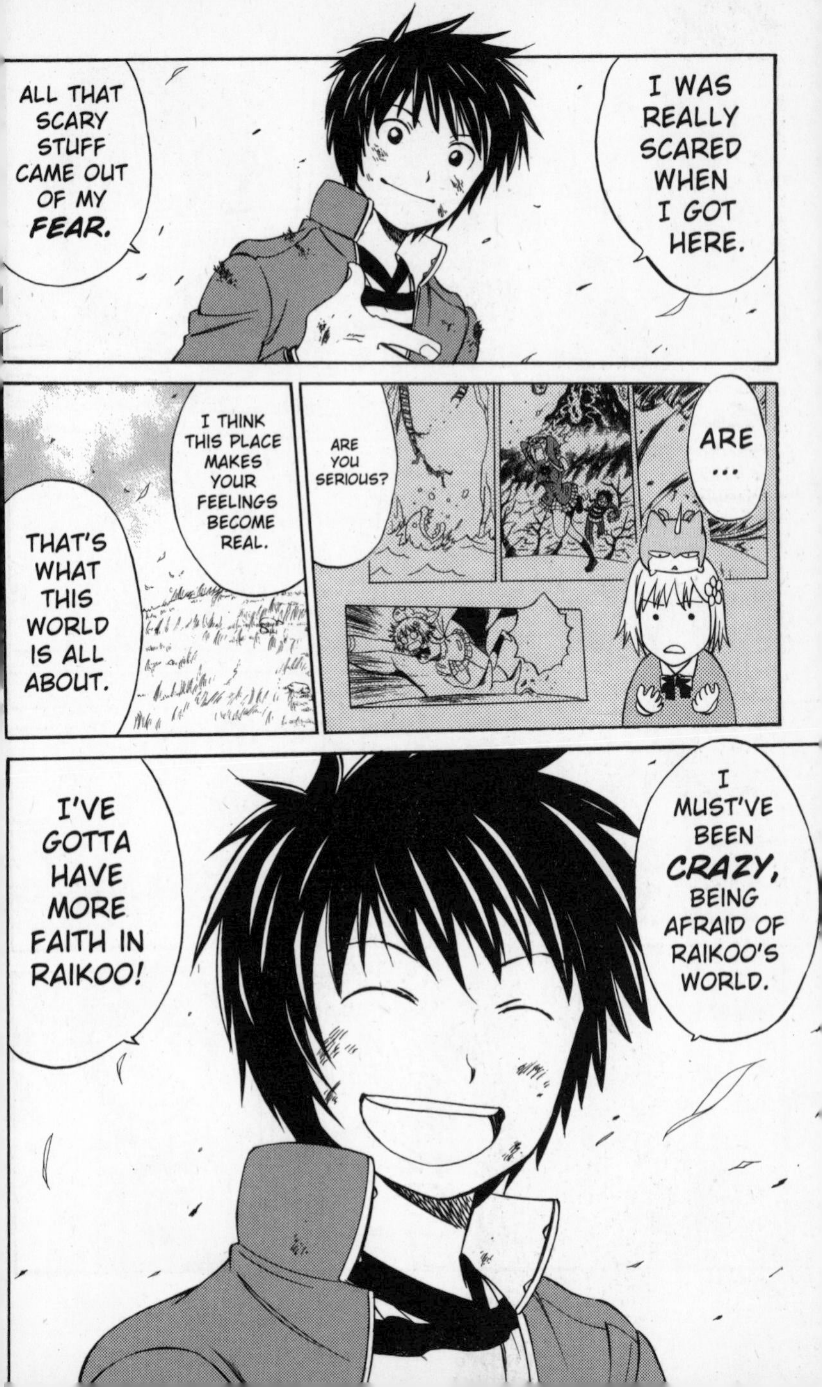
I WAS REALLY SCARED WHEN I GOT HERE.
ALL THAT SCARY STUFF CAME OUT OF MY ***FEAR.***
ARE ...
ARE YOU SERIOUS?
I THINK THIS PLACE MAKES YOUR FEELINGS BECOME REAL.
THAT'S WHAT THIS WORLD IS ALL ABOUT.
I MUST'VE BEEN ***CRAZY,*** BEING AFRAID OF RAIKOO'S WORLD.
I'VE GOTTA HAVE MORE FAITH IN RAIKOO!

READ THIS WAY

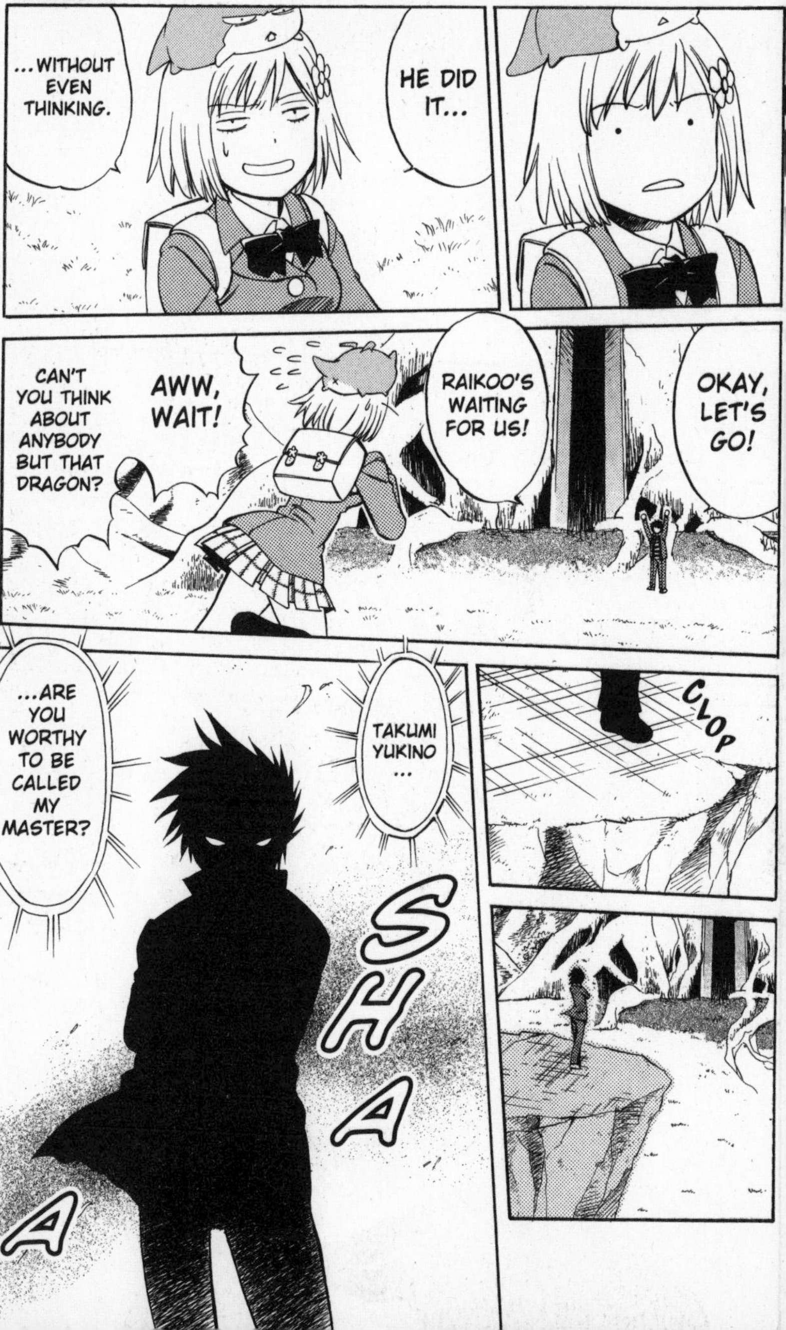
HE DID IT...
...WITHOUT EVEN THINKING.
OKAY, LET'S GO!
RAIKOO'S WAITING FOR US!
AWW, WAIT!
CAN'T YOU THINK ABOUT ANYBODY BUT THAT DRAGON?
CLOP
TAKUMI YUKINO ...
...ARE YOU WORTHY TO BE CALLED MY MASTER?
SHAA

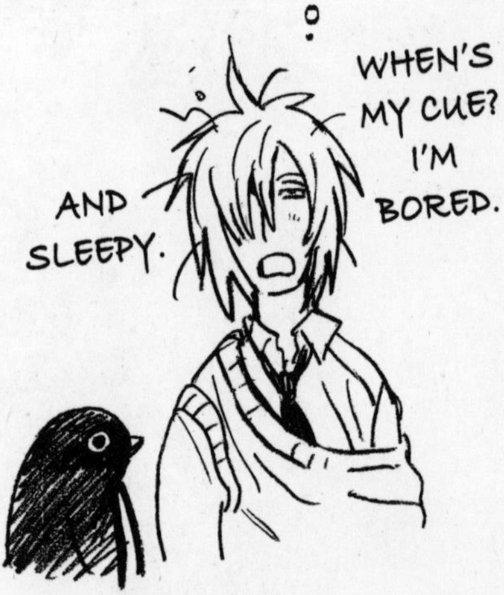
WHEN'S MY CUE? I'M BORED.
AND SLEEPY.

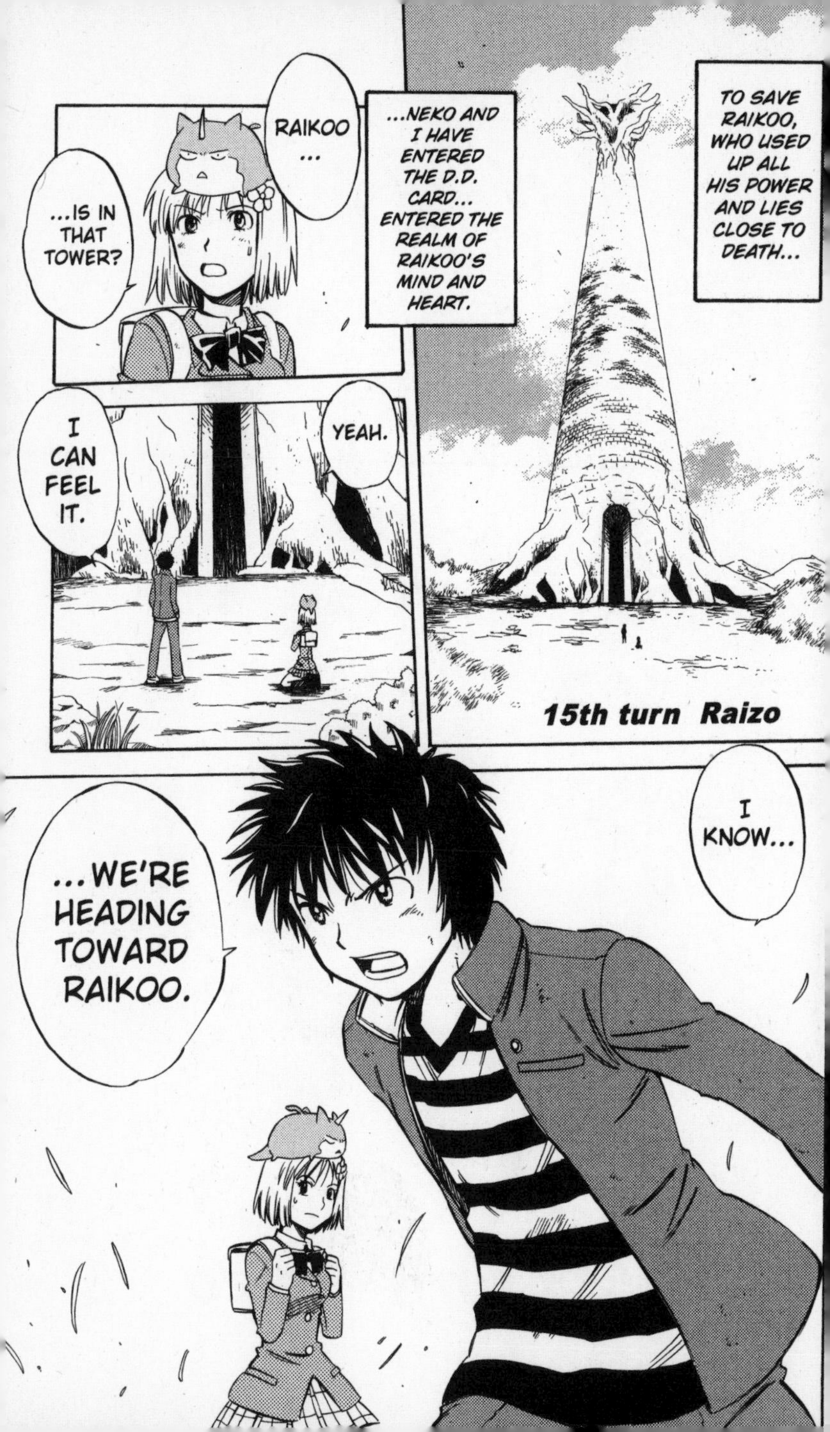
TO SAVE RAIKOO, WHO USED UP ALL HIS POWER AND LIES CLOSE TO DEATH...
...NEKO AND I HAVE ENTERED THE D.D. CARD... ENTERED THE REALM OF RAIKOO'S MIND AND HEART.
15th turn Raizo
RAIKOO ...
...IS IN THAT TOWER?
YEAH.
I CAN FEEL IT.
I KNOW...
...WE'RE HEADING TOWARD RAIKOO.

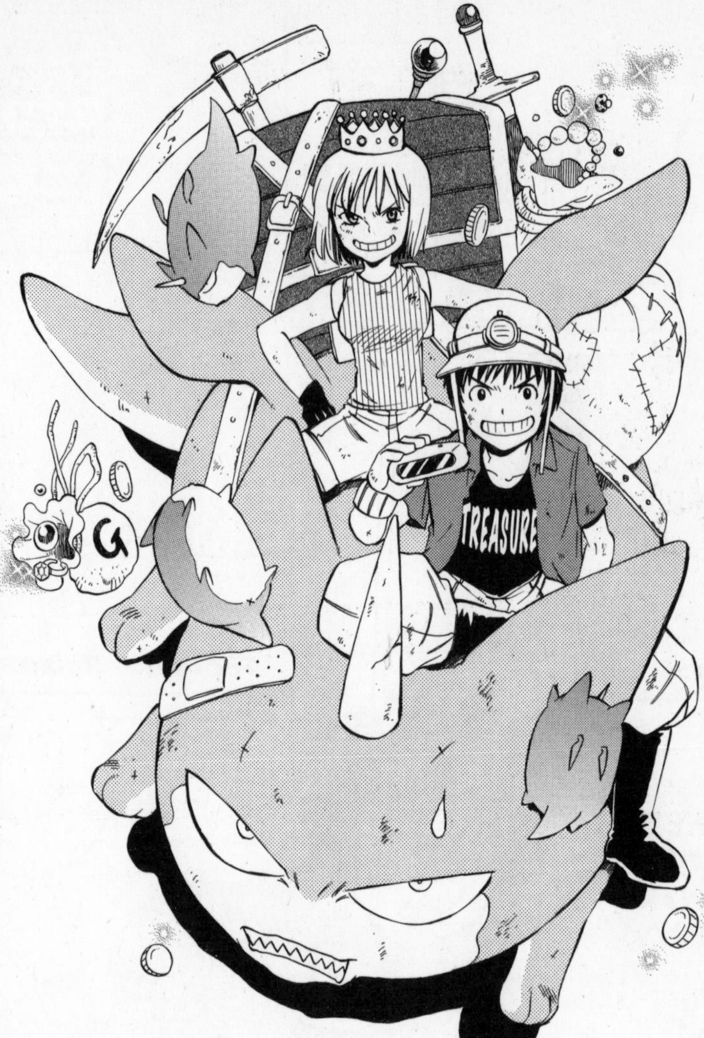
G
TREASURE

15th turn Raizo

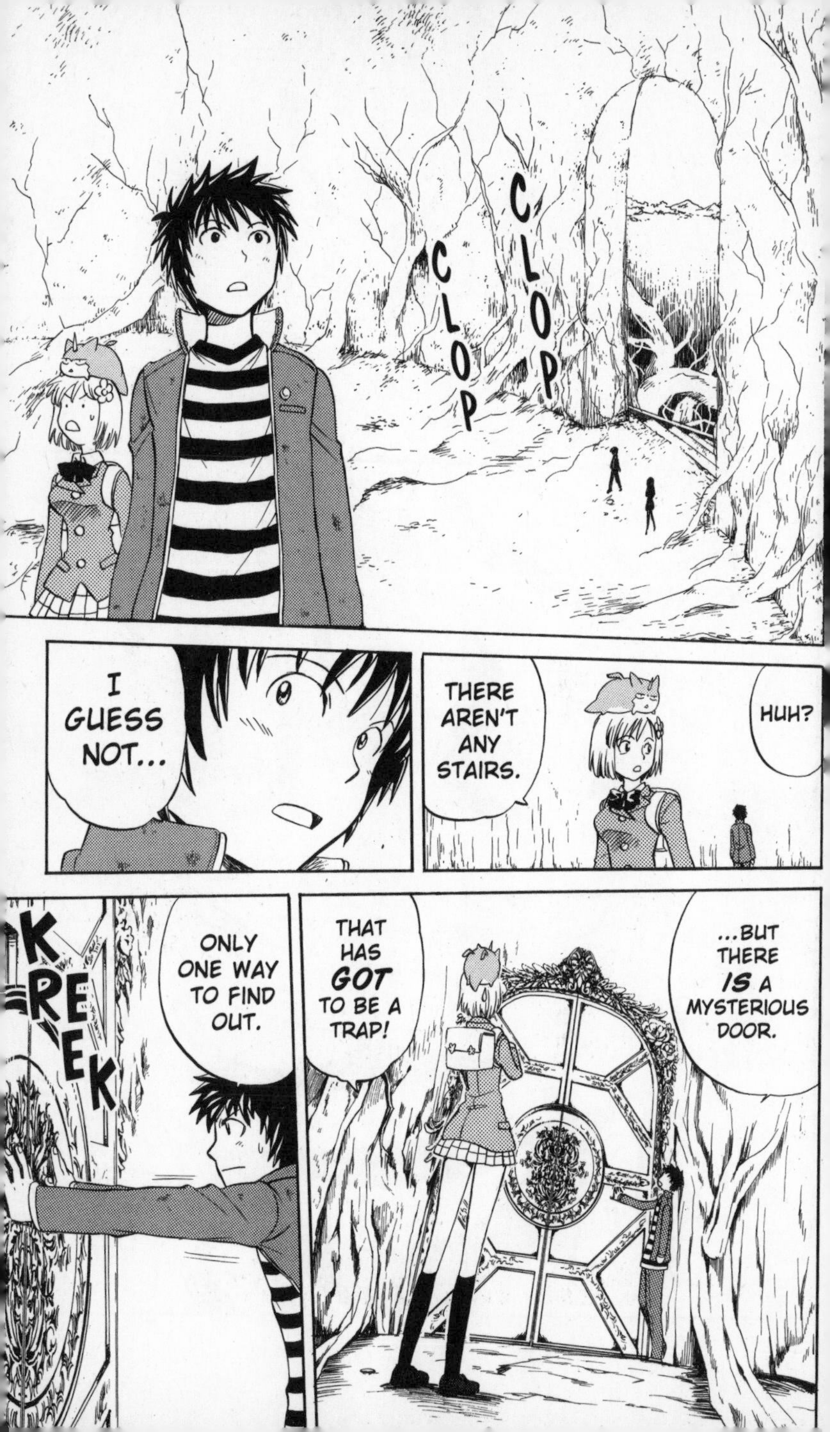
CLOP
CLOP
HUH?
THERE AREN'T ANY STAIRS.
I GUESS NOT...
...BUT THERE IS A MYSTERIOUS DOOR.
THAT HAS GOT TO BE A TRAP!
ONLY ONE WAY TO FIND OUT.
KREEK

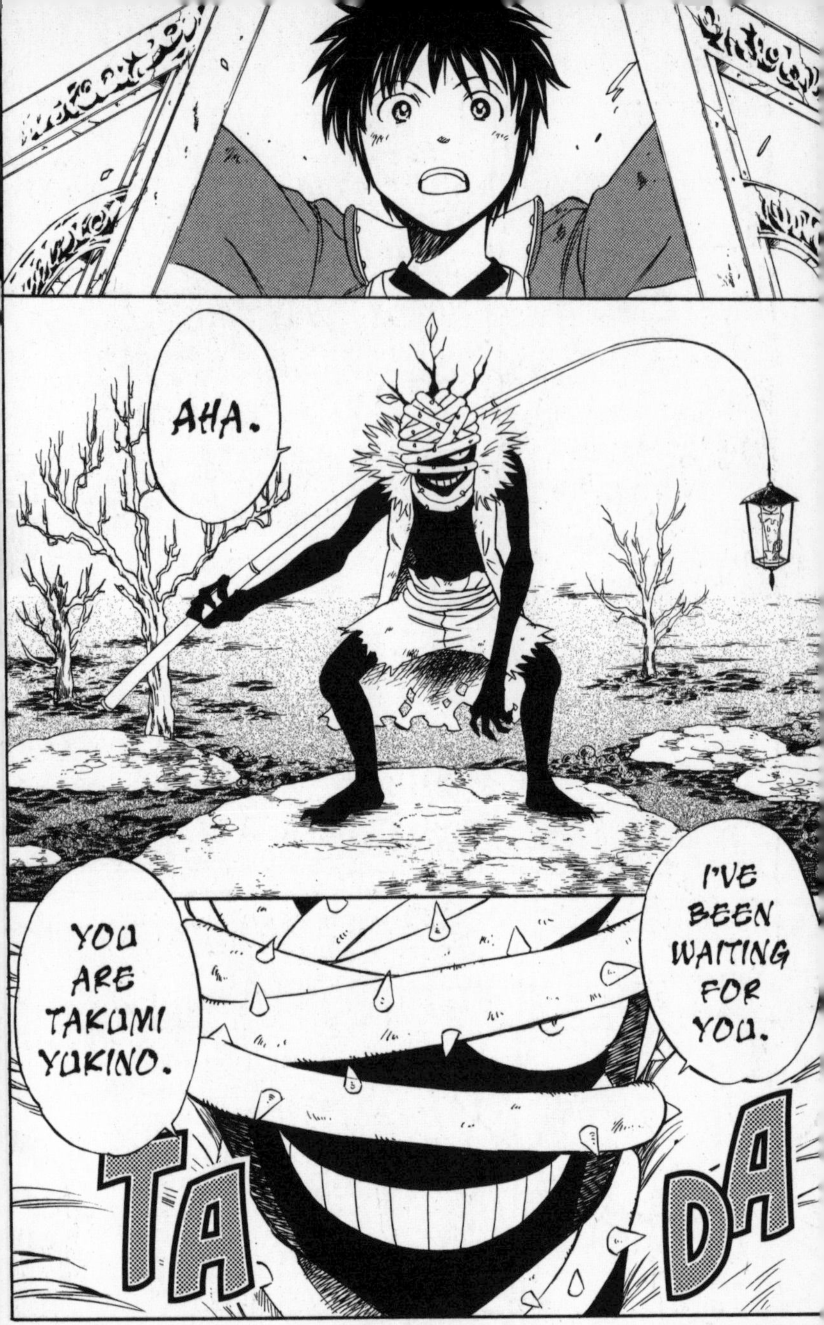
AHA.
I'VE BEEN WAITING FOR YOU.
YOU ARE TAKUMI YUKINO.
TA DA

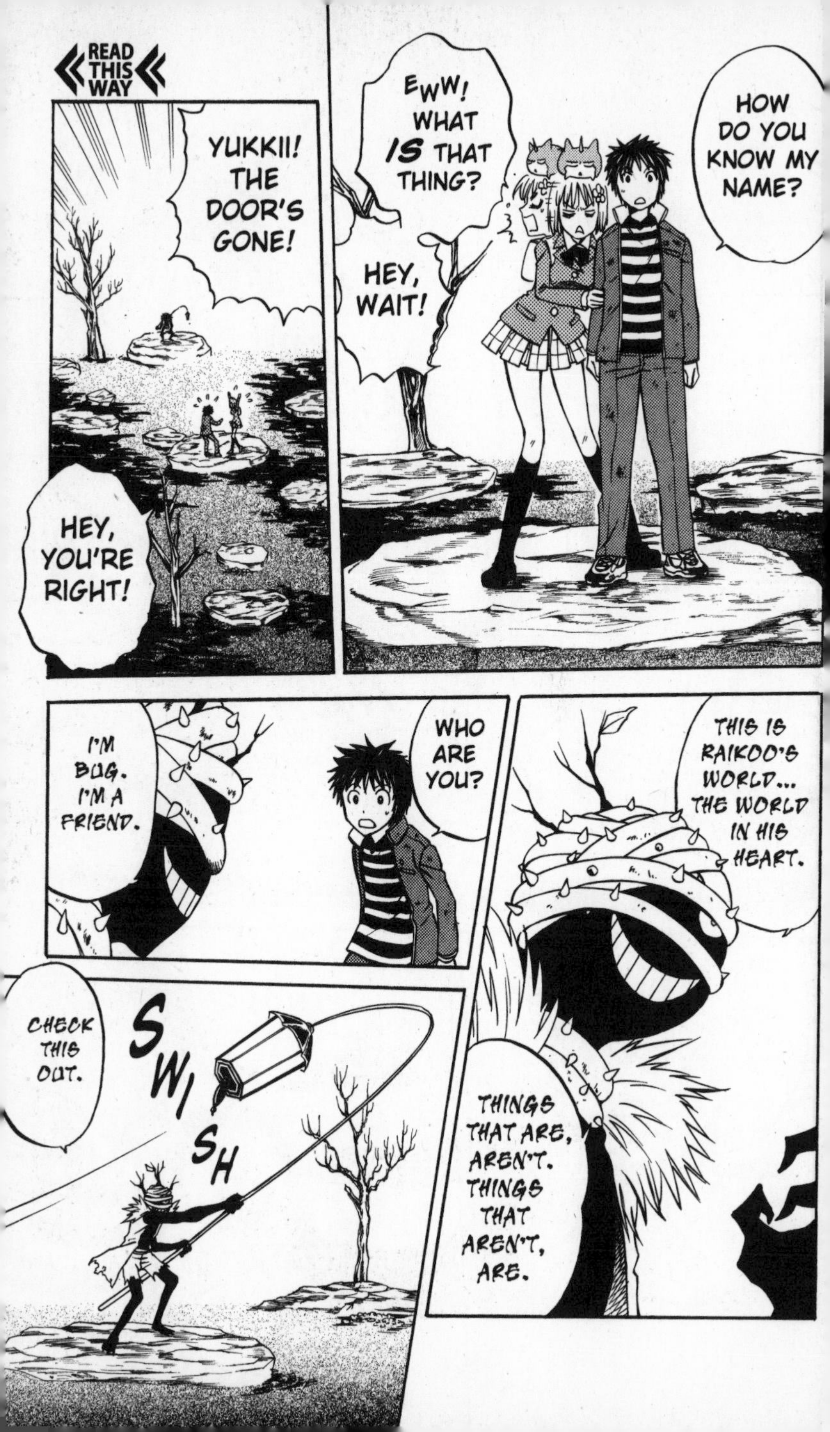
READ THIS WAY
HOW DO YOU KNOW MY NAME?
EWW! WHAT *IS* THAT THING?
HEY, WAIT!
YUKKII! THE DOOR'S GONE!
HEY, YOU'RE RIGHT!
THIS IS RAIKOO'S WORLD... THE WORLD IN HIS HEART.
THINGS THAT ARE, AREN'T. THINGS THAT AREN'T, ARE.
WHO ARE YOU?
I'M BUG. I'M A FRIEND.
CHECK THIS OUT.
SWISH

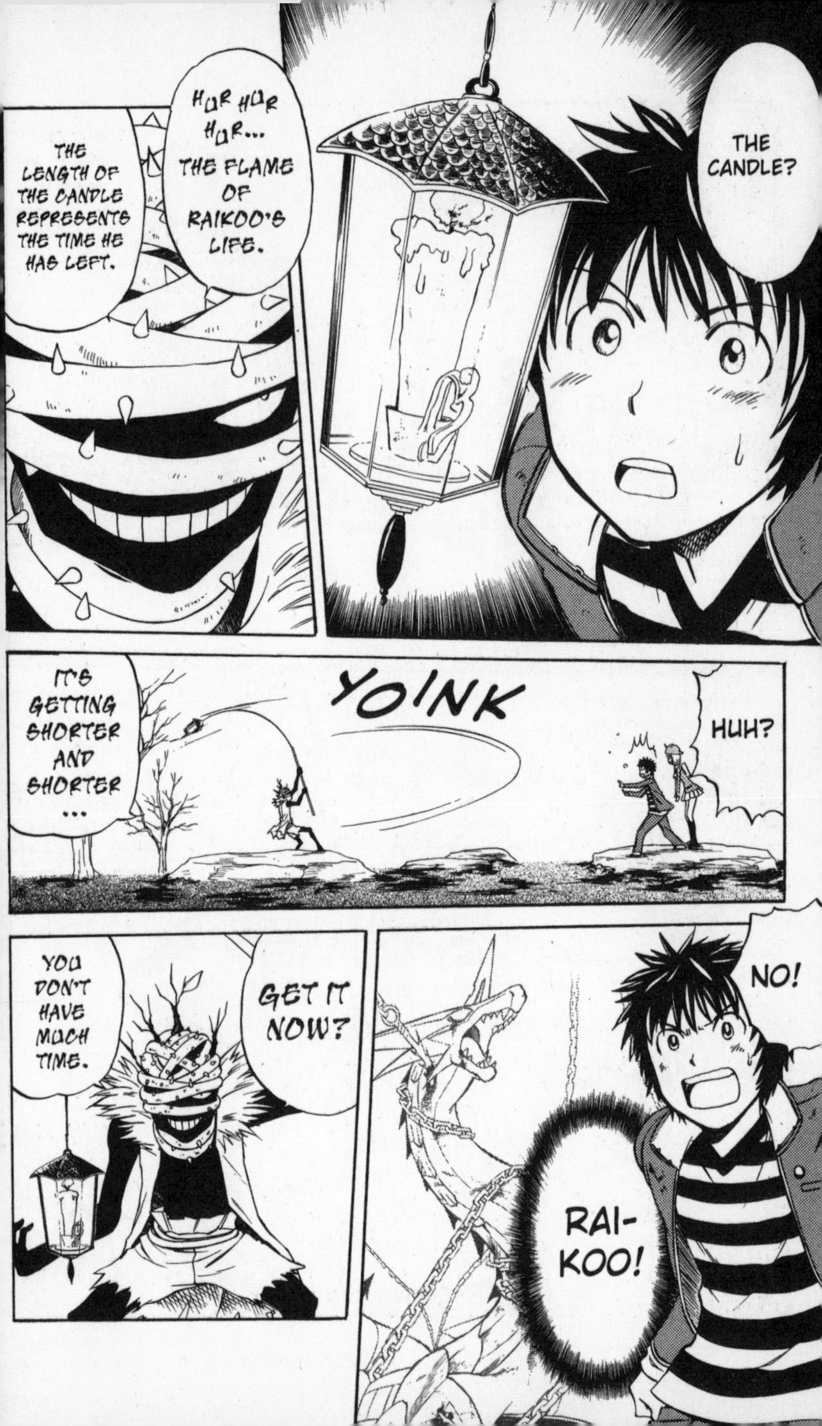
THE CANDLE?
HUR HUR HUR... THE FLAME OF RAIKOO'S LIFE.
THE LENGTH OF THE CANDLE REPRESENTS THE TIME HE HAS LEFT.
HUH?
YOINK
IT'S GETTING SHORTER AND SHORTER...
NO!
RAI-KOO!
GET IT NOW?
YOU DON'T HAVE MUCH TIME.

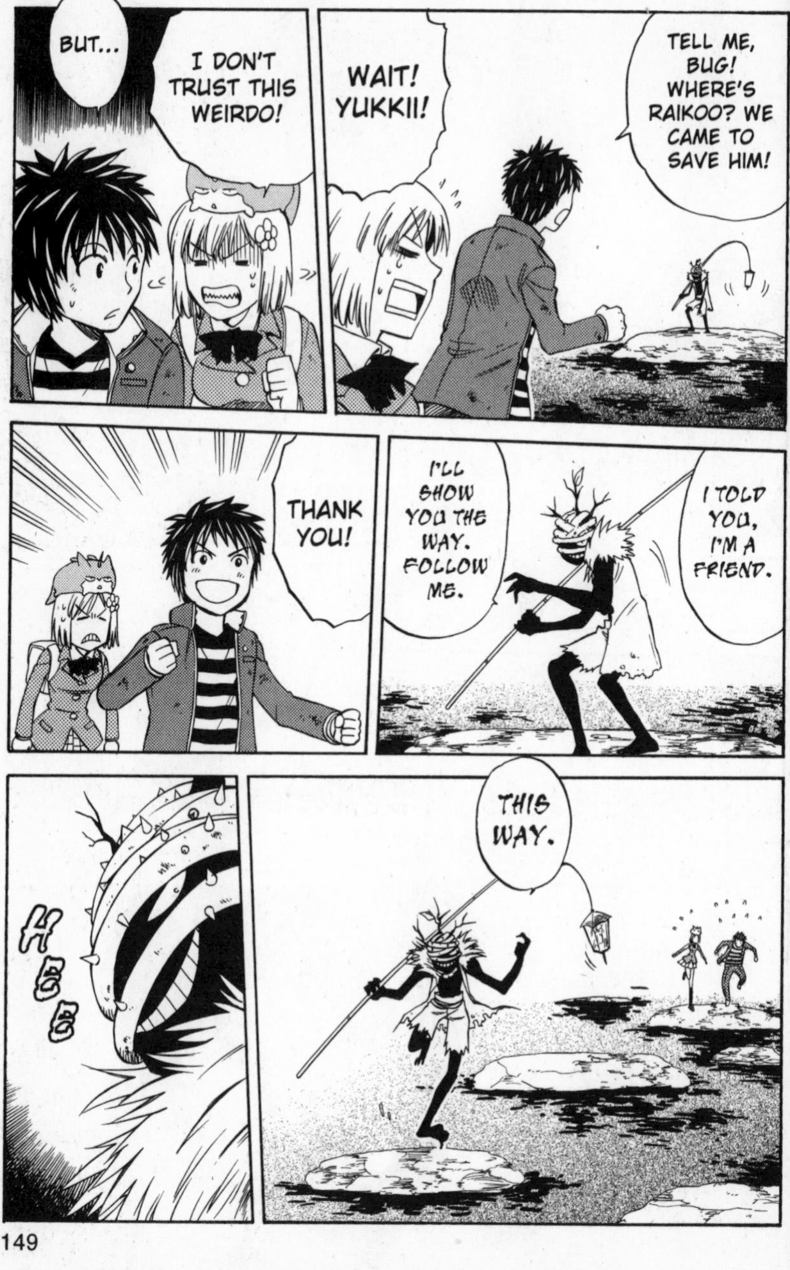
TELL ME, BUG! WHERE'S RAIKOO? WE CAME TO SAVE HIM!
WAIT! YUKKII!
I DON'T TRUST THIS WEIRDO!
BUT...
I TOLD YOU, I'M A FRIEND.
I'LL SHOW YOU THE WAY. FOLLOW ME.
THANK YOU!
THIS WAY.
HEE

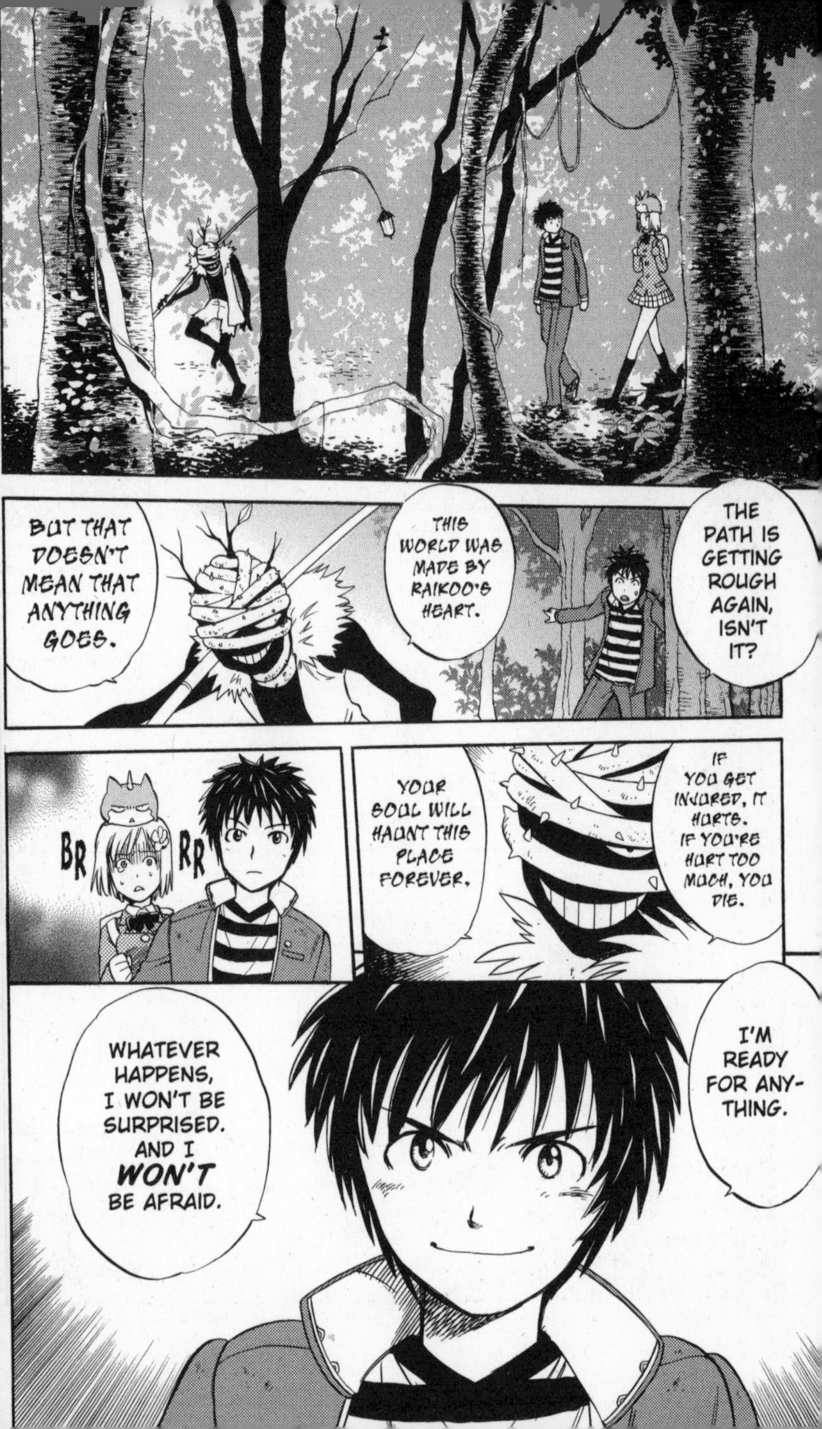
THE PATH IS GETTING ROUGH AGAIN, ISN'T IT?
THIS WORLD WAS MADE BY RAIKOO'S HEART.
BUT THAT DOESN'T MEAN THAT ANYTHING GOES.
IF YOU GET INJURED, IT HURTS. IF YOU'RE HURT TOO MUCH, YOU DIE.
YOUR SOUL WILL HAUNT THIS PLACE FOREVER.
BRRR
I'M READY FOR ANY-THING.
WHATEVER HAPPENS, I WON'T BE SURPRISED. AND I WON'T BE AFRAID.

READ THIS WAY

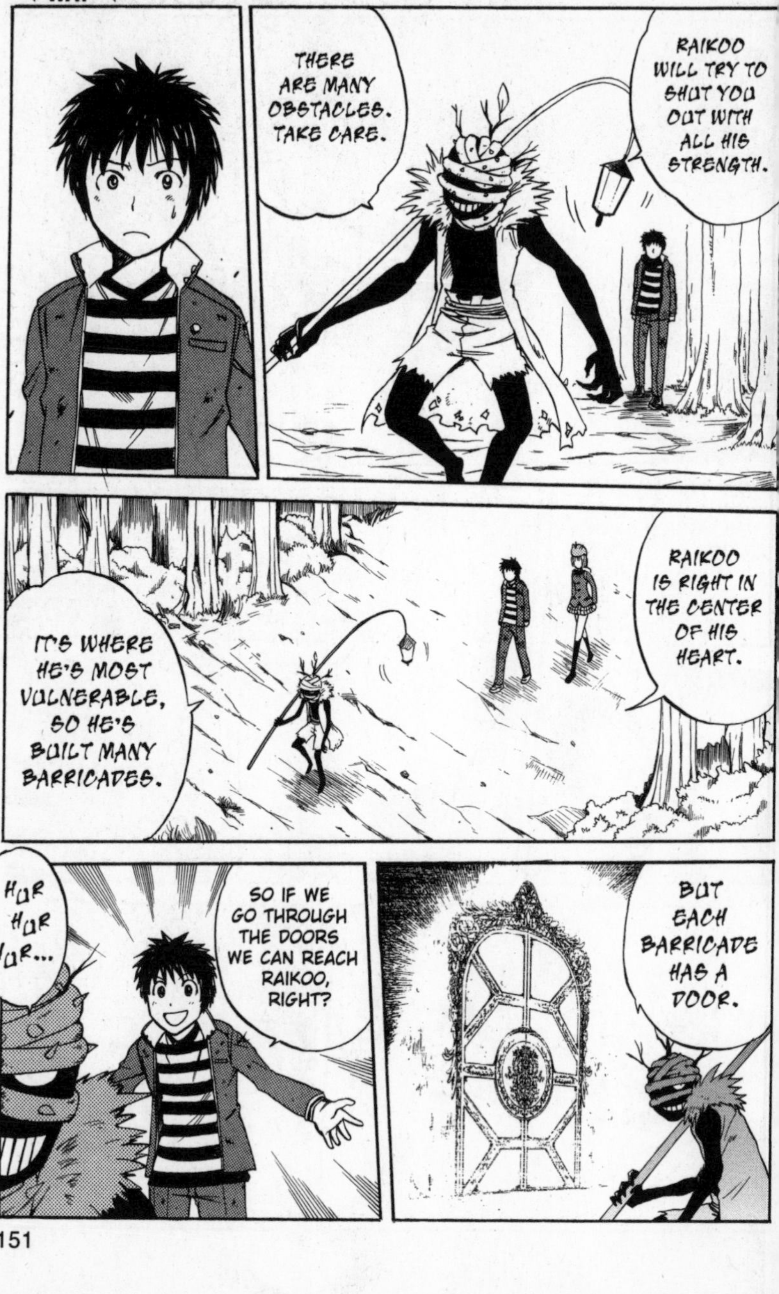
RAIKOO WILL TRY TO SHUT YOU OUT WITH ALL HIS STRENGTH.
THERE ARE MANY OBSTACLES. TAKE CARE.
RAIKOO IS RIGHT IN THE CENTER OF HIS HEART.
IT'S WHERE HE'S MOST VULNERABLE, SO HE'S BUILT MANY BARRICADES.
BUT EACH BARRICADE HAS A DOOR.
SO IF WE GO THROUGH THE DOORS WE CAN REACH RAIKOO, RIGHT?
HUR HUR HUR...

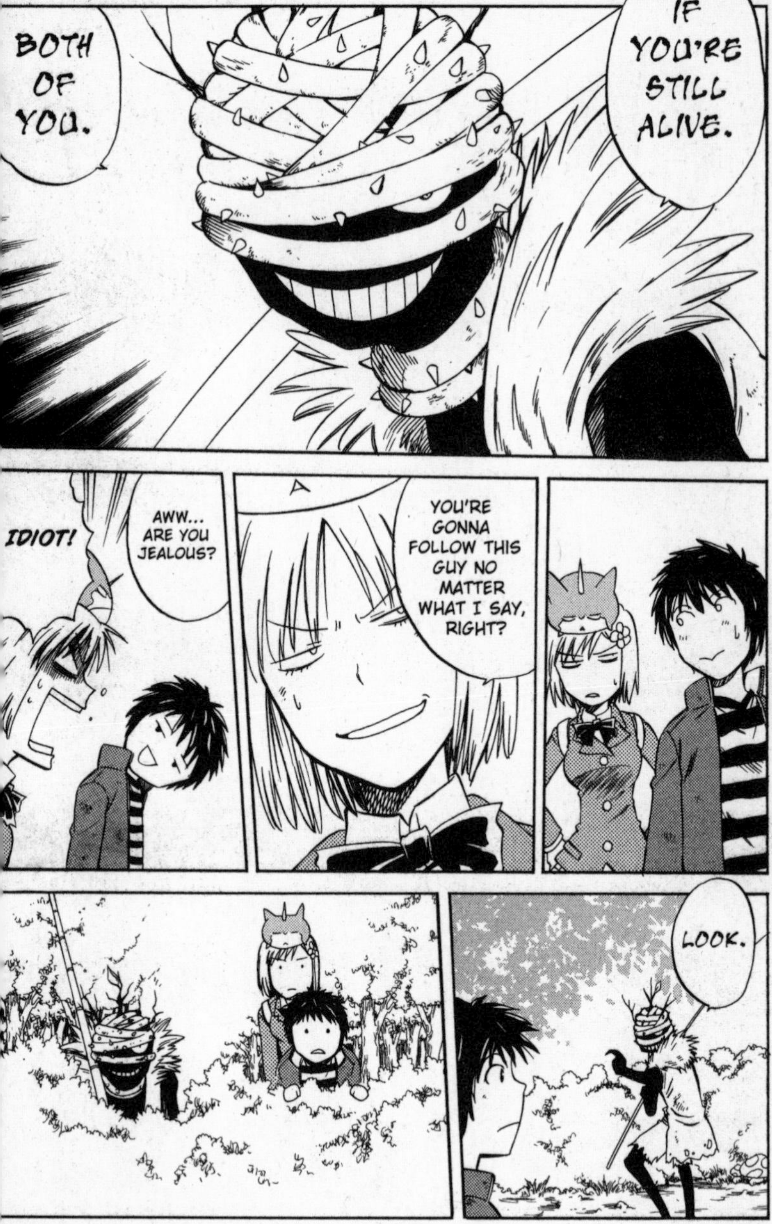
IF YOU'RE STILL ALIVE.
BOTH OF YOU.
YOU'RE GONNA FOLLOW THIS GUY NO MATTER WHAT I SAY, RIGHT?
AWW... ARE YOU JEALOUS?
IDIOT!
LOOK.

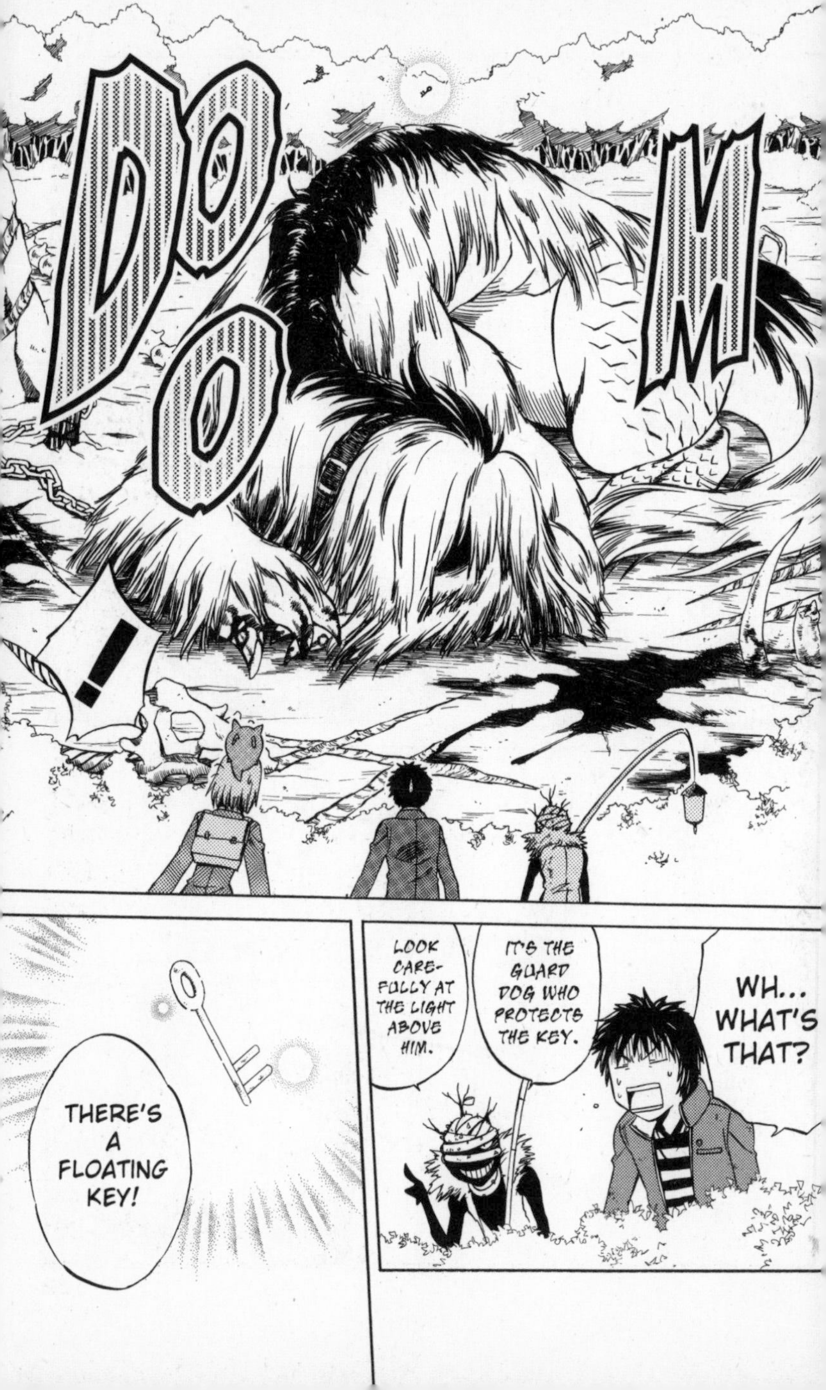
DOOM
!
WH... WHAT'S THAT?
IT'S THE GUARD DOG WHO PROTECTS THE KEY.
LOOK CAREFULLY AT THE LIGHT ABOVE HIM.
THERE'S A FLOATING KEY!

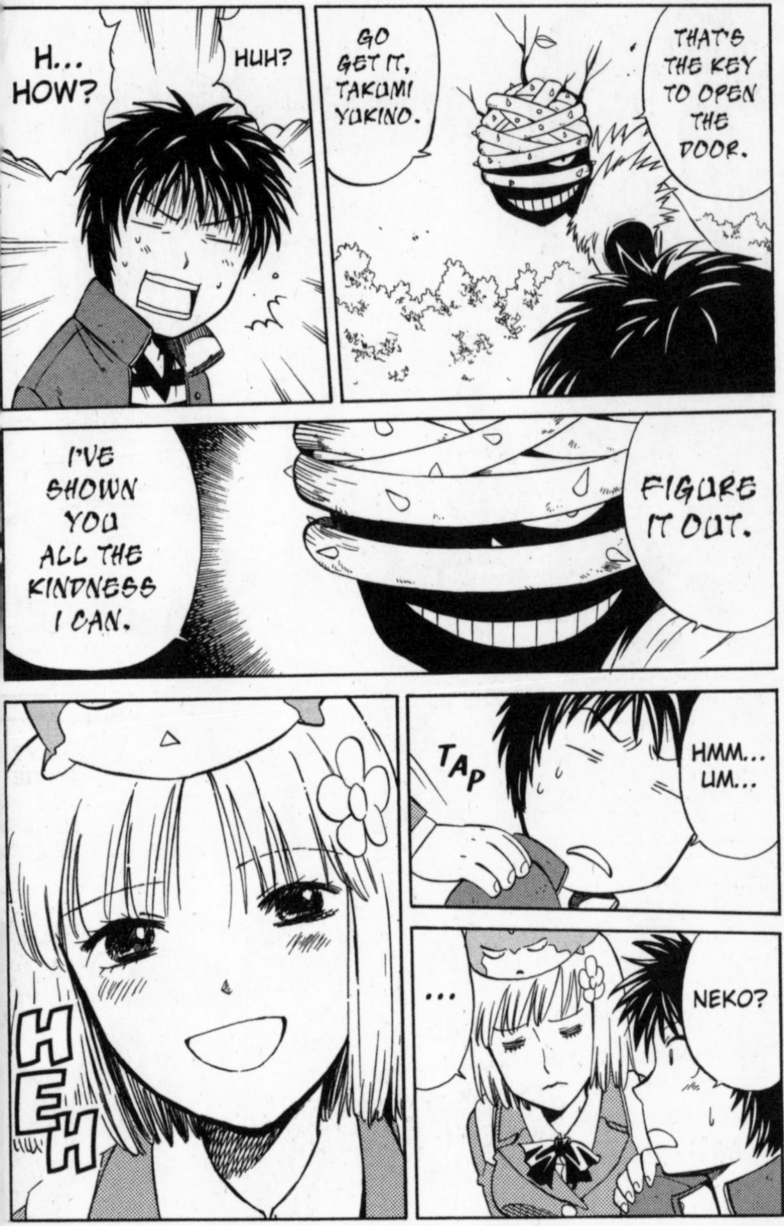
THAT'S THE KEY TO OPEN THE DOOR.
GO GET IT, TAKUMI YUKINO.
HUH?
H... HOW?
FIGURE IT OUT.
I'VE SHOWN YOU ALL THE KINDNESS I CAN.
HMM... UM...
TAP
NEKO?
...
HEH

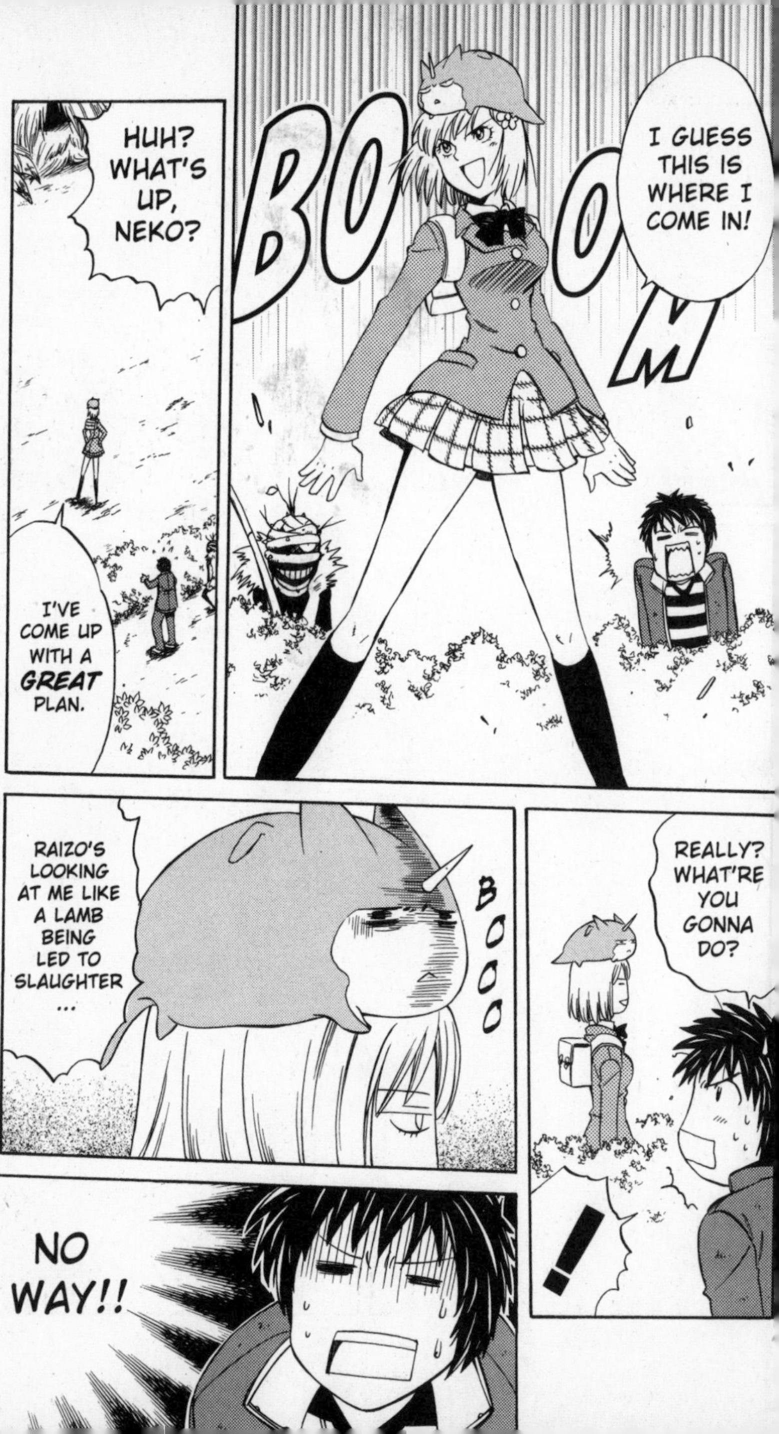
I GUESS THIS IS WHERE I COME IN!
BOOOM
HUH? WHAT'S UP, NEKO?
I'VE COME UP WITH A **GREAT** PLAN.
REALLY? WHAT'RE YOU GONNA DO?
!
RAIZO'S LOOKING AT ME LIKE A LAMB BEING LED TO SLAUGHTER...
BOOO
NO WAY!!

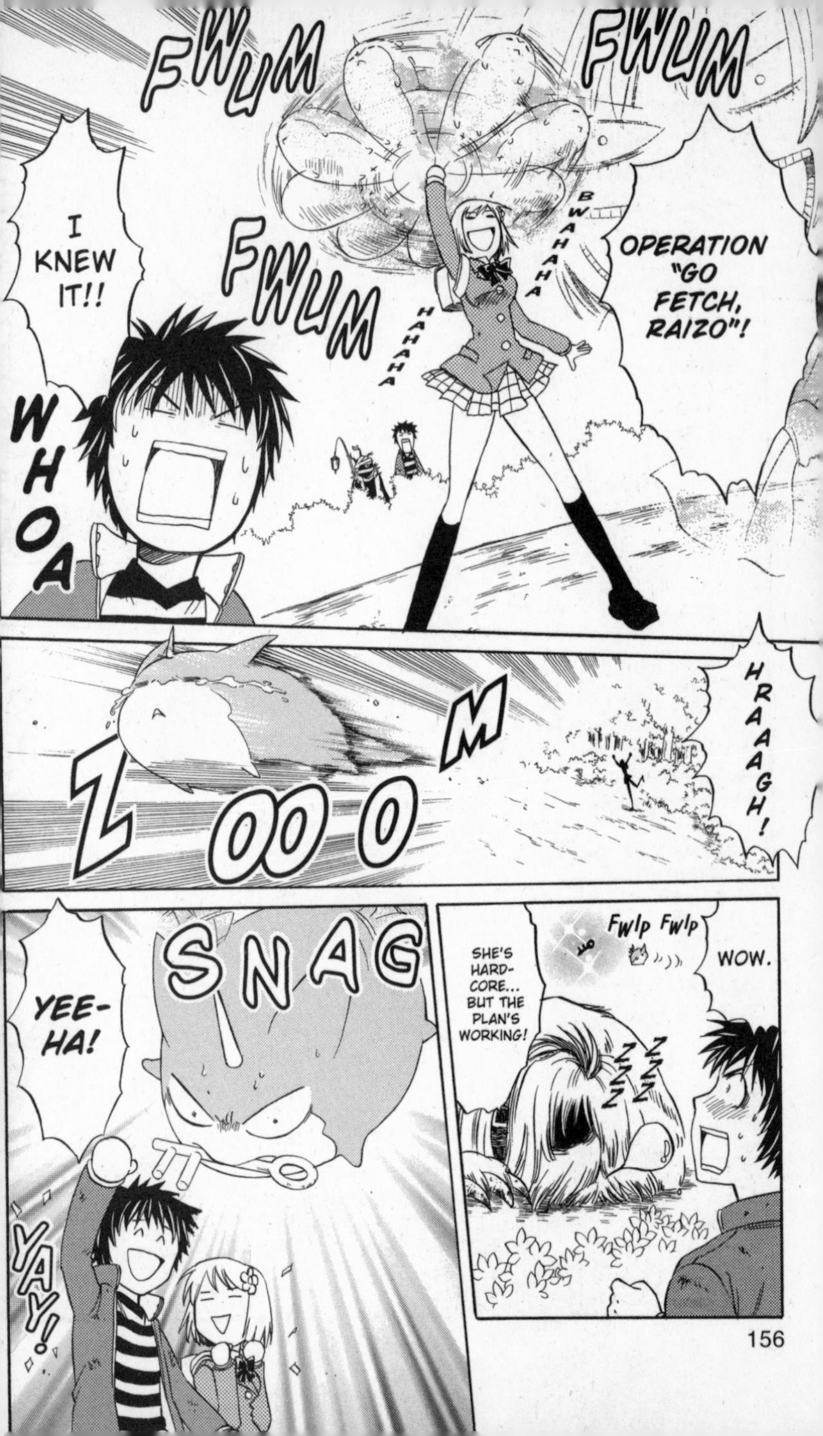
FWUM
FWUM
OPERATION "GO FETCH, RAIZO"!
BWAHAHA
HAHAHA
FWUM
I KNEW IT!!
WHOA
HRAAAGH!
ZOOOM
WOW.
Fwlp Fwlp
SHE'S HARD-CORE... BUT THE PLAN'S WORKING!
ZZZ
ZZZ
SNAG
YEE-HA!
YAY!

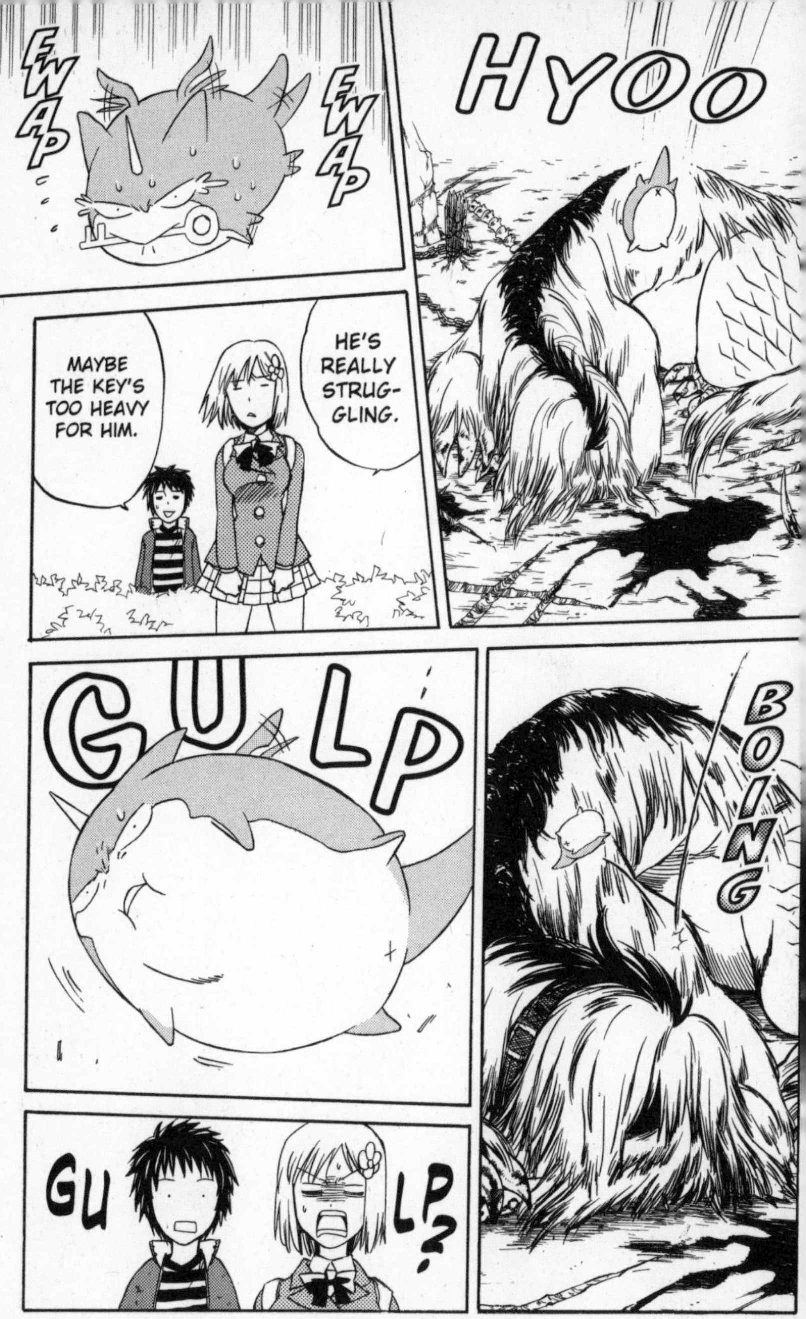
HYOO
FWAP
FWAP
HE'S REALLY STRUG-GLING.
MAYBE THE KEY'S TOO HEAVY FOR HIM.
BOING
GULP
GU LP?

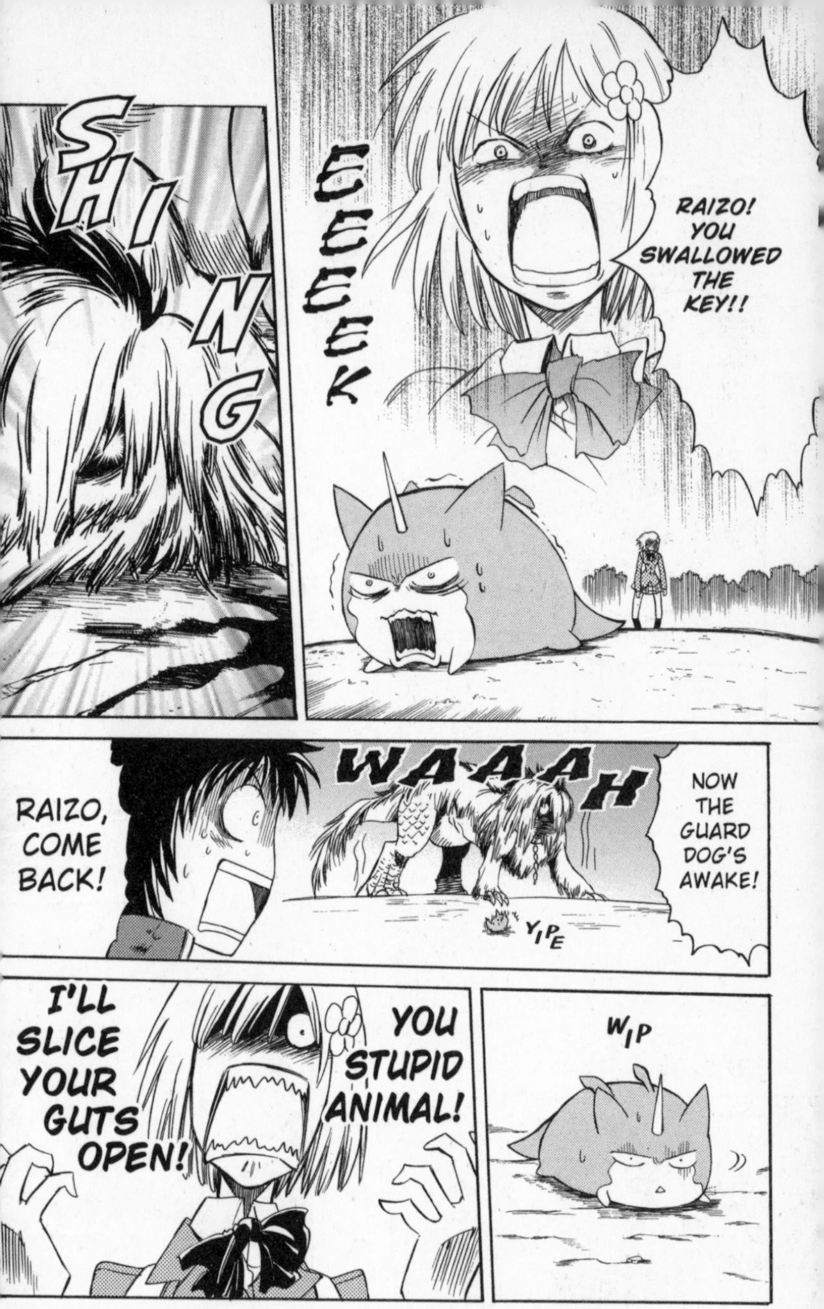
RAIZO! YOU SWALLOWED THE KEY!!
EEEEEK
SHING
NOW THE GUARD DOG'S AWAKE!
WAAAH
YIPE
RAIZO, COME BACK!
WIP
YOU STUPID ANIMAL!
I'LL SLICE YOUR GUTS OPEN!

READ THIS WAY

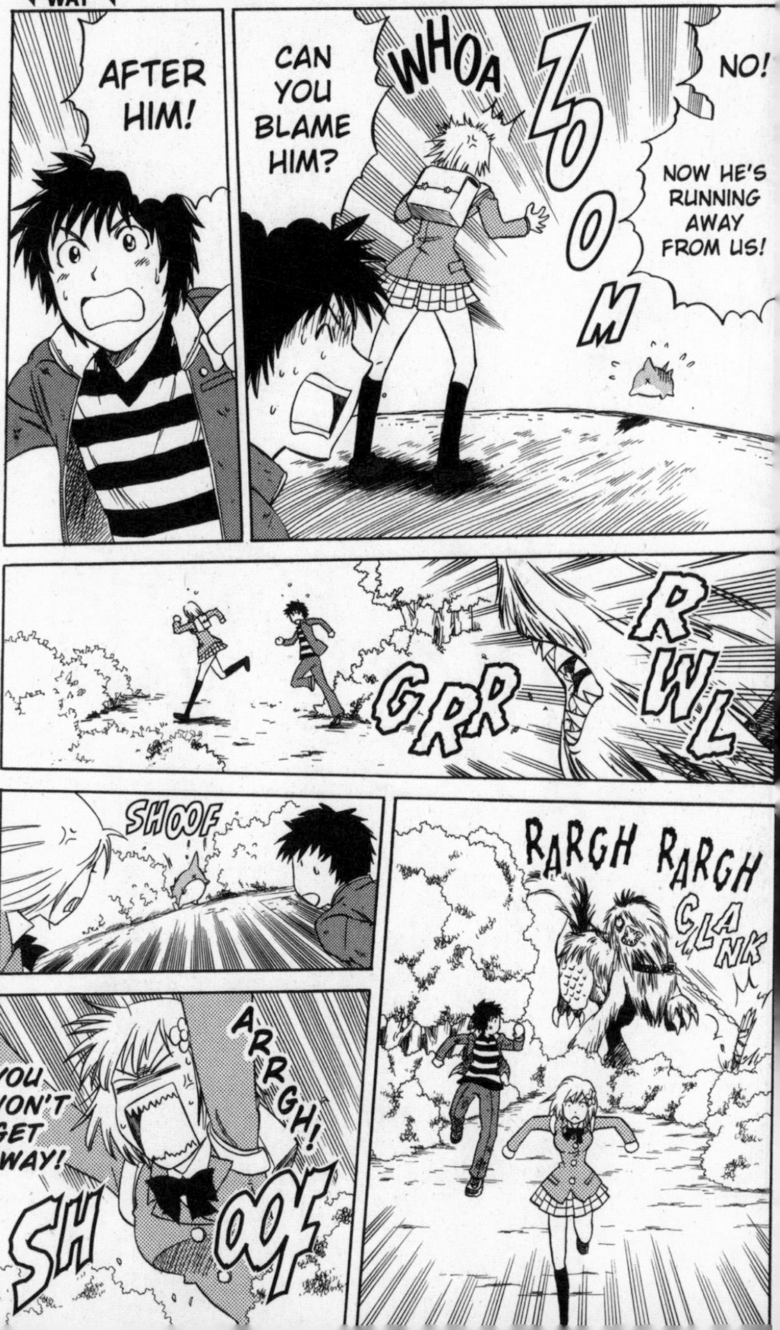
NO!
NOW HE'S RUNNING AWAY FROM US!
WHOA
ZOOM
CAN YOU BLAME HIM?
AFTER HIM!
RWL
GRR
RARGH RARGH
CLANK
SHOOF
ARRGH!
YOU WON'T GET AWAY!
SHOOF

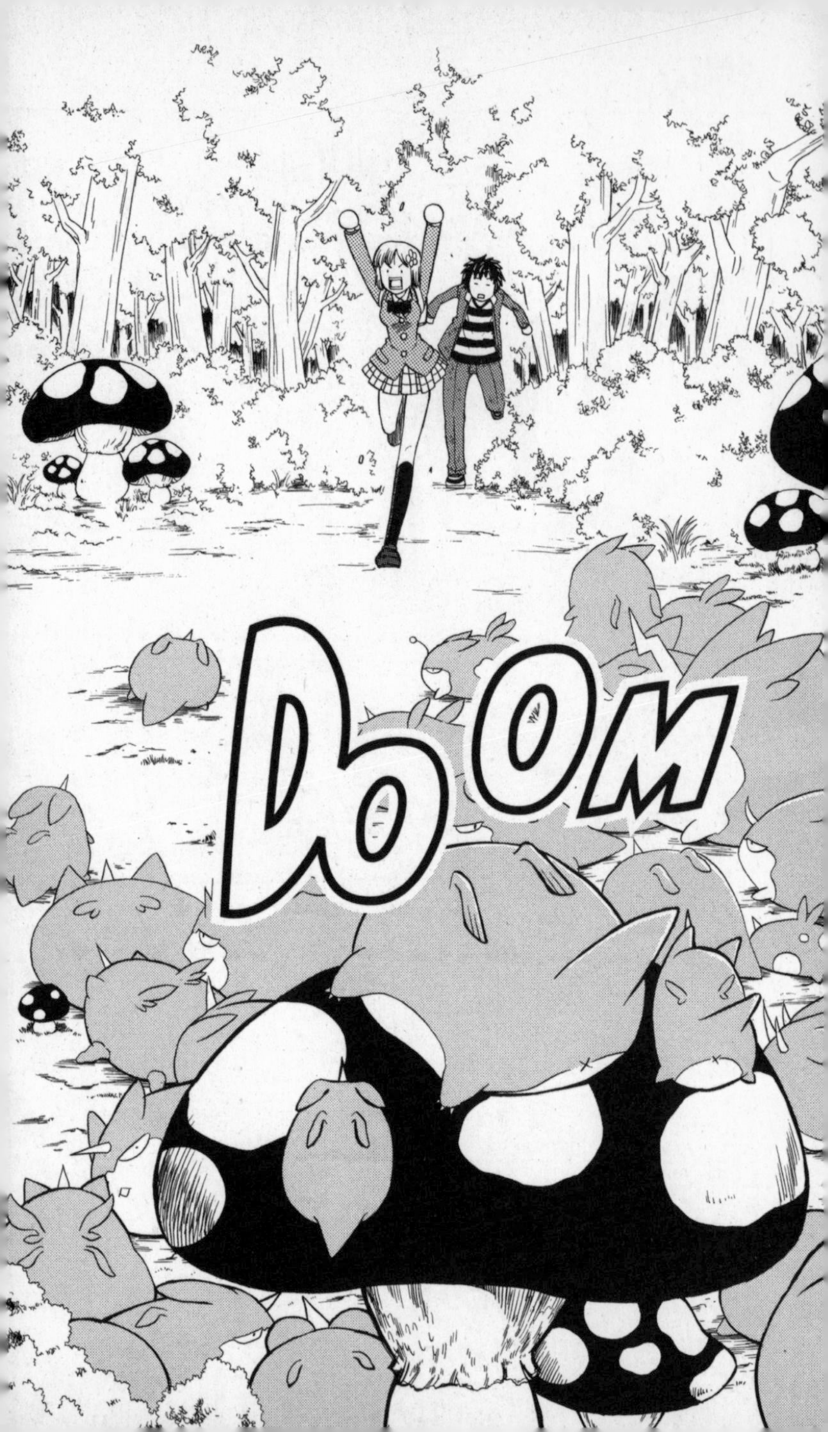
DOOM

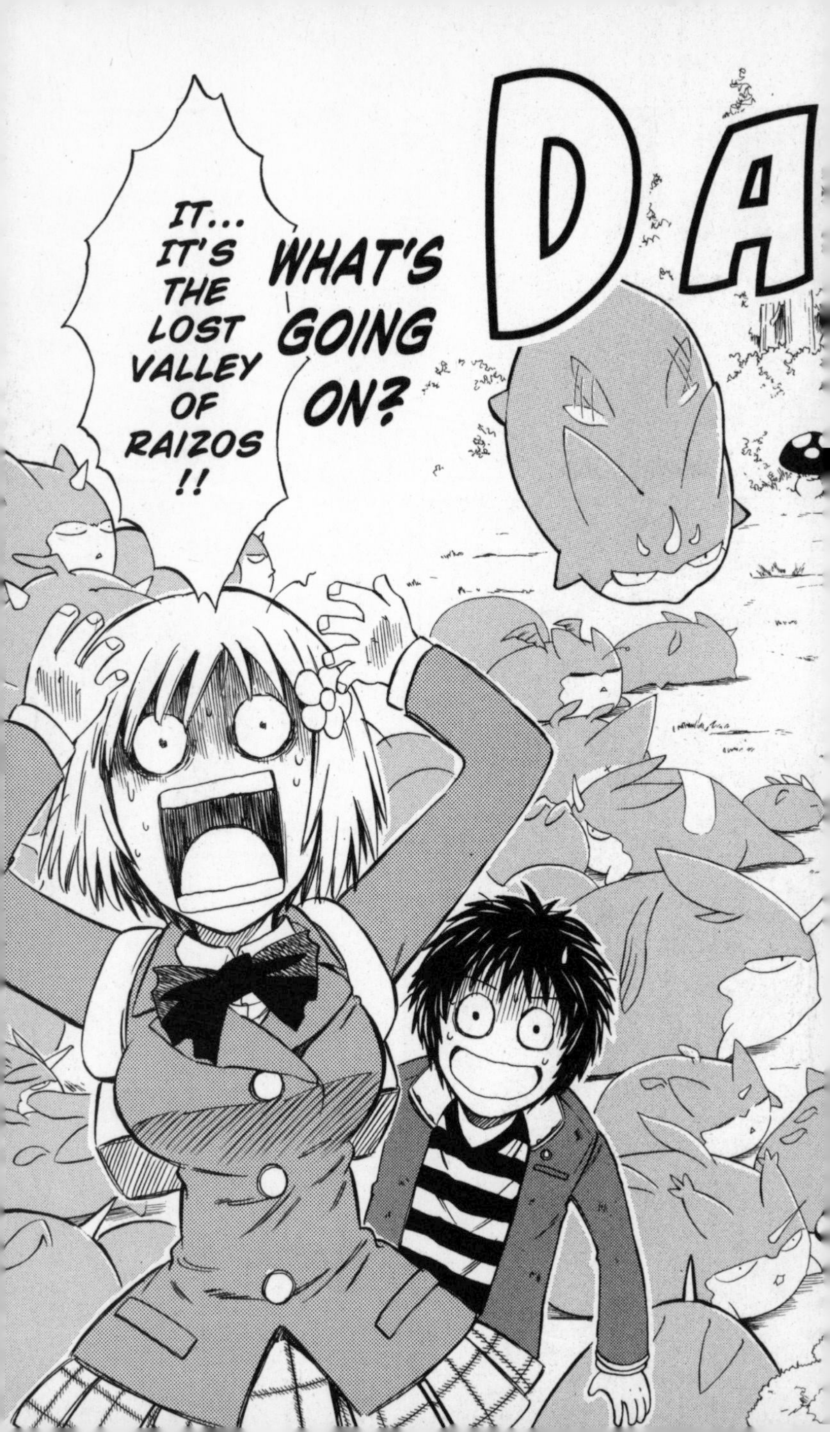
DA
WHAT'S GOING ON?
IT... IT'S THE LOST VALLEY OF RAIZOS!!

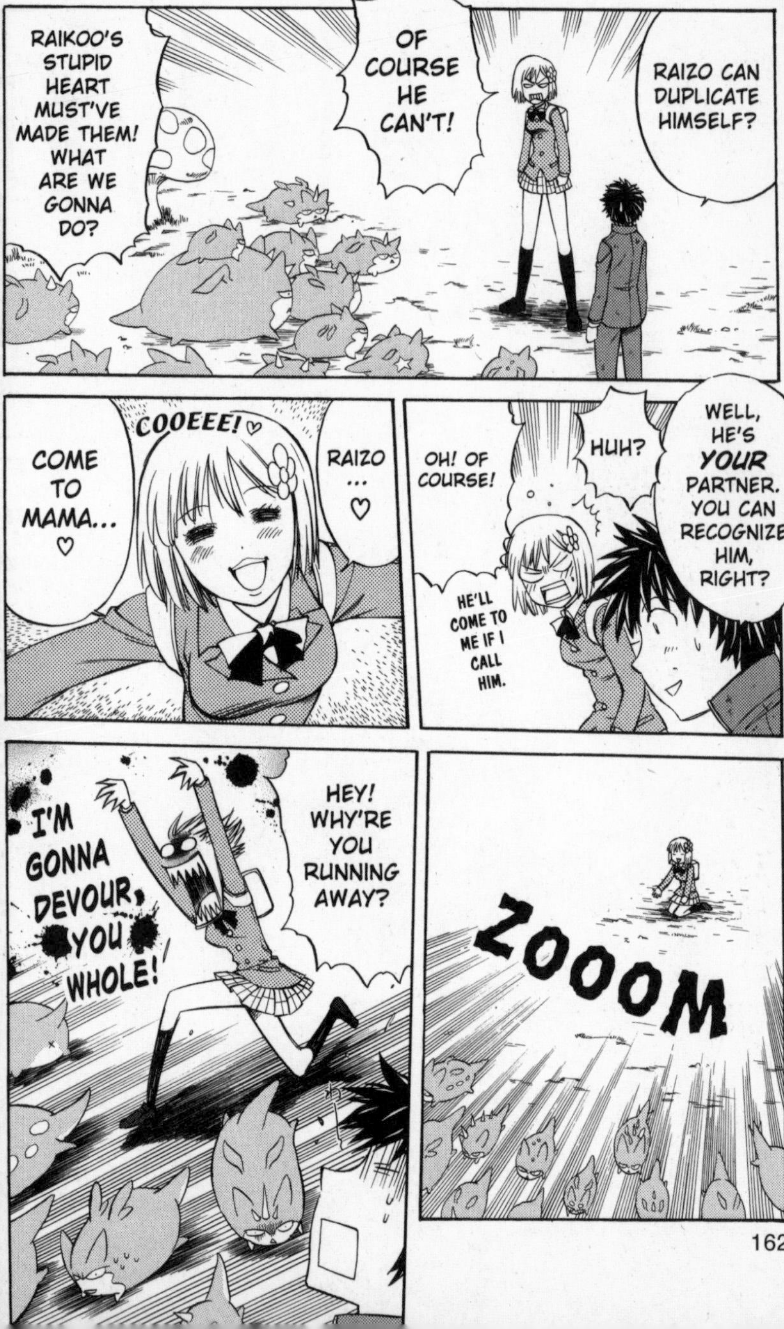
RAIZO CAN DUPLICATE HIMSELF?
OF COURSE HE CAN'T!
RAIKOO'S STUPID HEART MUST'VE MADE THEM! WHAT ARE WE GONNA DO?
WELL, HE'S YOUR PARTNER. YOU CAN RECOGNIZE HIM, RIGHT?
HUH?
OH! OF COURSE!
HE'LL COME TO ME IF I CALL HIM.
RAIZO ... ♡
COOEEE! ♡
COME TO MAMA... ♡
ZOOOM
HEY! WHY'RE YOU RUNNING AWAY?
I'M GONNA DEVOUR YOU WHOLE!

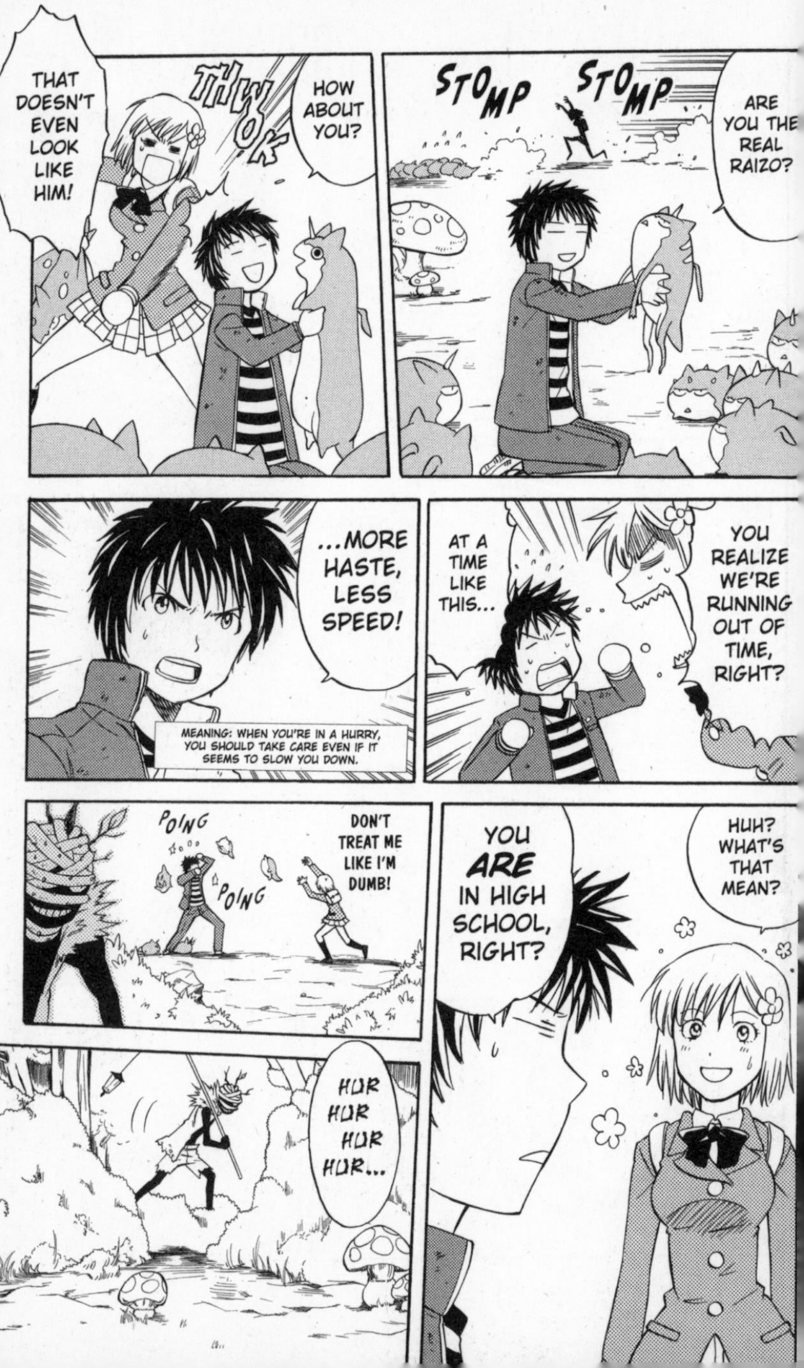
STOMP STOMP
ARE YOU THE REAL RAIZO?
HOW ABOUT YOU?
THWOK
THAT DOESN'T EVEN LOOK LIKE HIM!
YOU REALIZE WE'RE RUNNING OUT OF TIME, RIGHT?
AT A TIME LIKE THIS...
...MORE HASTE, LESS SPEED!
MEANING: WHEN YOU'RE IN A HURRY, YOU SHOULD TAKE CARE EVEN IF IT SEEMS TO SLOW YOU DOWN.
HUH? WHAT'S THAT MEAN?
YOU ARE IN HIGH SCHOOL, RIGHT?
DON'T TREAT ME LIKE I'M DUMB!
POING
POING
HUR HUR HUR HUR...

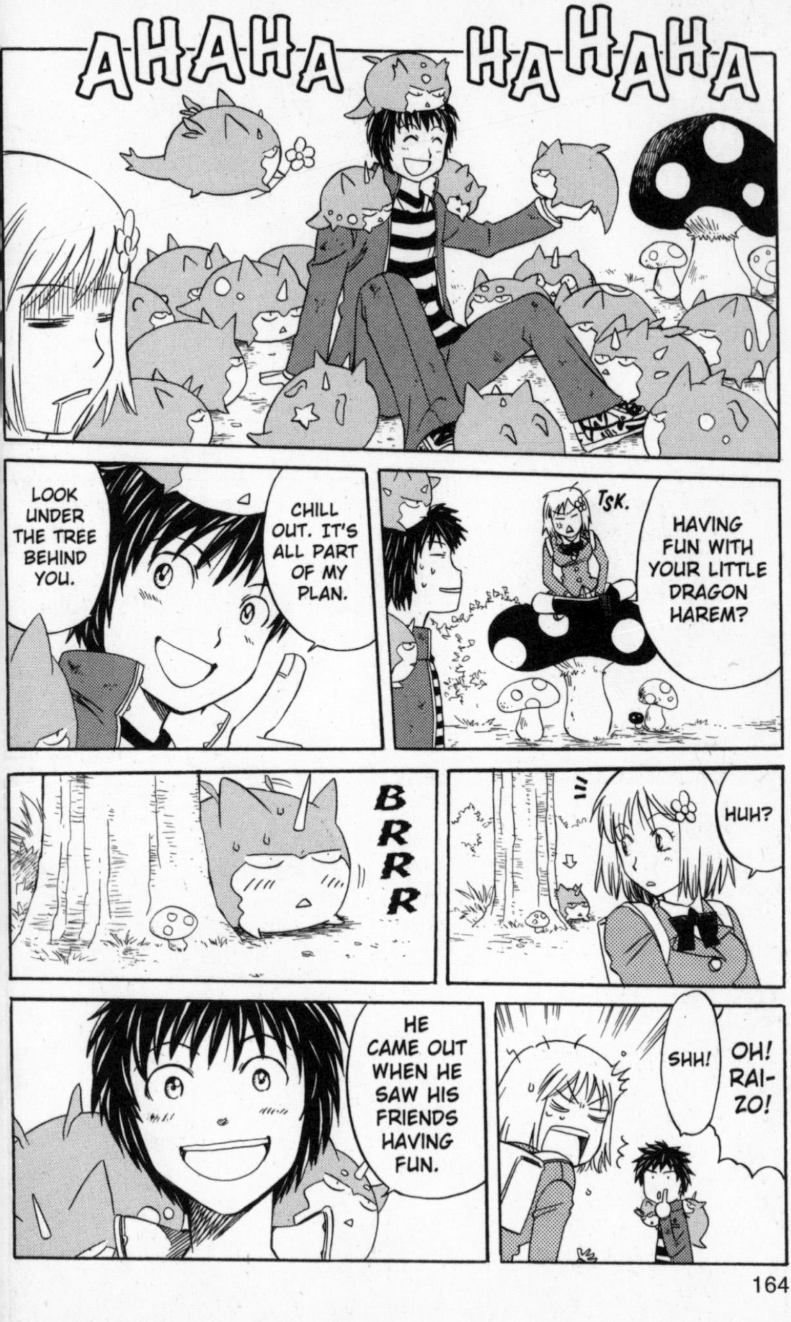
AHAHA HAHAHA
HAVING FUN WITH YOUR LITTLE DRAGON HAREM?
TSK.
CHILL OUT. IT'S ALL PART OF MY PLAN.
LOOK UNDER THE TREE BEHIND YOU.
HUH?
BRRR
OH! RAI-ZO!
SHH!
HE CAME OUT WHEN HE SAW HIS FRIENDS HAVING FUN.

READ THIS WAY

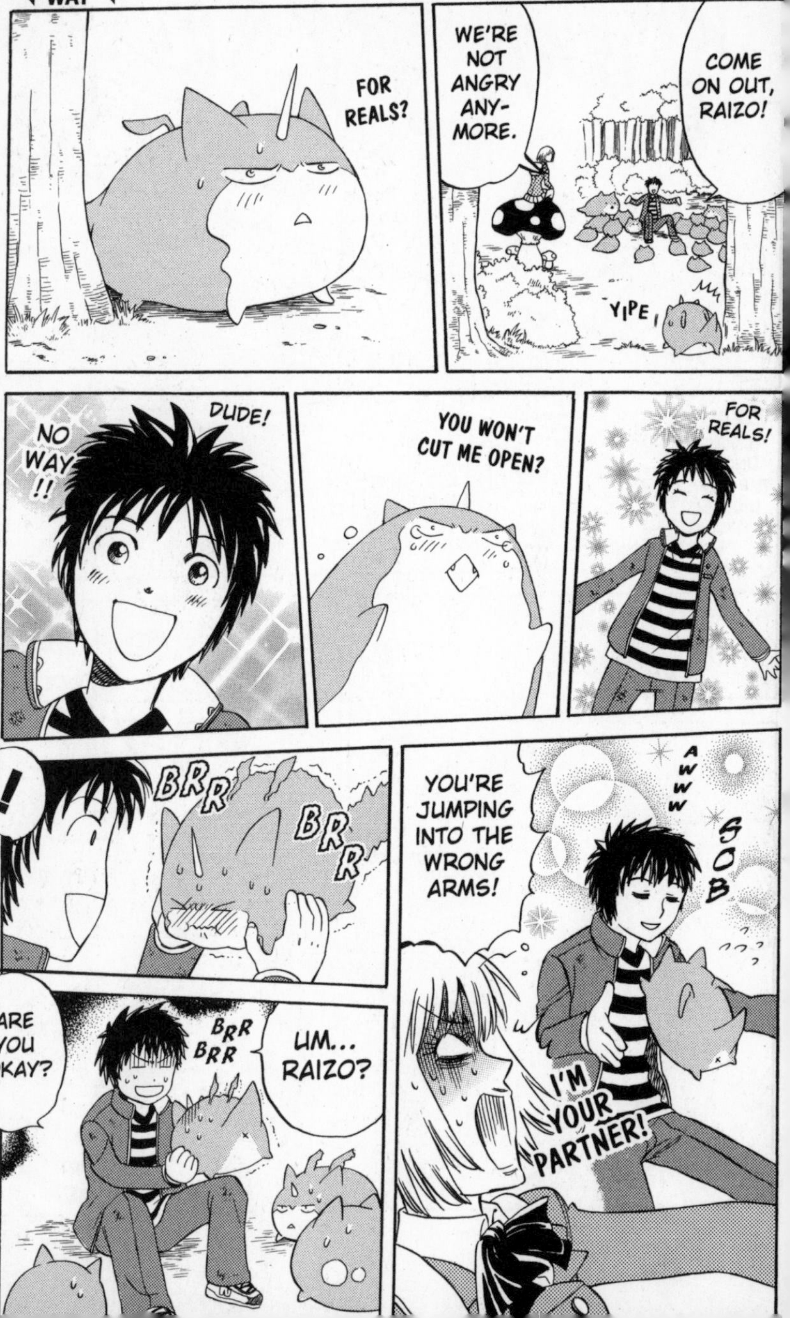
COME ON OUT, RAIZO!
WE'RE NOT ANGRY ANYMORE.
YIPE
FOR REALS?
FOR REALS!
YOU WON'T CUT ME OPEN?
DUDE!
NO WAY!!
AWWW
SOB
YOU'RE JUMPING INTO THE WRONG ARMS!
I'M YOUR PARTNER!
BRRR
BRR
!
UM... RAIZO?
BRR
BRR
ARE YOU OKAY?

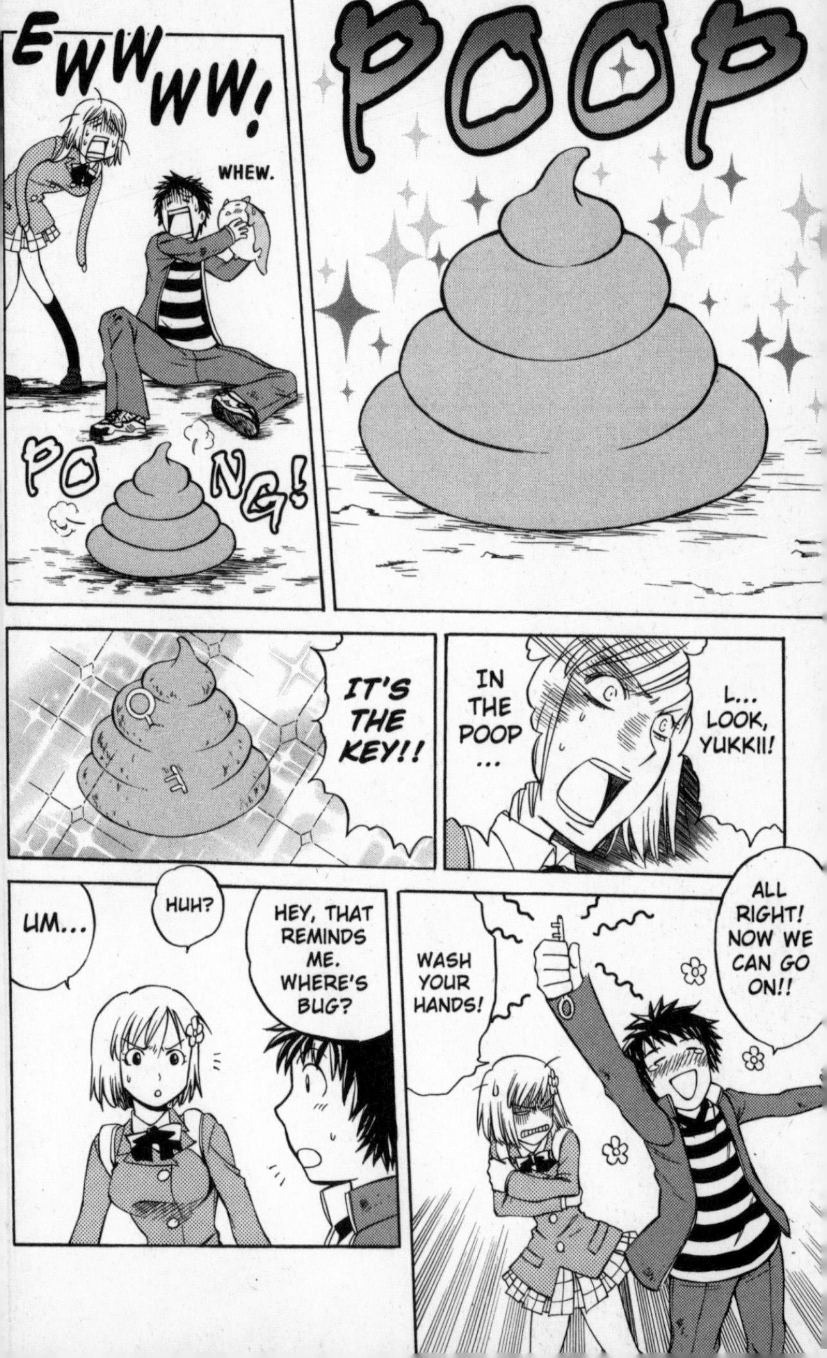
POOP
EWWWWW!
WHEW.
PONG!
L... LOOK, YUKKII!
IN THE POOP ...
IT'S THE KEY!!
ALL RIGHT! NOW WE CAN GO ON!!
WASH YOUR HANDS!
HEY, THAT REMINDS ME. WHERE'S BUG?
HUH?
UM...

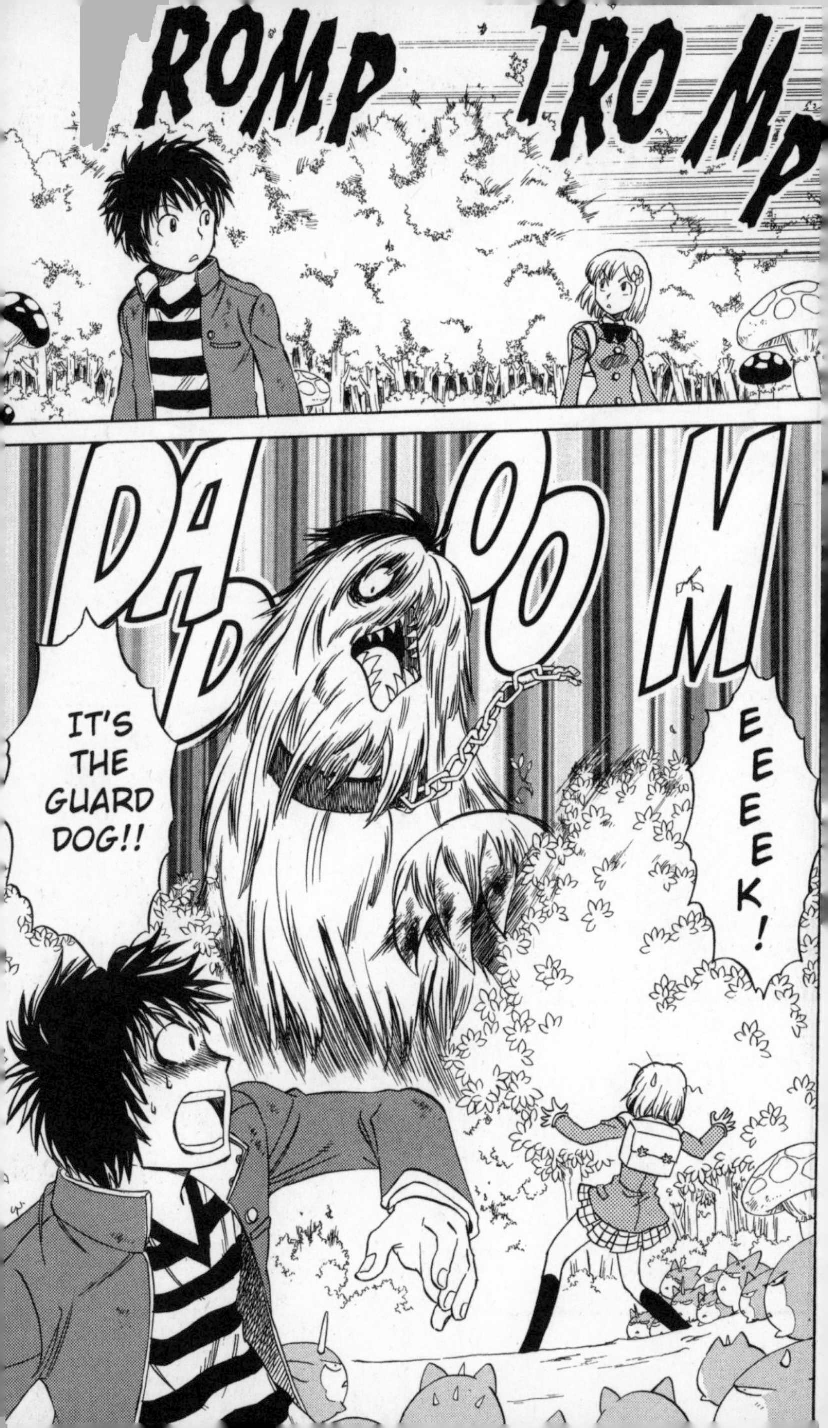
ROMP TRO MP
DADOOM
EEEEK!
IT'S THE GUARD DOG!!

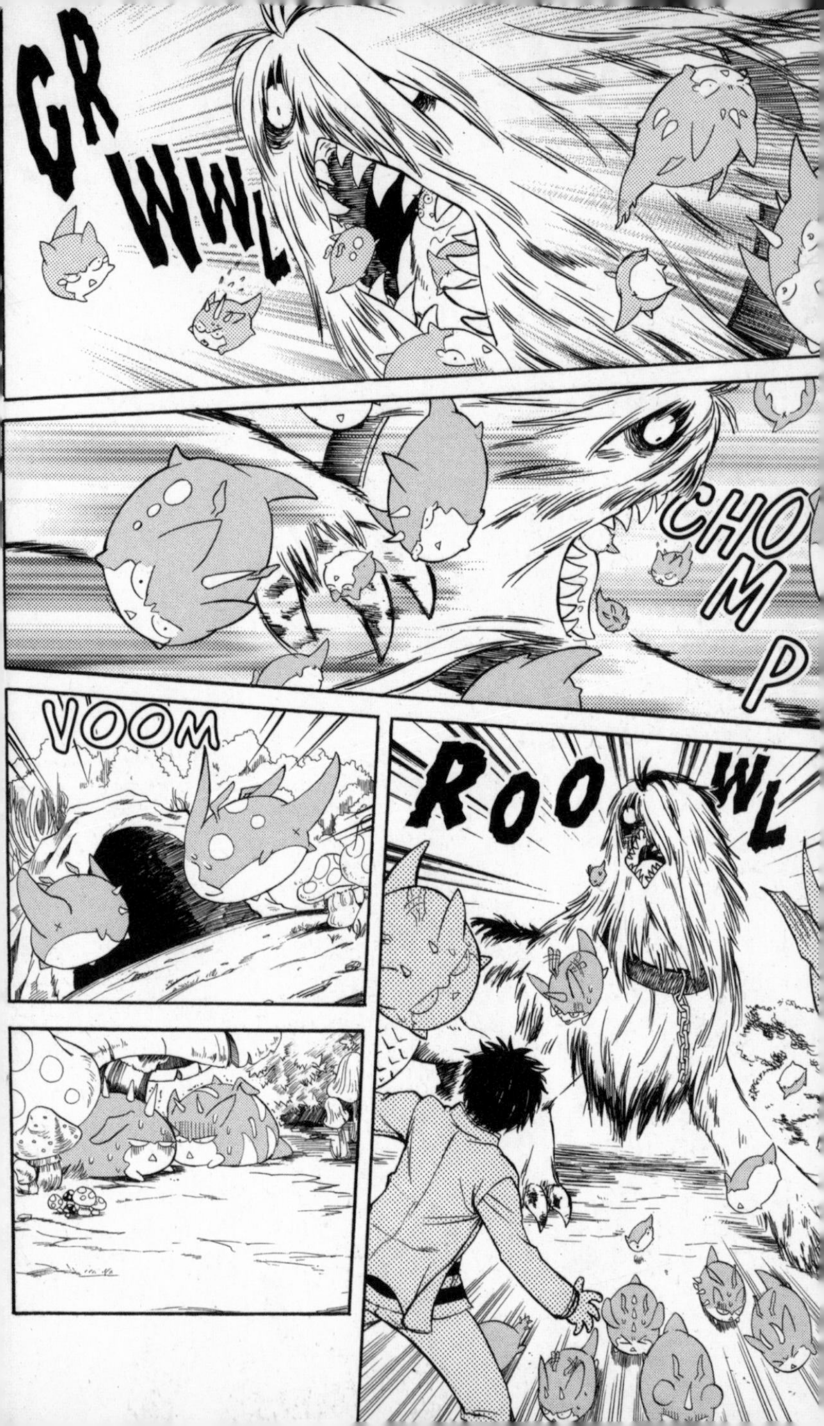
GRWWL
CHOMP
ROOWL
VOOM

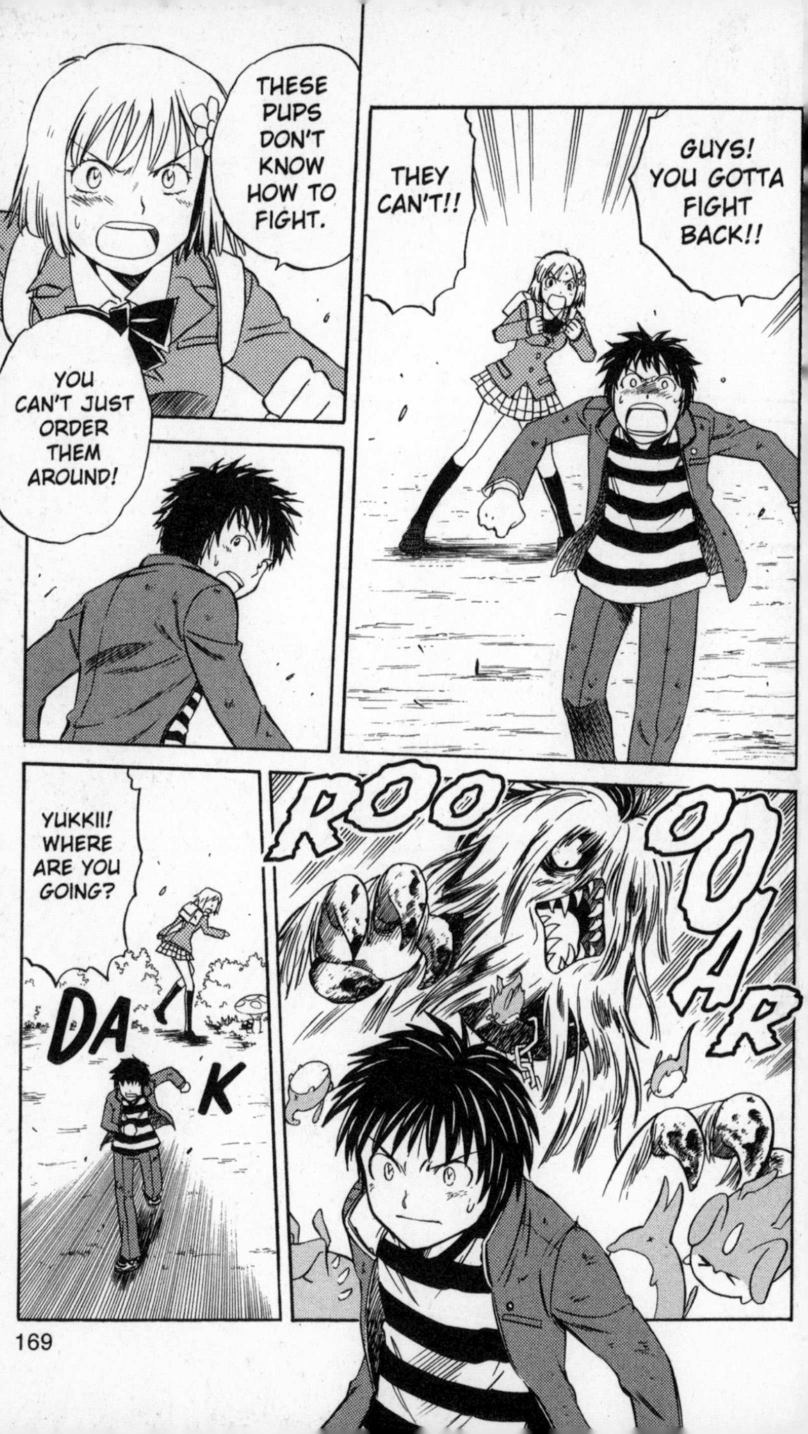
GUYS! YOU GOTTA FIGHT BACK!!
THEY CAN'T!!
THESE PUPS DON'T KNOW HOW TO FIGHT.
YOU CAN'T JUST ORDER THEM AROUND!
ROOOOAR
YUKKII! WHERE ARE YOU GOING?
DAK

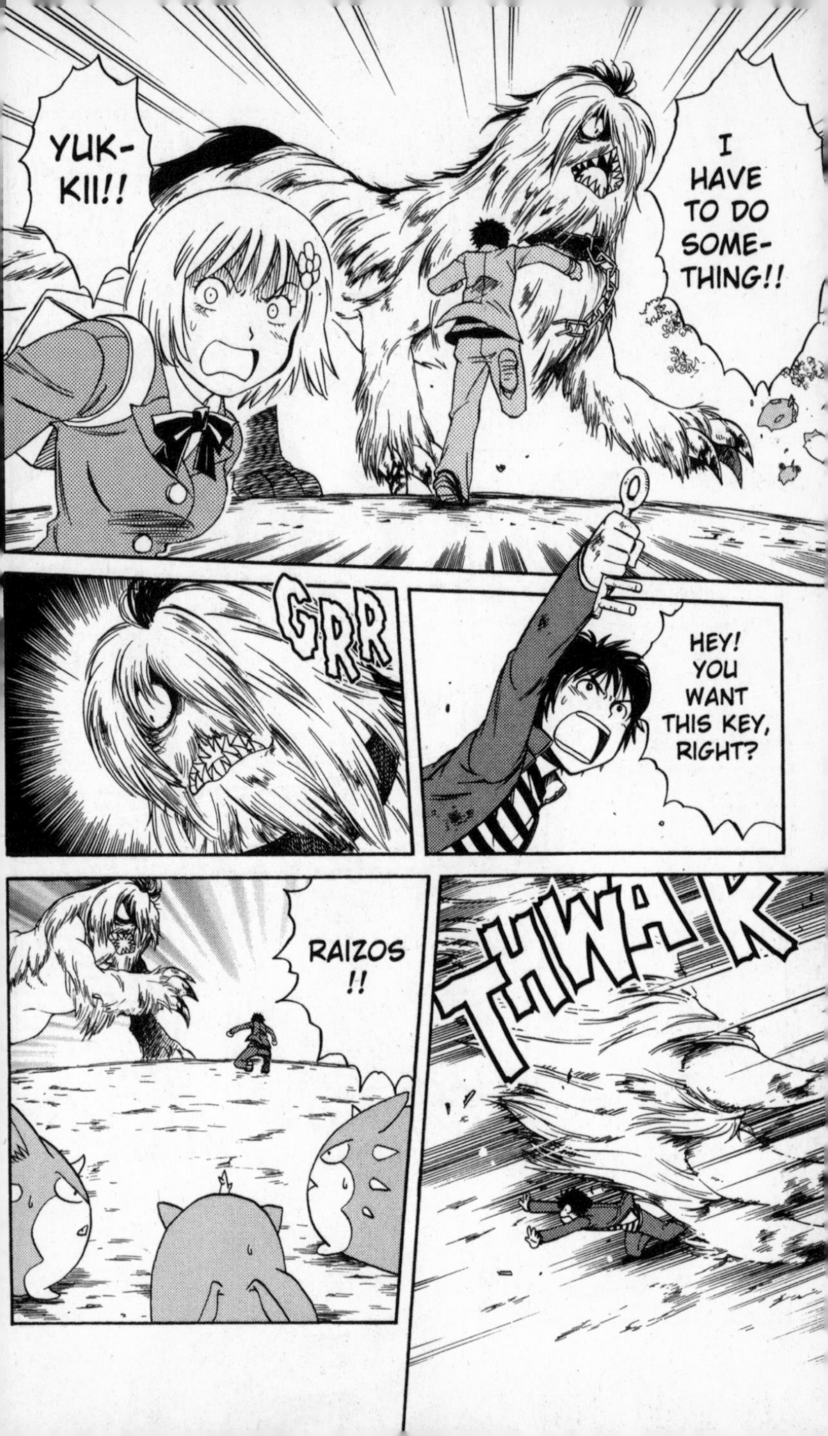
I HAVE TO DO SOME-THING!!
YUK-KII!!
HEY! YOU WANT THIS KEY, RIGHT?
GRR
THWAK
RAIZOS!!

READ THIS WAY

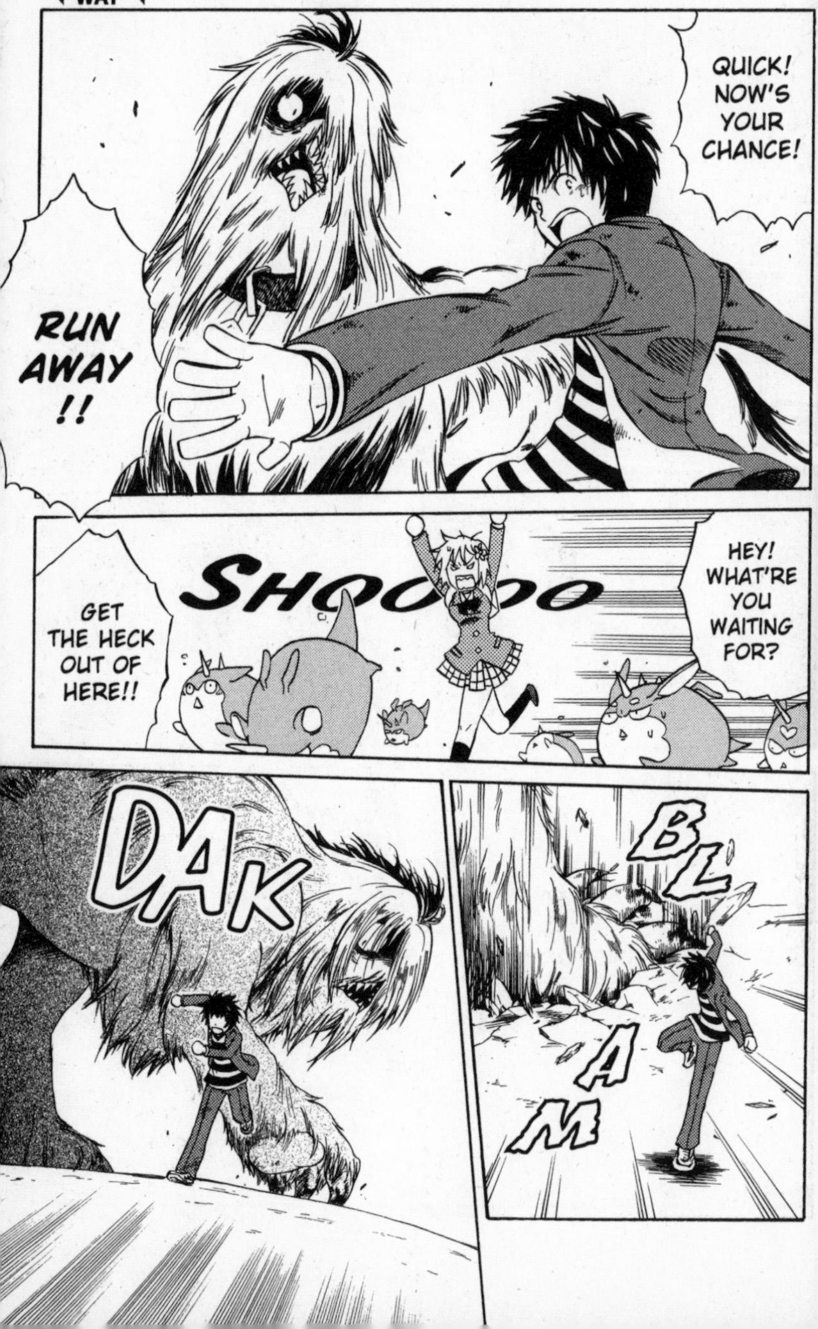
QUICK! NOW'S YOUR CHANCE!
RUN AWAY!!
HEY! WHAT'RE YOU WAITING FOR?
SHOOOO
GET THE HECK OUT OF HERE!!
BLAM
DAK

GRAB
YUK-KII !!
WHUM
QUICK! GET AWAY !!
WHUM
THWAK
WAAH!

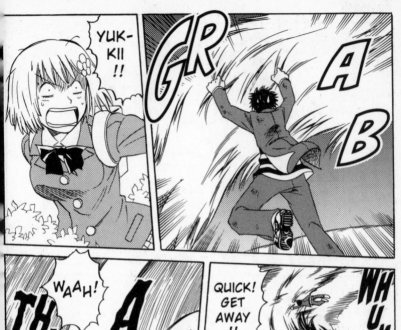

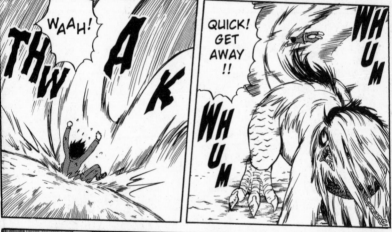

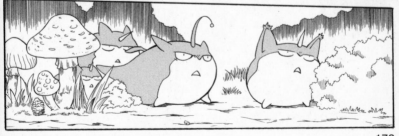

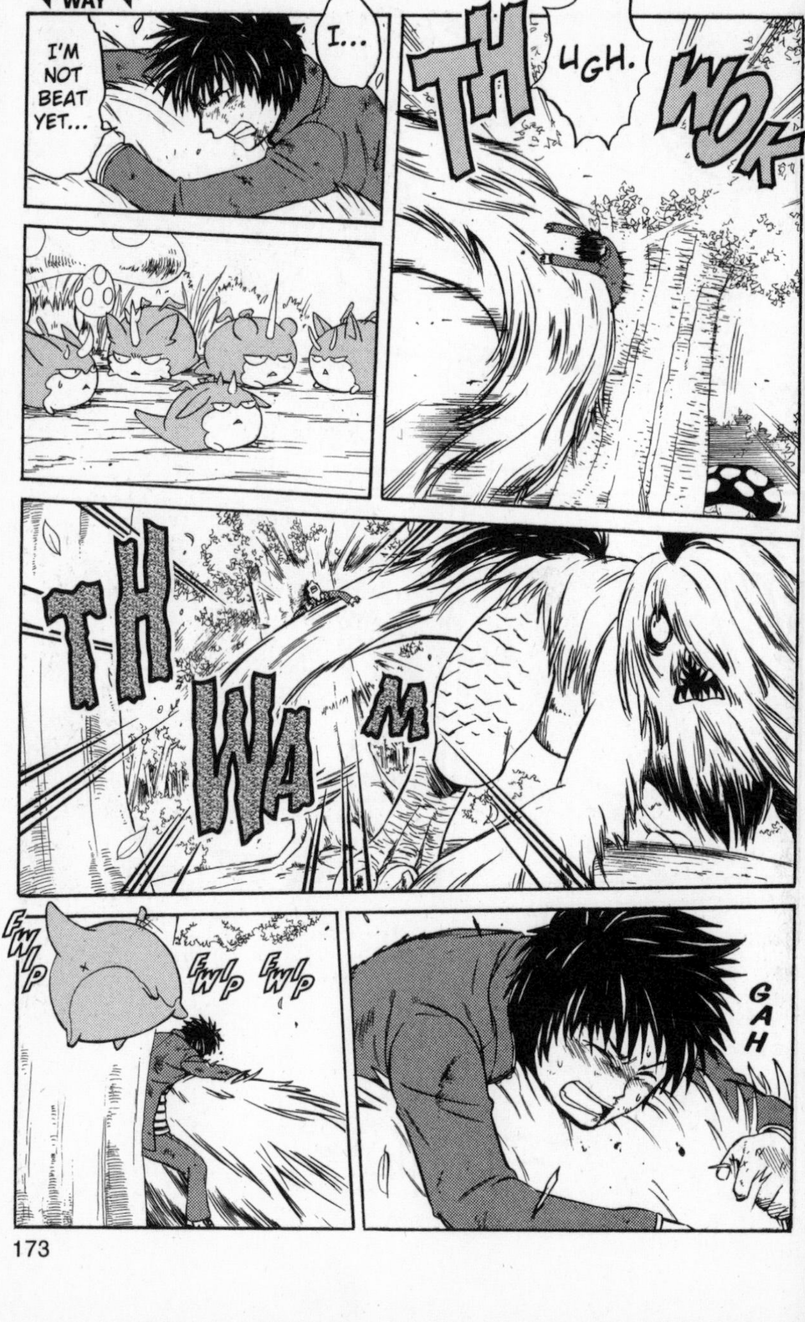
THWOK
UGH.
I...
I'M NOT BEAT YET...
THWAM
GAH
FWIP FWIP FWIP

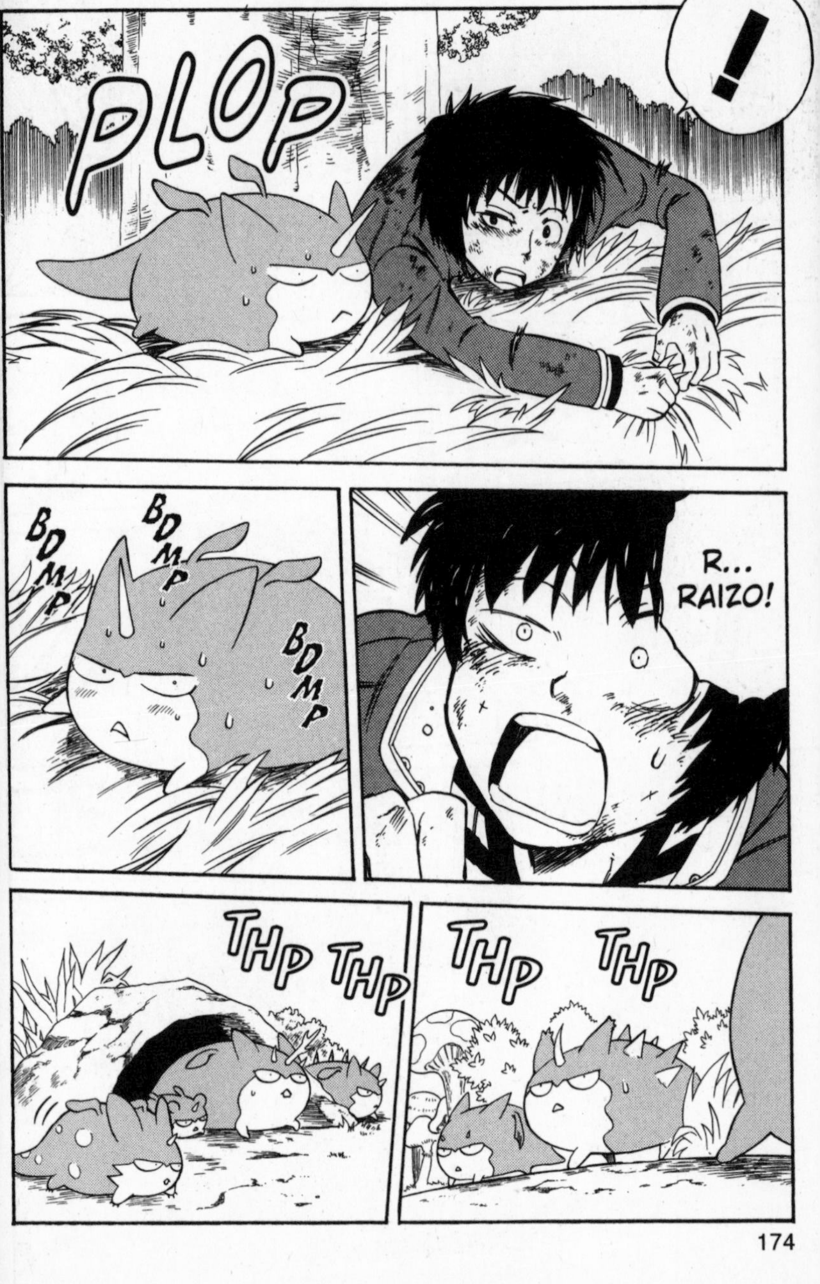

!
PLOP
R... RAIZO!
BOMP BOMP BOMP
THP THP
THP THP

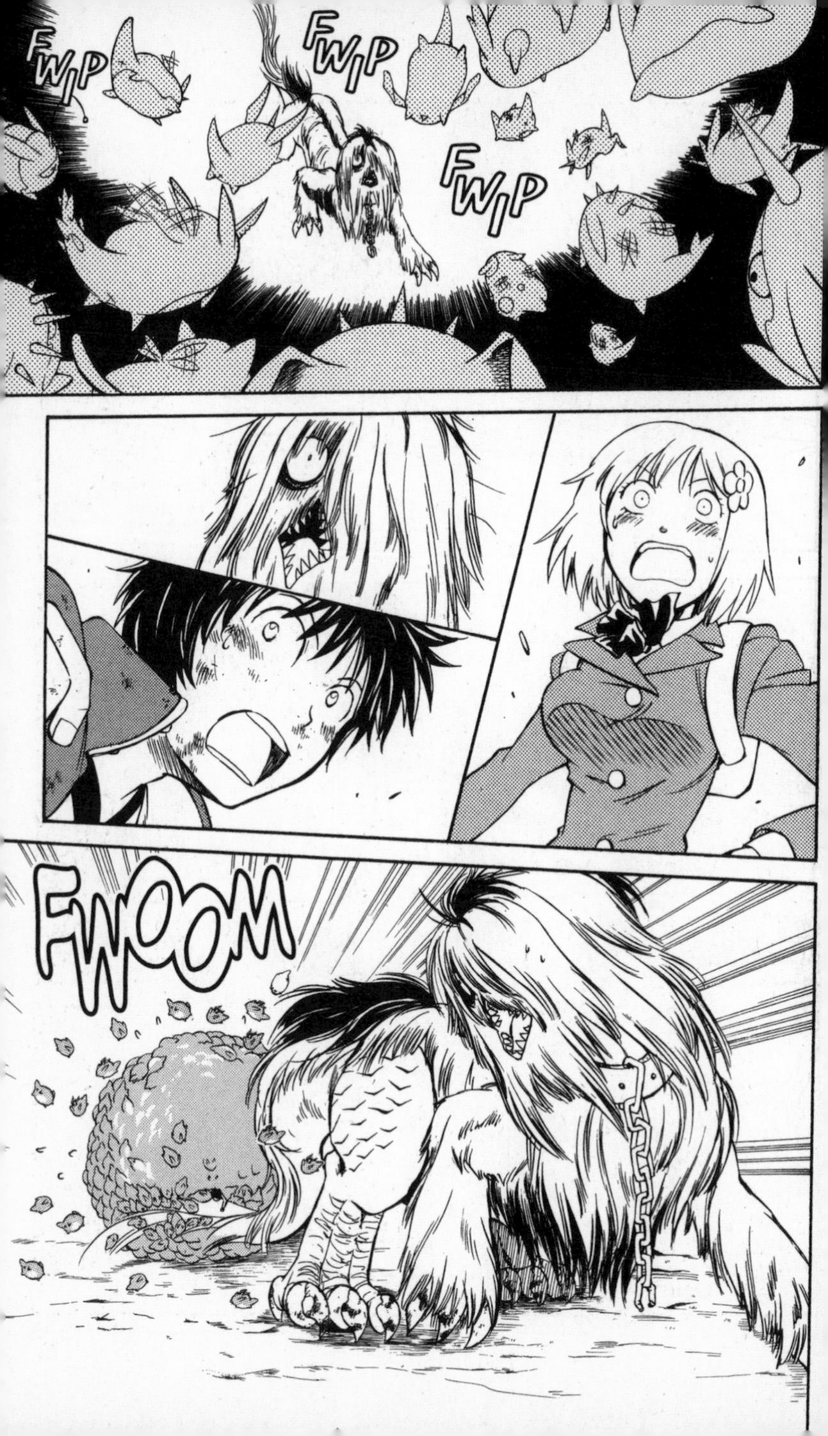
FWIP
FWIP
FWIP
FWOOM

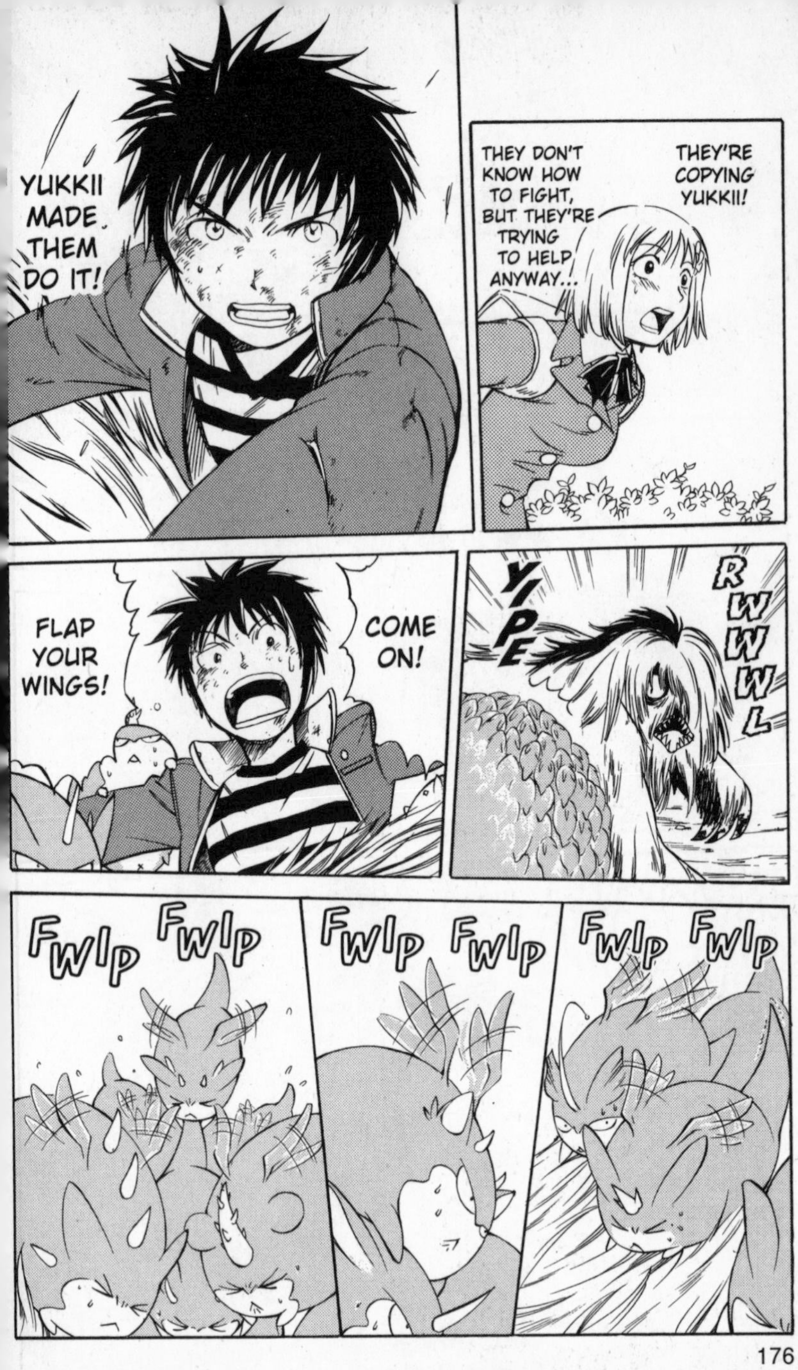
THEY'RE COPYING YUKKII!
THEY DON'T KNOW HOW TO FIGHT, BUT THEY'RE TRYING TO HELP ANYWAY...
YUKKII MADE THEM DO IT!
RWWWL
YIPE
COME ON!
FLAP YOUR WINGS!
FWIP FWIP
FWIP FWIP
FWIP FWIP

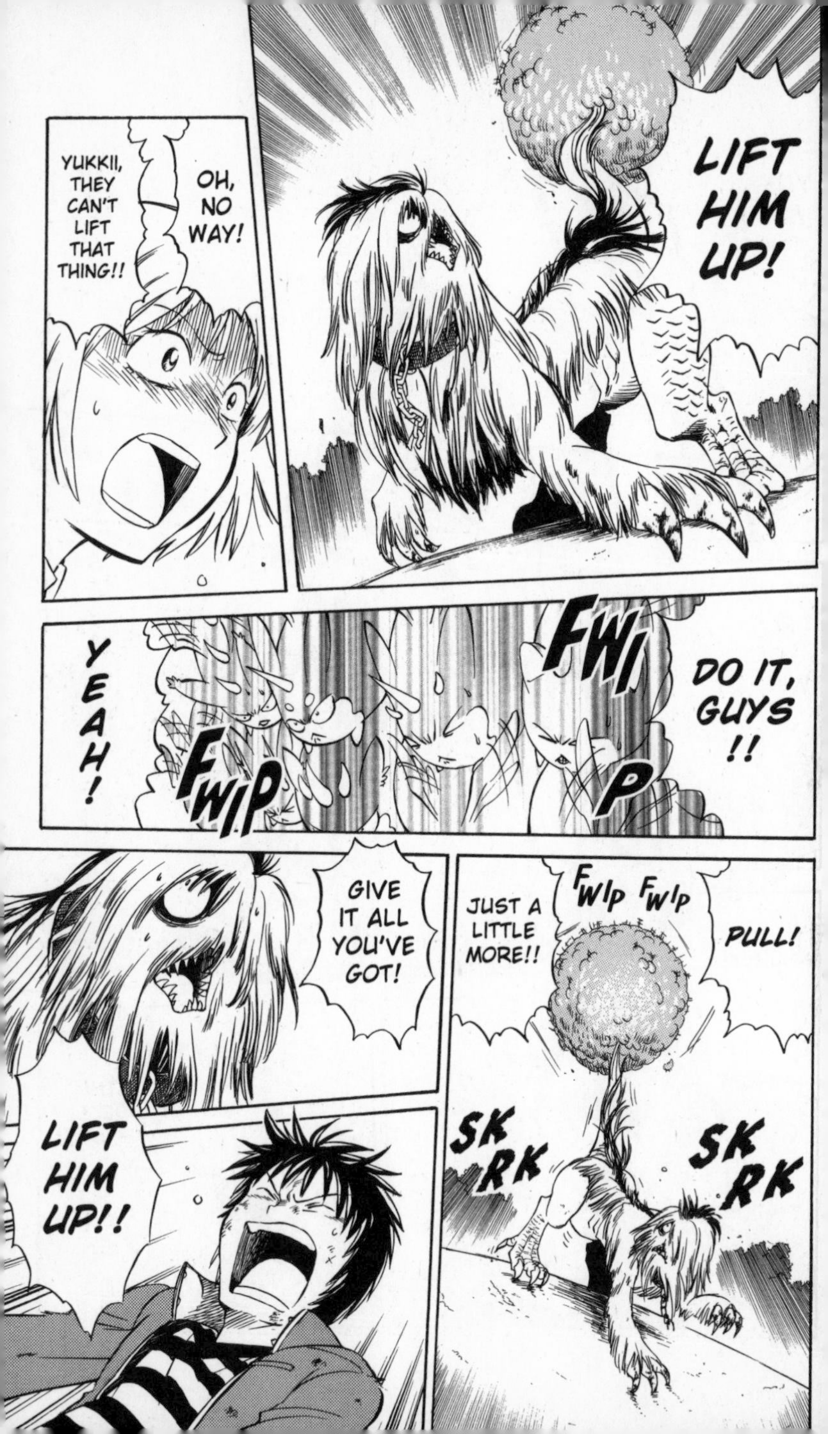
LIFT HIM UP!
OH, NO WAY!
YUKKII, THEY CAN'T LIFT THAT THING!!
DO IT, GUYS!!
FWIP
FWIP
YEAH!
PULL!
FWIP FWIP
JUST A LITTLE MORE!!
SKRK
SKRK
GIVE IT ALL YOU'VE GOT!
LIFT HIM UP!!

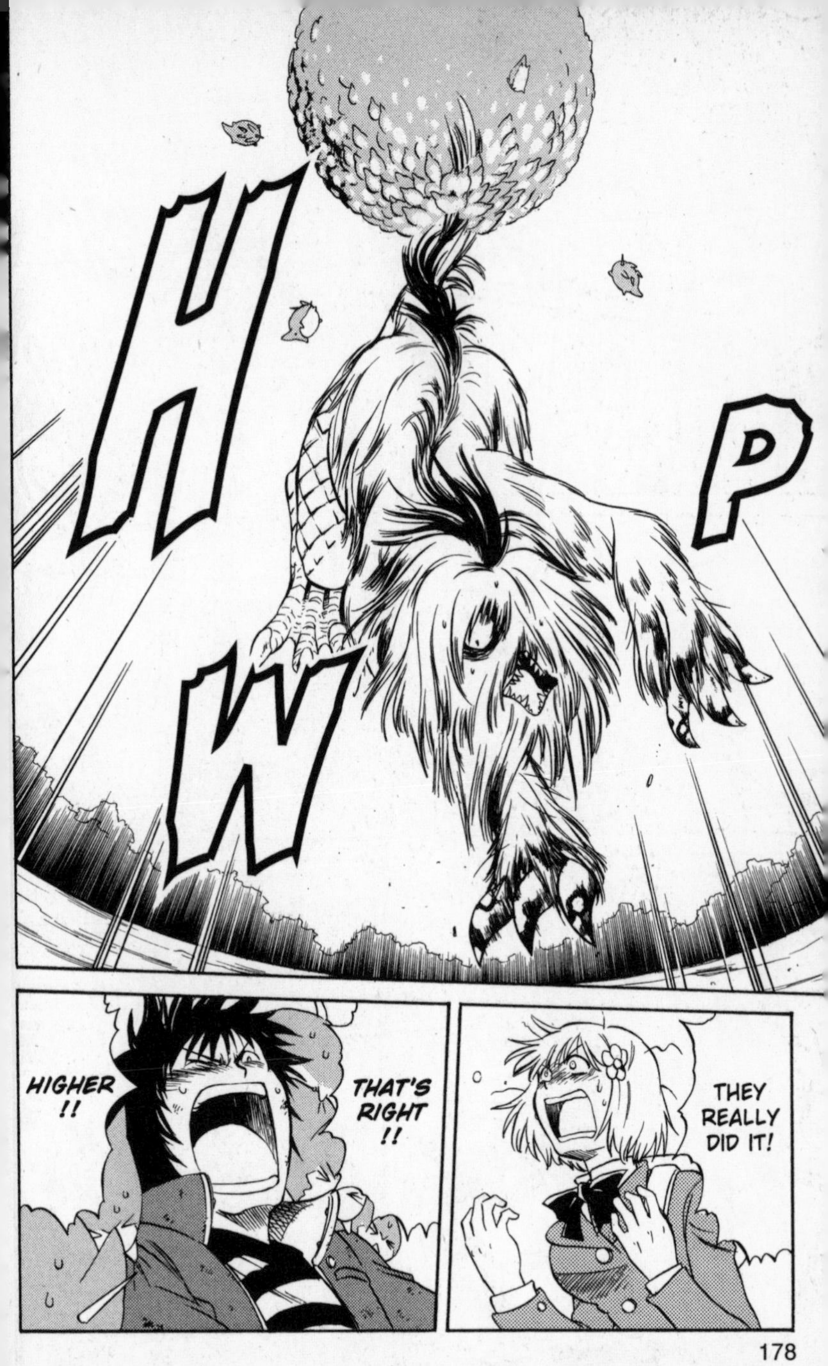
H
W
P
THEY REALLY DID IT!
THAT'S RIGHT !!
HIGHER !!

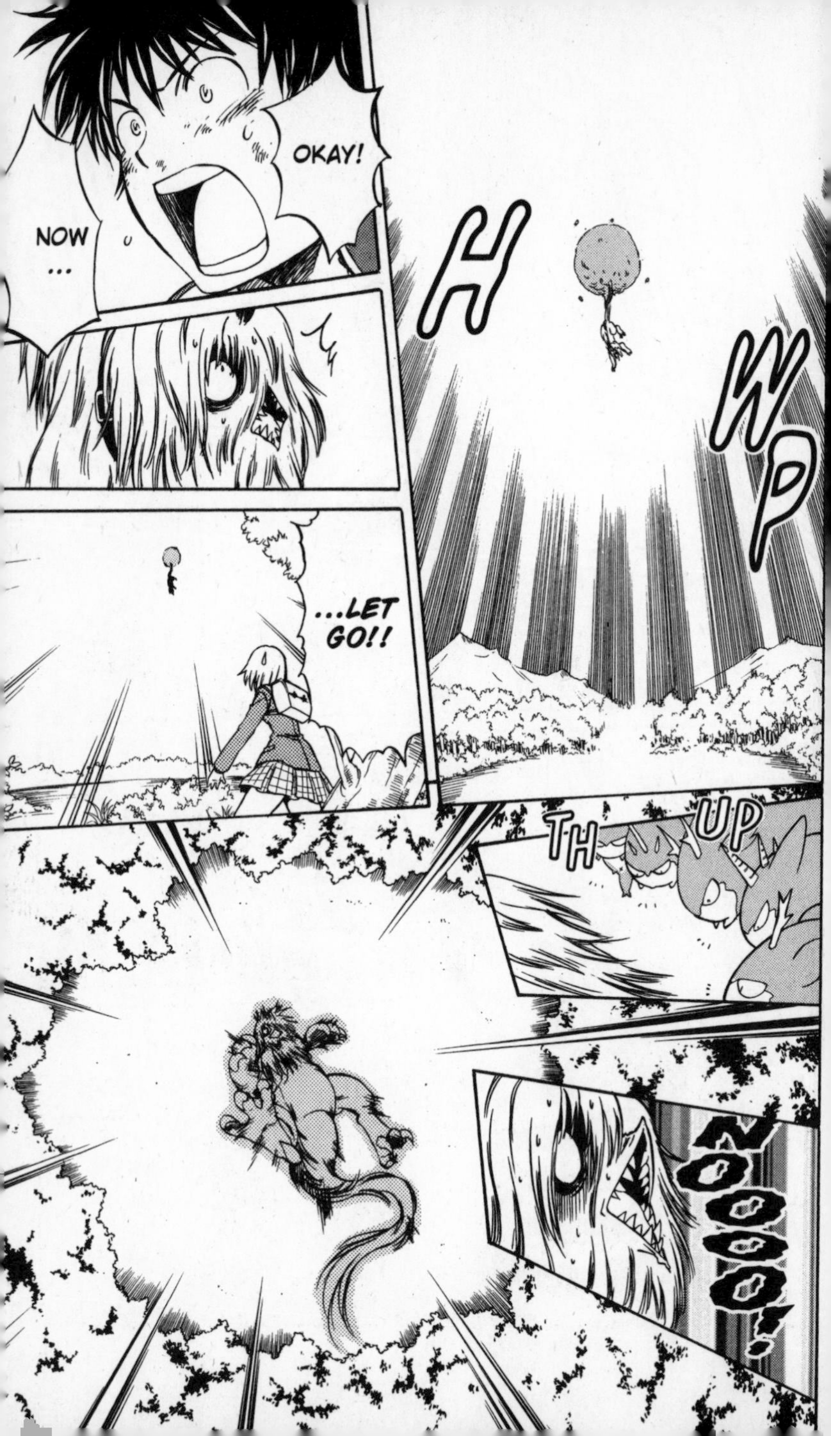

H WP
OKAY!
NOW...
...LET GO!!
TH UP
NOOOO!!

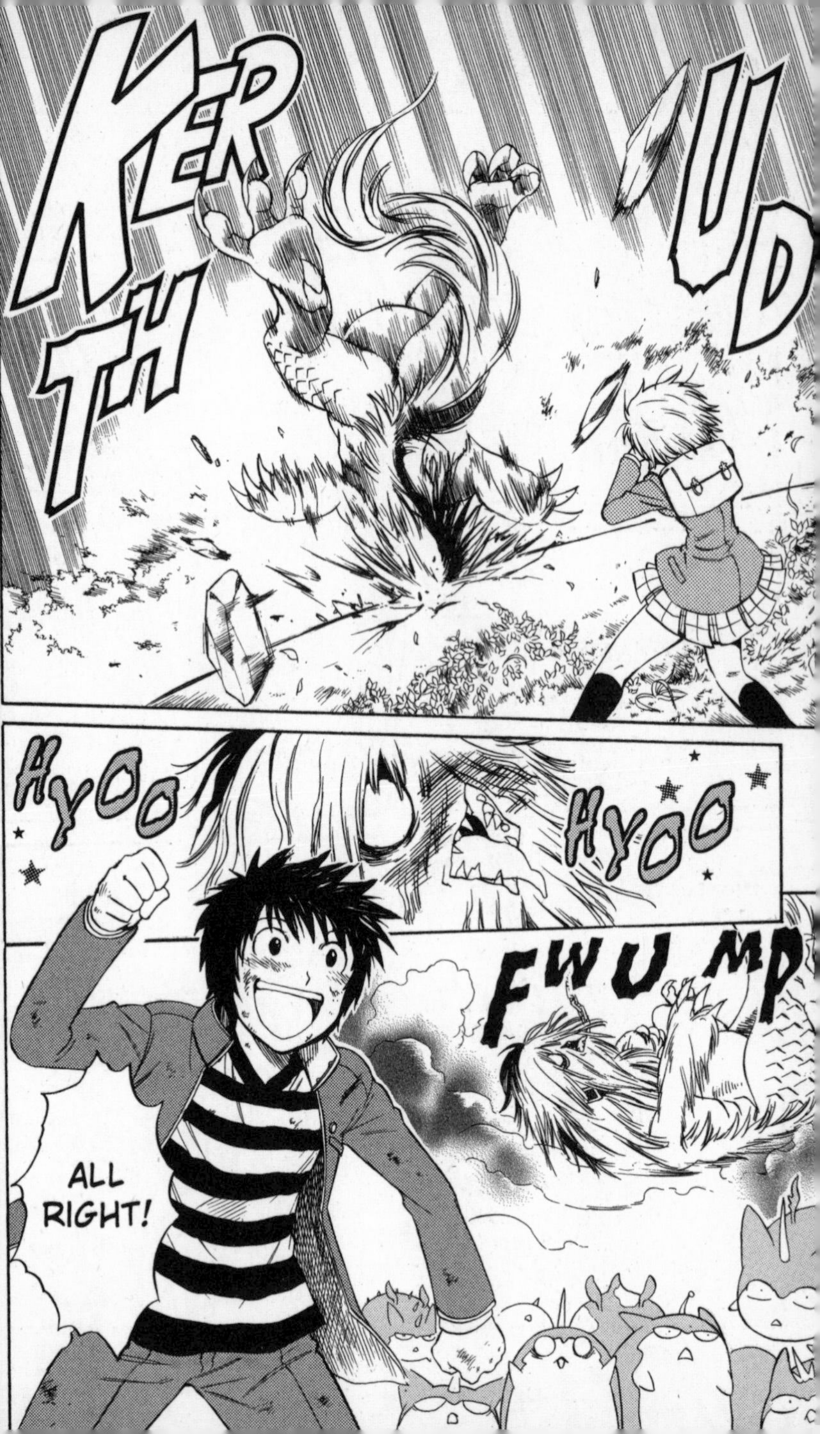
KERTHUD
HYOO
HYOO
FWUMP
ALL RIGHT!

READ THIS WAY

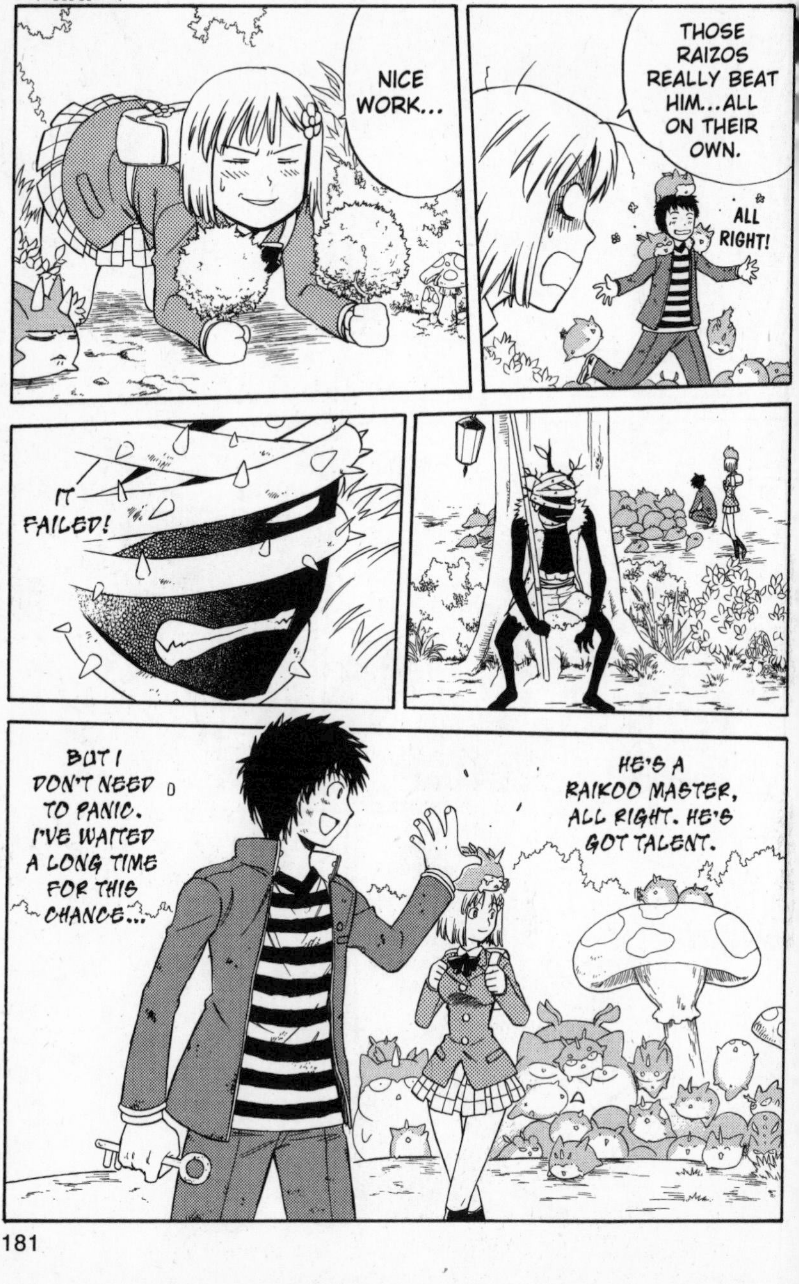
THOSE RAIZOS REALLY BEAT HIM...ALL ON THEIR OWN.
ALL RIGHT!
NICE WORK...
IT FAILED!
HE'S A RAIKOO MASTER, ALL RIGHT. HE'S GOT TALENT.
BUT I DON'T NEED TO PANIC. I'VE WAITED A LONG TIME FOR THIS CHANCE...

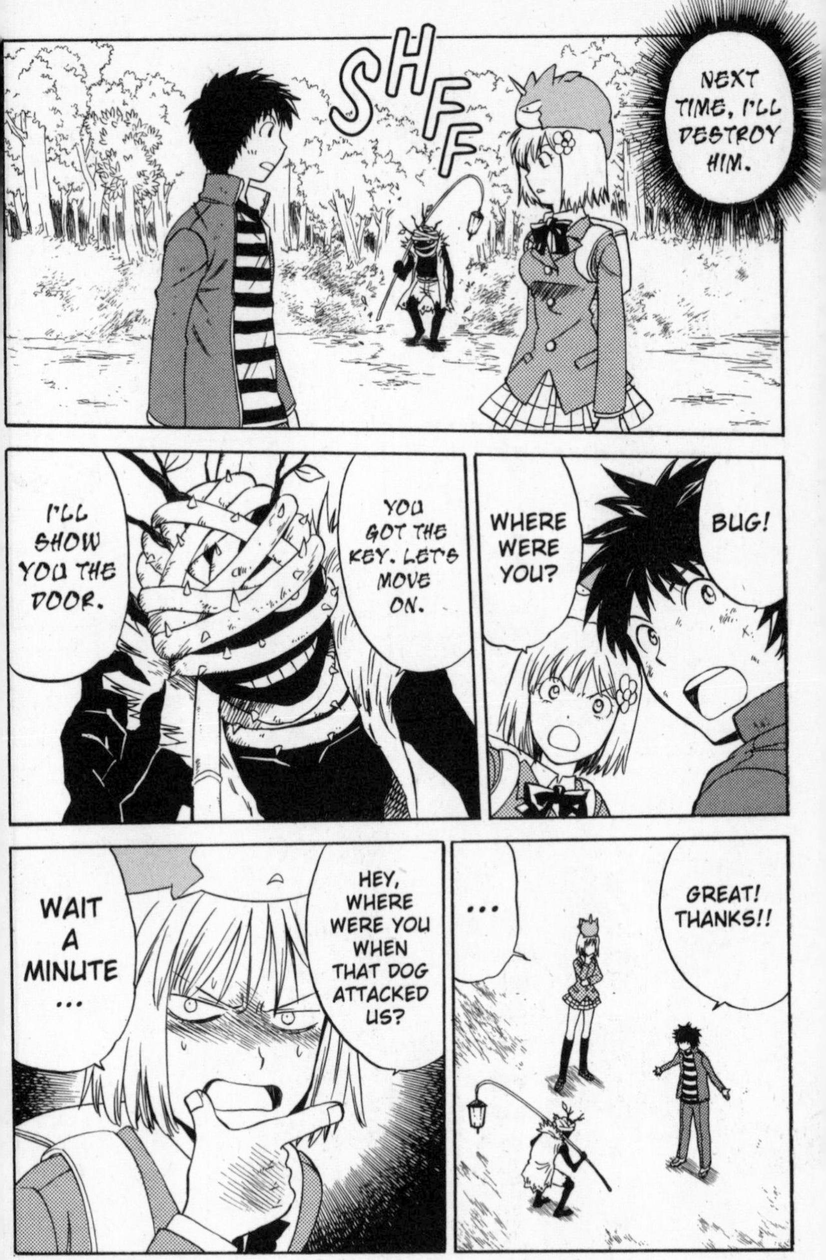
NEXT TIME, I'LL DESTROY HIM.
SHFF
BUG!
WHERE WERE YOU?
YOU GOT THE KEY. LET'S MOVE ON.
I'LL SHOW YOU THE DOOR.
GREAT! THANKS!!
...
HEY, WHERE WERE YOU WHEN THAT DOG ATTACKED US?
WAIT A MINUTE ...

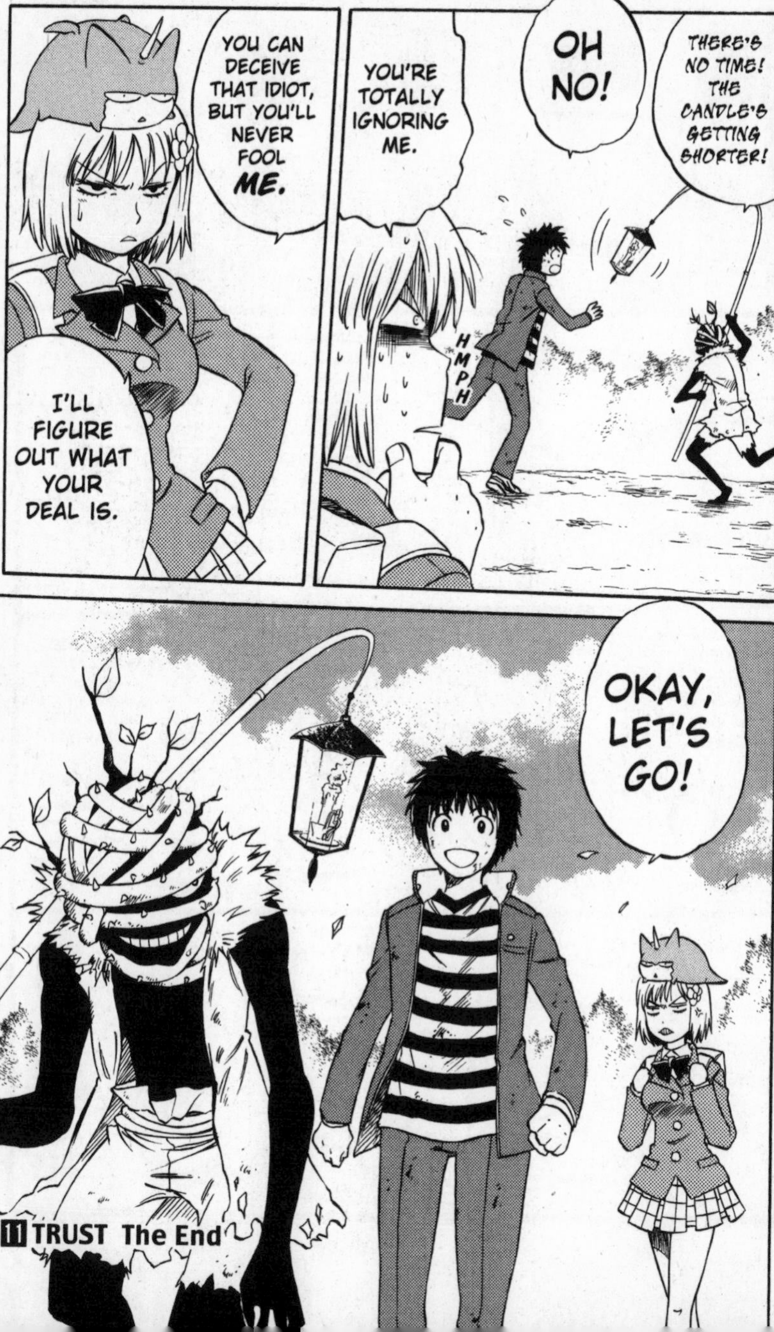
THERE'S NO TIME! THE CANDLE'S GETTING SHORTER!
OH NO!
YOU'RE TOTALLY IGNORING ME.
HMPH
YOU CAN DECEIVE THAT IDIOT, BUT YOU'LL NEVER FOOL ME.
I'LL FIGURE OUT WHAT YOUR DEAL IS.
OKAY, LET'S GO!

11 TRUST The End

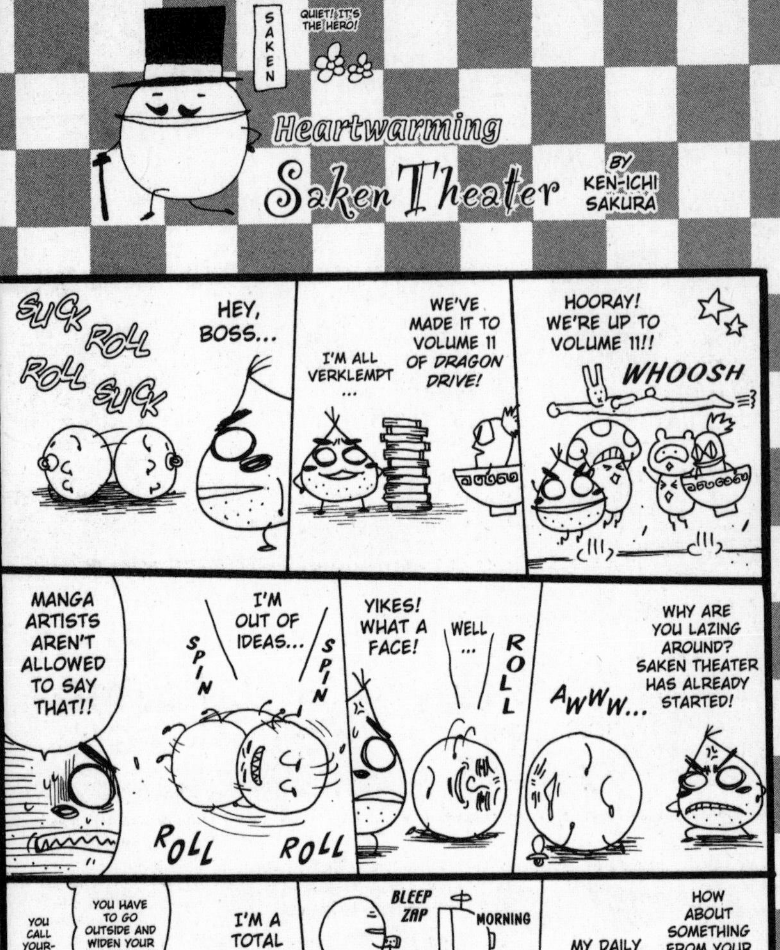
SAKEN
QUIET! IT'S THE HERO!
Heartwarming
Saken Theater
BY KEN-ICHI SAKURA
HOORAY! WE'RE UP TO VOLUME 11!!
WHOOSH
WE'VE MADE IT TO VOLUME 11 OF DRAGON DRIVE!
I'M ALL VERKLEMPT ...
HEY, BOSS...
SUCK ROLL
ROLL SUCK
WHY ARE YOU LAZING AROUND? SAKEN THEATER HAS ALREADY STARTED!
AWWW...
ROLL
WELL ...
YIKES! WHAT A FACE!
I'M OUT OF IDEAS...
SPIN
SPIN
ROLL
ROLL
MANGA ARTISTS AREN'T ALLOWED TO SAY THAT!!
HOW ABOUT SOMETHING FROM YOUR DAILY LIFE?
MY DAILY LIFE THESE DAYS...
BLEEP ZAP
MORNING
BLEEP ZAP
AFTER-NOON
BLEEP ZAP
EVENING
I'M A TOTAL HERMIT!
AND A GAME ADDICT!
HUH?
URGH
YOU HAVE TO GO OUTSIDE AND WIDEN YOUR EXPERIENCE!
YOU CALL YOUR-SELF A CARTOONIST ?!

Heartwarming

Saken Theater

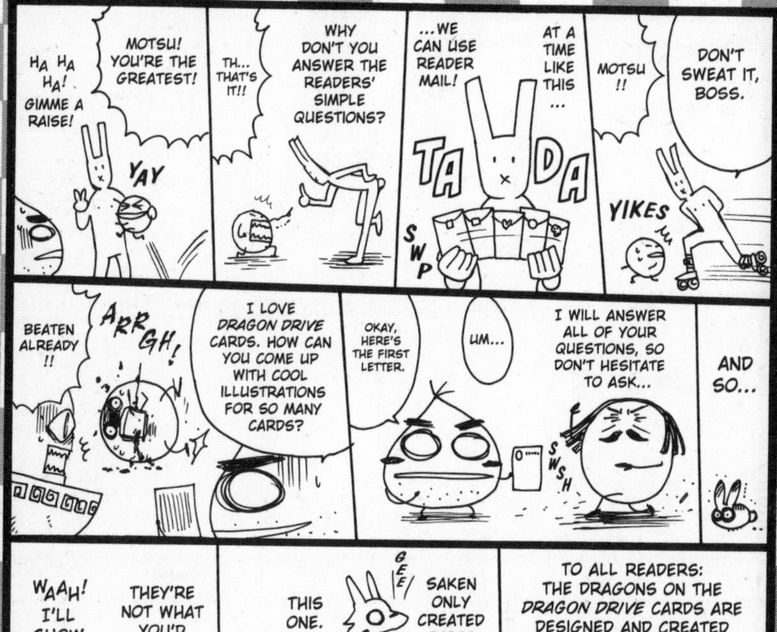
DON'T SWEAT IT, BOSS.
MOTSU!!
YIKES
AT A TIME LIKE THIS...
...WE CAN USE READER MAIL!
TA DA
SWP
WHY DON'T YOU ANSWER THE READERS' SIMPLE QUESTIONS?
TH... THAT'S IT!!
MOTSU! YOU'RE THE GREATEST!
HA HA HA! GIMME A RAISE!
YAY
AND SO...
I WILL ANSWER ALL OF YOUR QUESTIONS, SO DON'T HESITATE TO ASK...
SWSH
UM...
OKAY, HERE'S THE FIRST LETTER.
I LOVE *DRAGON DRIVE* CARDS. HOW CAN YOU COME UP WITH COOL ILLUSTRATIONS FOR SO MANY CARDS?
ARRGH!
BEATEN ALREADY!!
TO ALL READERS: THE DRAGONS ON THE *DRAGON DRIVE* CARDS ARE DESIGNED AND CREATED BY BANDAI ILLUSTRATORS. SAKEN LOOKS AT THE DESIGNS AND DRAWS COMICS BASED ON THEM. GOT IT?
SAKEN ONLY CREATED THESE DRAGONS:
GEE
THIS ONE.
AHEM!!
THIS ONE.
HOORAY!
THEY'RE NOT WHAT YOU'D CALL COOL...
WAAH! I'LL SHOW YOU! DARN IT!
TOO BAD!!

AND ARISA'S GLADIUS.

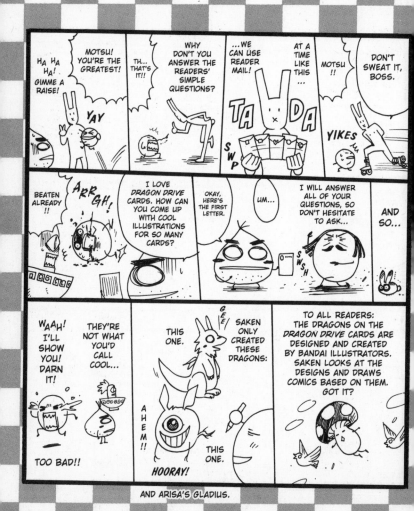

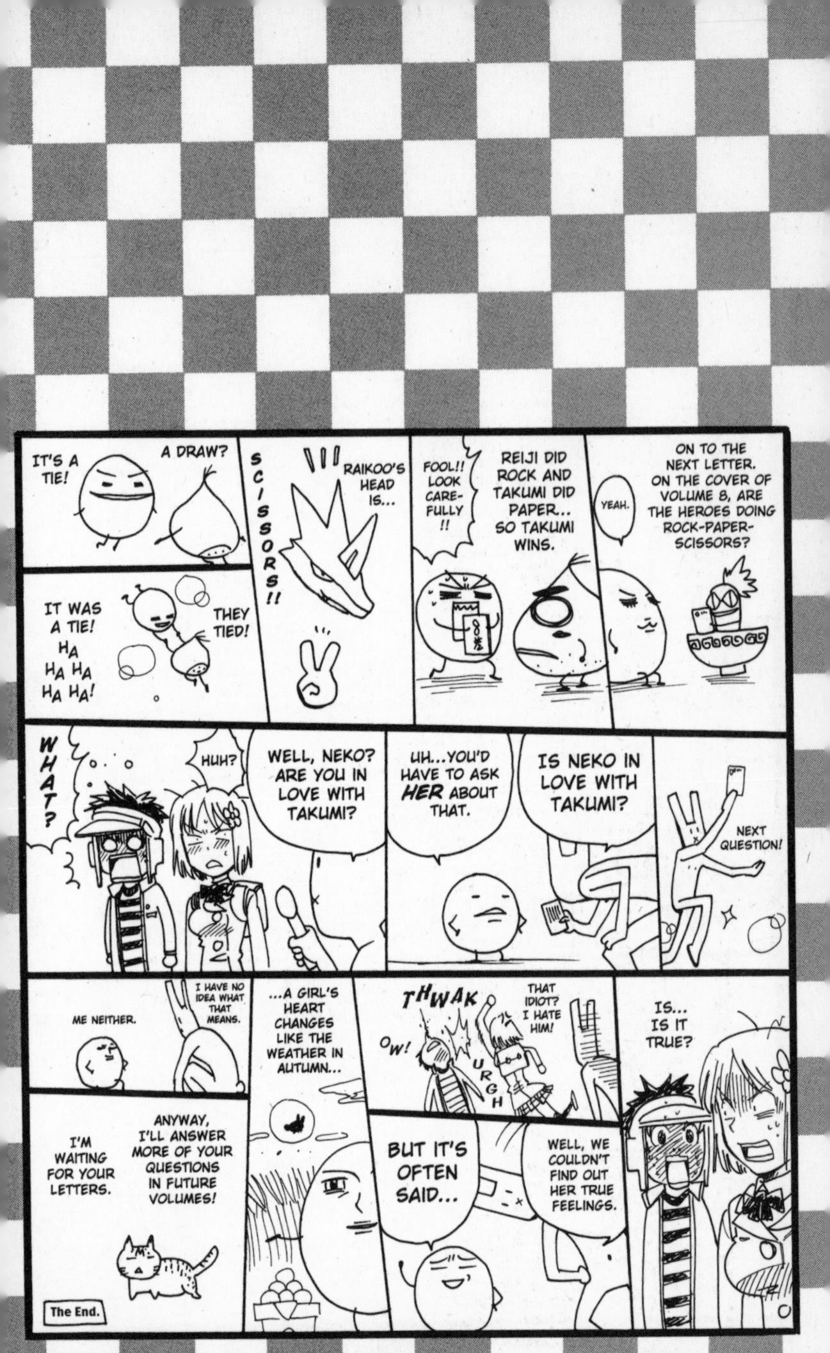
ON TO THE NEXT LETTER. ON THE COVER OF VOLUME 8, ARE THE HEROES DOING ROCK-PAPER-SCISSORS?
YEAH.
REIJI DID ROCK AND TAKUMI DID PAPER... SO TAKUMI WINS.
FOOL!! LOOK CAREFULLY!!
RAIKOO'S HEAD IS...
SCISSORS!!
A DRAW?
IT'S A TIE!
THEY TIED!
IT WAS A TIE! HA HA HA HA HA!
NEXT QUESTION!
IS NEKO IN LOVE WITH TAKUMI?
UH...YOU'D HAVE TO ASK HER ABOUT THAT.
WELL, NEKO? ARE YOU IN LOVE WITH TAKUMI?
HUH?
WHAT?
IS... IS IT TRUE?
THAT IDIOT? I HATE HIM!
THWAK
OW!
URGH
WELL, WE COULDN'T FIND OUT HER TRUE FEELINGS.
BUT IT'S OFTEN SAID...
...A GIRL'S HEART CHANGES LIKE THE WEATHER IN AUTUMN...
I HAVE NO IDEA WHAT THAT MEANS.
ME NEITHER.
ANYWAY, I'LL ANSWER MORE OF YOUR QUESTIONS IN FUTURE VOLUMES!
I'M WAITING FOR YOUR LETTERS.
The End.

RECENTLY,
WE'VE BEEN GETTING A
LOT OF MAIL WE CAN'T USE.
SO WE MADE THIS CAUTIONARY
GUIDANCE MANGA FOR THE
POSTCARD CORNER IN THE
JAPANESE *SHONEN JUMP*
MAGAZINE!

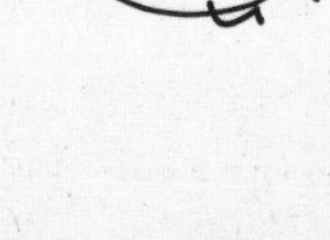

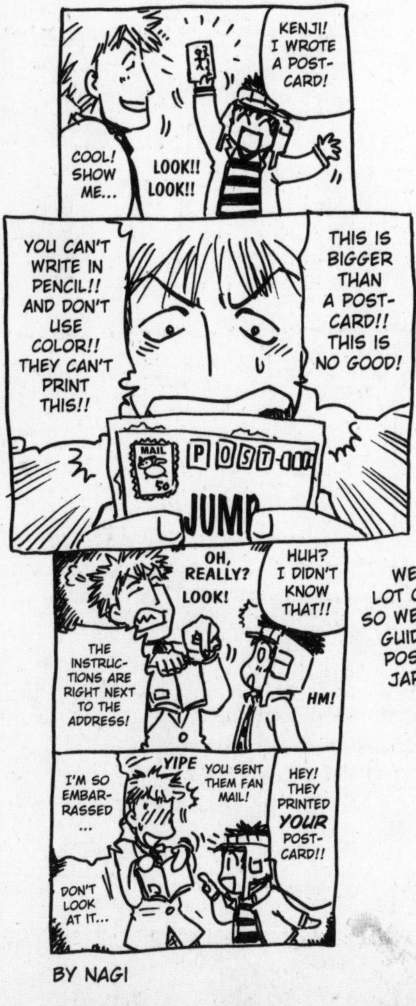
KENJI! I WROTE A POST-CARD!
LOOK!! LOOK!!
COOL! SHOW ME...
THIS IS BIGGER THAN A POST-CARD!! THIS IS NO GOOD!
YOU CAN'T WRITE IN PENCIL!! AND DON'T USE COLOR!! THEY CAN'T PRINT THIS!!
MAIL
50
POST-
JUMP
HUH? I DIDN'T KNOW THAT!!
OH, REALLY? LOOK!
HM!
THE INSTRUCTIONS ARE RIGHT NEXT TO THE ADDRESS!
HEY! THEY PRINTED YOUR POST-CARD!!
YOU SENT THEM FAN MAIL!
YIPE
I'M SO EMBARRASSED ...
DON'T LOOK AT IT...

BY NAGI

COMING NEXT VOLUME...

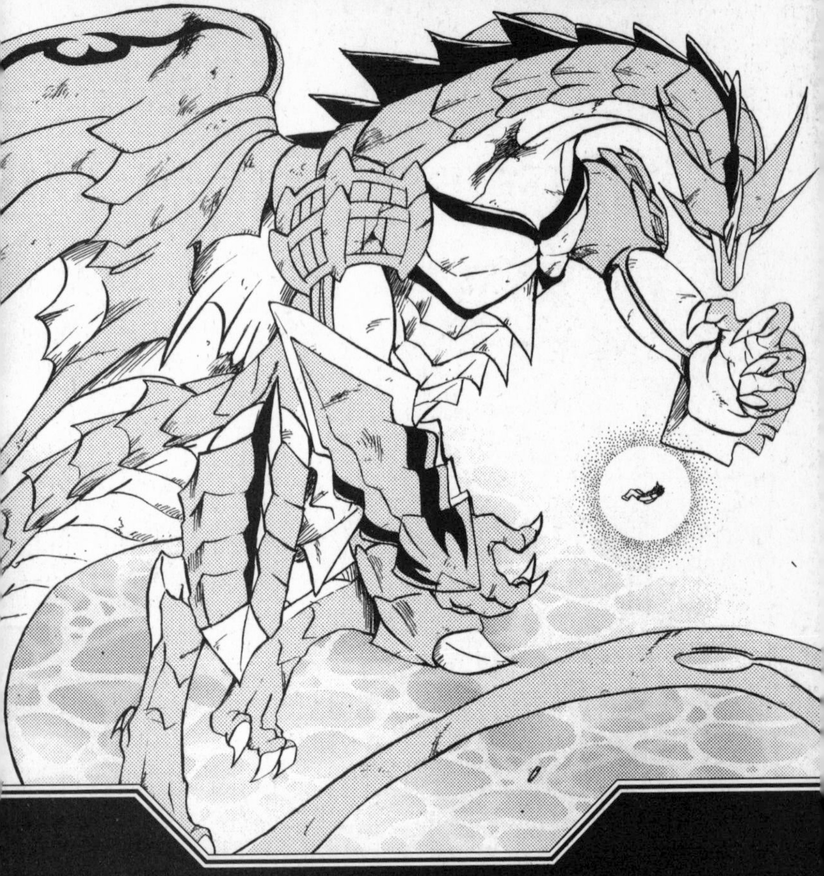

The world inside Raikoo's DD card just keeps getting weirder, and Neko soon figures out that their shifty guide Bug is bad news. But Takumi's determined not to give up on Raikoo or let Neko get spirited away. Can he defeat all the monsters in Raikoo's treacherous inner world... even his own evil duplicate?

AVAILABLE IN FEBRUARY 2009!

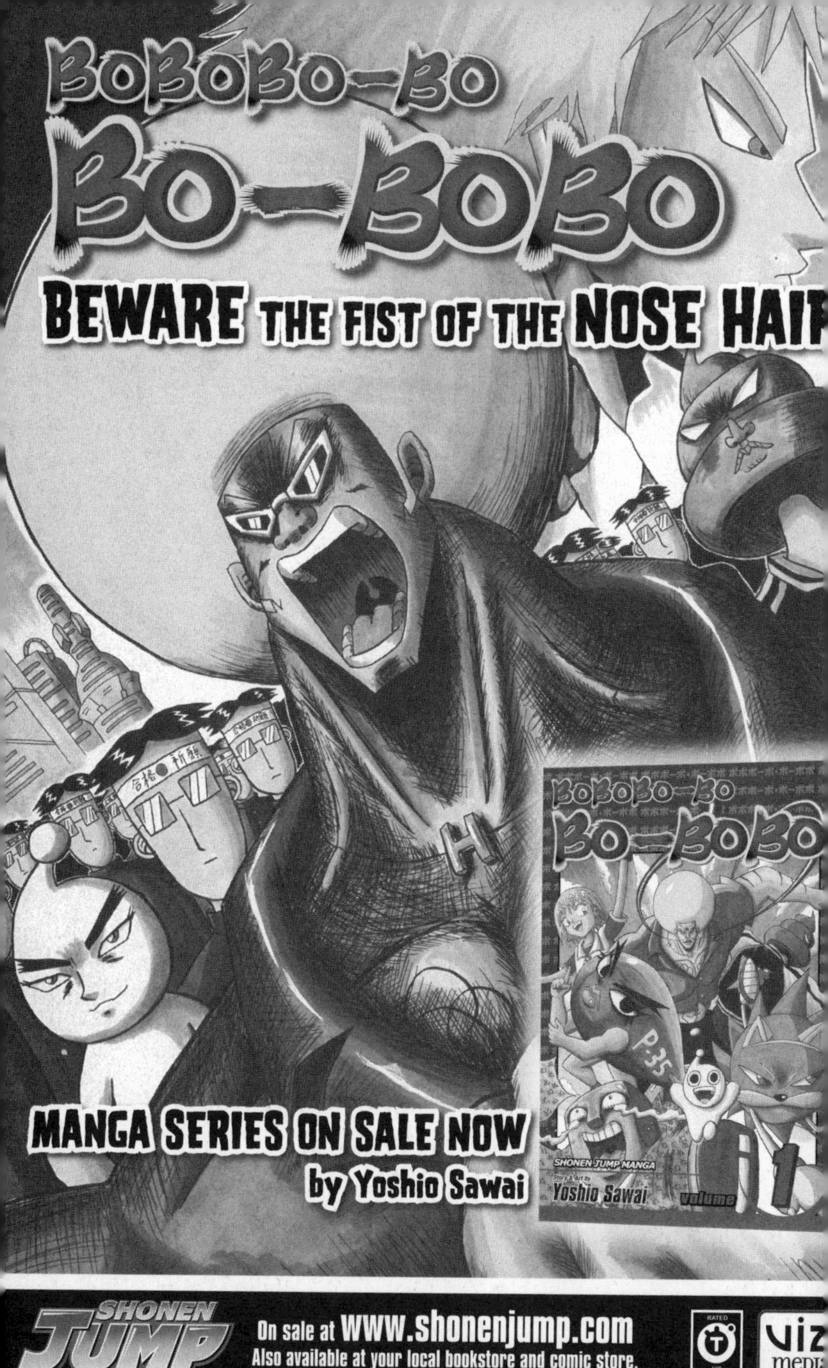
BOBOBO-BO
BO-BOBO
BEWARE THE FIST OF THE NOSE HAI
MANGA SERIES ON SALE NOW
by Yoshio Sawai
BOBOBO-BO
BO-BOBO
SHONEN JUMP MANGA
Story & Art by
Yoshio Sawai
volume 1
SHONEN JUMP
On sale at www.shonenjump.com
Also available at your local bookstore and comic store.
RATED T FOR TEEN
VIZ MEDIA

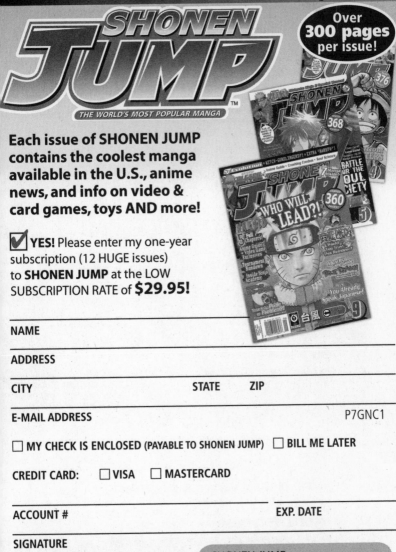